The American Journalist in the 21st Century

U.S. News People at the Dawn of a New Millennium

LEA'S COMMUNICATION SERIES
Jennings Bryant/Dolf Zillmann, General Editors

For a complete list of titles in LEA's Communication Series, please contact Lawrence Erlbaum Associates, Publishers, at www.erlbaum.com.

The American Journalist in the 21st Century

U.S. News People at the Dawn of a New Millennium

David H. Weaver
Randal A. Beam
Bonnie J. Brownlee
Paul S. Voakes
G. Cleveland Wilhoit
Indiana University

Routledge
Taylor & Francis Group

NEW YORK AND LONDON

First published 2007 by Lawrence Erlbaum Associates., Inc

This edition published 2014 by Routledge

Routledge   Routledge
Taylor & Francis Group   Taylor & Francis Group
711 Third Avenue   2 Park Square
New York   Milton Park, Abingdon
NY 10017   Oxon OX14 4RN

Routledge is an imprint of the Taylor & Francis Group, an informa business

Cover design by Tomai Maridou

Library of Congress Cataloging-in-Publication Data

The American journalist in the 21st century : U.S. news people at
the dawn of a new millennium / David H. Weaver . . . [et al.].
        p.   cm.
    Includes bibliographical references and indexes.
    ISBN 0–8058–5382–0 (cloth : alk. paper) — ISBN 0–8058–5383–9
(pbk. : alk. paper)
    1. Journalism—United States—History—21st century. 2. Journalists—
United States—History—21st century. 3. Journalists—United States—
Statistics. 4. Occupational surveys—United States. I. Weaver, David H.
(David Hugh), 1946- .
PN4867.2.A44 2006
071'.471—dc22   2006003215

10 9 8 7 6 5 4 3

Contents

Preface

This book builds on the work of many other scholars, most notably John Johnstone and his colleagues at the University of Illinois at Chicago, who did the first comprehensive national study of U.S. news people in 1971, which was reported in detail in their 1976 book, *The News People*. That landmark study produced baseline information about U.S. journalists' backgrounds, education and training, careers, working patterns, and attitudes about their jobs, their roles, and their responsibilities. It included journalists working for a wide variety of printed and broadcast news media.

Since then, David Weaver and G. Cleveland Wilhoit have carried out two additional national surveys, in 1982–1983, and in 1992, modeled on this 1971 study and reported in their books, *The American Journalist* and *The American Journalist in the 1990s*. The third study, conducted in 2002 and reported in this book, was done with the help of three additional colleagues at Indiana University—Bonnie Brownlee, Randal Beam (now at the University of Washington), and Paul Voakes (now at the University of Colorado). This 2002 comprehensive national survey of U.S. journalists includes many of the same questions asked by the Johnstone team 30 years ago, but also a number of new ones to measure the impact and use of new technologies, especially the Internet, and the changes in the working environments of journalists throughout the country.

As in the earlier books, our chief concerns in this book are with (a) changes in the backgrounds and education of those working in U.S. news media; (b) their working conditions and jobs, including the impact of new technologies; (c) their views concerning their roles and ethical values, and (d) their perceptions of what constitutes their best work. In addition to providing a fourth wave of information about these journalists, this book also includes a new chapter on journalists who work mainly for online or Internet media, and it includes more open-ended comments than the previous three studies that allow journalists to speak in their own words about why they chose journalism as an occupation, their job satisfaction (or dissatisfaction), journalistic freedom, the performance of their news organizations, and their best work.

ACKNOWLEDGMENTS

A study of this magnitude requires support from many people. Most important was the generosity of the John S. and James L. Knight Foundation in providing the funding needed for the telephone interviewing of 1,464 journalists across the United States. We are especially indebted to Dr. John Bare, who was Director of Program Development and Evaluation at the Knight Foundation in 2002 when this study was planned and conducted. His unwavering support of this project was crucial to its funding. Larry Meyer, Vice President of Communications, was very helpful in preparing the *Key Findings* printed report that we presented at the April 2003 annual meeting of the American Society of Newspaper Editors and the August 2003 convention of the Association for Education in Journalism & Mass Communication, and which appeared on the Poynter Web site. And Eric Newton, Director of Journalism Initiatives, kept us on our toes with his questions and critiques as he edited the Key Findings report and helped us present it to ASNE and AEJMC.

At Indiana University, we are grateful for support from the Roy W. Howard Chair held by David Weaver, which helped to fund research assistants and doctoral students Leigh Moscowitz, Peter Mwesige, and Eunseong Kim. They did a truly impressive job of complicated data analysis and table/chart preparation. The Howard Chair also provided release time for Weaver to take the lead on the initial report and this book. We are grateful to the Howard family and the Scripps Howard Foundation for establishing this Chair within the School of Journalism and to former Dean Trevor Brown for his support of this project.

Others who supported this project include Professor Lee Becker of the University of Georgia, who helped to get the Knight Foundation interested in supporting it, and John Kennedy, Director of the Center for Survey Research at Indiana University, as well as his talented staff member Kathy Matthews, who was Project Manager. Others at the Center for Survey Research who were helpful include Nancy Bannister, Associate Director, and Katy Adams, Field Director, as well as the dozens of interviewers who did their jobs so diligently. We are most grateful to the 1,464 U.S. journalists who took the time to answer our many questions. Finally, we thank Linda Bathgate, Senior Editor–Communications at Lawrence Erlbaum Associates, for her interest in this project and her patience as we missed several deadlines for producing the completed book manuscript.

ORGANIZATION OF THE BOOK

We divided the primary responsibility for the chapters in this book as follows: Randal Beam was the author of Chapters 3, "Journalists in the Workplace," and 8, "Journalists' Best Work," as well as Appendix III, "Coding Schedule for Journalists' Best Work." He also read all the other chapters carefully and made numerous helpful suggestions. Bonnie Brownlee was the lead author of Chapters 5, "Women Journalists," and 6, "Minority Journalists," and David Weaver also worked on these chapters. Paul Voakes was the author of Chapter 4, "Professionalism," and helped with Chapter 7, "Online Journalists." David Weaver was the author of Chapters 1, "Basic Characteristics," 2, "Education and Training," 7, "Online Journalists," 9, "Conclusions," and Appendix I, "Methods." G. Cleveland Wilhoit worked with Randal Beam on Chapter 3 and with Paul Voakes on Chapter 4, and made helpful suggestions on other chapters. All of us worked on Appendix II (the survey questionnaire) and made suggestions on most chapters. Doctoral student Eunseong Kim prepared the Bibliography and the Name and Subject Indexes.

A PERSONAL NOTE

With G. Cleveland Wilhoit retired as of summer 2004 and David Weaver planning to retire before 2012, which would be the next decennial date for this survey, this will be the last such study that they work on. They hope that younger scholars such as Professors Beam, Brownlee, and Voakes will take up the torch and keep alive this series of studies of U.S. journalists. These surveys of 1982, 1992, and 2002 have involved a great deal of detailed work, but we hope that the information they have produced will not only increase understanding of who U.S. journalists are, where they work, and what they think, but will also help to improve U.S. journalism. With the publication of this book, Weaver and Wilhoit have worked together on journalism and mass communication research for 37 years. They are proud of this record, but also ready to hand over this work to younger scholars with more energy and new ideas.

—*David Weaver*
Randal Beam
Bonnie Brownlee
Paul Voakes
G. Cleveland Wilhoit

Basic Characteristics of U.S. Journalists

The statistical "profile" of U.S. journalists in 2002 is similar to that of 1992. The typical journalist then was a White Protestant married male in his 30s with a bachelor's degree. In 2002, this average journalist was a married White male just over 40, less likely to come from a Protestant religious background, and slightly more likely to hold a bachelor's degree. But this journalist was still more likely to work for a daily newspaper than any other type of news medium in 2002, to have attended a public college or university, to work for a news organization owned by a larger company, and to have not majored in journalism in college. As in 1992, this picture, based on averages, masks many of the important differences in U.S. news people that are discussed in much greater detail throughout this book.

This opening chapter examines the size of the journalistic workforce in the United States in 2002 as compared with previous decades, the geographic dispersion of U.S. journalists, their age and gender, their ethnic and religious origins, their political views, and their media use patterns. (See Appendix I, this volume, for details of the survey methods.)

SIZE OF THE JOURNALISTIC WORKFORCE

In 1971, Johnstone and his colleagues estimated the total full-time editorial workforce in U.S. English-language mainstream news media to be 69,500, with more than half employed by daily newspapers.[1] In late 1982, we estimated this workforce to be 112,072, an increase of 61%, with slightly fewer than half employed by daily newspapers.[2] In 1992, we estimated the total number of U.S. journalists working for mainstream news media to be 122,015, an increase of just under 9%, with more than half employed by daily newspapers (see Table 1.1).[3] In late 2002, this number had dropped slightly to 116,148, a decrease of nearly 5%.

This estimated total includes only those journalists working full-time for daily and weekly newspapers, a handful of general interest news magazines that are published more than once a month, radio and television stations with news departments, and general wire service bureaus. It is likely that the growth in U.S. journalism during the past decade or two has been in specialized magazines and newsletters, both printed and online, and various cable TV network news organizations, rather than in the traditional news media included in our study. It is also likely that there has also been an increase in the number of part-time correspondents and freelancers working for U.S. news organizations. Thus, our estimate of the total number of full-time U.S. journalists is conservative, but it is consistent with the estimates of the previous studies conducted in the 1970s, 1980s, and 1990s.

Although it is very difficult to obtain estimates of employment for all journalists or branches of the communication field, there are data from the U.S. Census and the Bureau of Labor Statistics on the total number of employees in the printing and publishing and communications industries. These figures show that the field of "communication" (which includes telephones, radio and television broadcasting, and cable and pay TV) grew from 1.3 million employees in 1990 to

TABLE 1.1
Estimated Full-Time Editorial Workforce in U.S. News Media

News Medium	April 1971[a]		November 1982[b]		June 1992[c]		November 2002	
	Number	%	Number	%	Number	%	Number	%
Daily newspapers	38,800	55.8	51,650	46.1	67,207	55.1	58,769	50.6
Weekly newspapers	11,500	16.5	22,942	20.5	16,226	13.3	21,908	18.9
News magazines	1,900	2.7	1,284	1.1	1,664	1.4	1,152	1.0
Total print media	52,200	75.1	75,876	67.7	85,097	69.8	81,829	70.5
Television (& combined radio/TV stations & networks)	7,000	10.1	15,212	13.6	17,784	14.6	20,288	17.5
Radio	7,000	10.1	19,583	17.5	17,755	14.5	13,393	11.5
Total broadcast media	14,000	20.2	34,795	31.1	35,539	29.1	33,681	29.0
News services	3,300	4.7	1,401	1.2	1,379	1.1	638	0.5
Total workforce	69,500	100.0	112,072	100.0	122,015	100.0	116,148	100.0

[a] From John Johnstone, Edward Slawski, and William Bowman, *The News People* (Urbana: University of Illinois Press, 1976), p. 195.

[b] From David H. Weaver and G. Cleveland Wilhoit, *The American Journalist* (Bloomington: Indiana University Press, 1986, 2nd ed. 1991), p. 13.

[c] From David H. Weaver and G. Cleveland Wilhoit, *The American Journalist in the 1990s* (Mahwah, NJ: Lawrence Erlbaum Associates, 1996), p. 2.

1.6 million in 2000, an increase of 23%.[4] Most of this growth was in telephone and cable/pay TV services.

On the other hand, the field of "printing and publishing" (which includes newspapers, periodicals, books, commercial printing, and bookbinding) declined slightly from a total of 1.57 million employees in 1990 to 1.56 in 2000. The largest decline was in newspapers (from 474,000 to 445,000), and the largest increases were in periodicals (129,000 to 146,000) and commercial printing (552,000 to 565,000).[5]

These figures include many technical and clerical jobs, of course, so they are only rough estimates of growth (or lack of it) in news or journalistic jobs in these broader fields. But they do raise questions about whether there will continue to be a decline in the number of U.S. journalists working for traditional news media during the next decade. More specific occupational data from the U.S. census show some growth in the number of authors from 1992 to 2000 (125,000 to 138,000), designers (542,000 to 738,000), photographers (129,000 to 148,000), editors and reporters (264,000 to 288,000), and announcers (53,000 to 54,000), but many of these jobs are not in traditional news media.[6]

Our estimates of U.S. journalistic employment do not include part-time correspondents, freelancers, or stringers working on an occasional basis, and our estimates are subject to varying amounts of sampling error because they were based on different sized random samples of news organizations in relation to their actual numbers. (For more details on how these estimates were calculated and how our sample of journalists was drawn, see Appendix I, this volume.)

Table 1.1 suggests that the proportion of U.S. full-time journalists working for daily newspapers declined from 1992 to 2002, whereas those working for weekly or nondaily papers increased, and those working for news magazines declined slightly. Overall, the proportion working for these traditional print media remained virtually constant at 70% during this decade (see Table 1.1), but the actual numbers declined by more than 3,000. Likewise, the percentage working for the broadcast media of radio and television remained essentially constant at 29, but employment in radio decreased and in television it increased, both by 3 percentage points. The actual number of broadcast journalists declined by almost 2,000, however. The number of journalists working for the bureaus of the major wire services of Associated Press (AP) and Reuters also declined from 1992 to 2002, mainly because of the sharp decline of United Press International (UPI) during this decade.

On balance, then, we estimate nearly 6,000 fewer full-time journalists working for traditional mainstream U.S. news media in 2002 as compared with 1992. It should be remembered, however, that our definition of *journalist* follows that used in the previous studies of 1971, 1982–1983, and 1992—those who have editorial responsibility for the preparation or transmission of news stories or other information, including full-time reporters, writers, correspondents, columnists, news people, and editors. In broadcast organizations, only news and public

TABLE 1.2

Regional Distribution of Journalists Compared With Total U.S. Population
(Percentage in Each Region)

Region	Journalists				Total Population			
	1971[a] (N = 1,328)	1982–1983[b] (N = 1,001)	1992[c] (N = 1,156)	2002 (N = 1,149)	1970[d]	1981[e]	1990[f]	2002[g]
New England	7.5	9.7	5.0	3.3	5.8	5.4	5.3	5.0
Middle Atlantic	28.8	11.2	14.8	10.6	18.3	16.1	15.1	14.1
East North Central	15.3	19.2	12.0	17.6	19.8	18.2	16.9	16.1
West North Central	7.4	11.5	12.8	10.7	8.0	7.5	7.1	6.8
South Atlantic	11.0	12.8	20.6	27.7	15.1	16.5	17.5	18.4
East South Central	4.6	6.8	11.6	3.5	6.3	6.4	6.1	6.1
West South Central	9.1	13.3	6.0	6.2	9.5	10.7	10.7	11.2
Mountain	6.4	4.5	6.7	9.1	4.1	5.1	5.5	6.5
Pacific	9.9	11.1	10.5	11.1	13.1	14.1	15.7	16.0
Total	100.0	100.1[h]	100.0	100.0	100.0	100.0	99.9[h]	100.0
Total Northeast	36.3	20.9	19.8	13.9	24.1	21.5	20.4	19.1
Total Midwest	22.7	30.7	24.8	28.3	27.8	25.7	24.0	22.9
Total South	24.7	32.9	38.1	37.3	30.9	33.5	34.4	35.7
Total West	16.3	15.6	17.2	20.2	17.2	19.3	21.2	22.5

[a] From Johnstone, Slawski, and Bowman, The News People, p. 195.

[b] From Weaver and Wilhoit, The American Journalist, p. 16.

[c] From Weaver and Wilhoit, The American Journalist in the 1990s, p. 5.

[d] U.S. Bureau of the Census, Statistical Abstract of the United States, 1971, 92nd ed. (Washington, DC: U.S. Government Printing Office, 1971) Table 11, p. 12.

[e] U.S. Bureau of the Census, Statistical Abstract of the United States, 1982–1983, 103rd ed. (Washington, DC: U.S. Government Printing Office, 1982), p. 30.

[f] U.S. Bureau of the Census, Statistical Abstract of the United States, 1991, 111th ed. (Washington, DC: U.S. Government Printing Office, 1991), p. 20.

[g] U.S. Bureau of the Census, Statistical Abstract of the United States, 2002, 122nd ed. (Washington, DC: U.S. Government Printing Office, 2002), p. 29.

[h] Does not total 100% because of rounding.

affairs staff are included. Editorial cartoonists, but not comic-strip cartoonists, are included.

In this study and in 1992, we included photographers as journalists; in 1971 and 1982–1983 only photographers who were also reporters were included. We made this change in 1992 because we reasoned that photojournalists had more discretion than in the past about which pictures to shoot and were more likely to write text to accompany these pictures. As in the previous studies, we excluded librarians and visual and audio technicians because most of them are directed by reporters and editors (or assist them) and therefore do not have direct editorial control over the information that is communicated to general audiences.

GEOGRAPHIC DISTRIBUTION OF JOURNALISTS

Johnstone and his colleagues argue that, from its beginnings, the American news industry has been concentrated in the Northeast, largely because that region was the center of population of trade and commerce.[7] In 1971, the Johnstone study found journalists overrepresented by 12% in the Northeast, as compared with the total population, and underrepresented in all other major regions of the country (see Table 1.2). During 1982–1983, there was a dramatic decline in the percentage of journalists working in the Northeast, significant increases in the proportions employed in the North Central (Midwest) and South regions, and almost no change in those located in the West. In 1992, the proportion in the Northeast remained constant, with a small decline in the North Central (Midwest) and small increases in the South and West (see Table 1.2). In general, the changes in the 1980s were minor compared with those in the 1970s, as one might expect from the negligible growth in U.S. journalism in the 1980s. Likewise, the changes during the 1990s were not major. The largest decrease was in the Northeast (almost 6 percentage points), and the largest increases occurred in the Midwest (3.5 points) and the West (3 points).

The proportion of journalists living and working in different regions of the country in 2002 and 1992 matched the distribution of the overall population fairly closely—certainly more than in 1971. Table 1.2 shows a pattern of growth in journalists in the South and West regions of the country during the 1980s and 1990s that parallels the growth in overall population in these regions. But in terms of national prominence and influence, it is still true that the major broadcast networks, news magazines, news services, and some of the most influential newspapers tend to be heavily concentrated in the Northeast, so the regional imbalances in prestige and influence are much greater than Table 1.2 suggests, as was true in the three earlier studies. This point is reinforced by our data on journalists' media exposure patterns presented later in this chapter.

TABLE 1.3
Distribution of Journalists by Region and News Medium
(Percentage in Each Region in 2002)

| | News Medium | | | | | | |
Region	Daily Newspaper (N = 571)	Weekly Newspaper (N = 179)	News Magazine (N = 62)	News Service (N = 69)	Radio Station (N = 105)	Television Station/Networks (N = 163)	Total (N = 1,149)
Northeast	10.4	14.5	58.1	20.3	15.2	5.5	13.9
Midwest (N. Central)	19.4	37.4	8.1	11.6	45.7	53.4	28.3
South	43.7	35.2	29.0	37.7	25.7	28.8	37.3
West	26.6	12.8	4.8	30.4	13.3	12.3	20.2
Total	100.1[a]	99.9[a]	100.0	100.0	99.9[a]	100.0	100.0

[a] Does not total 100% because of rounding.

Table 1.3 also reflects the overall U.S. population growth in the South and the West. Only news magazine journalists continue to be disproportionately clustered in the Northeast, and radio and TV journalists in the Midwest region. Table 1.3 shows the majority of daily newspaper and news service journalists working in the South and West, but overall the Midwest and the South are the regions with the most full-time journalists.

AGE AND GENDER

On average, U.S. journalists were older in 2002 than in the three previous decades, but no more likely to be women, despite dramatic increases in women journalism students and increased emphasis on hiring more women in journalism in the 1980s and 1990s (see Tables 1.4 and 1.5). The median age of U.S. journalists was a bit higher than that of the U.S. civilian labor force, but the pattern is the same for both—a steady increase in average age since the early 1980s as the baby boomers move through the decades. The largest increase from 1992 to 2002 among journalists was in the 45–54 age category, whereas in 1992 the largest increase from 1982 was in the 35–44 bracket, and in 1982 it was in the 25–34 group.

In the early 1970s and 1980s, journalists were disproportionately clustered in the 25–34 age bracket as compared with the U.S. civilian labor force, and in the early 1990s journalists were most overrepresented in the 35–44 bracket even though their median age was virtually identical to that of the civilian labor force. In 2002, however, journalists were overrepresented in the 25–34 and 45–54 brackets, but less so than in previous years, and underrepresented in the under 20 and 20–24 age categories, reflecting only slight growth in the field in the 1980s and slight negative growth in the 1990s. But U.S. journalists have been notably underrepresented in the 20–24 age category as compared with the general labor force since the early 1990s, reflecting the lack of growth of the field since the 1970s.

Many of the journalists hired during the boom period of the 1970s were still in their late 40s or early 50s in 2002, still quite a few years away from retirement. With virtually no growth in the field of traditional mainstream journalism during the 1990s, this left little room for those seeking to enter the field in the first years of the new 21st century, as was true in the early 1990s. The youngest journalists, on average, were women with a median age of 35 (as compared to 42 for men) and Asian American journalists with a median age of 36. Unlike the early 1990s, other minority journalists were not significantly younger on average than were majority white journalists, nor did the different media types vary much in median age, except for television journalists with a median age of 38.

Although 54% of all full-time U.S. journalists hired between 1998 and 2002 were women, the lack of growth in traditional mainstream journalism jobs meant that not enough women in absolute numbers were hired to make a difference in the overall workforce percentage, especially considering the linear drop in the proportion of women by years of experience shown in Figure 1.1. Table 1.5 shows that the percentage of women working as full-time journalists for traditional mainstream U.S. news media has remained virtually constant since the early 1980s, despite the increase in women in the U.S. civilian labor force.

TABLE 1.4
Age Distribution of U.S. Journalistic Workforce (Percentage in Each Age Group)

Age Group	Journalists				U.S. Civilian Labor Force			
	1971[a]	1982–1983[b]	1992[c]	2002	1971[d]	1981[e]	1989[f]	2000[g]
Under 20	0.7	0.1	0.0	0.0	5.1	8.3	6.4	5.7
20–24	11.3	11.7	4.1	4.4	13.9	14.8	11.4	10.3
25–34	33.3	44.9	37.2	29.3	22.2	28.0	29.0	22.0
35–44	22.2	21.0	36.7	27.9	20.0	19.5	24.7	26.5
45–54	18.8	10.9	13.9	28.2	21.0	16.1	15.6	22.3
55–64	11.3	8.9	6.6	7.8	14.1	11.0	9.6	10.3
65 and older	2.3	1.6	1.5	2.3	3.9	2.8	2.8	3.0
Total	99.9[h]	99.1[h]	100.0	99.9[h]	100.2[h]	100.0	100.0	100.1[h]
Median age	36.5	32.4	36.0	41.0	39.2	33.6	36.1	39.1

[a] From Johnstone, Slawski, and Bowman, *The News People*, p. 197.

[b] From Weaver and Wilhoit, *The American Journalist*, p. 19.

[c] From Weaver and Wilhoit, *The American Journalist in the 1990s*, p. 8.

[d] U.S. Department of Labor, 1971, Table A-3, p. 29.

[e] U.S. Bureau of the Census, *Statistical Abstract of the United States, 1982–1983*, 103rd ed., p. 379.

[f] U.S. Bureau of the Census, *Statistical Abstract of the United States, 1991*, 111th ed., p. 392.

[g] U.S. Bureau of the Census, *Statistical Abstract of the United States, 2001*, 121st ed., p. 369.

[h] Does not total 100% because of rounding.

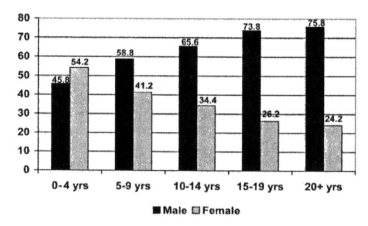

FIG. 1.1.   Gender of journalists by years in journalism (%).

The trend of decreasing proportions of women journalists by years of experience illustrated in Figure 1.1 is very similar to the pattern of a decade ago in 1992, and the percentages of women for all professional age categories except the least experienced (0–4) are nearly identical, suggesting that the attrition rate was about the same (roughly 5% for each 5 years of experience) in 2002 as compared with 1992. Among those journalists with only 0 to 4 years of experience, however, there were significantly more women in 2002 (54.2%) than in 1992 (44.8%). If the attrition rate doesn't change, that will mean more women journalists with more job experience in the future.

In 1992, the average number of years of journalism experience was 15 for men and 12 for women. In 2002, it was 18 years for men and 13 for women, suggesting

TABLE 1.5
Gender of U.S. Journalists (Percentage)

Gender	Journalists				U.S. Civilian Labor Force			
	1971[a]	1982–1983[b]	1992[c]	2002	1971[d]	1981[e]	1989[f]	2001[g]
Male	79.7	66.2	66.0	67.0	66.4	57.5	54.8	53.4
Female	20.3	33.8	34.0	33.0	33.6	42.5	45.2	46.6
Total	100.0	100.0	100.0	100.0	100.0	100.0	100.0	100.0

[a] From Johnstone, Slawski, and Bowman, *The News People*, p. 197.

[b] From Weaver and Wilhoit, *The American Journalist*, p. 19.

[c] From Weaver and Wilhoit, *The American Journalist in the 1990s*, p. 8.

[d] U.S. Department of Labor, 1971, Table A-2, p. 28.

[e] U.S. Bureau of the Census, *Statistical Abstract of the United States, 1982–1983*, 103rd ed., p. 379.

[f] U.S. Bureau of the Census, *Statistical Abstract of the United States, 1991*, 111th ed., p. 392.

[g] U.S. Bureau of the Census, *Statistical Abstract of the United States, 2002*, 122nd ed., p. 381.

that women were still not staying in journalism as long as men or were hired more recently than men, or both. There is evidence in our 2002 study that women were just as likely as men to have had 10 to 14 years of experience and even more likely to have had less than 10 years, supporting the more recent hiring explanation. Men were much more likely to have had 20 or more years of experience than were women, however (45% vs. 29%), which could mainly reflect the tendency for more men than women to be hired into journalism prior to 1982 during the period of large growth in U.S. mainstream journalism in the 1970s.

There are some fairly recent studies, however, that suggest that women are more likely to want to leave journalism than are men. A 2002 survey of 273 newspaper editors by the American Press Institute and the Pew Center for Civic Journalism found that 45% of women, as opposed to 33% of men, said they anticipated a better job at another newspaper or leaving the industry completely.[8] Our own data from 2002 support this tendency, with 21% of women journalists saying that they would most like to be working outside the news media in five years compared with 16% of males.

Even though women were just one-third of the full-time mainstream journalism workforce in 2002, as Table 1.5 indicates, this is a greater proportion than in some other professional occupations measured by the 2000 U.S. Census, such as lawyers and judges (30%), architects (23.5%), engineers (10%), physicians (28%), and dentists (19%).[9] However, for managerial and professional occupations combined, the 2000 U.S. Census reports 46.5% were women, and for the other occupations mentioned earlier, there were significant increases in the proportions of women from 1990 to 2000, unlike journalism, which remained constant during this decade and also during the 1980s.

In addition, our data indicate that 34% of the women journalists supervised other news or editorial employees compared with 45% of men, and 38% of women journalists said they had a great deal of influence in hiring and firing employees compared with 46% of men, suggesting that women journalists in general were somewhat less likely than men to have supervisory responsibilities in their news organizations in 2002. These differences may be explained, in part, by fewer average years of journalism experience among women as compared with men, but this finding does not reveal whether women are leaving journalism because of lack of promotion opportunities or whether they are not competitive for promotions because they are leaving before men, or both.

The gender of U.S. journalists was related to their marital status and family situation in 2002, just as it was in 1992 and 1982. As before, women journalists were significantly less likely to be married (48%) than were men (67%), and less likely to have children living with them (32.5%) than were men (46%). Professor Lee Becker of the University of Georgia, director of the annual surveys of journalism and mass communication enrollment and graduates, explained it this way to Mark Jurkowitz of *The Boston Globe*: "I think that while the newsroom can be friendly to women . . . you have to look at the occupation. There are some occupational characteristics . . . that are at odds with family social life, at odds with child rearing."[10] This view was echoed by University of Maryland journalism professor Maurine Beasley, who said, "If you stay in journalism with the kinds of hours required of you, unless you have a lot of money to pay for round-the-clock child care, you have a difficult row to hoe. Most journalism jobs don't pay that. So, young women go into the field, but they find it not 'family friendly' so they tend to leave the field."[11]

Becker also found, in reanalyzing his data after this *Boston Globe* article was printed in late August of 2003, that women were more than twice as likely as men to have majored in public relations in college, male students were more likely to have had a media internship while in college than were female students (who were more likely to have had an internship in public relations), salary and job benefits were more important to women in selecting a job than they were to men, women students were more likely to have sought jobs in public relations than were men in 2002, and public relations job holders reported that their employers were more likely to pay for more benefits, including maternity leave.[12]

But not all news media were equally attractive (or unattractive) to women in 2002, as our data in Table 1.6 indicate. The proportion of women journalists varied significantly by medium in 2002, with the highest percentage (43.5%) at news magazines and lowest percentages at the major wire service bureaus (20.3%) and radio (21.9%). Compared with 1992, there was a substantial drop in the percentage of women journalists in radio and weekly newspapers and a notable increase in television news, which moved up to second place in proportion of women journalists. Women held steady in daily newspapers and news magazines. It may be that the hours, pay, and benefits were more attractive at news magazines and television than at other news media. Our salary data presented in Chapter 3

TABLE 1.6
Representation of Women Journalists in Different Kinds of U.S. News Media

News Medium	Percentage Women				Case Base			
	1971[a]	1982–1983[b]	1992[c]	2002	1971[a]	1982–1983[b]	1992[c]	2002
Radio	4.8	26.3	29.0	21.9	89	118	100	105
Television	10.7	33.1	24.8	37.4	162	121	137	163
Wire services	13.0	19.1	25.9	20.3	46	47	58	69
Daily newspapers	22.4	34.4	33.9	33.0	920	462	635	569
Weekly newspapers	27.1	42.1	44.1	36.9	78	183	161	179
News magazines	30.4	31.7	45.9	43.5	33	63	61	62
Total	20.3	33.8	34.0	33.0	1,328	994	1,152	1,147

[a] From Johnstone, Slawski, and Bowman, *The News People*, p. 198.
[b] From Weaver and Wilhoit, *The American Journalist*, p. 21.
[c] From Weaver and Wilhoit, *The American Journalist in the 1990s*, p. 10.

TABLE 1.7
Representation of Woman Journalists in U.S. Media
and in U.S. Labor Force by Age (Percentage)

Age Group	Journalists				Total Labor Force			
	1971[a]	1982–1983[b]	1992[c]	2002	1970[d]	1981[e]	1989[f]	2000[g]
Under 25	25.5	42.0	48.9	60.8	40.9	46.5	47.6	47.8
25–34	17.9	35.1	37.9	44.9	32.3	42.5	44.5	46.1
35–44	15.5	28.6	30.6	24.8	35.6	42.6	45.7	46.3
45–54	22.5	33.0	30.6	23.8	38.4	41.8	45.2	47.5
55–64	25.5	24.7	27.6	33.3	36.8	40.1	42.9	45.7
65 and older	9.1	31.2	35.3	34.6	32.8	38.7	41.5	42.9

[a] From Johnstone, Slawski, and Bowman, *The News People*, p. 198.
[b] From Weaver and Wilhoit, *The American Journalist*, p. 22.
[c] From Weaver and Wilhoit, *The American Journalist in the 1990s*, p. 10.
[d] U.S. Bureau of the Census, 1971, Table 328, p. 211.
[e] U.S. Bureau of the Census, *Statistical Abstract of the United States, 1982–1983*, 103rd ed., p. 379.
[f] U.S. Bureau of the Census, *Statistical Abstract of the United States, 1991*, 111th ed., p. 392.
[g] U.S. Bureau of the Census, *Statistical Abstract of the United States, 2001*, 121st ed., p. 367.

indicate that news magazines offered the highest median salaries in 2001, but the wire services were second, followed by TV in third place.

The largest increase in women journalists during the 1990s was in the youngest age category (under 25), as was true a decade ago for the 1980s and as might be expected from the data in Figure 1.1 for women by years of experience. Table 1.7 shows that the proportion of U.S. journalists under 25 years of age who were women exceeded the total U.S. civilian labor force percentage by 13 points, confirming the success of mainstream media in hiring young women during the 1990s. But Table 1.7 also shows a steady drop in the proportion of women by age until the 55–64 age bracket, with dramatic drops of 16 and 20 percentage points between the first and second, and second and third, age categories.

A cohort analysis of these figures suggests that the largest decline in women journalists from 1992 to 2002 came from those who were 25–34 years old in 1992 and 35–44 in 2002 (13 percentage points). This is a larger decline than any in previous studies. There was no such decline in the total labor force, however, suggesting that the demands of journalism may be more difficult for women who have childrearing responsibilities than are other occupations in general. It will be interesting to see how many of the large number of young women journalists stay with this occupation during the 2002–2012 decade.

Among minority journalists, however, the percentage of women was considerably higher than the 33% for the entire main sample: 55.5% of Asian American journalists, 54.1% of African Americans, 46.2% of Hispanics, and 38.9% of Native Americans. This was also true in 1992.

ETHNIC AND RACIAL ORIGINS

In their 1971 study of U.S. journalists, Johnstone and his colleagues concluded that journalists come predominantly from the established and dominant cultural groups in society.[13] Table 1.8 suggests that in 2002 that still was the case, even when the percentages of racial and ethnic minorities were compared with their percentages in the U.S. population. There was a slight increase in the percentages of U.S. journalists with Jewish and Hispanic backgrounds. But except for Jewish journalists, all other groups were still underrepresented in U.S. journalism, especially African Americans and Hispanic Americans, as compared with their relative proportions in the overall U.S. adult population.

Excluding Jewish journalists, the overall percentage of racial and ethnic minorities in full-time U.S. mainstream journalism jobs increased slightly from 8.2% in 1992 to 9.5% if the 0.1% who identified themselves as Pacific Islanders and the 1.0% "Other" minorities are included. This figure of 9.5% lagged far behind the percentage of Hispanics and non-Caucasian races (30.9%) estimated by the 2000 U.S. Census for the total U.S. population. But when compared with the percentage of college-degree holders (effectively the minimum qualification for being hired as a journalist in the United States) who were minorities, the gap is not as

TABLE 1.8
Racial and Ethnic Origins of U.S. Journalists Compared With
Total U.S. Population (Percentage in Each Group)

Ethnicity	Journalists				U.S. Adult Population			
	1971[a]	1982–1983[b]	1992[c]	2002	1970[d]	1981[e]	1990[f]	2002[g]
African American	3.9	2.9	3.7	3.7	11.1	11.8	12.1	12.7
Hispanic	1.1	0.6	2.2	3.3	4.4	6.5	9.0	13.4
Asian American	—[h]	0.4	1.0	1.0	0.5	0.7	2.9	4.0
Native American	—[h]	—[i]	0.6	0.4	—	—	0.8	0.9
Jewish	6.4	5.8	5.4	6.2	2.6	2.6	2.4	2.0
Other (includes Caucasian)	88.6	90.3	87.1	85.4	81.4	78.4	72.8	67.0
Total	100.0	100.0	100.0	100.0	100.0	100.0	100.0	100.0

[a] From Johnstone, Slawski, and Bowman, The News People, pp. 26, 198, 225.

[b] From Weaver and Wilhoit, The American Journalist, p. 23.

[c] From Weaver and Wilhoit, The American Journalist in the 1990s, p. 11.

[d] U.S. Bureau of the Census, Statistical Abstract of the United States, 1972, 93rd ed., pp. 29, 33, 45.

[e] U.S. Bureau of the Census, Statistical Abstract of the United States, 1982–1983, 103rd ed., pp 32, 33, 54, 55.

[f] U.S. Bureau of the Census, Statistical Abstract of the United States, 1991, 111th ed., pp. 22, 56.

[g] U.S. Bureau of the Census, Statistical Abstract of the United States, 2003, 123rd ed., pp. 15, 67.

[h] Not reported by Johnstone, Slawski, and Bowman, The News People.

[i] Not reported by Weaver and Wilhoit, The American Journalist.

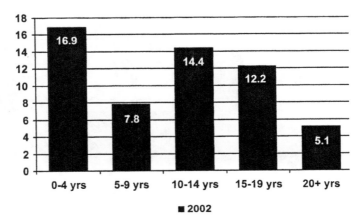

FIG. 1.2. Minority journalists by years in journalism (%).

great. The 2000 U.S. Census estimates that 24% of college-degree holders were minorities, with Asian Americans three times more likely to have earned college degrees than the other minority groups.

If only those full-time journalists hired during the past decade are considered, the overall percentage of minorities was considerably higher than 9.5% (16.9% for those with 0–4 years of experience, as Figure 1.2 indicates). This figure suggests that there have been increased efforts, and some success, in minority hiring in U.S. mainstream journalism during the 1990s.

But Figure 1.2 also shows that after 4 years of experience, the percentage of minority journalists drops sharply, most likely because of a tendency for minorities to leave journalism more quickly than majority Whites. Our data show that, in 2002, minority journalists had an average of 13 years of work experience in journalism, compared with an average of 17 years for nonminority journalists. In 1992, the major drop in the proportion of minority journalists came after 9 years of experience (from 12.4% to 6.4%), but in 2002 the major drop comes after only 4 years, not an encouraging sign for the retention of young minority journalists. The percentages of minority journalists in the 10–14 and 15–19 year categories in 2002 are more encouraging, however, when compared with those in 1992 (14.4% vs. 6.4% and 12.2% vs. 4.8%). These figures suggest that many of the minorities hired in the 1980s have stayed in journalism for 10 years or more.

As with women, some news media have done better than others in recruiting full-time minority journalists. Figure 1.3 shows that television had the highest percentage, whereas weekly newspapers had the lowest. It is likely that the low percentage for weeklies is related to the tendency for most racial minorities in the United States to live in larger urban areas rather than in the smaller towns where weeklies tend to be published. However, the same cannot be said for news magazines, which tend to be located in the largest urban areas and which are

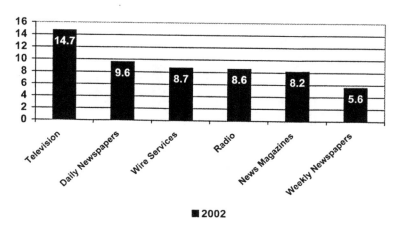

FIG. 1.3. Minority journalists by type of news medium (%).

next-to-last in employment of minorities. Nevertheless, all news media except radio gained in percentages of minorities from 1992 to 2002, and the differences between media, with the exception of television, were not as pronounced in 2002 as they were in 1992.

The higher percentages of minorities in broadcast news media were consistent with more interest in these media by minority journalism students in 1980[14] and in 1987.[15] In our 1982–1983 study of U.S. journalists, we speculated that "minorities are more likely to be attracted to the faster-growing broadcast media than to the more traditional print media of newspapers, news magazines, and news services."[16] This appears to have happened during the past two decades, perhaps because of additional efforts by broadcast news managers to recruit minorities, because of more interest in broadcast media by minority journalism students, or because stations had to demonstrate a commitment to affirmative action during re-licensing before deregulation began.

Although there were real increases in the proportions of racial and ethnic minorities working in some U.S. mainstream news media during the 1990s, it will likely be difficult to retain many of the brightest and most ambitious, given the limited opportunities for advancement in a field that has not grown much, if at all, during the past 20 years, and in which many journalists are still 10 years away from retirement.

RELIGION

Table 1.9 shows that U.S. journalists changed somewhat during the past decade in terms of religious backgrounds, and they reflected the overall U.S. population less closely than in the three previous decades. There was a notable drop in the percentage of journalists coming from a Protestant background (especially if the 4.7% who said Evangelical Christian are not included in the Protestant category), and an increase in the proportion claiming to be brought up in no religion or one other than Protestant, Catholic, or Jewish. Whereas journalists from a Protestant background were underrepresented, Catholics and Jews were somewhat overrepresented in journalism as compared with the overall U.S. population.

There was variation by news medium, however, with journalists working for news magazines and wire services being much more likely to be from Jewish backgrounds than the population at large (26% in news magazines and 13% in the news services). There were also some differences by race, with Blacks more likely to be from Protestant families (49%), Hispanics much more likely to be Catholics (73%), Asians more likely to be from nonreligious backgrounds (19%), and Native Americans more likely to be from another religion (28%).

A new question in our 2002 study asked what religion, if any, journalists practiced now, as contrasted with what religion they were brought up in. The answers to this question revealed that about one-third (34%) did not practice any religion, 27% were Protestants, 5% Evangelical Christians, 20% Catholic, 4% Jewish, and 10% mentioned another religion. If those who said "other or none" are combined, nearly half (44%) of U.S. journalists fall into this category, far more than the 20% reported by the 2000 U.S. Census in Table 1.9, suggesting that

TABLE 1.9

Religious Backgrounds of U.S. Journalists Compared With Religious Preference of Total U.S. Adult Population (Percentage in Each Group)

Religion	Journalists				U.S. Adult Population			
	1971[a]	1982–1983[b]	1992[c]	2002	1974[d]	1981[e]	1992[f]	2002[g]
Protestant	61.5	60.5	54.4	46.2	60.0	59.0	55.0	53.0
Catholic	24.5	26.9	29.9	32.7	27.0	28.0	26.0	25.0
Jewish	6.4	5.8	5.4	6.2	2.0	2.0	1.0	2.0
Other or none	7.7	6.8	10.2	14.8	11.0	11.0	18.0	20.0
Total	100.1[h]	100.0	99.9[h]	99.9[h]	100.0	100.0	100.0	100.0

[a] From Johnstone, Slawski, and Bowman, *The News People*, pp. 90, 225. Figures calculated from Table 5.9.

[b] From Weaver and Wilhoit, *The American Journalist*, p. 24.

[c] From Weaver and Wilhoit, *The American Journalist in the 1990s*, p. 14.

[d] From George H. Gallup, *The Gallup Poll: Public Opinion, 1972–1977*, Vol. 1 (Wilmington, DE: Scholarly Resources, 1973), p. 393.

[e] From *The Gallup Poll: Public Opinion, 1982*, p. 37.

[f] Gallup Organization national telephone survey of 1,001 U.S. adults, July 31–August 2, 1992. Question: What is your religious preference? Data provided by The Roper Center, University of Connecticut.

[g] U.S. Bureau of the Census, *Statistical Abstract of the United States, 2003*, 123rd ed., p. 67.

[h] Does not total to 100% because of rounding.

U.S. journalists in 2002 were far less likely to practice any mainstream U.S. religion than the public at large.

When it comes to the importance of religion or religious beliefs, U.S. journalists were also not in step with the larger society. Our survey results show that the percentage of journalists rating religion or religious beliefs as "very important" was significantly lower (36%) than in the overall U.S. population in December 2002 (61%). But 36% of journalists said religion was "somewhat important," compared to 27% of the population.[17] The results also indicate differences by news medium, with journalists working for news magazines (19%) and wire services (25%) least likely to consider religion very important, and those in radio (47%) and television (47%) most likely. African American and Native American journalists were also most likely to say that religion or religious beliefs were very important (59% and 56%, respectively), and Asian Americans were least likely to say so (28%).

POLITICAL VIEWS

Journalists often have been portrayed as social reformers who are likely to be more liberal than conservative politically.[18] Lichter and Rothman's 1981 study of elite journalists found 54% placed themselves to the left of center, compared to only 19% who chose the right side of the spectrum.[19] These elite journalists' voting records strongly supported the Democratic party in presidential elections from 1964 to 1976. In our 1982–1983 national survey of U.S. journalists, we found a slight left-leaning tendency among journalists, but it was much less pronounced than that found in Lichter and Rothman's sample of Northeastern elite journalists. In our 1992 study, however, we found a more pronounced tilt to the left, a dramatic decrease in those who claimed to be middle of the road, and a small increase in those on the right, as Table 1.10 indicates.

Political Leanings

Table 1.10 also shows that in 2002, U.S. journalists were somewhat less likely to place themselves on the left and somewhat more likely to claim to be a little to the right than in 1992. But compared with the general population, journalists in 2002 were less likely to think of themselves as on the right side of the political spectrum than was the public in general (25% of journalists vs. 41% of the public), and journalists were much more likely to consider themselves on the left (40%) than was the public (17%). Neither journalists nor the general public changed dramatically in political leanings from 1992 to 2002, in contrast to the major changes among journalists from 1982–1983 to 1992.

When we analyzed the political leanings of U.S. journalists separately for executives (those who supervised editorial employees) and staffers, we found

TABLE 1.10
Political Leanings of U.S. Journalists Compared With U.S. Adult Population
(Percentage in Each Group)

Leaning	Journalists				U.S. Adult Population		
	1971[a]	1982–1983[b]	1992[c]	2002	1982[d]	1992[e]	2002[f]
Pretty far to left	7.5	3.8	11.6	9.0	—	—	3
A little to the left	30.5	18.3	35.7	31.1	21	18	14
Middle of the road	38.5	57.5	30.0	33.3	37	41	38
A little to the right	15.6	16.3	17.0	20.4	32	34	37
Pretty far to the right	3.4	1.6	4.7	4.5	—	—	4
Don't know/refused	4.5	2.5	1.0	1.7	10	7	5
Total	100.0	100.0	100.0	100.0	100.0	100.0	100.1

[a] From Johnstone, Slawski, and Bowman, *The News People*, p. 93.

[b] From Weaver and Wilhoit, *The American Journalist*, p. 26.

[c] From Weaver and Wilhoit, *The American Journalist in the 1990s*, p. 15.

[d] From George H. Gallup, *The Gallup Poll: Public Opinion, 1983* (Wilmington, DE: Scholarly Resources, 1984), p. 82.

[e] From Gallup Organization national telephone survey of 1,307 U.S. adults, July 6–8, 1992, and 955 U.S. adults, July 17, 1992.

[f] From Gallup Organization national telephone survey, September 2002. Question: "How would you describe your political views—very conservative, conservative, moderate, liberal or very liberal?"

more staffers than executives classifying themselves as left-of-center and more executives than staffers saying that they were leaning to the right, as was true in the 1971 study (see Table 1.11). In 1982–1983 and 1992, however, there was almost no difference in the proportions of executives and staffers in self-reported political leanings, suggesting less of a gap in political views between managers and staffers than in 2002.

In both groups, there were significant increases from 1982–1983 to 1992 in the proportions of journalists saying that they were pretty far or a little to the left, but from 1992 to 2002, there was a noticeable decline in executives saying this and a slight decline in staffers who reported leaning to the left. There were increases in the percentages claiming to be middle-of-the-road politically, especially among executives, reflecting the general trend for all U.S. journalists. The proportions leaning to the right did not change significantly for staffers, but there was a substantial increase in those leaning to the right among the executives.

In the 1982–1983 study, with its dramatic shift from the left to the center of the political spectrum, we concluded that there was "almost no evidence to support Rothman and Lichter's prediction that the next generation of journalists is likely to be more to the left than is the current generation."[20] In 1992, we had evidence that Rothman and Lichter[21] were better forecasters than we were, although it seems that all journalists, not just the next generation, had swung toward the left during the 1980s, possibly in reaction against the conservative

TABLE 1.11

Political Leanings of U.S. Journalists, Executives, and Staffers (Percentage in Each Group)

Leaning	Executives				Staffers			
	1971[a] (N = 2,220)	1982–1983[b] (N = 471)	1992[c] (N = 487)	2002 (N = 470)	1971[a] (N = 3,075)	1982–1983[b] (N = 528)	1992[c] (N = 654)	2002 (N = 678)
Left	4.5	5.7	11.5	5.6	10.3	6.8	11.9	11.6
Leaning left	30.2	17.2	36.8	31.5	33.6	19.3	35.5	31.6
Middle of the road	43.1	56.9	31.0	36.1	38.0	58.1	29.8	32.5
Leaning right	17.7	18.3	16.8	23.8	15.3	14.4	17.4	18.6
Right	4.5	1.9	3.7	3.0	2.9	1.3	5.4	5.7
Total	100.0	100.0	99.8[d]	100.0	100.1	99.9[d]	100.0	100.0

[a] Calculated from Johnstone, Slawski, and Bowman, *The News People*, p. 226. Ns are weighted in this study, but not the others.

[b] Calculated from Weaver and Wilhoit, *The American Journalist*, p. 28.

[c] Calculated from Weaver and Wilhoit, *The American Journalist in the 1990s*, p. 17.

[d] Does not total 100% because of rounding.

climate of the 1980s. In 2002, there is evidence of a small shift back toward more middle-of-the-road or conservative leanings, especially among supervisors of journalists.

Political Party Identification

Another indicator of U.S. journalists' political views is political party identification. In 1971, Johnstone and his colleagues found that U.S. journalists were predominantly Democrats or Independents. We found the same to be true in 1982–1983, but to a greater degree because of a shift of about 7% from Republicans to Independents. In 1992, as Table 1.12 shows, there was an increase of more than 5 percentage points in those considering themselves Democrats, a slight decrease in those claiming to be Republicans, and a decline in those claiming to be Independents. These trends ran counter to those for the general public, where there was an increase in Republicans and a decrease in Democrats from 1982–1983 to 1992. In 2002, the journalistic trends were somewhat reversed, with significantly fewer journalists claiming to be Democrats, slightly more identifying with the Republican party, and slightly fewer Independents. The percentage identifying with the Democratic party (35.9) was the lowest since 1971.

When compared with the U.S. population in 2002, journalists were only about 4 percentage points more likely to say they were Democrats, but about 13 points less likely to say they were Republicans. Journalists were about as likely as the public to claim to be Independents. Thus, U.S. journalists were most likely to be Democrats and Independents, as was true in the three previous decades, but in 2002 they were closer than in previous studies to the proportions of the U.S. general public. Nevertheless, journalists were significantly less likely than the general public to identify with the Republican party, as has been true since 1982–1983, and much more likely than the public to report some other political affiliation.

In general, minority journalists were much more likely to consider themselves Democrats than were majority Caucasian journalists, especially African Americans (53%) and Asian Americans (55%). There was also a considerable gender gap, with women more likely to say they were Democrats (45%) than men (33%). Men were more likely (36%) than women (29%) to say they were Independents. There was no gender gap for Republicans, however, with 19% of the male and 18% of the female journalists. The most likely to identify with the Republican party were television journalists (26%), and the least likely were wire-service (5%) and Black (5%) journalists.

When we look at political party identification by position in news organizations, it is clear that the biggest decline in Democrats from 1992 to 2002 came from executives, although there was a small decline among staffers as well (see Table 1.13). The biggest gain for the Republicans also came from the managers,

TABLE 1.12
Political Party Identification of U.S. Journalists Compared With U.S. Adult Population
(Percentage in Each Group)

Political Party	Journalists				U.S. Adult Population			
	1971[a]	1982–1983[b]	1992[c]	2002	1972[d]	1982–1983[e]	1992[f]	2002[g]
Democrat	35.5	38.5	44.1	35.9	43	45	34	32
Republican	25.7	18.8	16.4	18.0	28	25	33	31
Independent	32.5	39.1	34.4	32.5	29	30	31	32
Other	5.8	1.6	3.5	10.5	—[h]	—	1	—
Don't know/refused	0.5	2.1	1.6	3.1	—	—	2	5
Total	100.0	100.1[i]	100.0	100.0	100.0	100.0	101.0[i]	100.0

[a] From Johnstone, Slawski, and Bowman, *The News People*, p. 92.
[b] From Weaver and Wilhoit, *The American Journalist*, p. 29.
[c] From Weaver and Wilhoit, *The American Journalist in the 1990s*, p. 18.
[d] From George H. Gallup, *The Gallup Poll: Public Opinion, 1983* (Wilmington, DE: Scholarly Resources, 1984), p. 43.
[e] From *The Gallup Poll: Public Opinion, 1983*, p. 42.
[f] Gallup Organization national telephone survey of 1,307 U.S. adults, July 6–9, 1992. Data provided by The Roper Center, University of Connecticut.
[g] Gallup Organization national telephone survey of 1,003 U.S. adults, July 29–31, 2002.
[h] Not reported by Gallup.
[i] Does not total to 100% because of rounding.

TABLE 1.13
Political Party Identification of U.S. Journalists, Executives, and Staffers (Percentage in Each Group)

Party	Executives				Staffers			
	1971[a] (N = 2,220)	1982–1983[b] (N = 471)	1992[c] (N = 484)	2002 (N = 470)	1971[a] (N = 3,075)	1982–1983[b] (N = 528)	1992[c] (N = 649)	2002 (N = 678)
Democrat	33.5	37.2	44.8	33.0	37.4	41.5	45.0	39.9
Republican	27.5	20.8	14.3	18.3	24.5	17.4	18.3	18.8
Independent	33.2	40.3	37.4	36.1	32.3	39.8	33.1	31.6
Other	5.8	1.9	3.5	12.6	5.8	1.3	3.5	9.7
Total	100.0	100.2[d]	100.0	100.0	100.0	100.0	99.9[d]	100.0

[a]Calculated from Johnstone, Slawski, and Bowman, *The News People*, p. 226. Ns for this 1971 study are weighted.
[b]Calculated from Weaver and Wilhoit, *The American Journalist*, p. 31.
[c]Calculated from Weaver and Wilhoit, *The American Journalist in the 1990s*, p. 20.
[d]Does not total 100% due to rounding.

and staffers held steady. The executives were slightly more likely than the staffers to say they were political Independents.

Attitudes About Abortion

Still another indicator of the political attitudes of journalists was their response to a question about a specific issue (abortion) asked by the Gallup polling organization in a national survey. Although this question — "Do you think abortions should be legal under any circumstances, legal under only certain circumstances, or illegal in all circumstances?" — by no means covers the issue fully, it does allow a comparison of journalists' opinions with those of the public.

Not surprisingly, given the above findings on political leanings and party identification, journalists were inclined to respond in a more liberal manner, with 39.5% saying that abortion should be legal under any circumstance as compared with 25% of the public.[22] Whereas 22% of the public agreed that abortions should be illegal in all circumstances, only 7% of journalists agreed. Journalists were closer to public opinion about abortion in 2002, however, than in 1992, when 51% said that abortions should be legal under any circumstances and only 4% agreed with a complete legal ban.[23]

There was a large gap in 2002 between men and women journalists on this issue, with 33% of the men agreeing that abortions should be legal under any circumstances compared with 53.5% of the women journalists. The least support for this position came from radio (24.5%) and television (31%) journalists, and the most came from news magazine (66%) and wire service (57%) journalists. Minority journalists, except for African Americans, were more likely than the overall sample to say that abortions should be legal under any circumstances.

Attitudes About Firearms

Another question from the Gallup Poll asked, "In general, do you feel that the laws covering the sale of firearms should be made more strict, less strict, or kept as they are now?" On this issue, journalists were somewhat more likely than the public to say that the laws should be more strict (65% of journalists vs. 51% of the public) and somewhat less likely to say that the laws should be less strict (4% of journalists vs. 11% of the public).[24] As for keeping the firearms laws as they are now, 31% of journalists agreed compared with 36% of the public, not a significant difference. This question was not asked of journalists in our 1992 survey.

Among journalists in 2002, women were somewhat more likely than men to favor more strict firearms laws (70% vs. 62%). News-magazine and wire-service journalists were most likely to favor stricter laws (82% and 85%), and those working for radio (47%) were least likely, again suggesting that women journalists and those working for news magazines and wire services were most liberal politically and those working for radio were most conservative. Asian American and African American journalists were more likely than the overall sample to favor stricter gun control laws.

In our 1982–1983 study of U.S. journalists, we concluded that there was a trend among U.S. journalists toward the center of the political spectrum and away from the right and the Republican party, but no visible swing to the left. In 1992, there was a noticeable swing to the liberal side of the spectrum and the Democratic party, almost entirely at the expense of the middle-of-the-road Independents. The swing to the left politically was especially apparent among women and minority journalists and also among staffers of the more prominent Northeastern news media.

In 2002, the pendulum moved back toward the center a bit, with fewer journalists claiming to be leaning left or identifying with the Democratic party, and slightly more claiming to be right-of-center and identifying with the Republican party. But the overall picture was still one of U.S. journalists being somewhat more liberal politically than the public at large, although this varied substantially by news medium, gender and racial and ethnic background, as indicated previously.

MEDIA USE

As was true in the past two decades, U.S. journalists in 2002 were heavy consumers of not only their own media but also the news produced by journalists in other media. Journalists in 2002 reported watching local TV news shows four days a week—about the same as in 1992 (4.2) and viewing TV network news shows an average of only 1.9 days each week—down from an average of 3.3 in 1982 and 2.2 in 1992 (see Table 1.14). This decline in network TV news viewing appears

TABLE 1.14
Frequency of Television News Use by U.S. Journalists
(Percentage of Number of Days Per Week)

Days per Week	Network News	Cable News	NewsHour With Jim Lehrer	Local News
0	40.4	16.6	74.1	14.5
1	13.7	10.0	14.9	7.7
2	12.4	9.0	5.1	8.3
3	11.9	11.1	3.7	11.3
4	4.6	7.5	0.8	8.6
5	10.1	18.7	1.4	18.5
6	2.6	3.8	—	5.7
7	4.3	23.2	—	25.3
Total	100.0	100.0	100.0	100.0
Mean days per week	1.9	3.7	0.5	4.0

to be due to more frequent viewing of cable television newscasts (3.7 days a week on average, up from 3.2 in 1992, and even more for broadcast, wire service, and minority journalists). The frequency of watching cable TV news was nearly equal to that of local TV news viewing in 2002 for the first time.

Newspaper Reading

Table 1.15 shows that the most frequently read newspapers by U.S. journalists were *The New York Times*, *The Wall Street Journal*, and *The Washington Post*. In 1992, *USA Today* was in third place behind the same top two, but it slipped into fourth place in 2002. In 1971, *The Washington Post* was in second place. Reader-

TABLE 1.15
Newspapers Most Often Read by U.S. Journalists
(Percentage Reading Once a Week or More)

Newspaper	Number Journalists Reading	Percentage of Journalists Mentioning (N = 1,149)*
New York Times	438	38.1
Wall Street Journal	263	22.9
Washington Post	230	20.0
USA Today	221	19.2
Los Angeles Times	85	7.4
Chicago Tribune	84	7.3
Atlanta Journal Constitution	45	3.9
New York Post	44	3.8
Boston Globe	40	3.5
Albuquerque Journal	36	3.1
Cleveland Plain Dealer	36	3.1
Denver Post	32	2.8
Dallas Morning News	31	2.7
(Norfolk) Virginian Pilot	29	2.5
New York Daily News	28	2.4
Charlotte Observer	28	2.4
Enterprise (Lexington Park, MD)	28	2.4
Washington Times	27	2.3
San Francisco Chronicle	25	2.2
Chicago Sun Times	24	2.1
Albuquerque Tribune	24	2.1
Rocky Mountain News (Denver)	23	2.0
Raleigh News & Observer	23	2.0
Oregonian	22	1.9
Pittsburgh Post Gazette	22	1.9

* Percentages total to more than 100% because each journalist could name up to 12 different newspapers. Only those newspapers mentioned by 2% or more of all respondents are listed here.

ship of *The New York Times* dropped from one-third in 1982–1983 to about one-fourth in 1992 and rose to nearly 40% in 2002, and readership of *The Wall Street Journal* dropped very slightly from nearly one-fourth in 1992 to just over one-fifth in 2002. But when the percentages of journalists reading these newspapers online are added (Table 1.16), it seems likely that *The Wall Street Journal* and *The Washington Post* have not suffered any loss in the percentage of journalists reading them from 1992. *USA Today* and *The Los Angeles Times* held steady, and the *Chicago Tribune* appears to have gained ground with online newspaper readers.

Regardless of these changes, those newspapers with nationwide visibility among substantial proportions of U.S. journalists were small in number and tended to be located in the Northeast or in the Washington, D.C., area, just as was true in the 1971 Johnstone study, except for *The Chicago Tribune* and *The Los Angeles Times*.

Magazine Reading

The same is true for the magazines that U.S. journalists read regularly, as Table 1.17 indicates. The percentages of journalists reading almost every issue of the top three magazines held steady from 1992 to 2002, but *The New Yorker* moved up from sixth place in 1992 to a tie with *Sports Illustrated* for third place. Other changes included *National Geographic* dropping off the list of magazines mentioned by 1% or more of all responding journalists and *Esquire* dropping from eighth place in 1992 to thirteenth in 2002. *Rolling Stone* held steady, as did *Atlantic Monthly*, but *U.S. News & World Report* dropped from fourth place in 1992 to eighth place in 2002 and lost nearly half of its journalist readers. *Vanity Fair* emerged from obscurity in 1992 (it was not on the list of the top 24 magazines read by journalists then) to climb to fifth place in 2002. In general, the list in 2002 focused on leading information and opinion publications rather than on the more mass-circulation entertainment ones, as was true in 1992, with a few exceptions.

In all, only four newspapers and four magazines were read regularly by 10% or more of U.S. journalists in 2002. All these publications were based on the East Coast, which reinforces the conclusions of the 1971 Johnstone study regarding the pyramidal shape of the prestige hierarchy within the news industry and the dominance of the eastern seaboard.[25] (For a discussion of journalists' exposure to specialized professional publications, see Chapter 4 on professionalism.)

CONCLUSIONS

This analysis of the basic characteristics of U.S. journalists in 2002 finds more similarities to than differences from those in the 1992 study. Among the most prominent **similarities** are these:

TABLE 1.16
Online Newspapers Most Often Read by U.S. Journalists

Newspaper	Number Journalists Reading	Percentage of Journalists Mentioning (N = 1,149)*
The New York Times	287	25.0
Washington Post	234	20.4
Chicago Tribune	65	5.7
USA Today	58	5.0
Los Angeles Times	54	4.7
Boston Globe	47	4.1
Atlanta Journal Constitution	40	3.5
Wall Street Journal	36	3.1
Dallas Morning News	30	2.6
Miami Herald	22	1.9
St. Petersburg Times (Minn.)	20	1.7
Baltimore Sun	20	1.7
St. Louis Post Dispatch	19	1.7
New York Post	18	1.6
Orlando Sentinel	18	1.6
San Francisco Chronicle	18	1.6
Charlotte Observer	17	1.5
Detroit Free Press	17	1.5
Denver Post	16	1.4
Chicago Sun Times	16	1.4
Indianapolis Star	15	1.3
Cleveland Plain Dealer	14	1.2
Guardian, London	14	1.2
Raleigh News & Observer	13	1.1
Philadelphia Inquirer	13	1.1
Houston Chronicle	13	1.1
Detroit News	12	1.0
New York Daily News	12	1.0
Seattle Times	11	1.0

* Percentages total to more than 100% because each journalist could name up to 12 different newspapers. Only those newspapers mentioned by 1% or more of all respondents are listed here.

1. The bulk of full-time U.S. journalists in 2002 were still concentrated in the print media, especially in daily newspapers.
2. Changes in the geographic distribution of U.S. journalists in the 1990s were minor compared with those in the 1970s, as one might expect from the lack of growth in U.S. mainstream journalism in the 1990s. The proportion of journalists living and working in different regions of the country also matched the distribution of the overall population fairly closely, especially in the South and West.

TABLE 1.17
Magazines Most Often Read by U.S. Journalists
(Percentage Reading Almost Every Issue)

Magazine	Number Journalists Reading	Percentage of Journalists Mentioning (N = 1,149)*
Newsweek	358	31.2
Time	321	27.9
The New Yorker	185	16.1
Sports Illustrated	184	16.0
Vanity Fair	73	6.4
Rolling Stone	65	5.7
People	58	5.0
U.S. News & World Report	57	5.0
Entertainment Weekly	51	4.4
Atlantic Monthly	49	4.3
Business Week	42	3.7
The Economist	42	3.7
Esquire	37	3.2
Harper's	35	3.0
Fortune	34	3.0
Consumer Reports	33	2.9
ESPN: the magazine	31	2.7
The New York Times Sunday Magazine	30	2.6
Sporting News	29	2.5
Smithsonian	28	2.4
The New Republic	27	2.3
Forbes	26	2.3
Mother Jones	21	1.8

* Percentages total to more than 100% because each journalist could mention any number of magazines. Only those magazines mentioned by 1.8% or more of all respondents are listed here.

3. U.S. journalists in 2002 were not more likely to be female, despite the increases in women journalism students and the emphasis on hiring more women in journalism in the 1990s. There was an increase in women among journalists hired from 1998 to 2002, but no increase in women among journalists with five or more years of experience.

4. Women journalists in 1992 were still less likely to be married than male journalists and less likely to have children living with them.

5. The New York Times and the Wall Street Journal were still the most regularly read newspapers among U.S. journalists, as were Newsweek and Time news magazines. Overall, as in 1982–1983, only a handful of newspapers and magazines were read regularly by more than 10% of all U.S. journalists—and all but one were based on the East Coast, reinforcing the dominance of the eastern seaboard in U.S. journalism.

This analysis also finds some notable **differences** from 1992, including the following:

1. The size of the mainstream news media full-time journalistic workforce in the United States in 2002 decreased by nearly 5% (almost 6,000 journalists) from 1992, the first estimated drop in the past 31 years.

2. U.S. journalists in 2002 were older, on average, than in 1992. The median age for all journalists increased from 36 to 41. Print journalists in 1992 were older on average (41 years) than were television journalists (38 years). Journalists from 25 to 44 years of age declined significantly as a percentage of all journalists in 2002, compared with 1992, and those 45 to 54 years old increased significantly, reflecting the aging baby boomers.

3. There was slight growth in the percentage of racial and ethnic minorities in U.S. journalism, from 8% in the early 1990s to 9.5% in 1992. Among journalists hired between 1998 and 2002, the percentage of minorities was significantly higher (17%). Television had the highest proportions of minorities, weekly newspapers the lowest, supporting our 1982 prediction that minorities would be more likely to be attracted to the faster growing broadcast media than to the more traditional print media.

4. Journalists in 2002 were less likely to identify with the Democratic party than a decade ago, and less likely to consider themselves to be left of center. They were slightly more likely to identify with the Republican party and to consider themselves right of center and middle-of-the-road politically. Nevertheless, U.S. journalists, in general, were more liberal politically than the U.S. public at large in 2002, although political attitudes varied considerably among journalists by gender, race, ethnicity, and type of news medium.

5. There was a slight decline among U.S. journalists in the average number of local and network TV news shows watched each week during the 1990s and an increase in the viewing of cable television network news from the early 1990s.

6. The Washington Post replaced USA Today as the third most widely read newspaper by U.S. journalists during 1992–2002, and Newsweek, Time, and Sports Illustrated remained the most popular magazines among U.S. journalists, joined by The New Yorker in a tie with Sports Illustrated.

These are the main similarities and differences in the basic characteristics of U.S. journalists working for both print and broadcast mainstream English-language news media from the early 1980s to the early 1990s. They suggest some progress in the recruitment of minorities, but some formidable problems for young people who want to advance in mainstream U.S. news organizations. Because of no growth during the 1990s, many of the most desirable jobs in U.S. journalism are held by people in their late 40s or early 50s, who are still years away from retirement. Without new growth in the field, there will be few opportunities for advancement for the next 10 years or so. This will make it very difficult to retain the brightest and most ambitious young journalists, especially women and minorities who have perceived their chances for advancement to be reduced in the past by their gender or race.

NOTES

1. John W. C. Johnstone, Edward J. Slawski, and William W. Bowman, *The News People: A Sociological Portrait of American Journalists and Their Work* (Urbana: University of Illinois Press, 1976), pp. 18, 195.
2. David H. Weaver and G. Cleveland Wilhoit, *The American Journalist: A Portrait of U.S. News People and Their Work* (Bloomington: Indiana University Press, 1986; 2nd ed., 1991), p. 13.
3. David H. Weaver and G. Cleveland Wilhoit, *The American Journalist in the 1990s: U.S. News People at the End of an Era* (Mahwah, NJ: Lawrence Erlbaum Associates, 1996), p. 2.
4. U.S. Bureau of the Census, *Statistical Abstract of the United States 2001* (Washington, DC: U.S. Government Printing Office, 2001), pp. 393–395.
5. *Statistical Abstract of the United States 2001*, pp. 393–395.
6. *Statistical Abstract of the United States 2001*, pp. 380–381.
7. Johnstone, Slawski, and Bowman, *The News People*, p. 20.
8. Crystal Bolner, "Women Want out of Newsrooms More than Men," *The American Society of Newspaper Editors Reporter*, Reston VA, April 9, 2003, p. 18. See also "The Great Divide: Female Leadership in U.S. Newsrooms," American Press Institute and Pew Center for Civic Journalism, September 2002, accessed on September 1, 2005, at http://www.asne.org/index.cfm?id=4051
9. U.S. Bureau of the Census, *Statistical Abstract of the United States 2001*, p. 380.
10. Mark Jurkowitz, "More Women in J-school Doesn't Translate to Jobs," *The Boston Globe*, August 27, 2003, p. C1.
11. Juli Duin, "Newsrooms' Distaff Divide," *The Washington Times*, September 28, 2001, www.washtimes.com.
12. Lee B. Becker, Tudor Vlad, Jisu Huh, and Nancy R. Mace, "Gender Equity Elusive, Surveys Show," *Freedomforum.org*, December 15, 2003, pp. 1–6. Accessed September 5, 2005, at http://www.freedomforum.org/templates/document.asp?documentID=17784
13. Johnstone, Slawski, and Bowman, *The News People*, pp. 25, 26, 198.
14. Paul V. Peterson, *Today's Journalism Students: Who They Are and What They Want to Do* (Columbus: School of Journalism, Ohio State University, 1981), p. 15.
15. Lee B. Becker and Thomas E. Engleman, "Class of 1987 Describes Salaries, Satisfaction Found in First Jobs," *Journalism Educator*, 43 (Autumn 1988), p. 6.
16. Weaver and Wilhoit, *The American Journalist*, p. 22.
17. Gallup Organization, National telephone survey, December 9–10, 2002. *The Gallup Poll: Public Opinion Two Thousand Two*, p. 397.
18. Leo Rosten, *The Washington Correspondents* (New York: Harcourt, Brace and Company, 1937; reprint ed. by Arno Press, 1974), p. 191; William L. Rivers, "The Correspondents After Twenty-five Years," *Columbia Journalism Review*, 1 (Spring 1962), p. 5; and Stephen Hess, *The Washington Reporters* (Washington, DC: The Brookings Institution, 1981), pp. 87–90.
19. S. Robert Lichter and Stanley Rothman, "Media and Business Elites," *Public Opinion*, 4(5) (October/November 1981), pp. 43–44.

20. Weaver and Wilhoit, *The American Journalist*, p. 29.
21. Stanley Rothman and S. Robert Lichter, "Are Journalists a New Class?" *Business Forum* (Spring 1983), p. 15.
22. Gallup Organization, National telephone survey of U.S. adults, May 6–9, 2002. *The Gallup Poll: Public Opinion Two Thousand Two*, p. 204.
23. Weaver and Wilhoit, *The American Journalist in the 1990s*, p. 19.
24. Gallup Organization, National telephone survey of U.S. adults, October 14–17, 2002. *The Gallup Poll: Public Opinion Two Thousand Two*, p. 327.
25. Johnstone, Slawski, and Bowman, *The News People*, p. 89.

Education and Training

In 1971, nearly 60% of all full-time U.S. journalists were college graduates, and 34% had majored in journalism.[1] In 1982–1983, nearly 75% of all U.S. journalists had completed a college degree, and 40% had majored in journalism.[2] In 1992, 82% of all U.S. journalists had earned a college degree, and 39% of these had majored in journalism.[3] In 2002, 89% of all U.S. journalists had a college degree, and 36% had majored in journalism.

Thus, in 31 years, the proportion of full-time U.S. journalists working for mainstream news media with at least a college bachelor's degree jumped from 58% to 89%, but the proportion of those college graduates with a journalism degree increased only slightly from 34% to 36%. If radio-TV, telecommunications, mass communication, and communication are added to journalism, however, the percentage of college graduate journalists who majored in any of these communications subjects increased from 41% to 50% during the 1971–2002 period. And in 2002, 73% of the college graduates had taken courses in journalism, and 74% had worked on a college newspaper or other campus medium, suggesting much more influence of college-level journalism education than the 36% figure for journalism majors.

This chapter discusses the educational backgrounds and preferences of U.S. journalists in light of a decade of significantly increased numbers of journalism school graduates entering the media job market. Comparisons are made with the earlier 1971, 1982–1983, and 1992 studies of journalists, and also with U.S. Census figures for the population in general.

PAST DEVELOPMENTS IN JOURNALISM EDUCATION

In an earlier book on American journalists, based on the 1982–1983 survey, we divided the history of journalism education in the United States into four rough periods: 1700s–1860s, 1860s–1920s, 1920s–1940s, and 1940s–early 1980s.[4] We do not repeat all the details of that brief historical sketch here, but pick up from the final part of it, where we traced the growth of schools and departments of journalism and mass communication since the turn of this century.

U.S. schools and departments of journalism have grown greatly in number, and in numbers of students, since the beginning of the 20th century. Lindley argues that journalism's emergence in the academic world was part of a great surge in education for the professions.[5] A tabulation of the number of schools with four-year journalism programs by the *Journalism Bulletin* showed an increase from 4 in 1910, to 28 in 1920, to 54 in 1927. These programs produced fewer than 25 graduates a year in 1910, but this figure ballooned to 931 in 1927.

Forty-four years later, in 1971, when the Johnstone survey of U.S. journalists was conducted, Peterson reported 36,697 undergraduate and graduate students who claimed journalism as a major, 7,968 degrees (undergraduate and graduate) granted, and "slightly more than 200 colleges and universities offering majors in journalism."[6] By the fall of 1982, just before our earlier national survey of U.S. journalists was carried out, 304 schools reported programs in journalism.[7] Of these, 216 participated in Peterson's annual enrollment survey and reported a total of 91,016 journalism or mass communication majors, and 20,355 degrees granted. In the fall of 1992, just after our summer 1992 survey of journalists was conducted, Becker reported a total of 413 U.S. degree-granting programs in journalism and mass communication, with a projected total enrollment of 143,370 students and 36,171 degrees granted for all 413 programs (Table 2.1).[8] Becker and his colleagues reported a total of 463 U.S. degree-granting journalism–mass communication programs for the fall of 2002 during the interviewing for our survey of journalists, with a projected total enrollment of 194,500 undergraduate and graduate students and 45,939 degrees (undergraduate and graduate) granted (see Table 2.1).[9]

RECENT DEVELOPMENTS IN JOURNALISM EDUCATION

It is obvious from these numbers that there has been tremendous growth in the number of college-level journalism–mass communication programs in the United States since early in the 20th century. Even during the 1980s and the 1990s, when there was little or no growth in mainstream news media full-time journalism positions, there was substantial growth in numbers of college programs (from 304 to 413 to 463) and in total enrollment of students (91,016 to 143,370 to 194,500). As Table 2.1 shows, the growth rates for programs, numbers of students, and degrees granted far outstripped the negligible growth in U.S. mainstream journalism during the 1982–2002 period. But the growth in the broader communication field and the printing and publishing industry from 1982 to 2002, as estimated by the U.S. Bureau of Labor Statistics, was greater than that in journalism enrollments in actual number of jobs, if not in percentage. Many of these jobs, if not most, were not journalism or news positions, however.

The nature of journalism and mass communication education has also changed over time, along with size. The early programs were concerned mostly with reporting, copy reading (editing), feature writing, editorial writing, criticism, history, comparative journalism, and ethics, according to a survey of about 40 institutions in 1924.[10] Modern journalism–mass communication education programs offer most of these same "news-editorial" subjects, but in addition often

TABLE 2.1

Number of U.S. College Programs, Majors, and Degrees
in Journalism–Mass Communication Compared With Number of U.S. Jobs
in Journalism–Mass Communication

Variable	1971[a]	1982–1983[b]	1992[c]	2002[d]	Growth, 1992–2002 (%)
Number of degree-granting programs	200+	304	413	463	12.1
Number of students enrolled	36,697	91,016	143,370	194,500	35.7
Number of degrees granted	7,968	20,355	36,171	45,939	27.0
Number of undergraduate degrees granted	6,802	18,574	33,752	42,060	24.6
Estimated full-time journalism jobs in mainstream U.S. news media[e]	69,500	112,072	122,015	116,148	-4.8
Estimated number of jobs in communication[f]	1.129 million	1.384 million	1.265 million	1.692 million	33.8
Estimated number of jobs in publishing[g]	1.104 million	1.292 million	1.538 million	1.492 million	-3.0

[a] Paul V. Peterson, "Journalism Growth Continues at Hefty 10.8 Per Cent Rate," *Journalism Educator*, 26, 4 (January 1972), pp. 4–5, 60.

[b] Paul V. Peterson, "J-school Enrollments Hit Record 91,016," *Journalism Educator*, 37, 4 (Winter 1983), pp. 3–4, 7, 8.

[c] Lee B. Becker, personal communication from 1992 annual enrollment census and 1991–1992 annual graduate survey, July 22 and 28, 1993.

[d] Tudor Vlad, Lee B. Becker, Jisu Huh, and Nancy R. Mace, "2002 Annual Survey of Journalism & Mass Communication Enrollments," August 1, 2003. Also available at www.grady.uga.edu/annualsurveys

[e] The 1971 figure is from John W. C. Johnstone, Edward J. Slawski, and William W. Bowman, *The News People: A Sociological Portrait of American Journalists and Their Work* (Urbana: University of Illinois Press, 1976), p. 195. The 1982 figure is from Weaver and Wilhoit, *The American Journalist*, 1986, p. 13. The 1992 figure is from David Weaver and G. Cleveland Wilhoit, *The American Journalist in the 1990s* (Mahwah, NJ: Lawrence Erlbaum Associates, 1996), p. 31.

[f] From *Statistical Abstract of the U.S. 2002*, p. 396. Figures are for 1970, 1981, 1989, and 2001, and are for all jobs, including technical, clerical, and production.

[g] From *Statistical Abstract of the U.S. 2002*, p. 395. Figures are for 1970, 1982, 1990, and 2001, and are for all jobs, including technical, clerical, and production.

include courses in mass media and society, communication law, photojournalism, visual communication, public relations, advertising, broadcast news, online or Web journalism, and telecommunications.

In a 1982 survey of 216 journalism schools, Peterson found that of 17,316 journalism bachelor's degrees identified by sequence, 26% were in news-editorial, 21% in radio-TV, 13% in public relations, 19% in advertising, and 21% in other areas.[11] A decade later, in their survey of 2,648 spring 1991 graduates of 79 journalism–mass communication programs, Becker and Kosicki found that bachelor's degrees in news-editorial had dropped to 17%, broadcasting (radio-TV) had stayed steady at 21%, public relations had increased to 18%, advertising had declined to 14%, and other areas had increased to 29%.[12]

In their annual survey of 2,963 journalism and mass communication 2001–2002 graduates from 103 programs, Becker and his colleagues found that news-editorial bachelor's degrees had dropped again during the 1991–2002 period from 17% to 14%, broadcasting had dropped slightly from 21% to 19%, public relations had increased slightly from 18% to 19%, advertising had dropped slightly from 14% to 12.5%, and other areas had increased from 29% to 34%.[13] These other areas included mass communication, in general, as well as other subjects such as magazines, photojournalism, graphics and design, interpersonal communication, journalism teaching, agricultural or technical journalism, and media studies.[14]

Employment Patterns

Of about 18,600 journalism–mass communication graduates who received bachelor's degrees in 1982, slightly more than one-half (53%) found mass communication jobs, with 12% going to daily newspapers, 10% to public relations, 8% to advertising agencies, and 6% to television stations. The remaining graduates who found mass communication jobs went to weekly newspapers, radio stations, magazines, and news services. Those who did not find such jobs went to graduate and law schools (about 9%) or to other work (nearly 23%). Nearly 12% were unemployed after graduation, and 3% said they were not looking for work.[15]

In 1991, of 34,000 bachelor's-degree graduates in journalism and mass communication, only 22% found jobs in mass communication, with 5% going to daily newspapers, 2% to public relations agencies, 4% to advertising agencies, and 3% to television stations. The remaining graduates who found mass media jobs went to weekly newspapers (about 3%), radio stations (3%), magazines (1.5%), and news or wire services (0.2%). Some of those who did not find media jobs went to other jobs in communication—about 26% in corporate public relations and advertising; educational, military, or government communications; or production/other companies. Some went into noncommunication work (27%) or continued in school (7.5%). About 16% were unemployed.[16]

In 2002, of 42,000 bachelor's-degree graduates from U.S. journalism and mass communication programs, about one-half of those who found jobs within

6 months were working in the communication field broadly defined, essentially the same proportion as in 1991.[17] About one-fourth (24%) found jobs in mass communication, with 6% going to daily newspapers, 2% to weekly newspapers, 0.6% to wire services, 2% to radio stations, 5% to television, 1% to cable, 1% to magazines, 3% to public relations agencies, and 3% to advertising agencies. Others working in communication went to corporate public relations and advertising departments (about 2%), newsletters and trade press (about 1%), book publishing (0.5%) and Web site publishing (0.4%).[18] The remainder working in communication (about 22%) were in educational, military, or government communications or in production. Some went into noncommunication work (24%) or continued in school (8.4%). About 16% were unemployed.

Thus, from 1982 to 2002, the proportion of journalism–mass communication bachelor's-degree graduates who went into mass communication jobs declined sharply from just over one-half (53%) to about one-fourth. The percentage going into other communication work (e.g., corporate, educational, military, or government) increased, and the unemployed proportion also rose from 12% to 16%. As in our earlier studies, but even more dramatically, the career patterns and interests of journalism–mass communication students have both reflected and spurred the expansion of journalism education into a more general mass or public communication field.

But what about the educational backgrounds of those journalists still working for the more traditional news media in this country? Did they change much during 1992–2002? How many graduated from college? From a graduate program? What fields of study did they pursue? Where did they attend university classes? Where did they end up working? How many journalists thought they needed additional training or education? In what subjects? To answer these and other questions about the education of U.S. journalists, we turn to our survey findings from interviews with them during the summer and fall of 2002.

EDUCATIONAL BACKGROUNDS OF U.S. JOURNALISTS

For most professionals, it would be redundant to ask about educational background because their professional standing is based on certain programs of studies.[19] Although that is certainly true for medical doctors, lawyers, licensed nurses and certified public accountants, it is not true for U.S. journalists. There is no single set of requirements for becoming a journalist, although it is more and more necessary for one to have at least a bachelor's degree from a college or university. As of 2002, there was still no specific credential necessary to enter the field of journalism, but it was clearer than ever before that a bachelor's degree in journalism–mass communication was becoming the most common qualification among those recently hired. Becker estimated that 75% of entry-level daily newspaper

TABLE 2.2

Amount of Formal Schooling by Age (Percentage of U.S. Journalists With Different Amounts of Schooling)

Highest Educational Attainment	Under 25				25-34				35-44			
	1971[a]	1982–1983[b]	1992[c]	2002	1971	1982–1983	1992	2002	1971	1982–1983	1992	2002
Some high school	1.7	0.9	0.0	0.0	0.8	0.0	0.0	0.0	1.8	0.0	0.2	0.0
Graduated from high school	3.8	8.6	2.1	5.9	8.6	3.3	2.6	0.6	11.4	5.2	2.6	1.6
Some college	44.4	16.4	19.2	3.9	26.6	14.0	7.9	6.3	22.7	21.4	12.8	7.5
Graduated from college	41.4	69.8	76.6	86.3	41.4	63.3	78.5	75.3	42.7	45.7	61.5	66.3
Some graduate training	6.0	1.7	0.0	0.0	13.9	10.2	3.3	3.0	9.9	9.5	8.3	6.3
Graduate degree(s)	2.7	2.6	2.1	3.9	8.7	9.1	7.7	14.9	11.4	18.1	14.5	18.4
Total	100.0	100.0	100.0	100.0	100.0	99.9	100.0	100.0	99.9	99.8	99.9	100.0
N	130	116	47	51	409	449	427	336	310	210	421	320

Highest Educational Attainment	45-54				55+				Total			
	1971	1982–1983	1992	2002	1971	1982–1983	1992	2002	1971	1982–1983	1992	2002
Some high school	1.8	0.9	0.0	0.0	3.9	1.9	0.0	0.0	1.8	0.6	0.1	0.0
Graduated from high school	12.3	16.5	8.8	1.5	28.8	20.2	11.8	5.2	12.2	9.4	4.2	1.8
Some college	29.9	26.6	20.7	10.8	21.8	20.2	29.0	17.2	27.9	19.7	13.6	8.9
Graduated from college	37.8	34.9	45.0	64.8	31.5	43.3	40.9	52.6	39.6	50.3	64.5	68.0
Some graduate training	10.6	8.3	10.0	6.2	7.4	6.7	6.5	3.4	10.5	8.7	6.2	4.7
Graduate degree(s)	7.6	12.8	15.6	16.7	6.6	7.7	11.8	21.6	8.1	11.1	11.4	16.6
Total	100.0	100.0	100.1	100.0	100.0	99.1	100.0	100.0	100.1	99.8	100.0	100.0
N	274	109	160	324	180	104	93	116	1,303	988	1,148	1,147

[a] 1971 figures from Johnstone, Slawski, and Bowman, The News People, p. 200.
[b] 1982–1983 figures from Weaver and Wilhoit, The American Journalist, p. 47.
[c] 1992 figures from Weaver and Wilhoit, The American Journalist in the 1990s, p. 34.

journalists in the early 1990s were graduates of journalism–mass communication programs.[20] Our data show that 76% of journalists in all news media under 25 years of age had majored in journalism or mass communication, and 75% of those with less than 5 years of experience in journalism had taken undergraduate courses in journalism.

Years of Schooling

Almost all U.S. journalists in 2002 had graduated from college (89%). Of those who did, about 36% majored in journalism, as noted earlier. The figures in Table 2.2 indicate significant increases in college graduates during the 1992–2002 decade among all age groups of U.S. journalists. Overall, the proportion of college graduate journalists rose from 82% to 89% during the past decade, and there was also an increase in the proportion holding a graduate degree (from 11.4% to 16.6%). This increase occurred in every age category. For those under 25 and from 45 to 54, however, the very slight increases in graduate degrees were not significant and could be due entirely to sampling error. The percentage of journalists with only a high school diploma decreased in every age category except those under 25 years old, and the percentage with only some college also decreased in every age category. Thus, a bachelor's degree was clearly the minimum requirement for a full-time job as a U.S. journalist in mainstream news media in the early 2000s.

When journalists were compared with the overall U.S. population, it became even clearer that a bachelor's degree was the necessary qualification for being a journalist. Whereas the percentage of U.S. journalists with 4-year college degrees increased by about 7 points to 89% during the 1992–2002 decade, the percentage of the overall population with college degrees increased by only about 5 points — from 21% to nearly 26%.[21]

In 1971, Johnstone and his colleagues argued that there was substantial heterogeneity in educational backgrounds of journalists. Then, there were sizable minorities of journalists who had never been to college, especially among those 55 and older (nearly one-third). But 31 years later, we found very few who had not attended college, even among the oldest journalists. The proportion of journalists without a college degree declined sharply from 42% to only 11%. Thus, the basic undergraduate college degree is much more the standard educational credential of U.S. journalists than 31 years ago, especially for those just entering journalism, as Table 2.2 indicates.

Variation Among Media

In 1971, Johnstone found that different kinds of news organizations varied greatly in the percentage of college graduates they employed. There was still some variation by news medium in 2002, but Table 2.3 indicates that it was less than in 1971, when the extremes were 37% for radio and 88% for news magazines. In

TABLE 2.3
Number of U.S. Journalists Who Are College Graduates by Media Type
(Percentage Who Graduated From College)

Media Type	1971 (%)[a]	1982–1983 (%)[b]	N	1992 (%)[c]	N	2002 (%)	N
News magazines	88.2	93.7	63	95.1	61	96.8	62
Wire services	80.4	95.7	47	94.7	58	98.6	69
Daily newspapers	62.6	74.4	462	84.3	634	91.9	571
TV	58.7	80.2	121	83.2	137	92.6	163
Weekly newspapers	43.6	69.8	182	77.0	161	79.3	179
Radio	36.6	52.5	118	59.0	100	76.5	105
Total print sector	59.4	76.4	754	84.4	914	90.2	881
Total broadcast sector	47.7	66.5	239	73.0	237	86.1	268
Total sample	58.2	73.7	998	82.1	1,151	89.3	1,149

[a] Johnstone's cases are not reported because they were weighted and not directly comparable to ours. From John Johnstone, Slawski, and Bowman, *The News People*, p. 200.

[b] From Weaver and Wilhoit, *The American Journalist*, p. 48.

[c] From Weaver and Wilhoit, *The American Journalist in the 1990s*, p. 35.

1992, the range of college graduates employed was still from radio to news magazines, but it had shrunk from 51 to 36 percentage points. In 2002, the range shrunk even more to about 22 percentage points, from 98.6% in the major wire services to 76.5% in radio.

The differences between the top four news media (news magazines, wire services, daily newspapers, and television) were much less pronounced than in the previous three studies. Radio and weekly newspaper journalists were least likely to hold a college degree, as in 1971, but even these journalists were much more likely than not to have a bachelor's degree in 2002 (three-fourths or more did). The largest increase in college graduates from 1992 to 2002 was among radio journalists, who jumped 17 points from 59% to 76.5%.

Johnstone and his colleagues attributed much of the difference in percentage of college graduates among the different news media to differences in sizes of media organizations and the communities in which they operated. Table 2.4 shows that differences by size of news organization were much less in 2002 than in 1971 but somewhat larger than in 1982–1983 or 1992. Only among the smaller news organizations in 2002 (those with 25 or fewer full-time journalists) was the proportion of college graduates less than in the larger news organizations. There was virtually no difference in the percentage of college graduate journalists in the other size categories, including the largest news organizations.

Thus, size of news organization and, by inference, size of community, were not significant predictors of holding a college degree in the early 1990s, as they were 21 years previous. Given the tremendous increase in the numbers of journalism-school bachelor's degrees from 1971 (6,802) to 2002 (42,060), it is not surprising that more college graduates have had to seek journalism jobs in the smaller news organizations.

TABLE 2.4
Number of Journalists Who Are College Graduates
by News Organization Size

Size of Editorial Staff	1971 (%)[a]	1982–1983 (%)[b]	N	1992 (%)[c]	N	2002 (%)	N
1–10	44.0	68.7	415	73.6	292	77.0	261
11–25	48.1	76.7	176	85.3	116	85.4	157
26–50	58.1	75.9	133	84.4	212	94.0	166
51–100	59.4	77.8	117	84.3	166	94.3	176
More than 100	76.2	81.0	142	85.4	343	94.9	294
Total			983		1,129		1,054

[a] Johnstone's cases are not reported because they were weighted and not directly comparable to ours. From Johnstone, Slawski, and Bowman, *The News People*, p. 201.

[b] From Weaver and Wilhoit, *The American Journalist*, p. 50.

[c] From Weaver and Wilhoit, *The American Journalist in the 1990s*, p. 35.

Regional Differences

In 1971, Johnstone and colleagues found "a surprising consistency" in the percentages of college-graduate journalists working in the nine census divisions of the country.[22] We found less such consistency in 1982–1983, with almost a 17-point difference between the divisions with the lowest and highest proportions of college-graduate journalists.[23] Ten years later, in 1992, we found even less consistency, with just over a 19-point difference between the lowest (East North Central) and highest (New England) divisions (see Table 2.5). But aside from these two extremes, there was not much difference among the other seven divisions (from 79% to 85% college graduates).[24]

In 2002, we found more consistency in college graduates by region as Johnstone et al. did in 1971, with only a 10-point difference between lowest (West South Central) and highest (Middle Atlantic). The other seven regions varied only from 86% to 92%, again suggesting that a bachelor's degree was the minimum qualification for becoming a full-time journalist in all parts of the country.

The proportion of college-graduate U.S. journalists increased from 1992 to 2002 in every region of the country, with the largest increases in the East North Central and Middle Atlantic areas. In 1971 and 1982–1983, the Middle Atlantic and Pacific divisions boasted the largest percentages of college graduates; in 1992, New England, the Middle Atlantic, and the South Atlantic areas were the leaders; in 2002, it was the Middle Atlantic and New England areas. These regions were also the leaders in the proportions of the general population with a college degree, especially New England, although these population percentages were far below those for journalists, as Table 2.5 shows.

Journalism–mass communication majors in 2002 varied more widely by area of the country than did college graduates, as Table 2.6 indicates. The highest

TABLE 2.5
College-Graduate Journalists by Region of Employment
(Percentage Graduating from College)

Region of Country[h]	Journalists				U.S. Population			
	1971[a]	1982–1983[b]	1992[c]	2002	1970[d]	1980[e]	1990[f]	2000[g]
New England	52.2	76.3	91.4	92.1	12.1	19.3	27.4	31.2
Middle Atlantic	61.0	81.3	84.7	94.3	10.9	17.1	22.6	27.6
East North Central	58.5	71.9	71.9	86.1	9.5	14.5	18.8	23.8
West North Central	52.4	71.9	82.3	88.6	9.8	15.1	19.3	27.2
South Atlantic	58.1	67.2	85.3	91.0	10.5	15.8	21.0	24.7
East South Central	59.1	64.7	82.0	90.0	7.7	12.0	14.7	20.7
West South Central	52.9	79.5	79.4	84.5	10.0	14.9	20.5	23.1
Mountain	58.2	68.2	79.2	89.4	14.6	18.3	22.7	26.1
Pacific	61.8	79.3	82.6	87.5	15.8	19.5	24.3	27.6
Total U.S.	58.2	73.9	82.1	89.3	10.7	16.3	21.3	25.6

[a] From Johnstone, Slawski, and Bowman, *The News People*, p. 202.

[b] From Weaver and Wilhoit, *The American Journalist*, p. 51.

[c] From Weaver and Wilhoit, *The American Journalist in the 1990s*, p. 37.

[d] From U.S. Bureau of Census, *Statistical Abstract of the U.S.*, *1973*, 94th ed., p. 117. Percentages are for those residing in each region.

[e] From U.S. Bureau of Census, *Statistical Abstract of the U.S.*, *1982–83*, 103rd ed., p. 144.

[f] From the U.S. National Center for Education Statistics, *Digest of Education Statistics*, *1992*, Table 12, p. 21.

[g] From U.S. Bureau of Census, *Statistical Abstract of the United States: 2001*, p. 141.

[h] **New England** includes Maine, New Hampshire, Vermont, Massachusetts, Rhode Island, and Connecticut. The **Middle Atlantic** region includes New York, New Jersey, and Pennsylvania. The **East North Central** region includes Ohio, Indiana, Michigan, Illinois, and Wisconsin. The **West North Central** area includes Minnesota, Iowa, Missouri, North Dakota, South Dakota, Nebraska, and Kansas. The **South Atlantic** region includes Delaware, Maryland, Washington DC, Virginia, West Virginia, North Carolina, South Carolina, Georgia, and Florida. The **East South Central** area includes Kentucky, Tennessee, Alabama, and Mississippi. The **West South Central** region includes Arkansas, Louisiana, Oklahoma, and Texas. The **Mountain** region includes Montana, Idaho, Wyoming, Colorado, New Mexico, Arizona, Utah, and Nevada. The **Pacific** area includes Washington, Oregon, California, Alaska, and Hawaii. Source is U.S. Bureau of the Census, *Current Population Reports*, Series p-25, no. 913.

proportion of these majors came from undergraduate colleges in the South Central states (Alabama, Arkansas, Kentucky, Louisiana, Mississippi, Oklahoma, Tennessee, and Texas) and Mountain states (Montana, Idaho, Wyoming, Colorado, New Mexico, Arizona, Utah, and Nevada), as was true in 1992. This was a notable change from 1982, when the largest percentages of journalism and communication majors came from colleges in the Midwest, an area that has been historically strong in journalism programs. But journalism–mass communication education still had the least influence in New England and the Middle Atlantic states, as was true in 1982–1983 and 1992, where the majority of the most prominent news media are located.

TABLE 2.6
College Major of U.S. Journalists by Region
of College (Percentage of College-Graduate
Journalists in 1982–1983, 1992, and 2002)

Region of Country[a]	Journalists Majoring in Journalism–Mass Communications[b]		
	1982–1983[c]	1992[d]	2002
New England	31.7	30.8	29.9
Middle Atlantic	33.3	34.0	41.8
East North Central	62.4	56.1	67.9
West North Central	68.9	60.7	68.3
South Atlantic	45.5	49.3	58.4
East South Central	44.1	65.7	75.0
West South Central	55.6	67.9	73.6
Mountain	56.7	65.6	77.2
Pacific	59.8	61.6	52.6
Total U.S.	53.2	53.5	59.7

[a] See Table 2.5 for a listing of states included in each region of the country.
[b] Includes journalism, radio and TV, telecommunications, and other communications.
[c] From Weaver and Wilhoit, *The American Journalist*, p. 52.
[d] From Weaver and Wilhoit, *The American Journalist in the 1990s*, p. 38.

There was some growth in percentages of journalism–mass communication majors in the Middle Atlantic and many other regions, but there was no growth in New England and negative growth in the Pacific region. Overall, however, the proportion of college-graduate U.S. journalists majoring in journalism or mass communication grew somewhat during the 1990s in contrast to the 1980s.

Did graduates of colleges in various regions of the country tend to work in the same areas where they attended college? As Table 2.7 shows, the majority did, especially in East North Central states (Illinois, Indiana, Michigan, Ohio, and Wisconsin) and in the West South Central (Arkansas, Louisiana, Oklahoma, and Texas), where three-fourths were working in the same region where they attended college. This was not as true in the Mountain, Middle Atlantic, and South Atlantic regions, where less than a majority of journalists who attended college ended up working in the same region, possibly because of out-migration from some states with limited journalism job opportunities and in-migration to the Middle Atlantic region where more and larger news organizations are located.

TABLE 2.7
Region of College by Region of Employment
of U.S. Journalists

Region of Country[a]	Percentage of Journalists Employed in the Same Region in Which They Attended College		
	1982–1983[b]	1992[c]	2002
New England	63.5	41.9	55.3
Middle Atlantic	54.1	65.8	46.3
East North Central	63.6	39.6	76.5
West North Central	55.6	56.4	68.1
South Atlantic	61.4	81.8	47.9
East South Central	70.6	69.1	56.4
West South Central	72.8	57.1	77.1
Mountain	61.3	57.4	39.2
Pacific	79.3	66.3	57.7

[a] See Table 2.5 for a listing of states included in each region of the country.

[b] From Weaver and Wilhoit, The American Journalist, p. 53.

[c] From Weaver and Wilhoit, The American Journalist in the 1990s, p. 38.

Fields of Study in College and Graduate School

Although journalism was the most popular major field of study for both undergraduates and graduates in 1971, formal training in journalism was not typical among practicing journalists (not just college graduates), because only 23% held journalism undergraduate degrees and just 7% had completed graduate degrees in journalism.[25] In 1982–1983, we found the same pattern, although the proportion of working journalists with an undergraduate journalism degree had increased to nearly 30%, and those holding a graduate journalism degree had inched up to 7.5%.[26] In 1992, 35% of all U.S. journalists held undergraduate journalism degrees, and just over 7% held graduate journalism degrees (see Table 2.8).[27] In 2002, about the same proportion of U.S. journalists held undergraduate journalism degrees (36%), but the percentage with graduate journalism degrees rose slightly to nearly 9%.

Thus, between 1971 and 2002, there was considerable growth in the proportion of all U.S. journalists (not just college graduates) holding undergraduate journalism degrees (from 23% to 36%) and slight growth in the percentage with journalism graduate degrees (from 7% to nearly 9%).

Table 2.8 shows that when radio and television (telecommunications) and other communication subjects (such as advertising, public relations, and speech communication) were combined with journalism, slightly more than one-half of all working journalists majored in communication in college, a slight increase from 1992 and a huge increase from the one-fourth who did so in 1971.

In addition to these increases in journalism and communication majors, our surveys of U.S. journalists indicate that 77% of those hired in 1991 had taken undergraduate courses in journalism or media studies and 75% of those hired between 1998 and 2002 had also done so. In addition, 76% of those journalists under 25 years of age had majored in journalism–mass communication (see Table 2.11). These figures suggest that formal college-level education in journalism–mass communication in 2002 was close to a necessary condition for an entry-level journalism job in U.S. mainstream news media during the 1990s.

In 1982–1983, we noted that the increase in journalism–communication majors had come largely at the expense of English and creative writing—from 23% of college graduates in 1971 to 15% in 1982–1983.[28] But in 1992 and 2002, there was little change in the percentages majoring in subjects other than communication (see Table 2.8). English as a major rose slightly from 1982 to 1992, history dropped a bit and political science was up slightly, but overall there were no significant changes in the majors of those journalists who completed college. There was a 5-point jump in the percentage of all journalists with a liberal arts and sciences major and a 13-point increase in communication majors, mainly because of the increase in the percentage of journalists who had completed a college degree.

Among those relatively few journalists who had completed graduate degrees, nearly one-half in 2002 had majored in journalism or communication, about the same proportion as in 1982–1983 but about 10 points lower than in 1992. The most popular other graduate majors were law, English, and business. In both 1982–1983 and 1992 those earning graduate degrees in journalism–communication were most likely to have majored in these subjects at the undergraduate level. In the 1992 survey, 37% of journalists who earned graduate degrees in journalism–mass communication also earned undergraduate degrees in these same subjects, compared with 40% in the 1982–1983 survey. But in 2002, this figure had dropped to 32%, indicating that only about one-third of journalists who earned graduate degrees in journalism–mass communication had majored in the same subject as undergraduates. The most popular other undergraduate majors were English, political science, and history.

Thus, the "high degree of educational diversity" of journalists found in the 1971 study eroded somewhat in the 1990s. In 2002, more journalists graduated from college, and more majored in journalism or communications at the undergraduate level. Still, in most undergraduate journalism programs, the major classes totaled only about one-fourth of all classes taken; in many of these programs, a second major or concentration was required that contributed to more educational diversity than the numbers majoring in journalism or communications suggest.

TABLE 2.8

Fields of Study of U.S. Journalists in College (Percentage of U.S. Journalists)

Subjects	Major Field in College (1971)[d]		Major Field in College (1982–1983)[e]		Major Field in College (1992)[f]		Major Field in College (2002)	
	Sample	College Graduates	Sample	College Graduates	Sample	College Graduates	Sample	College Graduates
Journalism	22.6	34.2	29.5	39.8	34.9	40.6	36.2	39.5
Radio and TV	1.8	2.8	4.4	5.9	4.3	5.0	3.0	3.2
Other communication specialty	3.1	4.7	6.7	9.0	9.2	10.7	14.1	15.0
Total communication field	27.5	41.7	40.6	54.7	48.4	56.3	53.3	57.7
English, Creative writing	15.1	22.9	10.9	14.7	13.9	16.2	13.7	14.9
History	6.4	9.7	4.7	6.3	3.8	4.4	4.4	4.8
Other humanities	2.9	4.4	4.9	6.6	4.8	5.6	4.0	4.4
Political science, government	5.0	7.5	3.6	4.9	5.3	6.1	5.4	5.8
Other social sciences	3.6	5.5	3.3	4.4	3.8	4.4	4.5	4.9
Liberal arts, unspecified	1.1	1.6	1.0	1.4	1.0	1.1	0.8	0.8
Mathematics	0.4	0.6	0.2	0.3	0.4	0.5	0.3	0.3
Physical or biological sciences	0.8	1.2	1.2	1.6	1.8	2.1	2.6	2.8
Total Liberal arts & sciences	35.3	53.4	29.8	40.2	34.8	40.4	35.7	38.7
Agriculture	0.2	0.3	0.4	0.5	0.1	0.1	0.1	0.1
Business	1.0	1.5	1.7	2.3	1.7	2.0	1.4	1.5
Education	0.5	0.8	1.3	1.8	0.8	0.9	0.9	1.0
Law	a	0.1	0.1	0.1			0.3	0.3
All other fields	1.5	2.3	0.3	0.4	0.2	0.2	0.4	0.5
Total other fields	3.2	5.0	3.8	5.1	2.8	3.2	3.1	3.4
Total	66.0[b]	100.1[c]	74.2[b]	100.0	86.0[b]	99.9[c]	92.6[b]	99.8[c]

[a] Less than one-tenth of 1%.
[b] Does not total to 100% because some journalists were not college graduates, and does not total to percentage of college graduates because some majored in more than one subject.
[c] Rounding error.
[d] From Johnstone, Slawski, and Bowman, The News People, p. 203.
[e] From Weaver and Wilhoit, The American Journalist, p. 56.
[f] From Weaver and Wilhoit, The American Journalist in the 1990s, p. 39.

ARE JOURNALISM MAJORS DIFFERENT?

Given the increases in proportions of all U.S. journalists majoring in journalism and mass communication in the past two decades, it is important to ask what difference that makes. In 1982–1983, we found no indication that majoring in journalism was correlated with job stability (number of previous jobs in journalism), job satisfaction, gender, race, or type of ownership of news organization.[29] In 1992, this was also true, except that journalism majors were more likely to be women (38%) than were other majors (32%).[30]

In 1982–1983, the most notable differences between journalism majors and others were in type of medium, size of media organization, region of employment, and age. A decade later, in 1992, there were still significant differences by type of medium, size of news organization, region of employment, and age. In 2002, there were significant differences by region, type of news organization (as shown in Table 2.9) and size of news organization (as shown in Table 2.10) but not in gender or age as compared with other majors. There were also a few other differences in attitudes about the ethics of certain reporting practices (paying for information, undercover employment, and use of hidden microphones or cameras, all of which were less likely to be approved by journalism majors), the importance of a few journalistic roles, perceptions of the goals of one's own news organization, the perceived influence of journalism training and wire service budgets on news judgment, and the percentage of social contacts connected to journalism.

But these differences between journalism and other majors were few compared to the overwhelming number of similarities, including supervisory responsibilities, frequency of reporting and editing, attitudes about different aspects of

TABLE 2.9
College Major of U.S. Journalists by Media Type
(Percentage of College-Graduate Journalists
in 1982–1983, 1992, and 2002)

Media Type	Journalists Majoring in Journalism–Mass Communication[a]					
	1982–1983	N	1992	N	2002	N
Magazines	25.9	58	24.1	58	23.3	60
Wire services	53.3	45	47.2	53	48.5	68
Daily newspapers	56.3	348	53.7	533	62.3	525
Television	62.9	97	78.6	112	73.5	151
Weekly newspapers	50.4	127	40.8	120	52.8	142
Radio	53.1	64	64.4	59	65.0	80
Total N		739		935		1,026

[a] Includes journalism, radio and TV, telecommunications, and other communications.

TABLE 2.10
College Major of U.S. Journalists by News Organization
Size (Percentage of College Graduate Journalists
in 1982–1983, 1992, and 2002)

Editorial Staff	Journalists Majoring in Journalism-Mass Communication[a]					
	1982–1983	N	1992	N	2002	N
1–10	53.3	287	54.9	215	59.7	201
11–25	62.5	136	67.7	99	54.5	134
26–50	54.5	101	52.6	171	68.6	156
51–100	58.7	92	55.7	140	66.3	166
More than 100	35.3	116	48.6	292	55.9	279
Total N		732		917		936

[a] Includes journalism, radio and TV, telecommunications, and other communications.

their jobs, income, years in journalism, views about most questionable reporting practices and professional roles, beliefs about civic journalism practices and influences on news judgment, political leanings, political party identification, attitudes about abortion and firearms laws, religious affiliation, marital status, and media use habits.

Table 2.9 shows that the college-graduate journalists working in news magazines, wire services, and weekly newspapers were less likely to have majored in journalism or mass communication than those working for other kinds of journalism organizations. Television, radio, and daily newspaper journalists were most likely to be journalism–mass communication majors. If only journalism majors are considered, rather than journalism and mass communication majors, the picture changes somewhat, with television and radio dropping considerably in rank. Daily newspapers were most likely to employ journalism majors (43%), followed by the wire services (36%), weekly newspapers (32%), television (31%), radio (22%), and news magazines (19%).

Table 2.10 indicates that journalism majors were more likely to work for medium-sized news organizations (between 26 and 100 editorial staff) than for the smallest and largest. Still, the median staff size for journalism majors was 60, compared to 40 for other majors, no doubt reflecting the high percentages of journalism majors working for larger daily newspapers. Notable changes from 1992 to 2002 were the increases in the percentages of journalism–mass communication majors in the three largest categories and the decrease in the 11–25 category. This pattern suggests that journalism majors were infiltrating the ranks of even the largest newspapers in the early 1990s, some of which have been resistant to hiring journalism graduates in the past.

Taken together, these findings, plus those illustrated in Tables 2.3, 2.5, and 2.6, suggest that the influence of journalism education was least where the percentages of college graduates were the highest for journalists and the general

TABLE 2.11
College Major of U.S. Journalists by Age
(Percentage of College Graduate Journalists
in 1982–1983, 1992, and 2002)

Age	Journalists Majoring in Journalism-Mass Communication[a]					
	1982–1983	N	1992	N	2002	N
Under 25	65.9	88	67.6	37	76.1	46
25–34	59.8	373	63.8	376	65.5	313
35–44	39.6	154	49.3	353	62.5	291
45–54	40.3	62	33.0	112	53.5	284
55 and over	45.8	59	44.4	54	41.4	90
Total N		736		932		1,024

[a] Includes journalism, radio and TV, telecommunications, and other communications.

population—in the Northeast and in news magazines. This was also true in 1992, probably because of the relative scarcity of major journalism schools in the Northeast, as compared to other regions of the country, as well as the tendency for news magazines to hire journalists who are more specialized in a subject (and more likely to have a graduate degree) than in the other news media.

In their 1971 study, Johnstone and his colleagues found that the number of journalists with undergraduate degrees in fields other than journalism and communication had decreased among more recent graduates, leading them to wonder whether this suggested a trend toward declining media recruitment of persons from other occupations.[31] We found in 1982–1983 and in 1992 that, among more recent college graduates, there were fewer majoring in fields other than journalism and communications, suggesting that the news media (except for news magazines) were indeed recruiting more heavily from journalism–mass communication schools than in the past.

Table 2.11 shows that among recent graduates in 2002 (those under 25 years of age), fewer than in earlier years majored in other fields, with slightly more than three-fourths majoring in journalism or mass communication and slightly less than one-fourth majoring in other fields. The percentage of journalism–mass communication majors increased in every age category except the oldest (55 and over) from 1992 to 2002, and for the first time these majors were in the majority in all age categories except the oldest, again suggesting that despite criticisms of journalism schools, hiring practices favored their graduates.

CONTINUING EDUCATION OF JOURNALISTS

In their 1971 study, Johnstone and colleagues found that just over one-third (36%) of the journalists in their national sample said they had participated in some kind of education program since becoming journalists. Twenty years later, in 1992, that figure had jumped to 58%, with daily newspaper journalists most likely to have done so (69%), and radio (39%) and television (40%) journalists least likely. In 2002, we found that nearly two-thirds (64%) had taken a short course, sabbatical leave, workshop, or fellowship since becoming a journalist, with those working for daily newspapers most likely to have done so (69%), followed closely by those in weekly newspapers (67%) and the wire services (65%). Those least likely to have had any continuing education were in news magazines (48%), television (56%) and radio (57%).

In addition to this trend of increased participation in short courses, sabbaticals, workshops, or fellowships by U.S. journalists, we also found an increase in the percentage who said they wanted additional training—from 62% in 1992 to 77% in 2002 (see Table 2.12). This 2002 figure was virtually identical to that of 1982, and it seems likely that the decrease to 62% in 1992 was due to a slight change in question wording when we asked if journalists felt they needed addi-

TABLE 2.12
Preferences of U.S. Journalists for Continuing Education
(Percentage of Total Sample Mentioning)

Variable	1971[a]	1982–1983[b]	1992[c]	2002
Total who said they would like some kind of additional training	57.7	76.8	61.6	77
Journalism	10.1	15.4	11.4	34.2
New technology, multimedia	—	—	—	12.4[d]
Political science, government	8.9	4.3	4.9	2.1
English, literature, writing	7.2	8.9	4.7	—
History	3.9	3.1	3.8	—
Economics	3.6	3.6	2.9	—
Law	2.7	3.3	2.2	5.2
Business	2.6	9.2	7.2	2.1
Photography	2.2	2.1	1.6	4.1
News analysis, clinics, seminars	1.7	12.9	9.8	8.2
Shorthand	1.5	0.0	0.3	—
Modern languages	1.5	2.2	2.6	6.2
Total who said they would not like additional training	42.3	23.2	38.4	23
	100.00	100.00	100.0	100.0
	(N ≅ 1,315)	(N = 987)	(N = 1,148)	(N = 1,149)

[a] From Johnstone, Slawski, and Bowman, *The News People*, pp. 45, 207. Subjects mentioned by fewer than 1.5% of journalists are not included in this table. Therefore, the percentages for the individual subjects do not total to the percentages wanting additional training.

[b] From Weaver and Wilhoit, *The American Journalist*, p. 61.

[c] From Weaver and Wilhoit, *The American Journalist in the 1990s*, p. 44.

[d] This category was not coded in the previous studies.

tional training, as contrasted with asking whether they would like additional training in 1982–1983 and in 2002.

Table 2.12 shows that the subject preferences for additional training in 2002 changed substantially from 1992. Many more journalists in 2002 were interested in training in journalism broadly defined (communications, advertising, broadcasting) and in new technology and multimedia skills. Compared with 1992, there was also some increased interest in law, photography, and modern languages. There were notable decreases in the proportions wanting additional training in government or political science, history, economics, and business (marketing, accounting, management, and computer science). In 1971, Johnstone found that academic subjects were cited more frequently than those he called *vocational*, whereas in 2002, we found (as we did in 1982–1983 and 1992) an increased tendency to mention more vocational subjects.

A similar pattern emerged from 652 daily and weekly newspaper journalists working at 123 newspapers in a 1992 study carried out by The Freedom Forum and the Roper Center for Public Opinion Research. The most often cited interests for additional training were in ethics, writing, privacy, libel law, management, editing, and reporting.[32] This study also found a fairly high ranking of computer-assisted or database reporting and a strong showing for special expertise in subjects such as environment, race, and gender.

A more recent 2002 telephone survey of 786 news executives and 1,178 news staff members from all U.S. mainstream news media, conducted by the Princeton Survey Research Associates with funding from the Knight Foundation, found that training in basic journalism skills was most likely to be offered on a weekly or monthly basis, but training in beat coverage areas such as politics, business, or health and in journalism ethics, values, and legal issues was generally scheduled only a few times a year at most.[33] This study also found that more journalism staffers thought that training in journalism ethics, values, and legal issues was very important compared to training in beat coverage areas or journalism skills.[34]

The Freedom Forum study found that those journalists who were under 40, women, college graduates, and journalism majors generally had more interest in continuing education than those older than 40, men, and nongraduates or nonjournalism majors. In our 1992 study, journalists most likely to want additional training were those who had worked in journalism five years or less, were minorities, were very dissatisfied with their jobs, and made less than $15,000 in 1991. In 2002, the profile was somewhat similar: women, minorities, less experienced, weekly newspaper, lower-income, and online journalists were most likely to say they would like additional training.

As in 1982–1983 and 1992, it was not surprising that in 2002 younger, less experienced journalists were more likely to want some form of continuing education, especially education that they thought would help them advance their careers. What was different from 1982–1983, however, was that plans to stay in journalism and college education were no longer associated with wanting additional training. Thus, commitment to journalism no longer seemed correlated with interest in continuing education. Instead, it was experience and job conditions, gender and race that predicted the desire for continuing education.

CONCLUSIONS

In 2002, it was more the case than ever before in American journalism that a bachelor's degree in journalism–mass communication was becoming the necessary qualification for being hired as a journalist by the mainstream news media, especially television, radio, and daily newspapers. At the same time, the lack of growth in mainstream news media jobs during the 1990s, coupled with dramatic growth in journalism-mass communication degrees granted, resulted in about the same proportion of journalism-mass communication graduates taking more traditional mass communication jobs as in the early 1990s—about one-fourth. From 1982 to 2002, however, the proportion of journalism–mass communication college graduates who went into mass communication jobs declined sharply from just over one-half to about one-fourth. The percentage going into other communication work such as corporate, educational, military, or government increased, and the unemployed rose somewhat.

In 1971, Johnstone and his colleagues concluded that there was substantial heterogeneity in educational backgrounds of U.S. journalists, but they also predicted that differences in these backgrounds would become less pronounced as those in the oldest age groups were replaced by younger journalists. This prediction was supported by our 1982–1983 study and was even more strongly confirmed in 1992 and 2002. As of 2002, there were very few U.S. journalists without a college degree (11%), as compared with 1971 (42%), and the percentage of all journalists who majored in journalism–mass communication was about twice what it was in 1971 (from 27% to 53%).

Differences in proportions of college graduates by media type and size of organization were markedly less in 2002 than in 1971 or in 1982–1983, but differences in college major by region of the country still persisted, with journalists who studied in the Northeast much less likely to have majored in journalism–mass communication than those who attended college in another region of the country. As in 1992, news magazines (nearly all located in the Northeast) were by far the least likely of all the news media to employ graduates of journalism–mass communication programs, although they were among the most likely to hire college graduates and those with graduate degrees.

In 1982–1983, we concluded that the increase in journalism–mass communication majors from 1971 to 1982–1983 had come largely at the expense of English and creative writing, but in 1992 and 2002, there was little change in the percentages of journalists majoring in subjects other than communication. At the graduate level, however, there was a significant increase in the proportion majoring in journalism–mass communication from 1982–1983 to 1992 (nearly 10 points to about 60%), largely at the expense of majors in other humanities and education, and a 6-point increase in English majors. From 1992 to 2002, however, the proportion majoring in journalism or communication in graduate school declined to the 1982–1983 level of 50%, and the most popular other graduate majors were law, English, and business. Only about one-third of U.S. journalists in 2002 who earned graduate degrees in journalism or communication had majored in the same subject during their undergraduate studies.

Thus, the "high degree of educational diversity" of journalists found in the 1971 study eroded somewhat in the 1990s. In 2002, more journalists had graduated from college, and more had majored in journalism or communications at the undergraduate level. Still, in most undergraduate journalism programs, the major classes totaled only about one-fourth of all classes taken, and in a number of these programs, a second major or concentration was required that contributed to more educational diversity than the percentages of journalism and communication majors might suggest. In 2002, we found a few differences between journalism and other majors by region, type and size of news organization, and in attitudes about the ethics of certain reporting practices, the importance of a few journalistic roles, and the goals of one's own organization, but these differences were few compared to the great number of similarities.

In addition to the increases in college graduates and in journalists majoring in journalism–mass communication, we also found an increase in those who had participated in a continuing education program (short course, sabbatical, workshop, or fellowship) since beginning work as a journalist, especially among daily newspaper journalists. The subjects of interest tended to be more applied or vocational than in 1971 and more closely tied to a desire to advance one's own career, again suggesting somewhat less educational diversity than three decades previous.

Because the educational backgrounds of U.S. journalists were not as diverse as they were 20 or 30 years ago, we might expect their views on the importance of different aspects of work and on professional values and ethics to be more homogeneous than in the earlier studies. But the following chapters on working conditions, professionalism, women, and minorities demonstrate that there is still much diversity (more attitudinal than demographic, perhaps) among U.S. journalists.

NOTES

1. John W. C. Johnstone, Edward J. Slawski, and William W. Bowman, *The News People: A Sociological Portrait of American Journalists and Their Work* (Urbana: University of Illinois Press, 1976), pp. 31, 36, 200, 203.
2. David H. Weaver and G. Cleveland Wilhoit, *The American Journalist: A Portrait of U.S. News People and Their Work* (Bloomington: Indiana University Press, 1986, 2nd ed., 1991), pp. 41, 46–47, 54–56.

3. David H. Weaver and G. Cleveland Wilhoit, *The American Journalist in the 1990s: U.S. News People at the End of an Era* (Mahwah, NJ: Lawrence Erlbaum Associates, 1996), pp. 29, 32–35, 38–41.

4. Weaver and Wilhoit, *The American Journalist*, pp. 41–44.

5. William R. Lindley, *Journalism and Higher Education: The Search for Academic Purpose* (Stillwater, OK: Journalistic Services, 1975), p. 3.

6. Paul V. Peterson, "Journalism Growth Continues at Hefty 10.8 Per Cent Rate," *Journalism Educator,* 26, 4 (January 1972), pp. 4, 5, 60.

7. Paul V. Peterson, "J-school Enrollments Hit Record 91,016," *Journalism Educator,* 37, 4 (Winter 1983), pp. 3–8.

8. Lee B. Becker, personal communication from 1992 annual enrollment census and 1991–1992 annual journalism–mass communication graduate survey, July 22 and 28, 1993. See also Lee B. Becker and Gerald M. Kosicki, "Annual Census of Enrollment Records Fewer Undergrads," *Journalism Educator,* 48, 3 (Autumn 1993), pp. 56–57, where the figure for total degrees granted was adjusted from 36,171 to 36,336.

9. See also Lee B. Becker, Tudor Vlad, Jisu Huh, and Nancy R. Mace, "Annual Enrollment Report: Graduate and Undergraduate Enrollments Increase Sharply," *Journalism & Mass Communication Educator,* 58, 3 (Autumn 2003), pp. 273–300, as well as the following Web site: www.grady.uga .edu/annualsurveys/

10. Lindley, *Journalism and Higher Education*, p. 4.

11. Peterson, "J-school Enrollments Hit Record 91,016," p. 9.

12. Lee B. Becker and Gerald M. Kosicki, "Summary Results from the 1992 Annual Enrollment & Graduate Surveys," paper presented at the 1993 convention of the Association for Education in Journalism, Table 2.

13. Lee B. Becker, Tudor Vlad, Jisu Huh, and Nancy R. Mace, "2002 Annual Survey of Journalism & Mass Communication Graduates," paper presented at the 2003 convention of the Association for Education in Journalism & Mass Communication, August 1, 2003, Table S1. See also the following Web site: www.grady.uga.edu/annualsurveys/

14. Personal communication from Dr. Tudor Vlad, Assistant Director, James M. Cox Jr. Center for International Mass Communication Training and Research, Grady College of Journalism and Mass Communication, University of Georgia, Athens, GA, July 15, 2004.

15. The Dow Jones Newspaper Fund, *1984 Journalism Career and Scholarship Guide* (Princeton, NJ: Dow Jones Newspaper Fund, 1984), p. 14.

16. Becker and Kosicki, "Summary Results," Table 9.

17. Becker, Vlad, Huh, and Mace, "2002 Annual Survey of Journalism & Mass Communication Graduates," Table 16.

18. Becker, Vlad, Huh, and Mace, "2002 Annual Survey of Journalism & Mass Communication Graduates," Tables S11–S14.

19. Johnstone, Slawski, and Bowman, *The News People*, p. 31.

20. Lee B. Becker, personal communication, July 28, 1993, based on unpublished research by him for The Dow Jones Newspaper Fund.

21. U.S. Bureau of the Census, *Statistical Abstract of the United States, 2001* (Washington, DC: U.S. Government Printing Office, 2001), p. 139.

22. Johnstone, Slawski, and Bowman, *The News People*, p. 34.

23. Weaver and Wilhoit, *The American Journalist*, p. 50.

24. Weaver and Wilhoit, *The American Journalist in the 1990s*, pp. 36–37.

25. Johnstone, Slawski, and Bowman, *The News People*, pp. 36, 203.

26. Weaver and Wilhoit, *The American Journalist*, pp. 54, 56, 57.

27. Weaver and Wilhoit, *The American Journalist in the 1990s*, p. 39.

28. Weaver and Wilhoit, *The American Journalist*, p. 54.

29. Weaver and Wilhoit, *The American Journalist*, pp. 55–60.

30. Weaver and Wilhoit, *The American Journalist in the 1990s*, pp. 41–43.

31. Johnstone, Slawski, and Bowman, *The News People*, p. 39.

32. Brian J. Buchanan, Eric Newton, and Richard Thien, *No Train, No Gain: Continuing Training for Newspaper Journalists in the 1990s* (Arlington, VA: The Freedom Forum, 1993), pp. 10–12.

33. *Newsroom Training: Where's the Investment?* "Twelve Key Findings" (Miami, FL: John S. and James L. Knight Foundation, 2002), p. 9.

34. *Newsroom Training: Where's the Investment?* "News Staffers Interview: Topline Results," p. 7.

Journalists in the Workplace

In Tampa, Florida, the newsroom gave way to the News Center at the start of this century. Media General, a Richmond, Virginia–based company that owns more than 100 U.S. media organizations, built the News Center to house three of its properties: the *Tampa Tribune*, WFLA-TV, and TBO.com, an online service.[1] Within this "converged" news operation, the journalists working for the television station, the newspaper, and the online service no longer compete with one another. They share. They share ideas, stories, tips, staff, equipment, and perhaps even the occasional joke around the water cooler. One Media General executive has called the $40 million News Center a "laboratory," and in a very real sense, an experiment is taking place there—an experiment in the organization of news work.[2]

A few months into the News Center experiment, broadcast journalist Jackie Barron wrote an article for the *Nieman Reports* describing her experience covering a federal murder trial for, simultaneously, the newspaper, the television station, and the Web site in Tampa.[3] The article captured her conflicting sentiments about the assignment—her exhilaration at learning how to handle multimedia reporting and her concern about the impact that this "juggling act" might have on the quality of her work; her appreciation for the way the experience improved her reporting techniques and her wariness about the exhausting demands of supplying information for three different outlets. "Convergence might mean that the old rules governing television and newspaper reporting will need to be altered as journalists construct this new media," she concluded in her article. "And editors, news directors, reporters and photojournalists—working together—can become parents of innovative forms of newsgathering and transmission."[4]

During the last decade, the work environment for many American journalists like Jackie Barron has been transformed. The changes undertaken in Tampa are undoubtedly at the extreme, but very few news organizations—and, as a consequence, very few journalists—have remained unaffected by the emergence of the Web as a vehicle for distributing news and information. Sometimes these consequences may be relatively mundane. The article that a reporter crafted for the morning newscast also finds its way onto the TV station's Web site. E-mail makes it easier to solicit and edit letters to the editor. But in other cases, the changes could be profound. A newspaper reporter is suddenly expected to do double-duty as an expert commentator on the nightly newscast. A TV videographer is asked to shoot still photos for the newspaper. A magazine writer is assigned to take part in a "chat" with readers via the publication's Web site. These are new professional obligations for journalists. As with Jackie Barron, some may be embraced with zeal and others with trepidation.

In 1992, at the time of the last American Journalist survey, the Web was just beginning to evolve into a vehicle for distributing news and information.[5] By 2002, virtually every sizable media organization in the country had a Web presence, and public use of online news sites was growing.[6] News organizations embraced the Web, in part, because technological change permitted it and, in part, because owners believed it was an economic necessity.[7] The growth of online journalism was perhaps the most visible change to occur in the workplace of American journalists during the last 10 years, but it was only one of several significant developments. News-media ownership became more consolidated.[8] Economic problems led to staff reductions and layoffs.[9] Potential threats to professional autonomy emerged as news organizations became more market driven.[10] Media observers and journalists alike grew concerned about the commitment that news organizations had to covering public affairs.[11] The "civic journalism" movement challenged the traditional relationship among journalists, sources, and audience members.[12]

All of these changes have created turbulence in journalists' work environment, and it is within the context of this turbulence that we have examined what American journalists think of the conditions of their work and the satisfactions they take from it. This chapter begins with an exploration of why journalists said they were drawn to this field and then goes on to examine:

- The characteristics of typical senior managers, junior managers, nonmanagement personnel and reporters;
- The perceived autonomy of reporters and the constraints that they believe affect their professional freedom;
- The communication between journalists and their supervisors, their sources, and their audience members;
- The assessment journalists have of their news organizations' efforts to inform the public and to strike a balance between commercial and professional goals;
- The salaries of news workers;

- The amount of satisfaction journalists have with their jobs; and
- The likelihood that journalists will change careers during the next 5 years.

WHY JOURNALISM?

Some found their way into journalism by plan, others quite by accident. ("I couldn't come up with anything else to do. That's all I could think of. Plus my parents were going to kick me out of the house if I didn't get a job," said a 44-year-old reporter for a Virginia daily newspaper.) One was drawn by the promise in college of free tickets "into a bunch of things," another by the promise of a career in which he "could make a difference in people's lives." Several wanted a front-row seat at sporting events, while others wanted a front-row seat on history. Some can't recall why they were attracted to this work. For others, it's all that they can ever remember wanting to do.

Many paths led to the front doors of the nation's newsrooms. In the two most recent American Journalist surveys, those who chose journalism as a career were asked what led them to do so. Their responses were notable both for the diverse circumstances that surrounded their decisions and for the similar themes that they evoked in explaining why they gravitated toward this occupation. Very often, the decision could be traced to a pivotal person, a pivotal choice, a pivotal interest, a pivotal event, as was the case for a 45-year-old Florida reporter:

> My grandmother was a Cherokee and I spent a lot of time with her when I was younger. She taught me a lot about nature and to ask questions. . . . Believe it or not that's how I first became interested in journalism. I was a writer—I wrote poetry, got published when I was young—but it was in that wanting to know the answers, and sometimes those answers were not easily found reading a paper and watching television. I wanted to go directly to the source for the information. . . . (My grandmother) taught me to look for the truth in whatever the subject, whatever the issue might be. And that it's not simply the facts—it's how it affects the lives of the people. And that's what I do for a living.

This very personal explanation for choosing a career in journalism touched on several common elements in the responses journalists gave—writing, searching for answers, seeking truth, serving the public. In general, the answers to the question "why journalism" fell into four broad categories:

- The intrinsic appeal of the tasks that journalists perform;
- The desire to be in a profession that has an important social or political role;
- The journalist's early experiences with or connection to the profession; and
- The belief that the work would be varied and exciting.

To get a sense about how often these answers occurred, we drew a sample of 123 responses and analyzed them. The results of that analysis are summarized below.

Intrinsic Appeal of the Tasks

About 40% of those whose responses we examined were drawn to the intrinsic tasks of journalistic work—writing, telling stories, talking to people, asking questions, covering events, and so forth. More than anything else, a love of writing is what drew people into journalism. As was the case in the 1992 American Journalists survey, this was the most common answer among the responses we examined. More than one in five journalists mentioned writing as a primary motivation for seeking a career in the news media, and many others listed it as a secondary consideration. "I just enjoy writing," a 38-year-old radio journalist from Ohio said. "I enjoy telling people what's going on, and after your years of experience, you get like an adrenaline rush from the really big stories."

Writing is a creative act, and that was appealing to many journalists as well. "I knew I needed an outlet to be creative in school," said an online editor, 46, who works in Florida. "I didn't want to take creative writing. I wanted something a little more substantial, so I went into journalism because I knew it would let me be more creative." A 32-year-old sports director from Illinois felt about the same way. "Basically, it was something that I always wanted to do. I always enjoyed writing, and I always enjoyed creative sports journalism. And this is something that I thought would give me an avenue to that."

While writing was what attracted the largest number of journalists, different aspects of news gathering appealed to others. About 14% of the responses that we examined spoke of things such as the chance to talk to a diverse group of people, to go out and cover events, to ask others questions, to engage in creative activities, or to investigate how things worked. That last reason was what appealed to a 28-year-old newspaper writer from Maryland. "I thought it was very interesting to find out how the world worked," she said. "I really enjoy working with people, finding out how things worked—everything along those lines." Another journalist, a 32-year-old editor for a news magazine who lives in Washington, D.C., said she was attracted by the challenge of news gathering, adding that journalists "seemed like my kind of people."

Finally, the chance to be a storyteller was a lure to about 7%. "Because I like to tell stories," responded a 54-year-old columnist for a daily newspaper in Ohio. "You deal with the truth, and you're exposed to real life on an infinite amount of aspects. You can help people."

An Important Job

Many in the survey said they were drawn to the profession because of the special role a journalist has in a democratic society. The "importance" of journalism, the chance to serve the public, the opportunity to witness important historical events, and the potential to effect social change were the primary motivations for about a quarter of those whose answers we examined. Those occupational characteristics also were mentioned in many of the responses that focused largely on other reasons for selecting this career.

Almost 16% alluded to the central role of journalism in public life. "Journalism, more than any other profession, provides you with a front seat to history," explained one 28-year-old news service journalist from Washington, D.C. "Most journalists are among the people in society who are most interested in what is going on in the world around them, interested in current events—in a broad spectrum of activities, not a narrow area of study or emphasis." A 50-year-old TV reporter-anchor from Missouri emphasized the opportunity to serve the community. "I just felt I could make a difference in people's lives—that there were problems that needed exposing and that exposing those problems could lead to possible solutions to those problems," he said. "I just felt that there was a certain amount of injustice and that it just needed a spotlight shined on (it). I just looked at the media in general as a good vehicle to invoke change."

A 52-year-old TV reporter from Illinois considered journalism a special calling. "I think it's a noble profession. I think it's exciting," he said.

> When I began I worked long, long hours and had great fun doing it. I couldn't wait to get to the office because I enjoyed covering stories and learning about the human condition, about how we govern ourselves, how we are good to each other, about how sometimes we are pretty inhumane with each other, and I've gotten to a point in my career that nothing really surprises me anymore. I'm kind of an idealist, and I think despite some of our shortcomings we still perform a noble function. . . . I think it is an important calling and important service.

Political life was the specific appeal for about 10%, and several journalists credited one of the most significant political stories of the last 35 years with igniting their interest in the profession. "The Watergate story had a lot to do with it," explained a 53-year-old city hall reporter from a New Mexico daily newspaper. "My father had been a journalist, and that probably also influenced me. But sort of the kicker was the Watergate story in 1972." Or this from a 60-year-old TV correspondent from Maryland: "I thought it was a very interesting career—great variety. At the time I was very interested in politics. I went to college when John Kennedy was president. We had the era of Camelot, and covering politics seemed like a very interesting thing to do."

College, High School, or Childhood Influences

About 20% of the journalists whose responses we analyzed traced their career choice to experiences in college or high school. And a substantial number said that they had always wanted to go into journalism or could at least remember wanting to do so since childhood, perhaps because they had a close relative in the profession.

One journalist, now a weekly newspaper editor in Kentucky, recalled becoming interested in the profession in elementary school. His second-grade teacher had decided that he had a knack for writing and encouraged him to begin reading magazines, on the theory that good writers were also avid readers.

"That was actually extremely inspirational to me, because it was the first time in my life somebody had told me I was good at something," he remembered. He said that during high school, the local newspaper recruited him to write sports. "(The editors) asked the English Department, 'Who do you think has a knack for this kind of thing?' and they were directed to me. I was flattered, and here I was once again being told I had a knack for that kind of thing. Next thing you know I'm in the newspaper business back in 1980."

This editor, now 38, was among about 8% of journalists who can recall a childhood experience that piqued their interest in journalism. More commonly, however, journalists decided on this career during high school or college. "I went to school—college—for journalism," said a 41-year-old radio news executive in the Northeast. "As a student I had small classes and great teachers, and I would say that being in college with the people that I was, I got very interested in writing and interviewing people. And I've always been exceptionally curious. So, I got a few skills under my belt and a little confidence. I just found that I was good at it and that I loved it and I couldn't do anything else."

It was not uncommon to find journalists who went to college intending to do something else:

- From a 46-year-old database editor at an Oklahoma newspaper: "I took a journalism class as an elective and decided I liked it. So I switched majors from political science."

- From a 33-year-old newspaper editor in Illinois: "I was a political science and speech major, and I started working at the student newspaper in college, and I loved it. So I stayed. I didn't intend to go into journalism, but I'm glad I did."

- From a 34-year-old newspaper bureau reporter working in Washington, D.C.: "'Wealthy author' was looking less and less likely. I was an English major in creative writing and I realized that wasn't going to pay the bills. So, I went to work for the school newspaper and enjoyed it. I found something I was good at and went with it."

- From a 56-year-old magazine writer from California: "I was studying astronomy and wasn't very good at it. So I decided to write about science rather than do it."

High school and college media provided an important connection to the profession. Dozens of journalists said that these experiences cemented their interest.

"I did a little bit of work on my high school paper and yearbook," explained a 27-year-old online editor from South Carolina, "and I guess I kind of got hooked there." A Florida television anchor, 56, got his start in college radio. "I fell in love with the radio station," he recalled. "I went there, they gave me an audition, they liked my voice, they asked me if I wanted a show and before I knew it, I was the news director of the radio station."

Several journalists gravitated to the profession because of family connections. "My mother was a journalist, so I became interested in doing the same thing at an early age," explained a 43-year-old reporter from a Virginia daily.

A Varied, Exciting Profession

Can't you choose a career just because it's fun? About 10% of those whose answers we analyzed did. They said they chose journalism because it was exciting, varied work or because they simply loved being involved with the news. "I just kind of dig it," said a 39-year-old newspaper photo editor from California. "I think it's interesting, and fun. . . . My job is important because the way I see a particular assignment is the way 33,000 people every day see it. And I think that's pretty cool." A TV anchor, 40, from Tennessee got hooked by the excitement and variety of the work. "The ability to see different sights, meet different people" was what appealed to him. "Always something unique, and like I tell grade school kids when I see them, it's grown-up show and tell."

Journalism also was the ideal profession for news junkies. "Even though I didn't study journalism in college, I kind of knew that that was what I always wanted to do," said a 40-year-old reporter in Virginia. "I love to read newspapers and read about people's lives," she said. "I would just get sucked into stories. My first job in journalism occurred accidentally. I'm just grateful for that accident because I can't imagine doing anything else."

Other Factors

It's a cliché, but an apt one for a few of the roughly 5% who were drawn to journalism because of an interest in sports. The cliché goes something like this: Sports journalists are frustrated jocks who, lacking the talent to compete in athletics, turn to writing about it instead. That's essentially the story of a 35-year-old radio news executive from Illinois: "I did so because when I was young I realized that if I couldn't be an athlete, the next best thing would be to be in broadcasting. I was able to pursue that dream through college at a cable television station and then here at the radio station." Others, however, were simply pursuing an interest in writing about a topic that they loved. "It combined a lot of interests of mine," said a 47-year-old California sports reporter. "I'd always been a newspaper reader, and I was always very interested in sports. It was a combination of the two that led me to a career in sports writing."

A handful of other factors came up occasionally in responses to "why journalism." They include the following:

- Family obligation. Some journalists were born into the profession, having had parents or other close relatives who owned media organizations.
- Accident. Several cited serendipity. For example, a radio host from Minnesota said he had been doing other work when he was approached by a network and offered a job.
- Advancement from a nonjournalism job in a news organization. One editor-publisher began as a part-time technician in a darkroom.
- Transfer from an allied profession. A typical example of this situation would be the meteorologist who subsequently sought work as a weather broadcaster or the advertising copy writer who became a newspaper reporter.

Though it's useful to categorize responses to better understand the main themes that emerge as journalists explain what brought them into the business, it's important to recognize that categorizing tends to simplify what, for many, were complicated reasons for choosing this profession. As a few of the previous comments suggested, often it was not just "the writing" or just "the opportunity for public service" or just "the excitement" that provided the lure. Rather, it was the prospect of being able to have them all, or at least many of them, in a single job.

The appeal of being able to meld a rewarding task, a meaningful purpose, and an exciting pursuit comes through in what a 49-year-old Florida photo editor said when asked "why journalism?" "Mainly because it was exciting," he said. "It dealt with people, it dealt with real life, it dealt with the making of history. I was very interested in capturing and recording the daily life of my community, and the aesthetic concerns of photography also interest me. So that's what got me into it— people, history and photography, and the desire to communicate."

PROFILES OF NEWS WORKERS

The American work force is getting grayer, and so is the American newsroom. Today, many news organizations are struggling to attract younger readers, viewers, and listeners to replenish their aging, shrinking audiences.[13] Increasingly, they face the challenge of doing so with staffs that are much older than the people whom they want to reach.

This aging of the newsroom is remarkable if one considers that after the initial American Journalists survey, in 1971, Johnstone et al. emphatically characterized journalism as a "young person's field," with a median age of 36.[14] Both the median age of journalists and of the overall labor force dropped in the decade that followed, and by 1982–1983, the median age for news workers was 32 (Table 3.1). During the past two decades, however, that median age climbed about 9 years. In 2002, half of all the journalists that we surveyed were between the ages of 32 and 49; two decades ago, the comparable figures were 27 and 42 (Table 3.2). The aging of the profession, one of the many consequences of the baby boom, has been more pronounced for journalists than for the workforce as a whole. In 1971 and 1982–1983, the median age of American journalists was 3 years younger than the overall labor force; today, it's 1 year older.[15]

Not only is the journalistic workforce becoming older, it is also more experienced and somewhat less occupationally mobile than in the past. An explosion in hiring during the 1970s dramatically reduced the median job tenure for journalists,[16] but it has been climbing steadily since then (Table 3.1). In 1982–1983, journalists had 9 years of professional experience and had been with their current employer for about 4 years.[17] By 2002, they had 15 years of professional experience and had been with their employer for 7 years. In terms of job tenure, journalists differ from other professional workers. For all professional workers in 2002, the median time spent with their current employer was about 4 years. But unlike journalists, that figure has changed little during the last 20 years.[18]

TABLE 3.1
Median Age, Years of Experience, Current Job Tenure for Journalists,
U.S. Labor Force

Characteristics	2002 (N = 1,147)[g]	1992[h] (N = 1,149)	1982–1983[i] (N = 991)	1971[j] (N = NA)
Median age of journalists	41	36	32	36
Median age U.S. labor force[a]	40	37	35	39
Journalists' years of professional experience	15	12	9	—[c]
Median years in current job for journalists	7	7	4	9[d]
Median years in current job for U.S. labor force[ab]	3.7	3.6[e]	3.5[f]	—[c]

[a] U.S. labor force 16 years and older.

[b] For U.S. professional workers, median years in current jobs was 4.2 years in 2002.

[c] Comparable data not available.

[d] This is a mean value; median not available.

[e] Figure is for 1991.

[f] Figure is for 1983.

[g] N varies slightly by variable because of missing data.

[h] Data on journalists from David H. Weaver and G. Cleveland Wilhoit, *The American Journalist in the 1990s: U.S. News People at the End of an Era* (Mahwah, NJ: Lawrence Erlbaum Associates, 1996).

[i] Data on journalists from David H. Weaver and G. Cleveland Wilhoit, *The American Journalist: A Portrait of U.S. News People and Their Work*, 2nd ed. (Bloomington: Indiana University Press, 1991).

[j] Data on journalists from John W. C. Johnstone, Edward J. Slawski, and William W. Bowman, *The News People: A Sociological Portrait of American Journalists and Their Work* (Urbana: University of Illinois Press, 1976).

TABLE 3.2

Median Age, Years of Experience, and Current Job Tenure by Managerial, Reporting Status

Characteristics	Senior Managers (N = 158)[a]	Junior Managers (N = 323)	Nonmanagers (N = 665)	Reporters Only (N = 750)[b]	All 2002 (N = 1,147)	All 1992[f] (N = 1,156)	All 1982–1983[g] (N = 1,001)
Age	48	42	37	40	41	36	32
Age range for 2 middle quartiles[c]	41–53	34–48	29–47	31–48	32–49	30–43	27–42
Years of journalistic experience	22	18	12	14	15	12	9
Range for 2 middle quartiles[d]	15–29	10–24	5–22	7–23	7–24	7–18	4–17
Years at current organization	12	8	5	6	7	6	4
Range for 2 middle quartiles[e]	5–22	4–17	3–13	3–14	3–16	3–12	2–11

[a] For all categories, N varies slightly by variable because of missing data.
[b] Reporters include respondents who said that they did reporting "regularly." Reporters are represented among all three management categories.
[c] Median ages for 25th and 75th percentiles.
[d] Median number of years of experience for 25th and 75th percentiles.
[e] Median number of years at current organization for 25th and 75th percentiles.
[f] From data collected for Weaver and Wilhoit, *The American Journalist in the 1990s*.
[g] From data collected for Weaver and Wilhoit, *The American Journalist*, 2nd ed.

TABLE 3.3
Job Functions by Type of Medium

Functions	Weeklies[a] (N=177) (%)	Dailies[a] (N=554) (%)	Magazine[a] (N=59) (%)	News Service[a] (N=69) (%)	Radio[a] (N=104) (%)	TV[a] (N=162) (%)	Online[a] (N=100) (%)	2002[b] (N=1,149) (%)	1992[b] (N=1,154) (%)	1982–1983[b] (N=1,001) (%)	1971[b] (N=1,328) (%)
News gathering											
Does reporting[c]	89.3	69.7	94.9	87.0	94.2	88.3	48.0	79.4	69.9	79.8	78.8
Covers specific beat[d]	41.4	55.6	44.6	55.0	20.6	31.5	25.0	44.5	44.7	38.4	34.7
Editing, processing											
Edits others' work[e]	86.4	73.8	69.5	85.5	83.8	70.4	93.0	77.1	75.7	71.4	64.8
Supervisory duties											
Manages, supervises[f]	52.5	35.9	30.5	52.2	55.8	34.0	63.0	42.0	42.6	47.1	41.9
Hiring, firing[g]	68.5	36.7	27.8	25.0	62.1	25.4	47.6	43.5	37.6	34.2	28.1
Sees reporters daily[h]	44.1	63.4	33.3	69.4	68.9	55.6	39.6	58.3	41.6	42.9	27.9

[a]Online category includes online journalists from the main sample and the special sample of the Online News Association. The other categories of media include journalists from only the main sample, excluding online journalists. N varies slightly by variable because of missing data.

[b]Includes only journalists from the main samples. N is for main samples and varies by variable because of missing data. Figures for 1971, 1982–1983, and 1992 from Weaver and Wilhoit, *The American Journalist in the 1990s*, p. 59.

[c]Percentage who said that they did reporting "regularly" or "occasionally."

[d]Percentage of those who did at least some reporting who said that they covered a specific beat or subject area.

[e]Percentage who said that they did "a great deal" or "some" editing of others' work.

[f]Percentage who said that they supervised news or editorial employees.

[g]Percentage with managerial or supervisory functions who said that they had a great deal of influence on hiring and firing.

[h]Percentage with managerial or supervisory functions who said that they met at least daily with reporters to discuss stories.

Not only have the characteristics of the journalists changed, but so has the distribution of tasks that they perform. Over all, about 80% of journalists in the 2002 survey said that they did reporting "occasionally" or "regularly" (Table 3.3). That's about 10 points more than in 1992 but roughly the same percentage as in 1971 and 1982–1983. The percentage of journalists devoted to this central function has always varied by the type of news organization. In 2002, 9 of every 10 journalists surveyed at weekly newspapers, news magazines, radio stations, news services, and television stations said they reported "occasionally" or "regularly." Among online journalists, fewer than half said they did so. For online news workers, editing was the key function. Ninety-three percent said they did "a great deal" or "some" editing of others' work.

Generally, the editing function has gained prominence over the years. In 2002, about three-quarters of all journalists said that they edited the work of others "a great deal" or "some" of the time, again with that figure varying by type of organization. That percentage is about 12 points more than in 1971, and it has risen by a few points in each survey. The high percentages who said they both reported and edited indicates that the work of most journalists is not highly specialized, because they perform multiple roles in the newsroom. Johnstone et al. pointed out this same phenomenon in 1971.[19] It persists even as the typical employing organization has become larger, which tends to produce more specialization in job functions (Table 3.5).[20]

Along with reporting and editing, managing others would be a third major job function in the newsroom. From time to time, journalism publications have reported about efforts to flatten the hierarchical structure of newsrooms.[21] Despite those assertions, the management cadre at news organizations—those who said they supervised the work of others—has remained more or less stable through the years (Table 3.3). In 1971, about 4 in 10 journalists reported having some management responsibilities; the 2002 figure was almost identical. What did change, however, was that substantially greater percentages of the journalists who had management responsibilities reported that they had influence on hiring or firing. In some industries, personnel decisions have become more of a collective than individual responsibility of the management.[22] That sharing of responsibility appears to be taking place within news organizations, too.

Finally, managers clearly are spending more time on communication with employees. One of the biggest newsroom changes detected in the American Journalist surveys relates to how much managers and reporters talk. Almost 60% of those with managerial or supervisory functions said they met daily with reporters. That percentage is double what it was in 1971 (Table 3.3).

Job Classifications

The job titles in newsrooms are hardly a study in uniformity. Depending on the organization, the top newsroom manager might be the editor, the editor-publisher, the executive editor, the managing editor, the news director, the executive news director, the executive producer, or the editorial director—and that's not an exhaustive set of titles for senior news managers. The grouping of tasks into jobs and the systems set up to orchestrate the efforts of individual news workers are equally diverse. Team structure? Hierarchical structure? Work groups? Each news organization is a little different, and the titles and responsibilities associated with a given job seem to be unique to each organization. Though mindful of this variation, journalists can be divided into three broad categories based on their key responsibilities in the newsroom:

- *Senior managers*, whose authority ranges across the entire newsroom or across large divisions within the newsroom and who constitute the top level of management at a news organization;
- *Junior managers*, who report directly to senior managers, who are the direct supervisors of the organization's rank-and-file journalists, and who typically are responsible for smaller divisions within the newsroom, such as a department, a desk, or a bureau; and
- *Nonmanagement staff*, who gather and produce the news and information that the organization distributes to readers, viewers, or listeners.

What follows are short demographic profiles of those three groups.

Senior Managers

Senior managers comprised about 14% of journalists in the 2002 survey. Senior managers included those with job titles such as publisher, editor in chief, editorial director, managing editor, general manager, news director, or executive producer.[23] Virtually all of these individuals supervised the work of other journalists.

As might be expected, senior managers were the oldest group in the newsroom. Their median age was 48,[24] and 75% of them were above the survey's overall median age of 41 (Table 3.2). Their relatively advanced age means, of course, that they tended to have spent a long time in the news business—about 22 years. They also had the longest job tenure with their current employer, suggesting that it was relatively uncommon for a senior manager to have parachuted in to his or her latest workplace from another job in another community. Indeed, senior managers typically had been working for their current organization for 12 years, and 75% of them had been there for 5 years or more.

More so than other news workers, they were White, married, and conservative (Table 3.4). In the latest survey, virtually all senior managers (97.5 percent) were non-Hispanic Whites. About three-quarters were male and were married, with more than half having children who lived at home. Whereas only a quarter of journalists overall reported that their political leanings were "a little" or "pretty far" to the right, among senior managers the figure was 36%. In terms of education, they were little different from other journalists. About 68% of senior managers had an undergraduate college degree, and another 14% had a graduate degree. Both figures were within a couple of percentage points of the overall figures. About three-quarters had attended a public university for their undergraduate degree, which was 6 to 10 percentage points higher than for the other groups in the survey.

Junior Managers

The senior managers of the future will most likely come from the ranks of junior managers, who made up about 28% of the journalists in the 2002 survey.[25]

TABLE 3.4
Demographic Characteristics by Management, Reporting Status

Characteristics	Senior Managers (N = 158)[a] (%)	Junior Managers (N = 324) (%)	Nonmanagers (N = 666) (%)	Reporters Only (N = 750)[d] (%)	All (N = 1,149) (%)
Political leanings					
To the left	26.6	41.3	43.8	39.6	40.7
Middle of road	37.3	35.3	32.5	35.3	33.9
To the right	36.1	23.4	23.7	25.1	25.3
Education					
High school	3.2	1.2	1.8	1.9	1.8
Some undergraduate	12.1	8.0	8.0	8.6	8.6
Undergraduate degree	68.2	70.3	67.3	67.1	68.3
Some graduate	2.5	4.0	5.6	4.7	4.7
Graduate degree	14.0	16.4	17.3	17.8	16.6
College attended					
Public undergraduate	77.3	67.6	71.4	70.4	71.1
Private undergraduate	22.7	32.4	28.6	29.6	28.9
Family life					
Single, never married	8.9	17.6	29.6	25.7	23.4
Unmarried, has partner[b]	1.9	5.6	7.1	6.1	5.9
Not now married[c]	11.4	11.1	8.8	9.2	9.8
Married	77.8	65.6	54.5	58.8	60.8
Children					
Has children at home	54.4	49.1	35.9	39.3	42.1
Race-ethnicity[e]					
Non-Hispanic White	97.5	90.0	89.1	90.2	90.5
Minority	2.5	10.0	10.9	9.8	9.5
Gender					
Male	74.7	71.6	63.0	66.0	67.0
Female	25.3	28.4	37.0	34.0	33.0

[a] For all categories, N varies slightly by variable because of missing data.
[b] Unmarried and living with partner.
[c] Separated, divorced, or widowed.
[d] Reporters include respondents who said that they did reporting "regularly." Reporters are represented among all three management categories.
[e] Non-Hispanic White versus all other categories of race and ethnicity combined.

But the junior managers were, in many respects, more like the rank-and-file journalists that they supervised than like their own bosses.

As a group, they were younger than the senior managers, with a median age of 42 (Table 3.2). About half of junior managers were between 34 and 48 years old. Because they were younger than the senior managers, they typically had less journalistic experience (about 18 years) and had spent substantially less time at their employing organization (about 8 years).[26]

About two-thirds of junior managers said they did reporting "regularly" or "occasionally," and more than 90% did editing or processing of others' work "a great deal" or "some" of the time. In those respects, their work routines were similar to senior managers. But their politics and life circumstances weren't. They were more liberal, less likely to be married, and less White (Table 3.4). More than 40% of junior managers characterized themselves as "a little" or "pretty far" to the left. About 65% were married, and only about half had children living at home.

The ranks of junior managers were slightly more diverse than for senior managers. Almost 10% were people of color, and about 72% were male. The survey results suggested the potential for more gender equity in the future. Roughly 47% of the junior managers who were under 35 were female. But it is likely to be a tougher slog toward greater racial or ethnic diversity. Among the junior managers under 35, 9 out of 10 were non-Hispanic Whites—the same percentage as for the group of junior managers as a whole.

In terms of educational background, this group differs little from others. Roughly 70% have an undergraduate degree, and another 16% have a master's degree. Two-thirds attended a public college or university for their undergraduate degree.

Nonmanagement News Workers

These news workers were primarily reporters, writers, anchors, announcers, news processors (such as copy editors), and desk editors without supervisory responsibilities.[27] They had a median age of 37, had 12 years of professional experience, and typically had been with their current employer for about 5 years (Table 3.2).[28] A quarter of them had been working at their current news organization for only one or two years.

This group was more liberal than the management ranks (Table 3.4). About 44% characterized themselves as left of center. They were more likely to be single and childless than the managers. About 55% were married, and about 36% had children at home. Thirty percent were single—three times as many as for senior managers. Women accounted for a larger portion of this group than for the managers: 37% were female and 63% male. But ethnic diversity was about the same as for junior managers, with 9 in 10 being non-Hispanic Whites. Again, there were few educational differences across the profession. As with both management groups, about 7 in 10 had an undergraduate degree, and about 7 in 10 had obtained that degree from a public institution.

Reporters. Because journalists who said they regularly did reporting comprised by far the largest percentage of the sample, we thought it would be useful to provide a short profile of their demographic characteristics too.[29] Approximately 65% of the journalists in the main sample fell into this group. Reporters accounted for such a large percentage of the nonmanagement news workers that their characteristics closely resembled that group, although they were not identical.

The typical reporter was 40 years old, about 6 years older than in 1992 (Table 3.2). He (two-thirds were male) had worked for his current employer for 6 years and had a total of about 14 years of professional experience.[30] Reporters were, then, slightly older and more experienced than the nonmanagement ranks over all. About half of the reporters surveyed were assigned to a beat, and the other half reported on varied topics. The percentage of beat reporters is about the same as 10 years earlier, when about 45% were assigned to a beat.[31] Journalists, in general, were more likely to be liberal than conservative, and the same was true for reporters. About 40% characterized their political views as left of center, about 25% right of center, and 35% as middle of the road (Table 3.4). This makes their political profile close to that of junior managers but more liberal than that of senior managers. About 70% attended a public college or university as an undergraduate, and approximately 90% have at least an undergraduate degree. Like the journalistic labor force as a whole, this is a group without much racial or ethnic diversity. Slightly more than 90% were non-Hispanic Whites.

Organizational Size

Our estimates indicated that the overall size of the journalistic workforce declined between 1992 and 2002. In 1992, approximately 122,000 people worked in the nation's newsrooms, about 6,000 more than in 2002. Still, the median size of the newsroom continued to grow during the last 10 years, though more slowly than in the decade before that (Table 3.5). Journalists in the latest survey reported working in newsrooms with a median size of 45 employees, up only slightly from 1992. The variation was considerable across types of media organizations. At 150, the news magazines, which are national publications, had by far the largest median staff size. The smallest were the intensely local weekly newspapers and radio stations.

Daily newspapers, which employed half of the journalists in the survey, exhibited the widest range. Daily newspaper journalists reported working for organizations with as few as three newsroom employees to more than 1,000. Fifty percent said they worked for dailies with between 32 and 150 news workers. The median staff size was reported to be 80. Television news organizations also showed great variation in size, reflecting the fact that the national networks employ large cadres of journalists while small local stations operate with only a handful of news workers. TV journalists reported working on staffs with a median

TABLE 3.5
Median News Staff Size by Type of Organization

Type of organization	2002	1992[a]	1982–1983[a]
News magazines	150.0	146.6	100.9
Daily newspapers	80.0	32.5	41.5
Television	40.0	25.7	21.8
News-service bureau	—[c]	7.0	6.2
Weekly newspapers	6.0	2.9	4.6
Radio	3.0	1.0	3.0
Online[b]	60.0	—[c]	—[c]
All types of media organizations	45.0	42.0	17.0

[a] From Weaver and Wilhoit, *The American Journalist in the 1990s*, p. 61.

[b] Values for this category are computed from the special sample of 100 online journalists. All other values are computed from respondents in the main sample.

[c] Comparable values not available.

of 40 employees, and half of the organizations had between 20 and 79 news workers.

Online news organizations emerged in the 10 years prior to the latest survey. Many online services were set up as auxiliaries of daily newspapers, broadcast outlets, and news magazines. The online journalists surveyed reported working in newsrooms with a median of 60 employees, no doubt reflecting the size of the parent organization of which they are part.

PROFESSIONAL AUTONOMY AND NEWSROOM INFLUENCE

One of the hallmarks of professional work—something that distinguishes a profession from other occupations—is the wide latitude that a practitioner has in carrying out his or her occupational duties.[32] On the assembly line, worker discretion is limited. A professional designs the tasks, and a worker simply executes them. The control and coordination of these tasks are handled largely by managers, not by the workers who complete them. Unlike assembly-line work, professional employment typically defies the precise specification of tasks in advance. It's too complicated. A physician examining a young man with the sore throat considers a wide range of possible causes and an equally wide range of possible treatments. She then relies on her training, judgment, and expertise to decide the best course of therapy. In doing so, she is exercising her professional autonomy. To the extent that her work is managed at all, it is supervised loosely by other physicians.

Journalism has been called a "semi-profession," in part because claims to work place autonomy have not been as firmly established as in many other professions.[33] Even though all professions face challenges to their autonomy (doctors would claim that insurance requirements or government regulations limit their autonomy), the threats can be even more acute for semi-professions like journalism. In their 1971 study, Johnstone, Slawski, and Bowman proposed that reporters' professional autonomy could be hindered by the fact that most worked in large, hierarchical bureaucracies.[34] They argued that this would lead to more formal control by managers over journalistic work, infringing on professional autonomy. In the years since, then, other potential threats to journalists' autonomy have emerged. They include the following:

- *The increasing commercialization of news.* In an influential 1994 book, John McManus concluded that journalism was becoming more market driven.[35] The market-oriented news organization draws heavily on audience research to identify the informational wants and needs of its readers, viewers, or listeners. Then it commits itself to fulfilling those needs. Scholars have argued that reliance on market research threatens journalists' prerogative to rely on well-established professional criteria in deciding what to publish or broadcast.[36]
- *The high profit expectations for media companies.* Daily newspapers and broadcast television outlets often have pretax profit margins of 25% and above — margins much higher than many other mature industries.[37] Media critics have complained that these "excessive" profit demands are forcing newsrooms to operate with too few staff members, leading to cutbacks in coverage and limiting journalists' ability to do their jobs properly.[38]
- *The erosion of the "wall" between a media organization's business and journalistic operations.* In 1999, The Los Angeles Times acknowledged that it had made a deal to share profits from a special section on the city's new sports arena with that arena's owner.[39] That put The Los Angeles Times in the position of being a business partner with an organization that it also covered. This arrangement became a high-profile example of what some have said is a trend toward integrating the journalistic and business functions within media companies. Another example would be the growth of cross-functional teams at media organizations.[40] Representatives of the newsroom have been enlisted in organization-wide efforts to develop new products or solve business problems unrelated to their responsibility to cover the news. Some fear that situations like these compromise journalists' ability to act independently should their professional judgment conflict with the business needs of their organization.
- *Scandals.* In 1981, The Washington Post returned a Pulitzer Prize won by its reporter, Janet Cooke.[41] She had earned the award for writing an article about a youngster who didn't exist. In 2003 and 2004, The New York Times and USA Today endured painful scandals when they discovered that reporters had fabricated information in stories written for the paper.[42] In the aftermath of these and

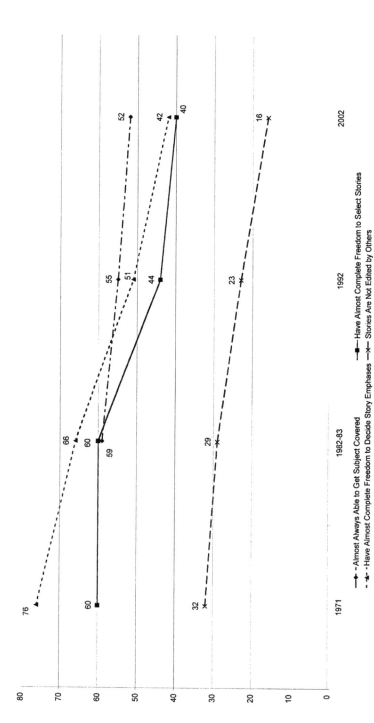

FIG. 3.1. Indicators of perceived autonomy and influence in getting subjects covered for journalists (excluding online) who do reporting "regularly" or "occasionally." Figures are percentages. N in 2002 = 910, in 1992 = 806, in 1982–1983 = 794; N varies slightly by variable because of missing data. Figures for 1992 from Weaver and Wilhoit, *The American Journalist in the 1990s*, p. 63; for 1982–1983 from Weaver and Wilhoit, *The American Journalist*, 2nd ed., p. 76; for 1971 from Johnstone et al., *The News People*, p. 222.

- ◆ - Almost Always Able to Get Subject Covered
- ▲ - Have Almost Complete Freedom to Decide Story Emphases
- ■ Have Almost Complete Freedom to Select Stories
- ✕ - Stories Are Not Edited by Others

other ethical breaches, many news organizations pledged to tighten procedures for monitoring reporters' work.

• *New media technologies.* Former journalists Bill Kovach and Tom Rosenstiel contend that a "journalism of assertion" has emerged during the last decade because cable news networks and Web sites have created a never-ending news cycle.[43] They maintain that traditional professional values such as proportion, verification, and relevance have given way to a perceived need to get an assertion into public circulation as quickly as possible. In this hypercompetitive news environment, they write, the need to be first sometimes takes precedence over the need to be right. Their argument implies that journalists' latitude for exercising professional judgment has become circumscribed because of the competitive pressures created by these 24-hour-a-day news organizations.

Against this backdrop, the surveys of journalists conducted since 1971 document continuing erosion both in the amount of professional autonomy that reporters perceived that they had and in their influence in the newsroom.[44] Two survey items seek to assess perceived autonomy. In each of the four surveys, reporters have been asked how much freedom they have (a) to select the stories that they work on, and (b) to decide what aspects of their stories to emphasize. Two other survey items assess, more indirectly, reporter influence in the newsroom. Those questions ask how often a reporter is able to get a subject covered that she or he thinks is important[45] and how much the reporter's work is edited by others.

Figure 3.1 documents the steady decline in all of these measures. In 2002, only about 40% of reporters said they had almost complete freedom to pursue the stories that they wanted, and about 42% said they had almost complete freedom to decide what to emphasize in their writing.[46] That's a drop of more than one-third during the last 30 years. The decline for the question about editing was steeper. About 16% reported that they were free to write what they wanted, with no editing from others.[47] That compares with 32% in 1971. The drop was less acute for the item asking reporters about their ability to get subjects covered. In 1982–1983, the first survey in which that question was asked, about 59% of reporters said they almost always had success getting an important subject covered. That percentage had slipped to 52% by 2002.

Perceived autonomy and influence varied widely across different types of news organizations and journalists. Reporters at larger organizations, which are often more bureaucratic and hierarchical, ranked lower on all the indicators. In 2002, only about a quarter of the reporters at the largest organizations (newsroom staffs of more than 100) reported having "almost complete freedom" to choose what stories to pursue and what to emphasize in those stories (Table 3.6). That's roughly half the level for reporters at the smallest organizations.

The levels of perceived autonomy also varied by the type of news organization. Reporters at weekly newspapers and radio stations (the organizations with

TABLE 3.6

Indicators of Perceived Reporter[a] Autonomy and Influence by Organization Size

Percentage Who Say . . .	10 or < (N = 248)[b] (%)	11–25 (N = 134) (%)	26–50 (N = 115) (%)	51–100 (N = 116) (%)	> 100 (N = 220) (%)
They have almost complete freedom in selecting stories they work on	57.9	51.5	36.8	26.1	26.8
They have almost complete freedom to decide aspects of a story to emphasize	59.3	53.0	39.3	31.1	28.2
They are almost always able to get a subject covered that they think should be covered	57.5	54.5	49.1	46.2	50.5
Their stories are not edited by other people	32.7	14.9	13.9	10.3	5.5

[a] Journalists (excluding online) who said they did reporting "regularly" or "occasionally."
[b] For all categories, N varies slightly by variable because of missing data.

the smallest news staffs) had the widest latitude (Table 3.7). Reporters at television stations, news magazines, and news services were the least likely to have said they had "almost complete freedom" to select their stories. Magazine reporters were the least likely to have said they had "almost complete freedom" to decide what to emphasize in their stories.

Among key personal characteristics, union members and minorities reported having less perceived autonomy and influence on getting subjects covered than others (Table 3.8). In the case of union members, this appears to be because the majority of them work at large organizations where reporter autonomy and influence are lowest. The explanation for the differences between minorities and non-Hispanic Whites is less apparent but may be affected, to some degree, by age, experience, and workplace. Minorities were more likely than non-Hispanic Whites to be working in television and less likely to be working at weekly newspapers. In general, TV reporters had less autonomy and influence, and weekly reporters had more autonomy and influence than others. In effect, minorities were overrepresented at organizations at which reporters had the least perceived autonomy and influence and underrepresented at organizations at which reporters had the most perceived autonomy and influence. Minorities also tended to be younger and less experienced journalists. Those two variables—age and years of journalistic experience—had a slight positive relationship with perceived autonomy and influence on getting subjects covered. The most recent survey found that differences based on gender were minimal.

TABLE 3.7

Indicators of Perceived Reporter[a] Autonomy and Influence by Type of Medium

Percentage Who Say . . .	Dailies (N = 391) (%)	News Services (N = 60) (%)	Magazines (N = 59) (%)	Weeklies (N = 160) (%)	TV (N = 144) (%)	Radio (N = 98) (%)	Online[b] (N = 76) (%)	All Reporters (N = 912)[c] (%)
They have almost complete freedom in selecting stories they work on								
2002	36	27	25	62	22	63	35	40
1992[c]	38	31	34	63	35	59	—[d]	44
1982–1983[c]	56	46	39	67	47	73	—[d]	60
They have almost complete freedom to decide the aspects of a story to emphasize								
2002	35	32	20	62	41	61	36	42
1992[c]	49	38	27	63	39	69	—[d]	51
1982–1983[c]	67	63	32	64	67	73	—[d]	66
They almost always can get a subject covered that they think should be covered								
2002	54	58	39	61	37	53	34	52
1992[c]	56	51	34	63	52	50	—[d]	55
1982–1983[c]	64	63	45	50	61	60	—[d]	59
Their stories are not edited by other people								
2002	7	3	5	20	23	49	30	16
1992[c]	12	0	7	34	32	59	—[d]	23
1982–1983[c]	14	8	23	29	39	59	—[d]	29

[a] Journalists who said they did reporting "regularly" or "occasionally."

[b] Respondents include journalists from the Online News Association special sample.

[c] N for the main sample only. N varies slightly by variable because of missing data.

[c] Figures for earlier years from Weaver and Wilhoit, The American Journalist in the 1990s, p. 63. For 1992, N = 806 and for 1982–1983, N = 794, though sample size varies slightly by variable because of missing data.

[d] Comparable data not available.

75

TABLE 3.8
Indicators of Perceived Reporter[a] Autonomy and Influence
by Gender, Minority Status, and Union Membership

Percentage Who Say . . .	Minority Status		Gender		Union Member?	
	Nonminority (N = 812)[b] (%)	Minority (N = 89) (%)	Men (N = 603) (%)	Women (N = 305) (%)	No (N = 737) (%)	Yes (N = 169) (%)
They have almost complete freedom to select stories they work on	41	38	39	43	43	27
They have almost complete freedom to decide aspects of story to stress	44	32	41	44	44	32
They almost always can get a subject covered that they think should be covered	54	37	52	51	55	40
Their stories are not edited by other people	16	13	17	13	17	8

[a] Journalists who said they did reporting "regularly" or "occasionally."
[b] For all categories, N varies slightly by variable because of missing data.

CONSTRAINTS ON PERCEIVED PROFESSIONAL AUTONOMY

In an effort to better understand what factors constrain professional autonomy, journalists were asked to describe the most significant limits on their workplace freedom.[48] A similar process was followed in 1992, permitting rough comparisons of the concerns expressed then and now. The responses offered in 2002 closely paralleled those of the 1992 study.[49] Indeed, the degree to which they overlap is striking, suggesting that limitations on professional autonomy may be an inherent characteristic of journalistic work and the media workplace. An examination of a sample of the 2002 responses on workplace freedom pointed toward four broad groups of limitations:

- Those imposed by agents outside the news organization, typically sources;
- Those imposed by the professional conventions that most journalists follow, such as ethical guidelines;
- Those imposed by the commercial imperatives of profit-making businesses; and
- Those imposed by policies, procedures, or customs of the news organizations for which the journalist worked.

Those categories covered the bulk of the concerns journalists expressed in 2002 and are discussed in detail next. Though most journalists described some limits on their professional freedom (the question's wording predisposed them to identify something), about 10% said that they had no significant limits on their autonomy.

Outside Agents

About 20% of the responses examined in 2002 focused on constraints imposed by agents outside the news organization. As in 1992, the most common complaint of this type was about a long-standing nemesis of the reporter—the government official. Many reporters expressed exasperation with the information control that public agencies exercised. "The biggest problem is getting public officials to follow the law and give us what we're entitled to," said a newspaper reporter, 40, from California. "Too frequently we have to fight, scratch and even file lawsuits over information that we're legally entitled to. Some public officials make a simple job too difficult." That point was echoed again and again. The "most significant limits are those imposed by courts and governments that try to keep the public's business secret," a news-service journalist, also 40 and from California, complained.

Occasionally, reporters said, the government seeks to directly limit their professional freedom. A Chicago-area TV journalist, 52, told of this dispute with officials at O'Hare International Airport over efforts to photograph airplane passengers:

> After 9/11 we were not allowed to take pictures of things that were part of a Congressional debate on new security equipment and procedures that all of us would go through as travelers. Someone with a small camera could take pictures, but we couldn't even take pictures to illustrate how the situation is changing because of fears that we are going to intrude with our cameras. . . . We were not allowed to take pictures of people at O'Hare. We fought that, and we won. . . . Why should we not be able to cover that? Why should we not be able to take pictures of things we can see with our own eyes?

Though reporters acknowledged that they could try to use open-records or open-meetings laws to pry information from government officials, many suggested it wasn't always practical to do that. One 59-year-old weekly journalist from North Carolina explained the situation this way:

> It's significant that government officials are not fully aware of the access newspapers should have to information under their control. I'm restricted because I would have to go to some lengths, getting legal counsel, to convince officials that they need to provide our newspaper with information under their control. With a small newspaper, the lack of resources—legal and monetary—would prevent me from tackling some controversial stories that otherwise I might feel so inclined to do.

Other forms of source resistance also concerned journalists. Coaches who limit access to athletes or teachers who limit access to students were cited as examples. And a Virginia broadcaster working for a company with a predominately Hispanic audience said it was sometimes hard to get sources to take minority-oriented media seriously:

> I sincerely believe there is a double standard when it comes to journalists who work for the Hispanic media. . . . The bottom line is you don't even feel comfortable picking up the phone or writing a letter, let's say, requesting an interview with the secretary of state because it's not given serious consideration. What they will classify as mainstream media can interview the secretary of state maybe four times in the year, and the Hispanic media can request an interview and never get an interview in a year. So I feel that limits my ability to ask questions that are pertinent to my audience, to the audience that watches (my network).

Though problems with sources predominated in this category, a few journalists referred to a more subtle external constraint—the sensibilities of the community in which they live. "You have to live with these people," explained a Missouri journalist, 35, who aspired to do more aggressive reporting at her weekly newspaper. "If I didn't live here, I'd go at (a story) in a completely different way. But I have ties to the community. I have a child in the school system." Another journalist, 35, who works at a daily newspaper in a small town in Kentucky, characterized it as a fear of public outcry. "A town this size is still pretty conservative. Usually this is on hard-news pictures and stories—how graphic pictures can get. If it's a subject people want to stay away from, people just don't want to see it. Take a bad wreck. (The public) doesn't like to see it."

Constraints of the Profession

About 10% of the comments about limits on autonomy were about professional constraints. These embraced a range of factors, from ethics to objectivity to the conventions of news work. Journalists were not necessarily unhappy about these constraints. Sometimes they were simply mindful that as members of a profession, they are expected to work within a code of conduct, either stated or implied. One, a 45-year-old journalist at a Georgia weekly, described the situation this way: "I guess certain moral things—that's the biggest limit (on professional freedom) we have. Moral rectitude. That's what it is. We pretty much do what we want to do—within the boundaries of journalistic ethics." A 49-year-old Washington State journalist from a daily newspaper endorsed professional conventions as a healthy way to work:

> I suppose the biggest limit is the amount of resources that are available at the place I work, whether it be in terms of staff size or financial considerations. And the other kind of limits are mostly what could be construed as conventions, whether it be conventions of the newspaper itself or of journalism. That suggests that restrictions may be a good thing in this case. Well, I think any profession or craft—any art, even—can only do its best if it abides by certain kinds of conventions and tradi-

tions. That's not to say that can't be challenged. And they should be challenged. But there are limits to what we should be doing.

It was occasionally possible to detect ambivalence about professional conventions. Here are comments from a journalist, 37, working at a weekly paper in Arizona:

Well, the only thing I can really think of is what I would call standard rules in the newspaper business. You must formulate your stories to fit the proper patterns that have already been outlined by the newspaper industry. You don't have overwhelming freedom sometimes to express yourself in a story in various ways. (There are) rules and regulations in everything, and the newspaper business has its own as well. I just try to work within the guidelines that have already been created.

Commercial Imperatives

Virtually all the journalists surveyed were employed by commercial media organizations, and news workers have always been cognizant of a prime imperative of commercial organizations, that is, the need to return an acceptable profit to owners. Commercial constraints come in various forms: the pressure from the advertisers who subsidize newsgathering; the need to make a product that the audience would want; and, most prominently, the absence of sufficient resources for making news. Concerns about these kinds of business constraints accounted for about 30% of the responses analyzed in 2002.

Advertiser influence arose either as direct attempts to shape content or as self-censorship by the journalists. The latter was mentioned more often. "Broadcast television tends to be a little more restrained when it comes to some kinds of advocacy," one 45-year-old Minnesota journalist explained. "Sponsors may be involved, and that sometimes results in a reluctance to pursue some stories." Or another, a 34-year-old TV reporter from Missouri: "Sometimes I think, whether subconsciously or consciously, story supervisors make decisions on stories based on advertiser influence. In other words, if it's a story that would hurt the advertisers, they may suggest that we don't do it or change the story."

The impact of market-driven journalism, which became more widespread starting in the 1980s, continued to be felt. Reporters were acutely aware of the pressure to make a commercially viable product and of its potential effect on their professional autonomy. Broadcast journalists cited the pressure produce stories that generated high ratings—stories that will "bring in numbers," as one put it. "Often news is chosen based on not the importance of it but the flashiness of it," the 26-year-old Arizona TV journalist explained. Another, a 32-year-old broadcaster from Ohio, described the situation this way:

Ratings limit what I can do as a journalist because when I pitch my story idea, our editorial committee has to decide if the viewers will like it. Will it appeal to the viewers? In other words, will it get us ratings? Even if it's an important news topic, if there are people on the editorial committees who think it won't be a ratings grabber, the story will get thrown out.

One print journalist lamented the need to tailor news product to what subscribers are looking for. Another, a 30-year-old journalist at a Virginia daily, said, "We have to consider the reaction from readers. . . . People in the newspaper business have to think about their circulation, so that's a marketing problem."

The most frequently mentioned commercial constraint (roughly a quarter of the responses analyzed in 2002 suggested it) related to a shortage of news-gathering resources: space, staff, or both. Often the limitation was described as a "lack of time," but this tended to be a euphemism for "too few people." Perhaps this concern was particularly resonant with journalists in 1992 and 2002 because the United States was in the midst of recessions in those years. Commercial media organizations are cyclical businesses—businesses that prosper when the economy is booming and that struggle when the economy stalls—so cutbacks are more common during recessions.

Journalist after journalist spoke of workplaces where too few people had too much to do. "Work loads and deadlines," responded one weekly newspaper journalist from Maine when asked about limits on professional freedom. "In other words our reporters are required to execute a great (number) of tasks every week, so that along with deadlines limits freedom." Or this from a radio journalist in Nebraska: "Probably time constraints and money. . . . I'm trying to cover an entire state with only four people, and that's very challenging." A Pennsylvania daily newspaper journalist explained it this way:

> I think this is a typical problem with a small paper. I'm talking under 20- to-30,000 circulation. I find the editor that I've worked for open-minded, but they can't afford to put a reporter on specialized stories, put a team of reporters on a project or provide the computer equipment and other technology, like scanners and digital cameras, or pay for data base that would enhance coverage.

Some blamed trends within the media industries for this state of affairs, such as a 54-year-old TV news executive from Alabama: "My freedom to gather information and to report is most limited by staff size—by staff size for the news department. And that's probably the product of consolidation—of station consolidation and staff compression and cutbacks." Others blamed the way their news organizations responded to the recession. A North Carolina daily newspaper journalist, 48, provided this analysis:

> With the economy in such poor shape and advertising revenue down, the company has less resources to put in the news operation. The increasing use of advertorial publications to bulk up advertising and masquerade as news—those publications are generated not because the news side wants to do them, or has the idea. Instead, the advertising side generates them because they can sell advertising for them. The point is, the motivation is all wrong.

Organizational Policies, Procedures, and Customs

In some cases, it was difficult to distinguish between commercial constraints and other organizational decisions that limit journalistic autonomy. For example, a news organization's reluctance to offend advertisers—a commercial constraint—quickly becomes embedded in the way a newsroom or its managers traditionally operate. But for this category, the emphasis is on constraints imposed by an organization's policies, procedures, and customs. About 25% of the responses that were analyzed alluded to constraints of these kinds. Some were related to decisions about the products that the organization produced or the way it organized work on those products. Others related to organizational dicta, stated or unstated. And still others related to the seemingly idiosyncratic rules imposed by newsroom managers. What they all had in common was that journalists believed that they infringed on their latitude to conduct their work.

Time was mentioned as a commercial constraint in discussions about staffing. It came up again as a constraint arising from organizational strategy—from organizational decisions about how to be successful in the long run. Several broadcast reporters mentioned the "minute-30" rule for stories. This comment, from a 53-year-old Washington, D.C., journalist, was typical: "Our guidelines generally call for our pieces to be about minute and a half. . . . I think that our most significant constraint is that of time—for the length of our story." Another broadcaster, 42, from Ohio, chafed at the policies governing time allotted in a newscast. "Probably having to work within a strict format," the journalist said in response to the question about limits on professional freedom. "For example, I do weather. If I get two-and-a-half minutes for a weather segment, I have very little time to talk about anything else of importance." In the print world, the equivalent concern was a lack of space. "It is hard to tell a complete story sometimes with a limited number of inches you are given for the story," one Oklahoma reporter, 42, said.

Several journalists suggested that organizational policies or customs nurtured "politically correct" content (though this also may reflect pressure from the broader culture). "I don't have many limits," said one Florida newspaper journalist, 52, who then added: "I think there is too much political correctness on how we describe things. The required descriptive terms to describe people's races and nationalities, and sometimes appearance, can be confusing to the reader and don't always present a true picture of our subjects." Another newspaper journalist, 37 and also from Florida, identified corporate and company policies as the primary limitations and offered this explanation: "We're constrained by what's politically correct. We're constrained in a way by diversity. Not to say that diversity is a bad thing, but in some cases we're only getting one side of the story, and the other side is shouted down if someone tries to bring it up."

Though many businesses, news organizations among them, have moved to flatten their organizational structures during the last decade, making them less hierarchical, the impact that supervisors have on reporter autonomy remained a sore point for some. "I would have to say my superiors," replied a Pennsylvania TV journalist, 30, when asked about limits on autonomy, "because they envision things their way, and so they want a story or a show crafted their way. You can bring up your own ideas, but if they're already set in their ways it's pretty hard to change that." A newspaper journalist, 35, from Oklahoma put it more succinctly: "My greatest limits are what my supervisors and higher editors want or limit me to do. That's about it."

PREDICTORS OF PERCEIVED AUTONOMY

In an effort to determine which factors have the most influence on the professional latitude that a reporter believes he or she has in the workplace, we conducted a statistical analysis of 20 potential predictors of perceived autonomy. That multiple-regression analysis is reported in Table 3.9. Three broad groups of factors were part of the analysis:

- Basic structural characteristics of the reporter's organization, such as its size, the nature of its ownership, and the type of media firm;
- The reporters' assessment of eight key organizational goals and practices, such as the organization's emphasis on profits or its reliance on market research to shape content; and
- Personal characteristics of the reporter, such as his or her years of experience, gender, or minority status.

The multiple-regression analysis makes it possible to simultaneously assess the impact of each of the 20 factors while controlling for (holding constant statistically) all other factors. For example, regression makes it possible to assess the impact of gender on perceived autonomy while at the same time controlling for the effects of the 19 other factors. This procedure permits four kinds of observations. First, it makes it possible to identify "significant" factors—those reaching a relatively stringent statistical standard of importance. Second, it makes it possible to describe the nature of the relationship between a specific factor and perceived autonomy. Third, it makes it possible to compare the relative importance of some of the significant factors to get a sense of which ones have the greatest impact. Finally, it permits an overall assessment of how helpful those 20 factors were, when taken as a group, in explaining the variation among reporters in their responses to the two fixed-response questions about journalistic professional autonomy: (1) how much freedom the reporter had to select the stories that he or she worked on and (2) how much freedom the reporter had to decide what to emphasize in the stories he or she worked on.[50]

The middle column of Table 3.9, labeled "standardized regression coefficients," shows key results of the multiple-regression analysis. Only 4 of the 20

TABLE 3.9
Predictors and Correlates of Perceived Reporter Autonomy[a,b]

Predictors	Standardized Regression Coefficient	Pearson's r
Organizational Characteristics		
Number of full-time employees	-.174[d]	-.18[d]
Owned by larger corporation	-.034	-.09[d]
Part of publicly owned corporation	.003	-.15[d]
News magazine[c]	-.104[d]	—
Radio[c]	.114[d]	—
Television[c]	-.164[d]	—
Weekly newspaper[c]	.154[d]	—
Daily newspaper[c]	-.049	—
Organizational Goals and Practices		
Organizational emphasis on earning high profits	-.025	-.11[d]
Organizational emphasis on high employee morale	.067	.15[d]
Organizational emphasis on keeping large audience	.063	.02
Organizational emphasis on high-quality journalism	.019	.08[d]
Belief that profits are a higher priority than journalism	-.006	-.09[d]
Belief that quality of journalism rising steadily	.040	.14[d]
Belief that newsroom resources have been shrinking	.031	-.10[d]
Belief that organization does a lot of audience research	-.023	.11[d]
Reporter Characteristics		
Supervises other employees	.070	.12[d]
Belongs to a union	-.066	-.16[d]
Years of experience in journalism	.072	.07[d]
Gender (is a female)	.047	.00
Personal income in 2001	.003	-.14[d]
Minority (not a non-Hispanic White)	-.095[d]	-.12[d]
Frequency of getting comments from supervisor	.029	.04
Covers a beat	.116[d]	.03

[a] Journalists from main sample who say they report "regularly" or "occasionally," excluding cases with missing values on predictor variables. Three aberrant cases also eliminated from analysis, leaving N = 736.

[b] Perceived autonomy was measured with a scale that combines responses to two questions about amount of freedom reporters have in selecting stories to work on and in choosing what to emphasize in their stories.

[c] Effects-coded variables with news services chosen as the excluded group. Zero-order correlations are not meaningful for effects-coded variables.

[d] Coefficients significant at $p \leq .05$. Total adjusted R^2 for the model = .14

factors were strong predictors of perceived autonomy: the size of the organization, the type of organization, the work assignment of the reporter (beat or general assignment), and the minority status of the reporter. The results show that while certain structural characteristics and personal characteristics were associated with perceived autonomy, none of the organizational goals and practices were influential.

As might be expected, the size of the organization was the most important factor associated with the perceived autonomy of reporters. This relationship was negative: As size increased, perceived autonomy declined. Those reporters working at smaller organizations felt that they had more latitude to choose the stories that they wanted to work on and to decide what to emphasize in those stories. This finding is consistent with similar analyses done after the 1992 survey and confirms the common assumption that smaller organizations tend to be less regimented, affording journalists more workplace freedom. This finding was affirmed again, indirectly, in examining the types of organizations at which journalists have the most autonomy. The analyses suggest that reporters at news magazines and television stations have less perceived autonomy than do journalists as a whole. Reporters at weekly newspapers and radio stations have more perceived autonomy than other journalists. Those at daily newspapers are about average. News or wire service reporters were not directly included in these analyses, for technical reasons, but other assessments show they tend toward having low perceived autonomy. Again, these findings are roughly comparable to the results of the 1992 study.

Two characteristics of reporters also were strong predictors of autonomy. Beat reporters had greater freedom in choosing what to write and what to write about than did reporters who did not cover a beat. This isn't a startling finding, as beat reporters often are responsible for generating their own story ideas. A more puzzling result, however, was that minority reporters perceived themselves to have less professional autonomy than nonminority reporters. An explanation for this was not readily apparent. This relationship persisted even after controlling for the other 19 factors considered in the analysis, including years of experience, gender, organization size, organization type, union membership, and so forth. A review of responses to the open-ended question about limits on journalistic freedom included only one or two direct references to race or ethnicity. In these responses, there was no hint that journalists of color perceived themselves as having less professional autonomy, though clearly the responses to the two fixed-response questions demonstrated that to be the case.

Among the four significant predictors of autonomy, the two organizational characteristics—size (indicated by the number of full-time newsroom employees) and the type of organization—stood out as the most powerful factors. Statistically speaking, they were more important than being either a beat reporter or a non-Hispanic White. That can be discerned by looking at the magnitude of the standardized regression coefficients.

In addition to what were significant predictors of autonomy, it's also worth noting a couple of factors that were not strong predictors. Overall, union members tended to report having less autonomy than reporters who did not belong to unions. But once all the 20 predictors are taken into account, that difference shrinks to nonsignificance. Similarly, reporters with more experience and those with some supervisory responsibilities tended to have somewhat greater perceived autonomy, though again not at statistically significant levels in the multiple-regression analysis. In the 1992 survey, gender and income also were associated with perceived autonomy. In 2002, they weren't. Overall, the prediction "model" for perceived autonomy was only modestly successful. Taken together, the 20 factors predicted only about 14% of the variance in the responses that reporters gave. That's sufficient to say that the model explained a statistically significant amount of the variance. Nonetheless, much remains unknown about the factors that constrain reporters' autonomy.

COMMUNICATING WITH AUDIENCE, SOURCES, AND SUPERIORS

Each day, the efforts of American journalists are read, watched, heard, and discussed by millions of people. Few other professions routinely produce work that is so visible to those outside the occupation group. In the last three surveys, journalists were asked about the extent to which they get comments about their work from three important groups: superiors, sources, and audience members. Over time, their responses consistently have shown that fewer than half received

TABLE 3.10

Comments by Superiors, Sources, and Audience Members on Journalists' Work by Type of Medium

Source of Comment	Dailies	Weeklies	News Magazines	News Services	Radio	TV	Online[b]	All 2002[c]	All 1992[d]	All 1982–1983[d]
Superiors	3.27	3.29	3.55	3.43	3.28	3.18	3.33	3.29	3.13	3.12
Sources	3.07	2.98	2.92	3.06	2.90	2.92	2.82	3.01	2.86	3.08
Audience	3.31	3.53	3.10	2.65	3.39	3.47	3.49	3.33	3.22	3.33

[a] Values are means. 4 = regularly, 3 = occasionally, 2 = seldom, 1 = never.

[b] Respondents are from the Online News Association sample and main sample, N = 100.

[c] Sample sizes vary slightly by variable because of missing values. Minimum sample sizes: dailies N = 571; weeklies N = 179; news magazines N = 62; news services N = 69; radio N = 105; TV N = 163; all 2002 N = 1,149. For comparability with previous surveys, total values exclude respondents from the Online News Association sample.

[d] From Weaver and Wilhoit, The American Journalist in the 1990s, p. 73. For 1992, N = 1,143; for 1982–1983, N = 993.

regular feedback from superiors, and only about a third heard from sources. From whom were journalists most likely to get comments? The audience.

Among journalists of all job classifications, about 48% reported regularly getting comments from audience members, about 45% from those above them in the organization, and about 32% from sources. (The question about sources was asked of all journalists but would be most germane for reporters. Their answers are reported in a separate section.) The frequency of comments from sources and audience members has changed only slightly during the last 20 years (Table 3.10). These figures were somewhat higher in the latest survey than in 1992 but not above what was reported in 1982–1983. Comments from superiors, however, have become more common.

Looking across types of media organizations, only the figures on comments from audience members showed much variation. Online news organizations often provide opportunities for instant audience feedback via e-mail or through participation in online polls. Consequently, journalists at online organizations reported relatively high levels of audience comment. They ranked only slightly below news workers at weekly newspapers, which tend to be in smaller communities where journalists often know their readers personally. Television journalists also reported relatively high levels of feedback from audience members, perhaps reflecting aggressive efforts to involve viewers with news programs through audience-involvement gimmicks such as call-in polls or news-tip lines. At the bottom of the audience comments list were news service journalists, who typically do not distribute their work directly to readers, viewers, or listeners.

Reporters are on the front lines in the news business, interacting with sources more than other journalists and often becoming the target when audience members take exception to work that is published or broadcast. The extent of reporters' communication with both sources and audience members has remained fairly stable for 20 years. Roughly half of the reporters surveyed in 2002 said that they received regular feedback about their work from audience members (Table 3.11). That's about five points higher than in 1992 but about the same percentage as in 1982–1983.

The frequency of audience comment has remained constant despite two workplace changes that would seem to encourage reporter-audience interaction. The first change is the evolution of market-driven journalism, which emphasizes the need to try to understand the informational wants and needs of readers, viewers, and listeners. The second change is the widespread use of e-mail, which gives audience members a relatively easy way to contact reporters about their work. Certain organizational goals were associated with the frequency of audience comments. Reporters at organizations that emphasized earning high, above-average profits, maintaining high employee morale, and conducting a lot of market research were the most likely to report receiving comments from audience members.[51]

Oddly, the group that's least likely to comment to reporters about their work continues to be sources. As in previous surveys, only about a third of the report-

TABLE 3.11

Reporters[a] Who Regularly Received Comments About Their Work
by Source of Comment, Type of News Organization, and Year

Source of Comment	Dailies (%)	Weeklies (%)	News Magazines (%)	News Services (%)	Radio (%)	TV (%)	Online[e] (%)	All[f] (%)
Superiors								
2002[b]	42	49	64	57	44	42	43	46
1992[c]	37	33	47	45	37	27	—[g]	37
1982–1983[d]	29	28	41	42	49	42	—[g]	35
Sources								
2002	45	35	22	35	24	27	27	36
1992	49	37	37	10	29	21	—[g]	38
1982–1983	48	32	33	21	33	36	—[g]	39
Audience								
2002	55	61	32	18	45	54	62	51
1992	44	60	41	8	50	49	—[g]	46
1982–1983	48	56	40	13	50	55	—[g]	49

[a] Journalists who said they did reporting "regularly" or "occasionally."

[b] Sample sizes vary slightly by variable because of missing data. Minimum sample sizes: dailies N = 391; weeklies N = 154; news magazines N = 58; news services N = 60; radio N = 58; TV N = 144; all N = 905.

[c] From Weaver and Wilhoit, The American Journalist in the 1990s, p. 75. Sample sizes = dailies N = 383; weeklies N = 144; news magazines N = 45; news services N = 51; radio N = 91; TV N = 92; all for 1992 N = 806.

[d] From Weaver and Wilhoit, The American Journalist, 2nd ed., p. 79. Sample sizes = dailies N = 254; weeklies N = 118; news magazines N = 30; news services N = 24; radio N = 90; TV N = 288; all for 1982–1983 N = 589.

[e] Respondents are from the Online News Association sample and main sample, N = 100.

[f] For comparability with previous surveys, "all" values exclude respondents from the Online News Association sample.

[g] Comparable data not available.

ers overall said they received regular comments from sources (Table 3.11). The frequency of feedback from sources was unrelated to the organizational goals involving profits, employee morale, and market research. However, it did vary considerably by organization type. Reporters from newspapers and news services were about twice as likely as reporters from news magazines and broadcast news organizations to hear back from sources.

The feedback that has increased most during the last 20 years is from supervisors. In 2002, about 46% of the reporters surveyed said that they regularly received comments from superiors about their work (Table 3.11). Overall, that figure was up about 11 percentage points from 1982–1983, when the question was first asked. The increase was largest among print and news-service reporters: up 13 points at daily newspapers, 21 points at weekly papers, 23 points at news magazines and 15 points at wire services. By contrast, the comparable percent-ages for broadcast reporters were about the same as, or down slightly, from 1982–1983, though there had been improvement during the previous 10 years.

Still, too many managers are missing a chance to bolster reporter morale. About 15% of reporters said that they seldom or never received comments about their work from superiors, despite evidence of a substantial positive correlation between job satisfaction and getting regular feedback from supervisors (see Table 3.23). There also was evidence that the amount of feedback reporters received was associated with an organization's management priorities. Organizations that valued keeping employee morale high and producing high-quality journalism were the most likely to have reporters who said they received regular comments about their work from supervisors.[52] Weaker relationships also existed between feedback to reporters and an organizational emphasis on keeping the size of the audience as large as possible and on conducting market research to get informa-tion about the audience. And there was a modest negative relationship between feedback to reporters and an organizational emphasis on achieving high, above-average profits. In other words, in those organizations perceived to emphasize high profits, there was less feedback to reporters from supervisors.

Among only supervisors with no reporting responsibilities, the extent of feed-back from superiors roughly paralleled that of reporters. About 54% of those supervisors reported receiving regular comments about their work from their superiors. But the percentage who received regular comments from sources and from audience members was slightly lower than for reporters. Only about 23% of those supervisors reported getting regular feedback from sources and about 45% from audience members.

Taken together, these two figures suggest that the supervisors were somewhat more isolated than reporters from both the individuals who supply the informa-tion that their organizations distribute and from those who consume it. The 2002 sample did not include enough supervisors with no reporting duties to break them down by media type. The analysis of relationships between organizational goals and feedback duplicated some of the findings for reporters. Feedback from superi-ors was highest at organizations with an emphasis on high employee morale and high-quality journalism.[53] Feedback from sources had a strong positive associa-tion with organizations that stressed high-quality journalism, and receiving com-ments from audiences was strongly associated with an emphasis on earning high, above-average profits.

HOW JOURNALISTS RATE THEIR ORGANIZATIONS

The media have never had a shortage of critics. In the early 20th century, news-paper publishers William Randolph Hearst and Joseph Pulitzer were excoriated for relying on scandal, sensationalism, and vivid graphics to woo readers to their stables of newspapers in cities like New York, San Francisco, and St. Louis.[54] Their "yellow journalism" eventually faded in the face of persistent criticism. From the 1940s into the 1960s, A. J. Liebling chastised the press regularly in his essays in *The New Yorker*. Among other things, he was chagrined about the declining number of newspapers and the subsequent growth of one-newspaper towns. "Diversity—and the competition that it causes—does not insure [sic] good news coverage or a fair champion for every point of view, but it increases the chances," he wrote.[55] In the 1980s, Ben H. Bagdikian began sounding the alarm about the concentration of ownership in his book *The Media Monopoly*. "Modern technology and American economics have quietly created a new kind of central authority over information—the national and multinational corporation," he wrote.[56] The consequence? "For the first time in the history of American journalism, news and public information have been integrated formally into the highest levels of financial and non-journalistic corporate control. Conflicts of interest between the public's need for information and corporate desires for 'positive' information have vastly increased."[57]

By the 1990s, the situation had become dire, Bagdikian argued. In the preface to the 1997 edition of his book, he described a "communications cartel" consisting of a handful of multinational media companies that possessed the power "to surround almost every man, woman, and child in the country with controlled images and words, to socialize each new generation of Americans, to alter the political agenda of the country."[58] He asserted that the "corporate controllers of public information" manipulated news toward their own financial and political goals even as they reduced "any sense of obligation to serve the noncommercial information needs of public citizenship."[59]

Slightly different versions of this critique have surfaced in other recent books. In *When MBAs Rule the Newsroom*, Doug Underwood described the rise of the hybrid editor—part journalist, part marketing executive.[60] In the market-oriented newsroom, he wrote, one casualty may be coverage of civic life. John McManus came to a similar conclusion in *Market-Driven Journalism: Let the Citizen Beware?* In his study of local television news, McManus found that "rational market journalism must serve the market for investors, advertisers, and powerful sources before—and often at the expense of—the public market for readers and viewers."[61] He said that too often, the result of this imperative is "informational poverty."

James Squires's memoir about his career as editor at *The Orlando Sentinel* and *The Chicago Tribune* is, in part, a chronicle of cost cutting and staff reductions during his years with the Tribune Co., one of the nation's largest publicly held media conglomerates.[62] The "corporate takeover" of news organizations, Squires asserted, has eroded the quality of U.S. journalism even as it has enhanced the profitability of the companies that produce it. David Croteau and William Hoynes juxtapose a "market model" for analyzing the media against a "public sphere model" in *The Business of Media: Corporate Media and the Public Interest*.[63]

Their thesis is that adherence by the news media to a market model—something that they believed was increasingly prevalent—would deprive society of the information about civic life that is necessary for a democracy to thrive.

Journalists themselves became so concerned about the state of their profession that in 1997, they joined with teachers, authors, critics, and even media executives to form the Committee of Concerned Journalists. That organization, which had grown to more than 1,900 members by the end of 2005, has pledged to "clarify and renew journalists' faith in the core principles and functions in journalism."[64] The committee's vice chairman, Tom Rosenstiel, wrote of his concerns in a 1997 article in *The Washington Post:*

> If the public does not trust the press, it will turn away from public dialogue. The deep sense of boredom the public feels toward Washington, chronicled in this newspaper and elsewhere, may be a warning sign. If the press turns away from the public service mission of journalism, from providing citizens with the information necessary to make self-government work, that has equally frightening implications. As Joseph Pulitzer said 93 years ago, "A cynical, mercenary, demagogic press will produce in time a people as base as itself."[65]

The scathing critiques of the news media have never quite matched journalists' own sense of their organizations' performance, at least as measured through responses to this question: "How good a job of informing the public do you think your own news organization is doing?" Figure 3.2 traces this self-assessment over the last 30 years. In the latest survey, almost 13% of those responding said that their organization was doing an "outstanding" job. That's about the same percentage as 10 years earlier, though down from the high-water mark of almost 18% in 1982–1983. The percentage rating their organization's performance as "fair" or "poor" declined slightly in 2002 to about 7%, its lowest point ever. "Very good" was the most prevalent rating in 2002, chosen by about half of the journalists in the main sample. Across time, survey results suggest a gradual swelling of the middle ratings on performance and a gradual decline of both the worst and best ratings. For example, in 1971, about 7 in 10 journalists judged that their organizations were doing a "good" or "very good" job of informing the public. By 2002, about 8 in 10 felt that way.

The performance ratings varied some by type of media organization (Figure 3.3). In 2002, journalists working for radio stations and for news services gave the most positive assessments of their organizations. Those journalists were the most likely to rate their organizations' performance "outstanding" and the least likely to rate them "fair" or "poor." The journalists at daily newspapers, news magazines, and TV outlets tended to be more critical of their organizations' performance. The ratings by type of media showed only modest changes from 1992. In the earlier survey, news magazines fared better. At that time, almost 19% of the news-magazine journalists said that their organization was doing an "outstanding" job—about 10 percentage points higher than in the most-recent survey.

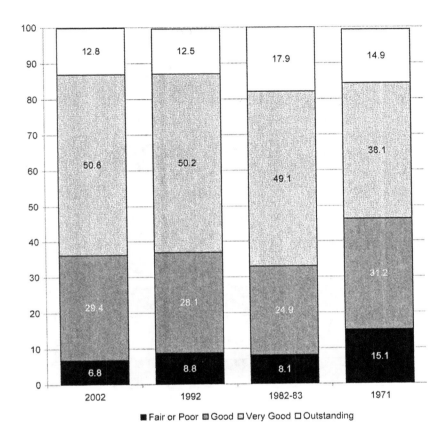

FIG. 3.2. Journalists' assessment of how good a job their organization does in informing the public by year. Values are percentages of the main sample. For 2002 N = 1,147; for 1992 N = 1,150; for 1982–1983, N = 999. Figures for 1971, 1982–1983, and 1992 from Weaver and Wilhoit, *The American Journalist in the 1990s*, p. 78. Figures do not add to 100% because of "no opinion" and rounding error.

The news services had an even larger drop, from 32.8% "outstanding" in 1992 to only 20.6% in 2002.[66] On the other hand, the assessments for radio improved from 1992 to 2002. The "outstanding" rating rose 7 percentage points and the "fair" or "poor" ratings declined about 5 points. The other organizations—TV, daily newspapers, and weekly newspapers—all stayed about the same.

The 2002 survey was the first in which online journalists were contacted, and they tended to be more extreme in their assessments. Eighteen percent of online journalists said that their organizations were doing an "outstanding" job informing the public, and 12% said that they were doing a "fair" or "poor" job.

Few differences in this performance assessment surfaced when considering other characteristics of the journalists or their employers. For example, men and

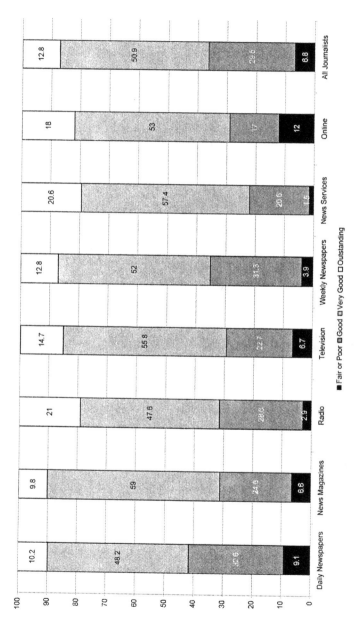

FIG. 3.3. Journalists' assessment of how good a job their organization does in informing the public, by type of media organization. N = 1,147 for "all journalists."

women assessed their organizations similarly, as did minorities and non-Hispanic Whites. Years of experience in journalism was not correlated with this performance rating. Nor did it matter if the journalist was a manager or a union member. And those who worked for publicly held corporations rated their organizations' performance about the same as those who worked for privately held companies.

But several other organizational characteristics were associated with journalists' judgments about how good a job their employer was doing informing the public. Journalists working for news organizations that were part of larger companies, such as newspaper, magazine, or television groups, rated their organizations' performance significantly lower than those working for independent properties. And journalists working at locally owned organizations rated performance higher than did journalists working at organizations owned by outsiders.

Some of the most pronounced differences occurred when examining the relationship between informing the public and the journalists' assessment of eight organizational goals, priorities, or conditions of their employers. In light of persistent criticism during the 1990s that news organizations were sacrificing journalistic quality in the pursuit of higher profits, the 2002 survey included eight new questions that asked about their employers' business and journalistic goals and priorities. Four questions asked journalists to assess the importance of these goals at their organization:[67]

- Earning high, above-average profits;
- Maintaining or securing high employee morale;
- Keeping the size of the audience as large as possible; and
- Producing journalism of high, above-average quality.

Journalists also were asked to say how much they agreed or disagreed with four other statements about their organizations:[68]

- Profits were a higher priority than good journalism at their organization;
- The quality of journalism at their organization had been rising steadily;
- Newsroom resources had been shrinking; and
- Their organization conducted a lot of market research to learn about the kind of information that the audience wanted or needed.

Tables 3.12 and 3.13 show the distribution of responses to the eight questions. The top organizational goal, in the view of journalists participating in the survey, was keeping the size of the audience as large as possible. The least important goal was maintaining high employee morale. For the agree-disagree statements about organizational priorities or conditions, journalists were most likely to agree with the statement that the quality of journalism at their organization had been rising steadily and least likely to agree with the assertion that their organization puts profits ahead of good journalism. The journalists' self-perceptions, then, seem

TABLE 3.12
Perceived Importance of Four Organizational Goals[a]

Organizational Goals	Not Really Important (%)	Somewhat Important (%)	Quite Important (%)	Extremely Important (%)	Mean Values[b]
Earning high, above-average profits	8	15	29	48	3.2
Maintaining or securing high employee morale	18	50	24	8	2.2
Keeping size of audience as large as possible	2	10	31	58	3.5
Producing journalism of high, above-average quality	4	23	35	38	3.1

[a] Analyses conducted on main sample, N = 1,149. N varies slightly by variable because of missing data.
[b] Mean value on 4-point scale ranging from "not really important" (1) to "extremely important" (4).

TABLE 3.13
Level of Agreement on Four Organizational Priorities, Conditions[a]

Organizational Priorities, Conditions	Strongly Disagree (%)	Somewhat Disagree (%)	Neutral (%)	Somewhat Agree (%)	Strongly Agree (%)	Mean Values[b]
Profits a higher priority than good journalism	29	23	10	24	14	2.7
Quality of journalism steadily rising	7	16	15	32	30	3.6
Newsroom resources have been shrinking	21	20	8	24	27	3.2
Organization does a lot of audience research	16	20	12	33	18	3.2

[a] Analyses conducted on main sample N = 1,149. N varies slightly by variable because of missing data.
[b] Mean value on 5-point scale ranging from "strongly disagree" (1) to "strongly agree" (5).

somewhat out of sync with the media critics' views that journalism in the United States is in decline.

The organizational goals, priorities, and conditions are linked, however, to journalists' assessments about how good a job their organization is doing informing the public. Table 3.14 shows the correlations between the eight organizational items and the "how good a job of informing the public" performance rating. At organizations that journalists said had a strong profit emphasis or where newsroom resources were shrinking, ratings on the informing-the-public item tended to be significantly lower. Conversely, journalists who felt that their employer val-

TABLE 3.14
Correlation Between Rating of Organization Success
in Informing Public and Eight Organizational
Goals, Priorities, or Conditions[a]

Organizational Goals	Pearson's r
Earning high, above-average profits	-.179[b]
Maintaining or securing high employee morale	.338[b]
Keeping size of audience as large as possible	.111[b]
Producing journalism of high, above-average quality	.474[b]
Profits a higher priority than good journalism	-.365[b]
Quality of journalism steadily rising	.337[b]
Newsroom resources have been shrinking	-.275[b]
Organization does a lot of audience research	.092[b]

[a] Analyses conducted on main sample N = 1,149. N varies
slightly by variable because of missing data.
[b] Correlation coefficient significant at p ≤ .05.

ued quality journalism and high employee morale were much more likely to say
that their organization was doing a good job informing the public.

Reasons for Performance Ratings

Why did journalists feel that their news organization was doing a good job or poor
job of informing the public? To answer that question, those in the survey were
asked to explain their assessment. A sample of about 150 of their responses was
analyzed, and among the 85% who rated their organizations' performance positively, three broad themes emerged.

The most common reason for a positive rating was the quality of news coverage. Roughly half said that the depth and breadth of coverage was a strength of
their organization. "As it regards to public affairs," a 29-year-old North Carolina
daily newspaper reporter said, "we cover the stories of the day, and there's not
much important going on that you won't find in our paper. We are able to get to
most things with a broad brush even if we don't get down to the details that we
would like." A 26-year-old news-magazine journalist from New York spoke of her
publication's ability to help the public understand complicated issues: "It (the
magazine) sifts through all the noise of the broadcasts and daily newspapers, and
boils it down and helps people determine what's important." Or this from a 50-
year-old New York radio journalist: "We try to address a broad range of issues in
a balanced way, including voices of just plain people, as well as people who influence policy or are news makers. . . . I think we do it in an interesting and acces-
sible way using both our on-air broadcast and a fairly extensive Web presence."

About a third of the responses pointed to staffing and resources as reasons that
their organization was doing an effective job of informing the public. "Talented,"

"skilled, "hard-working," and "smart" were among the adjectives that journalists often used to describe their colleagues. "I believe we have a group of extremely talented and dedicated reporters who know their coverage area extremely well, are very well connected to the people in their coverage areas, and understand the issues," a New Hampshire newspaper journalist, 43, explained. "They do a fantastic job of gathering information and presenting it in a fair and balanced way that our readers can understand." Journalists also cited their colleagues' professionalism. "I believe we are balanced and fair in reporting the news," said a 35-year-old radio sports reporter in Ohio. "We give the public both sides of the story without trying to sway them one way or the other. I believe we do a good job of interviewing the people and talking to the people who are involved in the stories so that the listeners can form their own opinions without having to rely solely on what we say or interpret."

Finally, about 15% of the journalists said their knowledge of the community was an important asset, as was their commitment to getting regular feedback from the community about their work. Some organizations relied regularly on formal public opinion research to keep tabs on community sentiment; others used more informal methods to try to understand what readers, viewers and listeners were concerned about. A TV news director in Iowa described the process that his organization used to stay connected with viewers:

> We have a Top Ten community issues list that we try to go by for our story assignments on a day-by-day basis. We try to provide continuing coverage of those issues so it is not just a hit and run. We have regular input from community leaders and . . . the public on what those Top Ten issues are, as well as polling (of) our reporters and producers on what they think those Top Ten issues should be. We have also developed relationships with three local daily newspapers to develop more in-depth coverage of those stories and issues through joint reporting projects. We've had numerous community town halls on a variety of issues, and we've pre-empted network primetime programming to carry those town halls.

A Florida journalist working for the Web site at a "converged" news organization said that her company used polls, message boards, and e-mail to get feedback from the community. "The public can comment on all aspects of print, broadcast, or online products," she said, using e-mail to share their views with journalists on the staff. "We respond to every e-mail, and we get dozens of e-mails every day."

Though quality news coverage, adequate staff and resources, and a strong link to the community accounted for the bulk of positive assessments, occasionally other reasons were mentioned. They included a strong belief in the watchdog role of the media; skeptical coverage of business and government; access to the latest news-gathering technology; and a clear sense of the organization's social role and mission.

A small minority of journalists—about 15% of the 150 responses that were analyzed—criticized their news organizations' efforts to inform the public. Typically their complaints focused on a lack of staff or on weak coverage. Sometimes those issues were linked, as they were in the opinion of a 54-year-old New Mexico daily newspaper journalist who said that a lack of resources made it difficult to report thoroughly or to dig deeply into stories. This reporter added, "The drive to gain subscriptions, I believe, colors the decisions about what news to run and how to run it, so that the paper is too close to what broadcast news has become." An Illinois journalist, 24, criticized her daily newspaper's traditional approach to government coverage, suggesting that what some had considered a strength others believed to be a weakness. "Because we cover county and city council board ad nauseam," she explained, "we have a dearth of national and international coverage." Other journalists complained that crime news or news about trivial events crowded out coverage of more important issues.

INCOME OF JOURNALISTS

Seasoned journalists sometimes tell students not to go into this occupation if they want to become rich. Though that's good advice, the typical journalist is hardly impoverished. In 2001, the estimated median personal income of journalists was $43,588, according to the latest survey results. Some journalists reported income well above the median (Figure 3.4): almost one in five earned $70,000 or more in 2001.[69] At the same time, about the same percentage earned less than $30,000. Journalists' estimated median incomes were higher than the 2002 annual median earnings of $39,520 for all white-collar occupations (excluding sales), but they were substantially below the $51,480 median of all professional and technical workers.[70]

The Bureau of Labor Statistics does not collect earnings information on journalists as an occupation group, but it does include "editors and reporters" among the roughly 450 job categories for which it gathers data. The BLS estimates that median annual earnings for editors and reporters was $39,562 in 2002—close to that of all white-collar occupations.[71] Keep in mind that comparisons with our survey data are inexact because the BLS definition of editors and reporters would include some workers who are not journalists (e.g., advertising copy writers, and book editors) and would exclude other workers who are journalists (e.g., photographers, designers, and producers).

Compared with all occupations, editors and reporters were within about the top quarter in annual earnings at the start of this decade, but they ranked in the lower half of all professional and technical occupations.[72] Certainly many other professional occupations offer better pay. For example, the median estimated annual earnings were higher for lawyers ($84,011), for urban planners ($53,435), for public-relations practitioners ($45,365), and for accountants and auditors ($45,053). Still, journalists outperformed other professional or technical workers, such as dieticians ($37,440), drafters ($37,211), licensed practical

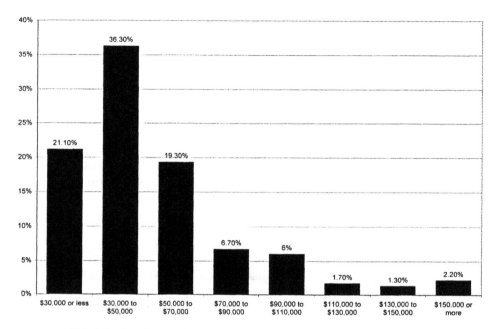

FIG. 3.4.   Distribution of journalists' personal income for 2001, N = 1,086. Data are from main sample.

nurses ($31,616), and social workers ($31,533). The professional or technical job categories with pay closest to editors and reporters included atmospheric or space scientists ($39,603), social scientists and electrical or electronic technicians (both $39,520), and religious workers ($39,458).

For journalists contacted in the 2002 survey, the 1990s were comparatively good salary years. For the second decade in a row, journalists' median personal income grew faster than the inflation rate. Between 1991 and 2001, median income increased about 39% while the inflation rate was only 30%. That was the good news. The bad news was that by the end of 2001, journalists still had not recaptured the purchasing power that they had in 1970, the year before the original Johnstone, Slawski, and Bowman survey was conducted. In inflation-adjusted dollars, the median 1970 personal income of $11,133 would have been equivalent to $50,810 in 2001. That's about $7,200 less than the actual median income of $43,588 in 2001 (see Figure 3.5).[73]

An increase in income above the inflation rate was not unexpected. Through much of the 1990s, journalism reviews, trade publications, and trade associations had reported that a tight labor market was pushing up salaries.[74] For part of that decade, the Internet-based media offered financially lucrative alternatives to traditional journalism jobs. "By expanding the number of jobs, new media is beginning to change the supply and demand equation in both new and traditional media," the *Columbia Journalism Review* reported in 1999. "And, the money that is lubricating the journalistic market is both the real kind, produced by profits in the business, and the 'funny kind' that results from the great boom that has been lifting prices of Internet stocks."[75] Within 2 years, of course, the Internet boom had become more of a whisper, the economy had lost its buoyancy and layoffs within the media industries were more common. Nonetheless, the 1990s roared economically and left a legacy of relatively healthy pay raises for journalists.

As in previous surveys, annual income figures differed significantly by type of media organization, region of the country, and individual characteristics of journalists. Since the surveys began in 1971, those working for news magazines consistently have been the best paid. That was true again in 2001 (Figure 3.6). Journalists working in radio and the weekly newspaper industry always have been the most poorly paid. Their rank also did not change. Previous surveys, of course, did not include estimates for online journalists. They are relatively well off within the field, with a median salary estimated at $64,000.[76]

Through the last 30 years, the spread between the best-paid and poorest-paid journalists has increased. In 1970, the median personal income for magazine journalists in the survey was about 1.8 times higher than for those working at weekly

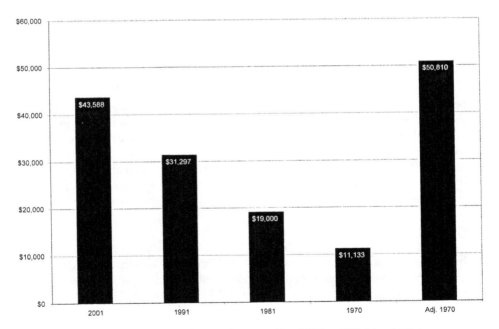

FIG. 3.5. Median annual personal income. N = 1,086 in 2001; N = 1,115 in 1991; N = 939 in 1981; N = 1,328 in 1970. Last column shows 1970 salary in 2001 dollars. Data are from main samples only. Figures for 1970, 1981 and 1991 from Weaver and Wilhoit, *The American Journalist in the 1990s*, p. 92.

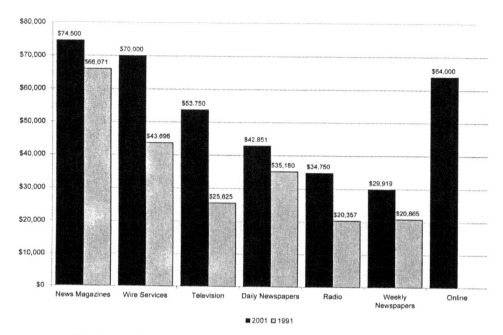

FIG. 3.6. Median annual personal income by type of medium. Data are from main samples only. Figures for 1991 from Weaver and Wilhoit, *The American Journalist in the 1990s*, p. 93.

papers. By 2001, the comparable figure was 2.5 times higher (Table 3.15). Median personal income typically has been the highest at large news organizations in the Northeast. That's true in this survey, as well. In 2001, the median income of journalists in the Northeast was about a third higher than for those working in Southern states, the poorest paid region. And journalists at the largest organizations (more than 100 editorial employees) continued to make substantially more than their counterparts in the smallest organizations (10 or fewer editorial employees).

Gender Differences

In the past, gender has been associated with income differences. In 2001, as in previous surveys, women reported making substantially less than men. The median income was $46,780 for men and $37,713 for women (Table 3.16). The magnitude of the difference—women made about 80.6% of what men made—is essentially unchanged from 1991. Though the magnitude of difference is smaller than it was in 1970 (64%) and in 1981 (71%), the trend toward income equity stalled in the 1990s. Within the managerial ranks, however, this gender difference was less pronounced. Female senior and junior managers reported having

TABLE 3.15
Median Personal Income from 1970 Through 2001
by Type of Medium, Region, and Organization Size

Factors	2001[a] (N = 1,086)	1991[b] (N = 1,115)	1981[c] (N = 939)	1970[d] (N = 1,328)
Media Sector				
News magazines	$74,500	$66,071	$34,750	$15,571
Wire services	70,000	43,696	24,100	11,833
Television	53,750	25,625	17,031	11,875
Daily newspapers	42,851	35,180	21,000	11,420
Radio	34,750	20,357	15,000	9,583
Weekly newspapers	29,919	20,865	14,000	8,786
Online	64,000	—[e]	—[e]	—[e]
Region				
Total Northeast	55,536	36,136	27,000	11,532
New England	32,500	33,461	30,000	11,274
Middle Atlantic	60,833	40,417	24,000	11,622
Total Midwest	42,632	26,964	16,999	11,187
East North-Central	43,500	24,500	18,000	11,702
West North-Central	41,667	30,147	15,933	9,600
Total South	41,346	29,542	17,550	10,005
South Atlantic	41,935	31,500	19,100	11,484
East South-Central	41,250	28,370	16,033	7,846
West South-Central	38,611	26,000	14,000	8,920
Total West	44,038	39,306	18,975	11,661
Mountain	47,292	35,833	15,933	9,118
Pacific	41,250	40,543	22,050	13,573
Size of News Organization				
1–10 editorial employees	31,875	20,319	15,000	8,632
11–25 editorial employees	32,045	24,342	15,985	9,866
26–50 editorial employees	39,808	28,167	21,000	11,657
51–100 editorial employees	50,238	32,574	23,960	10,892
> 100 editorial employees	60,781	42,799	30,025	13,550
Overall	43,588	31,297	19,000	11,133

[a] N for 2001 is for the main sample only. For all years, N varies slightly by variable because of missing data.

[b] From Weaver and Wilhoit, *The American Journalist in the 1990s*, p. 94.

[c] From Weaver and Wilhoit, *The American Journalist*, 2nd ed., p. 84.

[d] From Johnstone, Slawski, and Bowman, *The News People*, p. 235.

[e] Comparable data not available.

TABLE 3.16
Median Personal Income from 1970 to 2001
by Gender, Age, and Education

Factors	2001[a] (N = 1,086)	1991[b] (N = 1,115)	1981[c] (N = 939)	1970[d] (N = 1,328)
Gender				
Male	$46,780	$34,167	$21,000	$11,955
Female	37,713	27,669	14,984	7,702
Age				
Under 25	25,577	< 15,000	10,991	6,492
25–34	34,608	25,100	17,012	10,031
35–44	48,215	38,100	22,999	13,322
45–54	50,208	39,375	27,000	12,847
55 and older	48,654	40,333	22,000	12,000
Years of School				
High school grad or less	36,250	27,857	16,000	10,992
Some college	37,222	28,750	18,022	10,164
College graduate	42,579	29,717	17,999	11,617
Some graduate training	52,500	36,667	21,000	11,424
Graduate degree	55,500	39,333	25,012	12,823
Overall	43,588	31,297	19,000	11,133

[a] N for 2001 is for the main sample only. For all years, N varies slightly by variable because of missing data.

[b] From Weaver and Wilhoit, *The American Journalist in the 1990s*, p. 95.

[c] From Weaver and Wilhoit, *The American Journalist*, 2nd ed., p. 83.

[d] From Johnstone, Slawski, and Bowman, *The News People*, p. 236.

TABLE 3.17
Median Income by Employment Status

Employment Status	All (N = 1,085)	Men (N = 725)	Women (N = 360)
Senior managers	$46,310	$48,088	$41,875
Junior managers	$50,643	$52,404	$46,000
Nonmanagement employees	$39,156	$42,628	$34,722
Reporters[a]	$41,821	$44,734	$37,500

[a] Reporters include any journalist, regardless of his or her management status, who said that she or he reported "regularly" or "occasionally." For reporters, N = 861.

median personal incomes that were about 87% of what their male counterparts earned (Table 3.17).

A combination of factors contributed to the income difference between women and men. Women in this survey tended to be younger than men, to have fewer years of experience, and to work for smaller news organizations. They also were less likely to be managers than men. All these factors were associated with lower personal income. Looking ahead, evidence points toward growing salary equity between men and women. The single biggest factor affecting income is a journalist's years of experience.

Figure 3.7 shows the median annual personal incomes for men and women broken down by years of experience. In the youngest age groupings, the incomes of men and women are almost equal. If this pattern holds as younger women gain experience, and if they are afforded—and take—opportunities for advancement at the same rate as men, the salary gap could narrow. Whether this actually will happen may depend, in part, on whether women are as aggressive in negotiating for pay and promotions as men. Recent research indicates that for professional jobs in general, women are less likely than men to ask for salaries higher than the ones originally offered by an employer. That has the effect of giving men a head start on the salary ladder.[77] Closing the salary gap also could fall victim to women's aspirations, however. Catalyst, a nonprofit organization that seeks to advance women in business, estimates that concerns about family keep roughly a third

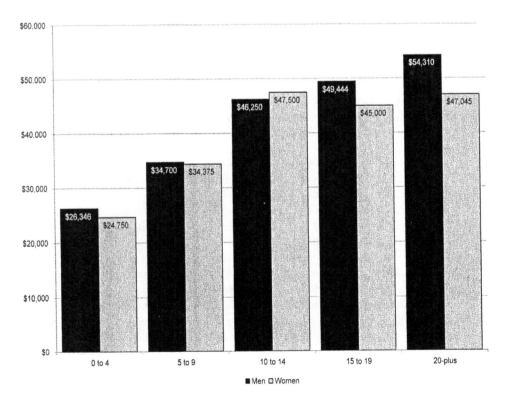

FIG. 3.7. Median personal income for 2001 by gender and years of professional experience (N = 1,085). Data are from main sample only.

of professional women from seeking senior executive jobs, where, other things equal, the pay is highest and the disparity with men's salaries the lowest.[78]

Other Factors

Age and education levels are other factors often associated with differences in personal income, and that was the case for journalists, too (Table 3.16). These differences followed predictable patterns. Median incomes rose with age until age 55 and then dropped slightly. The slight decline among the oldest journalists appears to reflect a higher-than-average concentration of weekly newspaper employees in that age group and a lower-than-average percentage of individuals with a college degree. As with age, median income tended to rise with education. Those with the most education have had the highest median income in each of the four American Journalist surveys. The most recent findings show that journalists with graduate degrees earned about 30% more than those with undergraduate degrees: $55,500 compared with $42,579. However, this income premium for a graduate degree has declined in each of the last three surveys. It was greatest in 1981, when journalists with a graduate degree earned about 39% more than those with an undergraduate degree.

Predictors of Income

One of the challenges in understanding income differences is that so many factors can influence what an individual makes. A multiple-regression analysis that simultaneously examined 14 factors that could influence income determined that 12 were significant predictors of journalists' income (Table 3.18).[79]

Among organizational characteristics, five mattered. The most important was no surprise: the size of the organization, as measured by the number of newsroom employees. The larger the organization, the higher the pay even after controlling for the 13 other factors. Similarly, publicly held media companies tended to offer higher salaries. Those salaries were about $400 higher annually, other factors held constant. Also, news organizations owned by larger corporations, typically organizations that were part of groups or chains, tended to pay more. The type of news organization for which a journalist worked was another factor that contributed significantly to income. In the latest survey, journalists working at news services, news magazines, and television stations were significantly better off than journalists overall, and journalists at newspapers and radio stations were significantly worse off.[80] Finally, the region in which a journalist worked affected pay. Other things equal, journalists in the South earned significantly less than journalists over all. Journalists in the Northeast earned more, though for technical reasons, a formal comparison could not be done.

Among the individual characteristics examined, a journalist's experience was far and away the most important consideration. More years of experience

TABLE 3.18
Predictors and Correlates of 2001 Annual Personal Income[a,b]

Predictors	Standardized Regression Coefficients	Pearson's r
Organizational Characteristics		
Number of full-time employees	.267[f]	.40[f]
Part of publicly owned corporation	.133[f]	.30[f]
Owned by larger company	.060[f]	.12[f]
Midwest region	-.026	—[c]
Southern region	-.043[f]	—[c]
Western region	.024	—[c]
Daily newspaper	-.076[f]	—[d]
Magazines	.303[f]	—[d]
Radio	-.129[f]	—[d]
Television	.124[f]	—[d]
Weekly newspaper	-.222[f]	—[d]
Individual Characteristics		
Years of experience in journalism	.388[f]	.45[f]
Gender (is a female)	-.097[f]	-.18[f]
Supervises other employees	.140[f]	.18[f]
Belongs to a union	.083[f]	.20[f]
Education level	.111[f]	.22[f]
Attended private college	.014	.14[f]
Undergraduate major in journalism, communications	.011	-.03
Belongs to journalism organization	.103[f]	.18[f]
American Indian or Pacific Islander	.003	—[c]
Asian American	-.053[f]	—[c]
African American	.023	—[c]
Hispanic	.008	—[c]
Non-Hispanic White	-.048[f]	—[c]

[a] Analysis of journalists from all samples after excluding cases with missing values. In addition, 11 aberrant cases also eliminated from analysis. N = 1,169.

[b] Dependent variable "personal income" was transformed to log (base 10) of income.

[c] Effects-coded variables with "Northeast" chosen as excluded group. Zero-order correlations are not meaningful.

[d] Effects-coded variables with "news services" chosen as excluded group. Zero-order correlations are not meaningful.

[e] Effects-coded variables with "race-other" chosen as excluded group. Zero-order correlations are not meaningful.

[f] Significant at $p \leq .05$. Total adjusted $R^2 = .56$.

translated into more money, other things equal. But other factors were relevant, too. Supervisors, union members, and the well educated had significantly higher incomes. Gender also was a significant predictor: women earned less. Those who belonged to journalism groups had significantly higher income. And among the racial and ethnic groups, non-Hispanic Whites and Asian Americans were paid somewhat less after other factors were controlled.

Taken as a whole, these 14 factors account for most of the differences that were found in 2001 personal income, explaining about 56% of the variance in pay. The most important predictors of income were similar to those in the 1992 survey, though differences in the analysis make precise comparisons difficult. As in 1992, organization size, type of organization, education, years of experience, supervisory responsibilities, race or ethnicity, gender, union membership, region, and public ownership all mattered in the previous survey just as in this one. In several instances, however, they mattered in different ways:

- While salaries for those working in television were significantly lower in 1992, they were above average in the latest survey.
- Being part of a larger company, a significant predictor in 2002, had not been an important influence in 1992.
- Salaries for journalists in the Midwest were significantly lower than for their comparison group in 1992 but not in 2002.[81] Salaries for journalists in the South were significantly lower than average for journalists in 2002 but not in 1992.[82]
- In 1992, Native American journalists had significantly lower salaries than their comparison group, but that was not the case in the latest survey.[83] In 2002, journalists who were non-Hispanic Whites and Asian Americans had significantly lower salaries than journalists over all.[84]

JOB SATISFACTION

How are morale and job satisfaction in the nation's newsrooms?

- Writer Neil Hickey answered that question this way in the September/October 2001 issue of *Columbia Journalism Review*:[85] "Low morale—is it common in newsrooms across America? An overwhelming percentage of journalists who participated in a nationwide CJR survey answered yes to that question." Specifically, about 84% of the 127 journalists contacted in CJR's informal survey said poor morale was a widespread problem.
- Deborah Potter answered the question this way in a 2002 article on the Journalism.org Web site: "More than half the news directors, 55%, said the mood in their newsrooms had suffered because of budget constraints or layoffs industry-wide. And in those newsrooms where morale was low, more than twice as many

bosses said things in general were going in the wrong direction than said the direction was right."[86] Potter's findings were in a report about the 2002 Local TV News Project, which included a survey of 103 TV news directors.

• Former newspaper editor Geneva Overholser answered the question this way in her Estlow Lecture, which she delivered at the University of Denver in October 2002:[87] "On and on go the sad pieces of news from surveys, about job satisfaction plummeting among journalists, about declining numbers of journalists expected to remain in the field until retirement, about increased numbers of mistakes associated with overloaded copy desks, about reporters with fewer and fewer hours to spend on stories, about the number of reporters news organizations have covering government at all levels." The economic pressures on journalism have fostered many of these problems, she said.

The decidedly pessimistic views of Hickey, Potter, Overholser, and others appeared to be the norm among media observers who were talking about journalists' morale and job satisfaction at the turn of the millennium. Because poor morale and declining job satisfaction tend to go hand in hand, their comments, plus ongoing news of recession-induced staff cuts and layoffs, seemed to point toward further declines in job satisfaction in this latest survey of U.S. journalists.[88] (Job satisfaction has been sinking steadily since the first survey in 1971.) But the journalists contacted in 2002 were slightly more upbeat. Almost 84% said that they were "fairly satisfied" or "very satisfied" with their jobs. The percentage of those who were "very satisfied" was up about 6 points from 1992 (see Table 3.19), reversing the trend from previous surveys. In the past, journalists' job satisfaction levels have tracked below those for the workforce as a whole, and that was true again in 2002. An October 2001 Harris poll of 656 working adults found that 58% were "very satisfied" with their jobs and another 36 were "somewhat satisfied."[89] By comparison, about 33% of journalists were "very satisfied" and another 51% were "fairly satisfied."

TABLE 3.19
Job Satisfaction by Year

Rating	2002 (N = 1,149) (%)	1992[a] (N = 1,156) (%)	1982–1983[b] (N = 1,001) (%)	1971[c] (N = 1,328) (%)
Very satisfied	33.3	27	40	49
Fairly satisfied	50.6	50	44	39
Somewhat dissatisfied	14.4	20	15	12
Very dissatisfied	1.7	3	2	1

[a] From Weaver and Wilhoit, *The American Journalist in the 1990s*, p. 100.
[b] From Weaver and Wilhoit, *The American Journalist*, 2nd ed., p. 89.
[c] From Johnstone, Slawski, and Bowman, *The News People*, p. 238.

TABLE 3.20
Job Satisfaction by Type of Medium

Rating	Dailies (N = 445) (%)	Weeklies (N = 177) (%)	News Magazines (N = 59) (%)	Radio (N = 105) (%)	TV (N = 162) (%)	News Services (N = 69) (%)	Online[a] (N = 100) (%)
Total satisfied	82.7	84.7	78.0	90.5	83.4	89.9	87.0
Very satisfied	30.7	30.5	33.9	47.6	38.3	29.0	38.0
Fairly satisfied	52.0	54.2	44.1	42.9	45.1	60.9	49.0
Total dissatisfied	17.3	15.3	22.0	9.5	16.6	10.1	13.0
Somewhat dissatisfied	14.8	14.7	20.3	9.5	15.4	10.1	10.0
Very dissatisfied	2.5	0.6	1.7	0.0	1.2	0.0	3.0

[a] Includes respondents from the main sample and the special sample of the Online News Association.

The level of job satisfaction varied slightly by media type (Table 3.20) and, to a greater extent, by the characteristics of journalists (Figure 3.8) themselves and of the organizations for which they worked. Those employed by news magazines were a little below average in job satisfaction, and those working for radio stations and news services were a little above average. Women had somewhat lower levels of job satisfaction than men. Satisfaction levels were exceptionally high for the youngest journalists but dropped substantially between the ages of 25 and 34 before beginning to climb as journalists became older.

Managers differed only slightly from nonmanagers. About 88% of senior managers and 85% of junior managers were either "very satisfied" or "fairly satisfied" with their jobs. Among nonmanagers, the comparable figure was 82%. Minority journalists and non-Hispanic Whites reported similar levels of job satisfaction in the main 2002 sample, though in the expanded sample, which included representatives from the African American, Asian American, Native American, and Hispanic journalism associations, the satisfaction levels for some minorities were lower (Table 3.21). Overall, the percentage of most minority journalists who were very or fairly satisfied was a few points lower than for non-Hispanic Whites, except for Native Americans and Alaska Natives, who were a bit more likely to be satisfied.

The factors most closely associated with job satisfaction were related to journalists' perceptions about their work environment. For example, for reporters in the 2002 survey, higher levels of perceived autonomy and influence were closely associated with higher levels of job satisfaction.[90] Reporters were asked two questions about autonomy: how much freedom they had to select the stories that they worked on and how much freedom they had to choose what to emphasize in their stories. Those questions were combined into a scale of perceived autonomy, and Figure 3.9 shows the relationship between that scale and job satisfaction.[91] As perceived autonomy increased, so did job satisfaction. Similarly,

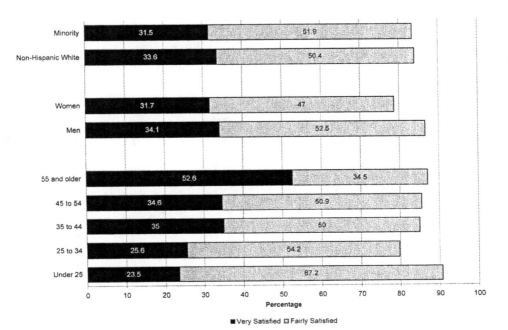

FIG. 3.8. Job satisfaction by minority status, gender, and age. Main sample N = 1,149, though N varies slightly by variable because of missing data.

TABLE 3.21
Job Satisfaction by Race-Ethnicity[a]

Rating	Whites (N = 1,120) (%)	African Americans (N = 61) (%)	Hispanics (N = 132) (%)	Asian Americans (N = 110) (%)	Other[b] (N = 58) (%)
Total satisfied	84.5	77.0	78.0	80.9	89.7
Very satisfied	34.5	29.5	26.5	28.2	39.7
Fairly satisfied	50.0	47.5	51.5	52.7	50.0
Total dissatisfied	15.5	23.0	22.0	19.1	10.3
Somewhat dissatisfied	13.8	21.3	20.5	19.1	10.3
Very dissatisfied	1.7	1.7	1.5	0.0	0.0

[a] Includes respondents from the main sample and the special samples from the African American, Asian American, Native American, Hispanic, and online journalism associations.

[b] Includes non-Hispanic respondents who classified themselves as American Indian, Alaska Native, Pacific Islander, or other.

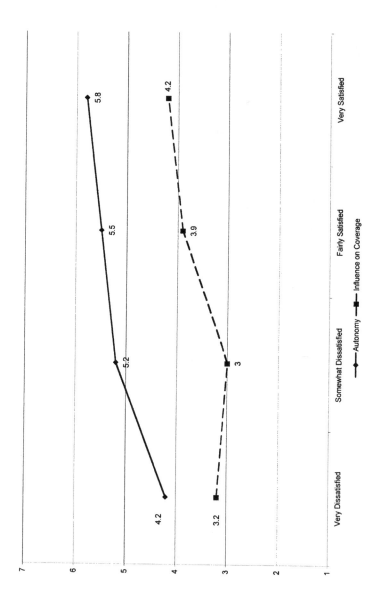

FIG. 3.9. Reporters' job satisfaction by values on perceived autonomy scale (N = 911) and on perceived influence on coverage (N = 910). Reporters are journalists who say they report "regularly" or "occasionally." Values on the autonomy scale ranged from a low of 1 to a high of 7. Values on the influence on coverage item ranged from a low of 1 to a high of 5.

reporters were asked how successful they usually were in getting a story covered that they believed needed to be covered. This indicator of perceived newsroom influence also was positively related to job satisfaction: the more influence, the higher the job satisfaction.[92]

In addition, job satisfaction was linked to the perceptions that journalists had about the performance of their news organization. Among all journalists in the main sample, those who said their organization was doing an "outstanding" or "very good" job of informing the public were much more satisfied with their work than journalists who said their organization was doing only a "good," "fair" or "poor" job (Figure 3.10).

In the 2002 survey, journalists were asked for the first time to say how important that they believed that four key goals were to the senior managers or owners of their organizations. Those goals were earning high, above-average profits; securing high, above-average employee morale; keeping audience size as large as possible; and producing journalism of high, above-average quality.

Job satisfaction had a strong, positive association with the second and fourth goals (securing high morale and producing high-quality journalism). It was negatively associated with an emphasis on earning high profits and had a weak positive

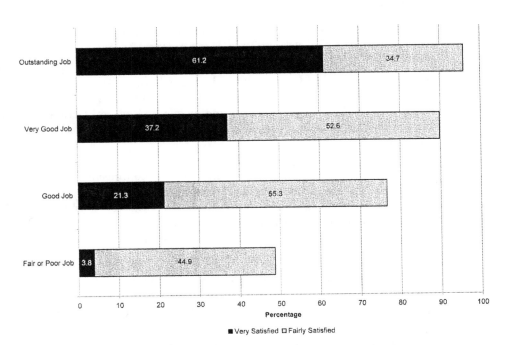

FIG. 3.10. Percentage of journalists who were "very satisfied" or "fairly satisfied" with their job by rating of their organization's performance in informing the public, N = 1,147.

TABLE 3.22
Correlation of Job Satisfaction With Organizational
Goals, Priorities, and Conditions

Organizational Goals, Priorities, Conditions	r^{ab}
Importance of the following goals . . .[c]	
Earning high, above-average profits	-.19
Securing high, above-average employee morale	.38
Keeping size of audience as large as possible	.09
Producing journalism of high, above-average quality	.36
Agreement with statement that . . .[d]	
At my organization, profits are a higher priority than good journalism	-.33
Quality of journalism at my organization has been rising steadily	.31
At my organization, newsroom resources have been shrinking	-.23
My organization does a lot of audience research	.06

[a] Pearson product-moment correlation coefficient for respondents in main sample, N = 1,149. N varies slightly by variable because of missing data. All correlation coefficients are significant at $p \leq .05$.

[b] Possible responses on job satisfaction were (4) "very satisfied," (3) "fairly satisfied," (2) "somewhat dissatisfied" and (1) "very dissatisfied."

[c] Possible responses were (4) "extremely important," (3) "quite important," (2) "somewhat important" and (1) "not really important."

[d] Possible responses were (5) "strongly agree," (4) "somewhat agree," (3) "neutral," (2) "somewhat disagree" and (1) "strongly disagree."

relationship with the goal of keeping the audience as large as possible (Table 3.22). These findings hint that there may be some truth in the observations of media critics that staff reductions were hurting morale and job satisfaction in newsrooms, assuming journalists believed that those reductions were undertaken to prop up high profits.

The larger picture, however, suggests that job satisfaction was not as low as the critics had surmised. These findings point toward a contingent relationship—that levels of job satisfaction depend, to some extent, on how newsrooms are managed. Further evidence of the contingent nature of this relationship was found in the analysis of four additional statements about the workplace to which journalists responded in the 2002 survey. Those items asked about the extent to which journalists agreed with these statements:

- That profits were a higher priority than good journalism at their news organization;
- That the quality of journalism at their organization had been steadily rising;
- That newsroom resources had been shrinking at their organization; and
- That their organization did a lot of audience research (an indicator of the strength of its market orientation).

Job satisfaction was negatively related to agreement with the profits and resources statements (Table 3.22). That is, the more that journalists agreed with the statements that profits were a higher priority than good journalism or that newsroom resources had been shrinking, the lower their job satisfaction was. The relationship was just the opposite for the quality item. The more that journalists agreed that quality had been rising, the higher their job satisfaction was. The relationship with the market-orientation item was weak and positive, suggesting that at a minimum, being a market-driven news organization wasn't undermining job satisfaction.

Predictors of Job Satisfaction

Previous research has established that many factors can influence a journalist's job satisfaction.[93] Table 3.23 shows results of a multiple-regression analysis that seeks to identify those factors that most strongly predict how satisfied a journalist is with his or her work. This analysis considered 25 such factors, which are listed in the left column of the table. These "predictors" of job satisfaction fall into three broad categories: organizational characteristics; assessments of organizational goals, priorities or conditions; and individual and work-environment characteristics of journalists. Multiple regression allows each of the 25 predictors to be assessed individually while statistically controlling, or "holding constant," all of the other predictors. The middle column in the table labeled "standardized regression coefficients," contains the most important results of this multiple-regression analysis.

In the analysis, 10 items emerged as significant predictors of job satisfaction. Two organizational characteristics were important: whether the news organization was owned by a larger corporation (typically a company that owns a group of newspapers, magazines, or broadcast stations) and whether the organization's owner was local. Both of those characteristics were associated with higher levels of job satisfaction, holding constant other factors. Similarly, three of the items assessing organizational goals or practices also were associated positively with job satisfaction. Journalists who said their employer emphasized keeping morale high and who believed that the quality of journalism at their organization was rising also were more likely to be satisfied with their jobs. The same was true for journalists who believed that their organization was doing a good job informing the public. None of the other factors in those two groups of predictors had a significant predictive impact on job satisfaction.

Five individual and work-environment characteristics appeared to be predictors of job satisfaction. Not surprisingly, journalists who were paid more and who had more experience were much more likely to be more satisfied with their jobs, other factors held constant. But three other factors were significant, too. Those journalists who perceived that they had substantial autonomy to decide which stories to work on and to choose what to emphasize in their stories were happier,

TABLE 3.23
Predictors and Correlates of Job Satisfaction[a]

Predictors	Standardized Regression Coefficients	Pearson's r
Organizational Characteristics		
Owned by larger corporation	.106[b]	.00
Owner is local person or organization	.085[b]	.08[b]
Part of publicly owned corporation	.033	.03
Number of full-time employees	-.023	.06[b]
Staff size growing	-.012	.12[b]
Assessment of Organizational Goals, Priorities, Conditions		
Rating of performance in informing public	.177[b]	.32[b]
Organizational emphasis on earning high profits	-.053	-.19[b]
Organizational emphasis on high employee morale	.139[b]	.37[b]
Organizational emphasis on keeping large audience	-.022	.09[b]
Organizational emphasis on high-quality journalism	.062	.36[b]
Belief that profits are a higher priority than journalism	-.037	-.32[b]
Belief that quality of journalism rising steadily	.098[b]	.30[b]
Belief that newsroom resources have been shrinking	-.043	-.21[b]
Belief that organization does a lot of audience research	.017	.08[b]
Individual and Work-Environment Characteristics		
Level of perceived autonomy	.081[b]	.23[b]
Influence on getting subjects covered	.161[b]	.31[b]
Frequency of receiving comments from supervisors	.097[b]	.26[b]
Frequency of receiving comments from sources	.035	.14[b]
Frequency of receiving comments from audience	-.034	.11[b]
Supervises other employees	-.018	.09[b]
Years of journalistic experience	.071[b]	.17[b]
Gender (female)	-.026	-.10[b]
Personal income in 2001	.140[b]	.19[b]
Racial or ethnic minority	.027	-.03
Had short course, sabbatical, workshop, fellowship	.025	.05

[a] Analysis of journalists from main sample after excluding cases with missing values. Four aberrant cases also eliminated from analysis, for total N = 919.

[b] Significant at $p \leq .05$. Adjusted $R^2 = .32$.

as were journalists who perceived themselves as having greater influence within the newsroom.[94] And journalists who reported receiving frequent comments from supervisors tended to be more satisfied, as well.

Taken as a whole, the survey findings about job satisfaction suggest that journalists were not particularly disillusioned with their work—certainly no more disillusioned than in previous surveys and perhaps not as disillusioned as critics have suggested. And the factors that influenced job satisfaction were sometimes counterintuitive.

For example, group ownership of media organizations has been widely lamented. Critics have been concerned about not only concentration of ownership but also that media groups—particularly publicly held groups—manage too aggressively for profits and tend to undervalue journalistic quality.[95] Given those assertions, one might expect to see evidence of that in low job satisfaction ratings. But according to the 2002 survey results, working for a publicly held company didn't appear to affect job satisfaction negatively, and working for a news organization owned by a larger corporation was positively associated with job satisfaction—the opposite of what might be expected. What seemed to matter most when it came to job satisfaction were the values of the news organization and the treatment journalists received from their employer, which can vary independently of ownership structure. Organizations that had employees who believed that they were valued and who believed that good journalism was valued by their owners or senior managers had more satisfied workers.

An analysis of predictors of job satisfaction was also done for the 1992 survey.[96] A precise comparison with those results is not possible because additional variables were considered in the multiple-regression analysis reported above and because the analysis done then was different from what was done this time. However, some informal comparisons are possible. In both 1992 and 2002, factors such as salary, perceived autonomy, the performance rating of the organization, and the frequency of comments from supervisors all were positively associated with higher levels of job satisfaction. Attending a short course, which was negatively associated with job satisfaction in some of the 1992 results, was not a significant predictor in 2002.

CHANGING CAREERS

The fact that U.S. journalists were a bit more content with their jobs in 2002, compared with a decade earlier, appears to have translated into a slight increase in the percentage planning to remain in the occupation during the next five years. About 77% of the journalists in the 2002 survey said that they anticipated continuing to work for the media (Figure 3.11). Another 17% said they intended to be working elsewhere, and about 5% either expected to be retired or were unsure of their plans. These results reflect a 3.5-point uptick from 1992 in the percentage of journalists who remain committed to media jobs.

The overall figures mask a few important differences among journalists (Table 3.24). Those working at news magazines and, to a lesser extent, at weekly newspapers were more likely to want to leave journalism than employees at other kinds of news organizations. Journalists at news services were the least likely to be planning to leave; that was true in 1992 as well. Between 1992 and 2002, radio, television, and news-service journalists became much less likely to "defect" to another career. The percentage of journalists in those three types of organizations who anticipated working outside the media within 5 years declined by about 40%.

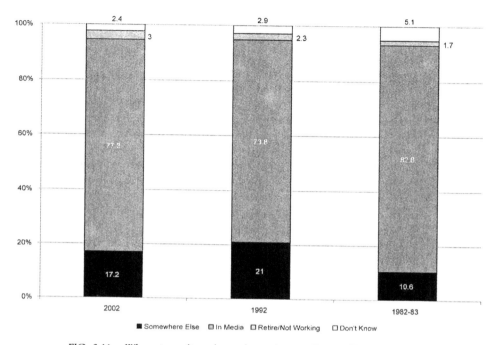

FIG. 3.11. Where journalists plan to be working in 5 years. For 2002, N = 1,121. Figures for 1982–1983 and 1992 from Weaver and Wilhoit, *The American Journalist in the 1990s*, p. 112.

Other organizational characteristics didn't show much association with plans to leave the profession. Journalists at organizations that had downsized newsrooms seemed slightly more likely to be planning to change careers: 19% versus 14% at those where the staff size grew in recent years. Otherwise, there was essentially no difference in "defection" plans between journalists working for stand-alone organizations and those working for media conglomerates, nor was there a significant difference between journalists at publicly held versus privately held media companies. Those working at organizations with 11 to 25 employees were somewhat more inclined toward career changes than their counterparts elsewhere; otherwise, the anticipated defection rate was about the same at both large and small organizations.

Personal characteristics had a much stronger relationship to future plans than organizational characteristics (Table 3.25). Women and minorities were more inclined to be planning to work outside the media within 5 years. If both female and minority journalists in those groups follow through on their intentions, that could frustrate efforts to diversify news staffs on the basis of gender and race or ethnicity. The journalists with the least experience (4 or fewer years) were about 7 percentage points above average in their intention to change careers. Not sur-

TABLE 3.24
Intention to Be Working Outside the Media
Within Five Years by Organizational Characteristics

Organizational Characteristics	Intends to Be Working Outside Media Within 5 Years (%)[a]	
	2002	1992
Type of medium[b]		
Dailies	19	20
News magazines	25	27
Radio	18	30
Television	14	24
Weeklies	21	24
News services	5	9
Online	15	—[c]
Staff size		
10 or fewer	18	24
11 to 25	24	21
26 to 50	14	22
51 to 100	17	26
More than 100	17	19
Staff size change		
Size has shrunk in recent years	19	—[c]
Size the same in recent years	18	—[c]
Size has grown in recent years	14	—[c]
Ownership characteristics		
Publicly owned	17	20
Privately owned	18	23
Part of larger corporation	17	23
Not part of larger corporation	19	19

[a] Analyses conducted on main sample for all but type-of-medium variable. N = 1,121 for 2002 and N = 1,156 for 1992. N varies slightly by variable because of missing data. Data for 1992 from Weaver and Wilhoit, *The American Journalist in the 1990s*.

[b] Analyses for type of medium conducted on main sample excluding online journalists, N = 1,126. Online category includes both respondents from main sample and from special sample of Online News Association, N = 100.

[c] Comparable data are not available.

prisingly, those who are toward the top in both income and organizational status and those who were the most satisfied with their jobs were the least likely to be planning to leave journalism. Only about 13% of senior managers were intending to find work outside of the media, compared with 20% of nonmanagers. And about 23% of journalists earning $35,000 annually or less were planning to defect compared with only 14% of journalists earning more than $55,000 a year. The impact of job satisfaction was even more dramatic (Figure 3.12). Among those

TABLE 3.25
Intention to Be Working Outside the Media
Within Five Years by Individual Characteristics

Individual Characteristics	Intends to Work Outside Media Within 5 Years (%) [a]	
	2002	1992
Gender		
Men	16	20
Women	21	24
Years in Journalism		
4 or fewer	24	19
5 to 9	17	25
10 to 14	15	25
15 to 19	17	24
20 or more	17	15
Race or ethnicity		
Minority	23	—[b]
Non-Hispanic White	17	—[b]
Undergraduate major		
Journalism, communications	15	—[b]
Other major	20	—[b]
Union status		
Union member	15	17
Non-union member	18	22
Supervisory status		
Senior manager	13	—[b]
Junior manager	15	—[b]
Not a manager	20	—[b]
Income		
$35,000 or less	23	25
$35,501 to $55,000	17	17
$55,001 or higher	14	20

[a] Analyses for conducted on main samples, N = 1,121 for 2002 and N = 1,156 for 1992. N varies slightly by variable because of missing data. Data for 1992 from Weaver and Wilhoit, *The American Journalist in the 1990s*.
[b] Comparable data are not available for 1992.

who were very satisfied with their jobs, only 7% planned to be working outside of the media in 5 years. Among those very dissatisfied, the figure rose to 59%.

Predictors of an Intention to Leave Profession

Because many of the variables discussed above are correlated with one another, a more sophisticated analysis of the data was done to try to determine the most

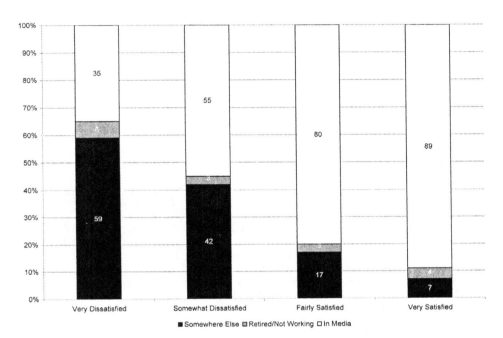

FIG. 3.12. Where journalists intend to be working in 5 years by job satisfaction, N = 1,121.

important factors that distinguish between those who planned to stay in journalism and those who planned to seek jobs outside the media (Table 3.26). Logistic regression allows a large number of variables, 29 in this case, to be examined simultaneously for their impact on the decision to stay or to go. In this process, the impact of each "predictor variable" is examined while at the same time controlling for the influence of other predictors in the analysis. For example, the impact of gender can be considered while holding constant the other 28 predictor variables. Ultimately, six factors appeared to have the most impact on plans to stay in or leave the profession:

- *Profits versus journalism.* Journalists were asked how strongly they agreed or disagreed with a statement that "profits were a higher priority than good journalism" at their organization. As agreement with the statement increased, so did the odds that the journalist would leave the profession. This item was included for the first time in the 2002 survey, so no comparisons were available with previous surveys.
- *Years of experience.* On the surface, the least experienced group of journalists appeared to be the most likely to abandon the profession within five years. But once other factors were taken into consideration in the regression analysis, that

TABLE 3.26

Factors That Distinguish Between Journalists Who Plan to Stay in Journalism
and Those Who Plan to Be Working Outside the Media in Five Years[a]

Factors (Predictor Variables)	Logistic Regression Coefficients[b]	Odds Ratios[b]
Organizational Characteristics[c]		
Part of public/private corporation	-.027	.976
Owned/not owned by a larger corporation	.147	1.158
Owner is/is not local person or organization	-.115	.891
Number of full-time employees	-.001	.999
Organizational Goals[d]		
Rating of performance in informing public	.292	1.245
Organizational emphasis on earning high profits	-.029	.972
Organizational emphasis on high employee morale	-.076	.927
Organizational emphasis on keeping large audience	.006	1.006
Organizational emphasis on high-quality journalism	.010	1.010
Belief that profits are higher priority than journalism	.193[f]	1.213
Belief that quality of journalism rising steadily	-.095	.909
Belief that newsroom resources have been shrinking	-.033	.968
Belief that organization does much audience research	-.002	.998
Individual and Work-Environment Characteristics[e]		
Level of perceived autonomy	-.012	.989
Frequency of receiving comments from supervisor	.000	1.000
Frequency of receiving comments from sources	-.079	.924
Frequency of receiving comments from audience	-.046	.955
Years of journalistic experience	.034[g]	1.035
Supervises/doesn't supervise other employees	.307	1.359
Personal income in 2001	-.278	.757
Member/not member of guild or union	.054	1.056
Level of job satisfaction	-.506[h]	.603
Level of education	.033	1.034
Gender	-.105	.901
College major is/is not journalism, communication	.355[i]	1.426
Marital status	.327	1.387
Currently has/does not have children in household	.358	1.430
Minority status	-.501[j]	.606
Belongs/doesn't belong to journalism organization	.482[k]	1.620

[a] These analyses were based on a question that asked journalists whether they intended to be working in the news media in 5 years, intended to be working somewhere else or intended to retire. Those journalists who intended to retire were eliminated from the analyses, as were journalists who failed to answer all 29 items included in these analyses. For these analyses, total N = 852. Model X^2 = 131.48, df = 29, p ≤ .05. Overall successful classification rate was 83.2%.

(Continued)

TABLE 3.26 (continued)

---

[b] Logistic regression coefficients and odds ratios help assess the association between the predictor variables and the dependent variable. The dependent variable, a dummy variable, indicated whether a journalist planned to be working in the media in 5 years (0) or to be working outside the media in 5 years (1). The interpretations of the logistic regression coefficients and the odds ratios vary from predictor to predictor. The values of the coefficients are not directly comparable to one another because the predictor variables are measured on different scales. Only items with superscripts "f" through "k" are significantly associated with the journalist's response on the dependent variable. For these analyses, the criterion for significance was a Wald value of $p \leq .10$ or lower.

[c] This block of variables was not a significant set of predictors of journalists' responses on the dependent variable. Block $X^2 = 6.15$, df = 4, not significant; cumulative Nagelkerke $R^2 = .012$.

[d] This block of variables was a significant set of predictors of journalists' responses on the dependent variable. Block $X^2 = 45.23$, df = 9, $p \leq .05$; cumulative Nagelkerke $R^2 = .096$.

[e] This block of variables was a significant set of predictors of journalists' responses on the dependent variable. Block $X^2 = 80.11$, df = 16, $p \leq .05$; cumulative Nagelkerke $R^2 = .234$.

[f] Journalists were asked how much they agreed or disagreed with the statement that "profits are a higher priority than good journalism" at their news organization. As agreement with the statement increased, the odds of leaving the profession increased. Wald statistic = 3.877, $p \leq .05$.

[g] As years of journalistic experience increased, odds of leaving the profession increased. Wald statistic = 7.761, $p \leq .05$.

[h] As job satisfaction increased, odds of leaving the profession declined. Wald statistic = 36.943, $p \leq .05$.

[i] Journalists whose undergraduate major was something other than journalism or communication had higher odds of leaving the profession than those who had been undergraduate journalism majors. Wald statistic = 3.122, $p \leq .10$.

[j] Minority journalists had higher odds of leaving the profession than non-Hispanic White journalists. Wald statistic = 2.755, $p \leq .10$.

[k] Journalists who did not belong to a journalism organization had higher odds of leaving the profession than other journalists. Wald statistic = 4.735, $p \leq .10$.

relationship reversed. In fact, the results suggested that as experience increased, so did the odds that a journalist planned to leave the media, other things equal. This result is at odds with the 1992 survey but is consistent with what was found in 1982–1983.[97]

• *Job satisfaction.* This was a critical factor in determining future plans. As job satisfaction increased, so did the likelihood that a journalist planned to remain in the profession. This is consistent with similar findings in all previous surveys.

• *College major.* Those who had undergraduate majors in journalism or communication were less likely to be planning career changes than those who majored in something else. This finding is inconsistent with the 1992 results, where no effect was found, but is in line with findings from the 1982–1983 survey.

• *Minority status.* Racial and ethnic minorities were more likely to be planning to leave the profession than were non-Hispanic Whites. Similar comparisons were not undertaken in earlier surveys.

• *Membership in journalism organizations.* Membership in organizations such as the Society of Professional Journalists or local press clubs appears to be an indicator of commitment to the profession. Journalists who belonged to these organizations were less likely to be planning to change careers than were those who did not belong to these organizations. That finding is consistent with all previous surveys.

Reasons for Career Change

Why are some journalists planning to change careers? Most cited low pay, poor working conditions, or personal considerations as the reasons that they intended to be working outside the media in five years, according to a sample of 75 responses to a follow-up question that asked those journalists who were planning to change careers why they intended to do so. About 20% complained about pay and job security and another 25% about stress, burnout, or an unfavorable work environment.

"Money," said a 46-year-old Florida newspaper journalist when asked about plans to leave the profession. "I'm older, and if I stay in the business 20 more years I won't make as much money in the 20 as I would in almost any other field with my experience." Some linked pay and working conditions. "The pay is not very good at all, and, also, the pay doesn't make up for the level of stress that comes with the job," another newspaper journalist, this one a 28-year-old from Indiana, said. "Also the hours that a journalist keeps — it gets really hectic sometimes." A potential "defector" who is 42 and who works at a weekly newspaper in Colorado echoed that sentiment: "To make better money — the only reason. Take it back. Better money and more control over schedule."

Another weekly newspaper journalist was tiring of the demands of her job. "I am getting tired," a 72-year-old New England editor explained. "We are a weekly in a resort community. I have a wonderful staff, and we all work as a team. The older you get, the more the deadlines become stressful. At some point I think I would like to relieve myself of that stress." The sacrifices associated with working in this 24-hour-a-day occupation surfaced again and again in the explanations of those planning to leave journalism. "Well I'm hoping to have a family, and this career is not conducive to having a family," said a 31-year-old Missouri TV reporter. "A daytime schedule is starting to become more important to me." Another, a 30-year-old North Carolina radio journalist, lamented that "there (were) certain pressures with reporting that don't go with family or with raising children."

The need for personal growth or change was motivating other journalists to think about new careers. In the sample of 75 responses, about 40% said that, for various reasons, they needed or wanted to try something else. "I've done it for 13 years, and I think it's good to try new things to keep yourself fresh over the course of a lifetime," an Illinois newspaper journalist, 35, said. Or, after a quarter of a century in the profession, another explained that it was simply "time to do something else." Several wanted to continue careers as writers but outside the confines of journalism. "I find journalism to be a particular kind of writing—public-service writing, which is useful and has its place," said a weekly journalist, 40, from California. "I really would prefer to write without that obligation. And that has less to do with the value of journalism and my satisfaction with the job than it does with my own creative fulfillment."

Another, a daily newspaper journalist from New Jersey, who is 51, spoke about the need for different challenges. "I have done a lot of different things already in journalism, so I feel that I have a varied and long experience in this line of work," the journalist said. "And I feel I'd like to test and check out something else—to refresh oneself. And I think journalists more than others tend to think that way. They feel—and I guess I share that feeling—that you need to experience other things and be less of an observer and more of a participant."

For about 15% in the sample of 75 responses, the motivation for a career change reflected pessimism about the profession or the future of the media. "It's not so much that I want to (change)," said a 46-year-old magazine journalist based in New York. "It's just that I'm concerned (that) the consolidation in the past year is going to be permanent." A television journalist from Texas complained about no longer feeling in sync with the values of that industry. "Because the news on television has changed so dramatically," she said in elaborating on her reasons for contemplating a career change. "(It) has become so money orientated that all the journalistic values that I have been allowed to use in my daily reporting have been thrown out the window. Now we're into drama, performances on the air, blood and guts reporting—almost anything that will grab the attention of the public so we can draw the audience, so we can sell time. Now, I know that we have to make money for the organization to stay in business. But I never thought that we would be pressured into doing some of the things that we are now doing on the air."

A 50-year-old print journalist, this one from a daily paper in Virginia, was equally discouraged: "The news media has changed so drastically. The newspaper which used to encourage enterprise reporting seems to be driven to compete with local TV. It's not that much fun anymore. It used to be fun and exciting, but that has not been the case in recent years." Another newspaper journalist, also 50 and from Virginia, expressed similar sentiments but more directly. "During the evolution of my career, things have changed so vastly," he said. "I no longer have the attachment that I once did for the business."

CONCLUSIONS

The news media's embrace of the Internet, the graying of its labor force, the struggles to maintain profit levels, the ongoing consolidation in ownership, the battle to hang on to audiences—all these upheavals affecting news people during the years from 1992 to 2002 seemed to portend big changes in American journalists' views about their work and their workplaces. However, the overall impression left by the findings in this chapter is one of stability or, perhaps, incremental shifts in attitudes or conditions.

Certainly changes did occur, but they were more evolutionary than revolutionary. Journalists were slightly more satisfied with their work than a decade ago, bringing to a halt a downward trend in job-satisfaction ratings. The percentage of journalists planning to leave the profession during the next 5 years dipped slightly. Salaries outpaced inflation. The "average grade" journalists gave their organizations' efforts to inform the public improved somewhat. Supervisors were meeting more often with their staff. Journalists tended to agree that the quality of work was rising at their news organizations.

The news was not all good, though. Despite the fact that job satisfaction rose over all, women journalists rated their level of satisfaction below that of men, and the youngest journalists—those under 25—tended to be considerably more pleased with their jobs than journalists in the next age group, the 25- to 34-year-olds. Given the close connection between job satisfaction and intent to leave the profession, media managers should be concerned about these gaps. Though salaries have been rising faster than the inflation rate, it's discouraging to find that purchasing power still remains below that of the early 1970s. And it's equally disconcerting to see that the pay gap between men and women stopped shrinking. Women are already underrepresented in the news workplace. Gender disparities in pay and job satisfaction certainly can't be helpful in recruiting and retaining women journalists. It is encouraging, however, that the median salaries of men and women journalists hired during the 1990s are essentially equal.

Another area of concern would be reporter autonomy and influence in the newsroom. Both have been declining, and both continued to decline during the last decade. Perceived autonomy and perceived influence are both predictors of higher levels of job satisfaction. Though the report on job satisfaction is good this time, it may be hard to sustain that improvement if two of the key influences on job satisfaction continue to decline.

These are a few of the changes from a decade ago that American journalists say have occurred in their workplaces. But they also report that many other things are about the same as in 1992. With one exception (reporting), the percentages of journalists involved in news gathering, news processing, and news supervision are largely unchanged. The amount of feedback that they report from sources and audiences has climbed, but only a little bit. The median size of the newsrooms in which they work is a bit larger but by fewer than a handful of employees. (The growth was not nearly as dramatic as between 1982–1983 and 1992, when the median size of the newsroom increased almost 50%.) The reasons that journalists cited for choosing this profession have a familiar ring. They were many of the same ones given in the last survey. And for those thinking about leaving journalism, the reasons for getting out also were familiar. Though reporters' perceived autonomy continues to slip, the forces that they say limit their professional freedom, including uncooperative sources, commercial constraints, and craft practices, were reminiscent of earlier surveys.

For journalists, big changes often are the catalysts for doing stories. But for the most part, American journalists in 2002 see their work environment in much the same way as they saw it in 1992. Small differences, yes. But this time, the "story line" is mostly about the lack of significant change.

NOTES

1. Joe Strupp, "Three Point Play," *Editor & Publisher*, Aug. 21, 2000, p. 18.
2. Brent Cunningham, "In the Lab," *Columbia Journalism Review*, May/June 2000, pp. 29–31.
3. Jackie Barron, "Multimedia Reporting in a Never-Ending News Cycle: A Tampa Reporter Covers a Murder Trial for TV, Newspaper and the Web," *Nieman Reports*, 54, 4 (Winter 2000), pp. 52–53.
4. Barron, "Multimedia Reporting in a Never-Ending News Cycle," p. 53.
5. David Carlson, *Online Timeline*, accessed on June 29, 2004, at http://iml.jou.ufl.edu/carlson/1990s.shtml
6. Steve Outing, "News Site Audiences Closing In," *Editor & Publisher*, April 3, 1999, p. 29; H. Denis Wu and Arati Bechtel, "Web Site Use and News Topic Type," *Journalism & Mass Communication Quarterly*, 79, 1 (Spring 2002), pp. 73–86.
7. John V. Pavlik, "The Future of Online Journalism: Bonanza or Black Hole?" *Columbia Journalism Review*, July/August 1997, pp. 30–36; Steve Outing, "An Inevitable Mix: Old and New Media," *Editor & Publisher*, Jan. 29, 2001, pp. 115–116.
8. Ben H. Bagdikian, *The Media Monopoly*, 5th ed. (Boston: Beacon Press, 1997), p. xlv.
9. Deborah Potter, "Local TV News Project — 2002: Pessimism Rules in TV Newsrooms," accessed on Feb. 26, 2004, at http:www.journalism.org/resources/research/reports/localtv/2002/pessimism.aps; "Newspapers Face Ongoing Challenges," *Quill*, 90, 6 (July/August 2002), p. 8.
10. Randal A. Beam, "What It Means to be a Market-Oriented Newspaper," *Newspaper Research Journal*, 19, 3 (Summer 1998), pp. 2–20.
11. Randal A. Beam, "Content Differences Between Daily Newspapers With Strong and Weak Market Orientations," *Journalism & Mass Communication Quarterly* 80, 2 (Summer 2003), pp. 368–390.
12. Jay Rosen, *What Are Journalists For?* (New Haven: Yale University Press, 1999).
13. Janet Whitman, "Gannett Takes Aim at Younger Readers," *The Wall Street Journal*, Nov. 5, 2003, p. 1; Mary Ellen Podmolik, "Numbers Crunch," *Advertising Age*, May 8, 2002, pp. S12–S13; Tom Rosenstiel, Carl Gottlieb, Lee Ann Brady, Dan Rosenheim, "Time of Peril for TV News," *Columbia Journalism Review*, November/December 2000, pp. 84–93.
14. John W. C. Johnstone, Edward J. Slawski, and William W. Bowman, *The News People: A Sociological Portrait of American Journalists and Their Work* (Urbana: University of Illinois Press, 1976), p. 22.
15. Mitra Toossi, "Labor force projections to 2012: The Graying of the U.S. Workforce," *Monthly Labor Review*, February 2004, p. 54.
16. The estimated size of the journalistic workforce grew from 69,500 in 1971 to 112,072 in 1982–1983. David H. Weaver and G. Cleveland Wilhoit, *The American Journalist: A Portrait of U.S. News People and Their Work*, 2nd ed. (Bloomington: Indiana University Press, 1991), p. 13.
17. The ages and years in this section are median values unless otherwise indicated.
18. Bureau of Labor Statistics, "Employee Tenure in 2002," accessed on July 2, 2002, at http://www.bls.gov/news.release/tenure.t06.htm
19. Johnstone et al., pp. 74–77.

20. Johnstone et al., pp. 83–84.
21. Kathleen A. Hansen, Mark Neuzil, and Jean Ward, "Newsroom Topic Teams: Journalists' Assessments of Effects on News Routines and Newspaper Quality," *Journalism & Mass Communication Quarterly*, 75, 4 (Winter 1998), pp. 803–821; Peter J. Gade and Earnest L. Perry, "Changing the Newsroom Culture: A Four-Year Case Study of Organizational Development at the St. Louis Post-Dispatch," *Journalism & Mass Communication Quarterly*, 80, 2 (Summer 2003), pp. 327–347.
22. "Case Study: At the Vanguard of Successful Recruitment," *HR Focus*, 75, 5 (May 1998), p. 9.
23. Senior managers included individuals who provided the following job titles: publisher, editor-publisher, owner, editor, editor in chief, executive editor, editorial director, executive director, managing editor, editorial-page editor, general manager, news director, executive news director, executive producer, or senior manager (nonspecific). Almost 94% report that they supervise the work of other journalists.
24. The ages and years in this section are medians unless otherwise noted.
25. Junior managers included those with titles such as assistant managing editor, associate editor, deputy managing editor, bureau chief, senior editor, any title signaling status as a department head, assignment editor, senior editor, program director, associate news editor, deputy news director, producer, managing producer, Web content manager, and so forth. This is not an exhaustive list. Junior managers included any individuals who supervised other employees and who had job titles suggesting that they were not at the top of the newsroom hierarchy.
26. The ages and years in this section are medians unless otherwise noted.
27. Nonmanagement employees included any respondent who said he or she did not supervise other journalists. Approximately 82% had job titles such as reporter, writer, correspondent, copy editor, layout editor, copy chief, anchor, anchor-reporter, weather person, or host/reporter. This is not an exhaustive list of job titles.
28. Figures in this section are median values unless otherwise noted.
29. Individuals who "regularly" do reporting are represented in both of the management groups and among nonmanagers.
30. The ages and years in this section are median values unless otherwise noted.
31. David H. Weaver and G. Cleveland Wilhoit, *The American Journalist in the 1990s: U.S. News People at the End of an Era* (Mahwah, NJ: Lawrence Erlbaum Associates, 1996), p. 57.
32. Randal A. Beam, "Journalism Professionalism as an Organizational-Level Concept," *Journalism Monographs*, 1990, 121.
33. Beam, "Journalism Professionalism."
34. Johnstone et al., p. 85.
35. John McManus. *Market-Driven Journalism: Let the Citizen Beware?* (Thousand Oaks, CA: Sage Publications, 1994).
36. Randal A. Beam, "Content Differences Between Daily Newspapers With Strong and Weak Market Orientations," *Journalism & Mass Communication Quarterly*, 80, 2 (Summer 2003), pp. 368–390.
37. David Laventhol, "Profit Pressures: A Question of Margins," *Columbia Journalism Review*, May/June 2001, pp. 18–19; Lucia Moses, "Nervous in the Newsrooms," *Editor & Publisher*, March 20, 2000, pp. 4–6; Louis Chunovic, "Close Up: ABC Stations Group," *Broadcasting & Cable*, July 12, 2004, p. 28.
38. Potter, "Local TV News Project—2002"; Greg Mitchell, "Outlook: The Worst May Be Over," *Editor & Publisher*, Jan. 7, 2002, pp. 10–13.
39. James Risser, "Lessons from L.A.: The Wall Is Heading Back," *Columbia Journalism Review*, January/February 2000, pp. 26–27.
40. Tony Case, "Nowhere But Up," *Editor & Publisher*, October 30, 2000, pp. 20–25.
41. Robert Reinhold, "*Washington Post* Gives Up Pulitzer, Calling Article on Addict, 8, Fiction," *New York Times*, April 16, 1981, p. A1.

42. Paul D. Colford and Evan Jenkins, "The *Times* After the Storm: Jayson Blair, Howell Raines, and the Rest of Us," *Columbia Journalism Review*, July/August 2003, pp. 14–17; James Bandler, "Report Cites 'Virus of Fear' at USA Today," *Wall Street Journal*, April 23, 2004, p. B1.

43. Bill Kovach and Tom Rosenstiel, *Warp Speed: America in the Age of Mixed Media* (New York: Century Foundation Press, 1999).

44. For these analyses, reporters were defined as journalists who said they did reporting "regularly" or "occasionally."

45. The question wording was "If you have a good idea for a subject which you think is important and should be followed up, how often are you able to get the subject covered?" Possible responses were "almost always," "more often than not," "only occasionally," and "don't make such proposals."

46. Possible responses to these questions were "almost complete freedom," "a great deal of freedom," "some freedom," or "none at all."

47. Possible responses to this question were "a great deal of editing," "some editing," or "none at all."

48. The analyses for this section included only journalists from the main sample.

49. A probability sample of responses from 95 journalists was selected and content analyzed. Additional responses were examined to get quotations that illustrated issues mentioned in the content analysis.

50. Response categories were "almost complete freedom," "a great deal of freedom," "some freedom," or "none at all." Responses to the two items were combined to form a simple additive scale with alpha = .70.

51. The Pearson correlation coefficients were .117 between frequency of comments from the audience and profit emphasis, .076 between audience comments and an emphasis on high employee morale and .104 between audience comments and market research. All of those coefficients were significant at $p \geq .05$.

52. Respondents were asked to indicate the importance, at their news organization, of "maintaining high, above-average employee morale" and "producing journalism of high, above-average profits." The Pearson correlation coefficients between those items and an item asking how often the respondent received comments about his or her work from superiors were .270 (morale) and .262 (journalism), respectively. The coefficients between the supervisor feedback item and indicators of a strong emphasis on keeping the audience as large as possible, on conducting market research to learn about audience interests and on achieving high, above-average profits were .083 (large audience), .071 (market research) and -.072 (profits). All five correlation coefficients were significant at $p \leq .05$.

53. Pearson correlation coefficients were .191 for the relationship between feedback from superiors and employee morale and .255 for feedback from superiors and high-quality journalism. The coefficient for feedback from sources and high-quality journalism was .184. The coefficient for feedback from audiences and a strong profit emphasis was .184. All of those coefficients were significant at $p \geq .05$.

54. Michael Buchholz, "Yellow Journalism," in Margaret A. Blanchard (Ed.), *History of the Mass Media in the United States: An Encyclopedia* (Chicago: Fitzroy Dearborn Publishers, 1998), pp. 709–710.

55. A. J. Liebling, *The Press* (New York: Ballantine Books, 1961), p. 33.

56. Bagdikian, *The Media Monopoly*, p. xlv.

57. Bagdikian, p. xlviii

58. Bagdikian, p. ix.

59. Bagdikian, p. xii.

60. Doug Underwood, *When MBAs Rule the Newsroom* (New York: Columbia University Press, 1993), pp. 15–20.

61. McManus, *Market-Driven Journalism*, p. 197.

62. James D. Squires, *Read All About It: The Corporate Takeover of America's Newspapers* (New York: Times Books, 1993).

63. David Croteau and William Hoynes, *The Business of Media: Corporate Media and the Public Interest* (Thousand Oaks, CA: Pine Forge Press, 2001).

64. Committee of Concerned Journalists, "About CCJ," accessed on Dec. 19, 2003, at http://www .journalism.org/who/ccj/about.asp

65. Tom Rosenstiel, "U.S. Press: Paying for Its Sins," *The Washington Post*, September 14, 1997, p. C03.

66. It is important to note, however, that numbers of magazine and news-service journalists in the surveys were small. There were 59 news-magazine journalists in the 1992 survey and 62 in 2002; the number of news-service journalists was 58 in 1992 and 69 in 2002.

67. The four-point response scale for these items was "extremely important" (4), "quite important" (3), "somewhat important" (2), and "not really important" (1).

68. The five-point response scale for these items was "strongly agree" (5), "agree" (4), "neutral" (3), "disagree" (2), or "strongly disagree" (1).

69. Median salary estimates were computed from responses to a question that asked journalists to indicate the amount of their total 2001 personal income, before taxes, by choosing one of 29 income categories ranging from "less than $15,000" to "$150,000 and over." Except for the first and last category, each response category represented a range of $5,000 (e.g., "between $15,000 and $20,000" or "between $90,000 and $95,000"). Estimated medians were calculated from this grouped data following a procedure that Blalock described. See Hubert M. Blalock Jr., *Social Statistics*, 2nd ed. (New York: McGraw-Hill Book Co., 1972), pp. 66–68.

70. Bureau of Labor Statistics, "National Compensation Survey: Occupational Wages in the United States, July 2002 Supplementary Tables," accessed at http://www.bls.gov/ncs/home.htm on July 20, 2004. Figures are estimates from the Bureau of Labor Statistics' National Compensation Survey reported for July 2002. The data collection period was between December 2001 and January 2003. Median salary data for the 2001 calendar year—the reference period for the American Journalists survey—were not available. Median annual earnings for white-collar (excluding sales) and professional-specialty and technical workers were projected by multiplying the median hourly wage by 2,080, the number of hours that would be worked per year for a job with a 40-hour week. The estimated average earnings are higher. Average annual earnings for white-collar, non-sales employees are estimated at $47,840 and earnings for professional-specialty and technical workers are $57,346.

71. Median hourly earnings were estimated at $19.02 based on data from the Bureau of Labor Statistics. Average earnings are higher than median earnings for virtually all occupations, including editors and reporters. Average hourly earnings for editors and reporters was $22.43 in July 2002, which produces estimated average earnings of $46,654.

72. Among the 427 occupational categories examined by the Bureau of Labor Statistics in 2000, "editors and reporters" ranked 86th in average hourly earnings. They ranked 68th among 115 professions.

73. Inflation calculations obtained from National Aeronautics and Space Administration Web page, accessed at http://www.jsc.nasa.gov/bu2/inflateCPI.html on July 18, 2004.

74. Anne Colamosca, "Pay for Journalists Is Going Up," *Columbia Journalism Review*, July/August 1999, pp. 24–28.

75. Colamosca, p. 24.

76. Salary estimates for the types of media are subject to relatively wide fluctuations from survey to survey because the numbers of respondents in those categories is sometimes small. For the 2002 survey's salary estimates, the number of respondents for each media type was as follows: news magazines = 57; news wires = 64; online = 92; television = 152; daily newspapers = 538; radio = 102; and weekly newspapers = 173.

77. Laura D'Andrea Tyson, "New Clues to the Pay and Leadership Gap," *Business Week*, October 27, 2003, p. 36.

78. Tyson, 2003.

79. The multiple-regression analysis was conducted on respondents from both the main probability sample and the oversamples of minority and on online journalists.

80. Effects coding was used for the region and media type variables in these analyses. News services functioned as the reference group for media type and the Northeast region functioned as the reference group for region. In both instances, journalists in these categories had the highest annual median personal incomes.

81. The 1992 regional salary comparisons were made using a group of dummy-coded variables, with the reference group being journalists from the Western region. For 2002, the regional salary comparisons were made using effects-coded variables, with the reference group being journalists from the Northeast, who were the highest paid journalists.

82. These analyses were conducted with the main sample plus the special samples for minority and online journalists.

83. The 1992 race-ethnicity salary comparisons were made using a group of dummy-coded variables, with the reference group being journalists from the "other" category for race and ethnicity. For 2002, the race-ethnicity salary comparisons were made using effects-coded variables, with the reference group being journalists from the "other" category of race-ethnicity.

84. These analyses were conducted with the main sample plus the special samples for minority and online journalists.

85. Neil Hickey, "Morale Matters: Low and Getting Lower," Columbia Journalism Review, September/October 2001, pp. 37–39.

86. Potter, "Local TV News Project—2002."

87. Geneva Overholser, "What is Good Journalism? Fighting to Keep It Working for Us," comments delivered to the Anvil Freedom Award, Estlow Lecture, University of Denver, Denver, CO, October 22, 2002.

88. Meesook Kim and Kyung-Ho Cho, "Quality of Life Among Government Employees," Social Indicators Research, 61, 1 (April 2003), p. 387; Julie Abbott, "Does Employee Satisfaction Matter? A Study to Determine Whether Low Employee Morale Affects Customer Satisfaction and Profits in the Business-to-Business Sector," Journal of Communication Management, 7, 4 (2003), pp. 333–339.

89. Humphrey Taylor, "The Impact of Recent Events and Fears About the Economy on Employee Attitudes," The Harris Poll # 57, November 21, 2001, accessed at http://www.harrisinteractive.com/harris_poll/index.asp?PID=268 on October 27, 2003.

90. For these analyses, reporters were defined as journalists who said they did reporting "regularly" or "occasionally."

91. The values on the autonomy scale ranged from 1 to 7.

92. The values on the influence item about getting subjects covered ranged from 1 to 5.

93. Weaver and Wilhoit, The American Journalist in the 1990s, pp. 107–111.

94. Influence was measured with an item that asked: "If you have a good idea for a subject which you think is important and should be followed up, how often are you able to get the subject covered?" Possible responses ranged from "almost always" (5) to "only occasionally" (1).

95. Gilbert Cranberg, Randall Bezanson, and John Soloski, Taking Stock: Journalism and the Publicly Traded Newspaper Company (Ames: Iowa State University Press, 2001), pp. 6–13; Bagdikian, The Media Monopoly, pp. ix–xxxv.

96. Weaver and Wilhoit, The American Journalist in the 1990s, pp. 108–110.

97. Comparisons with previous studies are inexact because different techniques were used to analyze the data in 1992 and 2002.

Professionalism:
Roles, Values, Ethics

The irony simply could not be ignored. On May 1, 2003, at the conclusion of the Society of Professional Journalists' annual Ethics Week, American journalism's most controversial ethics scandal in the new century erupted. It reared its head not among the tabloids or other outlets commonly associated with ethical breaches, self-serving values, or a lack of professionalism, but rather at the venerable *New York Times*.[1]

Jayson Blair, a fast-rising young reporter on the *Times* staff, was found to have copied major parts of a story of his from an article previously published in the *San Antonio Express-News*. Further internal investigation revealed that Blair had committed plagiarism, fabrication, and misrepresentation in a number of stories he had written for the *Times*. The *Times* printed an extraordinary 14,000-word explanation of Blair's misdeeds and how they had escaped the attention of *Times* editors for so long. A month after Blair was fired, Editor Howell Raines and Managing Editor Gerald Boyd resigned.

The revelations raised several troubling questions about the state of American journalism in the 21st century: If such practices are allowed at the most hallowed news organization, what practices are allowed among news media at the other, less scrutinized organizations? Have journalistic values changed in recent years? If the pinnacle of journalistic professionalism permits behavior that violates many of the traditional values of journalism, has journalism forfeited its claim to be a profession? Although our survey was conducted 6 months before the Jayson Blair story broke, its data help create a profile of the roles, values, and ethics that underlie the work of Blair's contemporaries in American journalism. The data suggest that while these characteristics changed somewhat over the

1990s, American journalists still regarded their work with a generally high degree of responsibility.

The survey did not (nor could it presume to) settle the question as to whether journalism is a profession, or even whether it should be. Many scholars and commentators argued for most of the 20th century that journalists shared a core set of values that sought to serve society, that they were trained to regard phenomena with disinterested expertise, that they enjoyed great personal autonomy in determining the nature and outcome of their work, and, therefore, that journalism could be considered a profession. Others responded that if a profession is an autonomous practice of work based on strict educational requirements and licensing, then journalism is far from a profession. Our survey discovered evidence, as others have in the past, of some characteristics that "professionalize" journalists but of others that place them outside the description of most American professions.

Much of the debate over whether journalists *should be* of a profession centers on values—both journalistic and professional. Media scholar Theodore Glasser has argued that professionalism implies standardization and homogeneity, thus precluding individual differentiation and inviting ethnocentric assumptions.[2] Critic James Bowman sees the chief danger in journalistic professionalism to be its promotion of "detached objectivity," which keeps journalists from feeling outrage (which Bowman takes as a prerequisite to good journalism).[3] Hard on the heels of detached objectivity, Bowman argues, are "shallow sophistry and cynicism," superficiality, and audience-building for marketing purposes.

There are shared professional values, of course, that would seem to benefit the greater society as well as journalism's practitioners: independence, pursuit of the truth as one sees it, humaneness, fairness, to name a few. Media scholars Pamela Shoemaker and Stephen Reese have examined the production of journalistic content from the perspective of "hierarchies of influence,"[4] which sheds light on the debate over professionalism. Professional values operate simultaneously at several different levels of analysis: individual, organizational, or ideological, for example. From this perspective, some "professional" values are often at odds with other professional values.

At an individual level of analysis, for example, professional values may include personal sensitivity and the desire to minimize harm to news subjects, even if that means allowing a news subject to read an article before the reporter submits it. At an organizational level, however, it may be considered "professional" to possess certain technical skills and to follow company policies—one of which may be the refusal to allow news subjects to read articles before publication. A reporter trying to act "professional" may receive conflicting directives from two different conceptions—at two different levels—of professionalism.

Professional values sometimes conflict even at the same level of analysis. Fred Brown, a former Ethics Committee chair for the Society of Professional Journalists (SPJ), has written that the SPJ's own code of ethics—a broad, institutional level of analysis—reveals some schizophrenia.[5] Of the code's four pillar concepts, two elicit "Mr. Nice Guy"—"minimize harm" and "be accountable"—whereas the other two represent "Mr. Tough Guy"—"seek and report the truth" and "act independently." Brown, an editor himself, counsels journalists to strike a middle ground by being "civil, respectful and determined,"[6] while Reese offers no advice other than to view professional values operating at a variety of levels (the media scholar's obligation) and to seek to determine which have the most influence on journalistic behavior.[7] Our coauthor Randal Beam has determined through his studies of newsrooms that the organization, not the individual or the institution, is the most influential source of values for the journalist.[8]

With such a complex dynamic involved in the parsing of professional values, why should journalists (or anyone else) care whether journalism is a profession? Journalism is an occupation whose survival, more so than most professions, depends on its credibility. Journalists don't heal sick bodies or keep clients out of prison; they provide information. If their clients no longer trust the information, then the occupation has lost its cache. Journalism gains credibility through the collective behavior of journalists, whose behavior is guided by their values.

Many commentators argued that journalism began the 21st century with a credibility deficit. Before the Jayson Blair story emerged, Stephen Glass was fired at the *New Republic* for fabricating much of his work, and two years later he profited from an autobiographical novel and subsequent film. In 2002, two reporters at *The Salt Lake Tribune* sold information to *The National Enquirer* about a local kidnapping case and then lied to their editor about it. A photographer for *The Los Angeles Times* was fired in 2003 for digitally altering a photo of a British soldier guarding a group of Iraqi civilians during the U.S.-led war in Iraq.

Several commentators in 2003 marveled at the low level of public outrage after the Jayson Blair affair. Was news media credibility so low, *Newsweek* columnist Jonathan Alter asked, that Americans simply assume that reporters usually fabricate their material? Columbia University journalism professor Richard Wald echoed that concern: "When people simply don't believe what they read or hear on the news, or when they don't care whether it's true or not, then we really are in trouble."[9] Alter offered a number of causes of the trouble: that people resent the news media as they do any other large, ubiquitous institution; that the media have blurred the traditionally distinct line between entertainment (fiction) and news (nonfiction); that cable television presents news as it is being gathered, not after it has been verified; and that many Americans accord the same level of believability to claims on the Internet as they do to traditional news media.[10]

Media scholar James Carey traced the *Times*'s Blair problem—and the paper's subsequent loss of credibility—back to a fundamental hypocrisy of professional values at the *Times*. Blair's rapid rise to stardom at the *Times*, despite the presence of factual and ethical breaches, indicates a gap between the newspaper's private professional values and public professional values. Publicly, the *Times* valued "loyalty to truth, thoroughness, context and sobriety," Carey wrote. The actual events at the *Times*, however, revealed that a greater importance was being attached to "prominence, the unique take, standing out from the crowd, and a riveting narrative."[11]

Often when an occupation has been beset by public criticism or indifference, its practitioners have coalesced behind shared values and behaviors. A series of studies of journalism's professionalism over the last 30 years, however, indicates that this is one occupation whose members have been in basic disagreement over journalism's role in society, its ethical standards, and several other characteristics of a profession. This study reaffirms that the journalistic workforce is still "unprofessional" in many regards. Nonetheless, significant shifts have occurred in the makeup of all that disagreement.

THE JOURNALIST'S PROFESSIONAL COMMUNITY

As Shoemaker and Reese would suggest with their method of studying different levels of influence on media content, professional values can be measured at both institutional and personal levels. Most professions exhibit evidence of a national or global community. Do journalists across the country belong to the same professional organization? Read the same professional journals? Gather socially with other journalists?

Professional Group Memberships

In the 1990s, journalists reversed a 20-year trend of declining membership in professional organizations. The percentage of journalists surveyed who said they belonged to at least one professional organization had slipped from 45% in 1971 to 36% in 1992, but that rebounded to 41% in 2002, as Figure 4.1 indicates. As

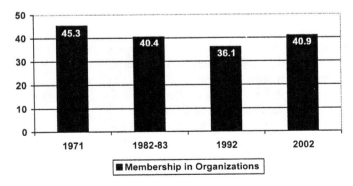

FIG. 4.1. Membership in professional organizations (percentage of all journalists saying they belong to one or more).

TABLE 4.1
Membership in Professional
Associations by Medium
(Percentage Saying One or More)

Medium	%	N
Daily newspaper	40.5	571
Weekly newspaper	40.2	179
News magazine	22.6	62
Wire service	55.1	69
Television	42.9	163
Radio	42.9	105
Total	40.9	1,149

in past studies, no single group dominated the list of organizations. The Society of Professional Journalists was the group most often mentioned: Ten years earlier, 7% said they belonged to SPJ; in 2002, that rose only to 9%. By comparison, about 30% of the medical doctors in the United States belong to the American Medical Association,[12] about 35% of the lawyers in the country belong to the American Bar Association,[13] and about 53% of America's certified public accountants belong to the American Institute of Certified Public Accountants.[14] But not all professions are composed of joiners. Only about 5% of the country's university and college instructors belong to the American Association of University Professors.[15]

Only five journalism-related organizations were mentioned by more than 20 journalists in the survey: SPJ, Investigative Reporters & Editors, the National Press Photographers Association, the National Association of Television Arts and Sciences, and the Society of American Business Editors & Writers.

The portrait of the typical journalistic "joiner" is quite similar to its 1992 counterpart. As in previous years, more experienced journalists and journalists who were members of trade unions were more likely to belong to a professional association. Newsroom supervisors also tend to join professional groups. There was little difference among radio, television, daily newspaper, or weekly newspaper journalists in the rate of joining these groups—about 4 in every 10 belong (see Table 4.1). But those percentages represent major increases for the broadcast and wire-service journalists over the 1992 results (28% for radio journalists, 34% for television and 31% for wire services), and a major decline in professional association for the news-magazine journalists (formerly at 34%).

Somewhat surprising are the factors that seemed not to make a difference in whether a journalist belonged to a professional association. Journalists with degrees in a journalism or communication field were no more likely to join an association than journalists with other degrees. Journalists at large newspapers were no more likely to join than journalists at small papers. These patterns were in evidence in the 1992 survey as well.

Readership of Professional Publications

The journalists mentioned a total of 77 professional publications and about 123 separate Web sites when asked which journalism-related publications or Web sites they regularly read, but, as in past surveys, there seems to be sparse readership of any single publication. As Table 4.2 shows, *Editor & Publisher*, *Columbia Journalism Review*, and *American Journalism Review* are the only publications read regularly by more than 12% of journalists in 2002. After those three, no magazine or journal was mentioned by more than 3% of the journalists surveyed. And the most popular trade magazine, *American Journalism Review*, was read regularly by only 15%. If there's any good news here for professionalism, it is that regular readership is inching upward over time (despite a slight falling off of "occasional" readership).

The most striking finding on readership, however, was that *American Journalism Review* was not really the top source of news and contemplation about journalism. Survey respondents were also asked about Web sites, and Poynteronline, the Web site of the Poynter Institute (a Florida-based journalism think tank), was mentioned by 17% of the respondents. Another 9% said they regularly read the Romenesko site—an online column written by media critic Jim Romenesko—which was actually posted at Poynteronline. That combination suggests that about one-fourth of American journalists are getting their journalism news from some or all of Poynteronline.

TABLE 4.2
Readership Among All Journalists of Professional Journals
and Trade Publications (Percentage Naming Each Publication)[a]

Publication	Frequency of Readership					
	Regularly		Occasionally		Never	
	1992[b]	2002	1992[b]	2002	1992[b]	2002
Editor & Publisher	13	14	26	20	61	66
Columbia Journalism Review	12	13	21	21	67	66
American Journalism Review	8	15	14	14	78	71
Quill	4	3	6	3	90	94
Poynter Report	—	3	—	3	—	94
News Photographer (NPPA)	4	3	1	2	95	95
RTNDA Communicator	—	2	—	2	—	96
IRE Journal	—	1	—	1	—	97
ElectronicMedia	—	0	—	2	—	98
Other	—	45	—	33	—	—

Note. 1992 N = 1,156; 2002 N = 1,149.
[a]Numerous other publications were mentioned, with 1% or less readership.
[b]Data are from David Weaver and G. Cleveland Wilhoit, *The American Journalist in the 1990s*, p. 131.

Perhaps the easy availability of Web sites, coupled with a site's ability to update its news and commentary several times a day, explains the Web's rise in readership. In fact, some media watchers credited the Web with the resignations of Raines and Boyd after the Jayson Blair scandal. Romenesko regularly posted *New York Times* internal memos, which staff members had leaked to the Web site. Suddenly a fascinated nation of journalists (at least 25% of them, at any rate) were watching the *Times's* management, and the staff's dissatisfaction with that management, every day. Because of the ubiquity of the Web, wrote Duke University professor Susan Tifft, "Every copy clerk and stringer can make his or her unhappiness known to millions."[16]

The frequent use of Poynteronline is the other bit of good news for professionalism here. In a time of widespread criticism of journalism, a regular readership of 10% to 15% for each of the three leading trade publications would be a poor sign of professionalism. But the substantial interest in journalistic Web sites suggests that journalists were more interested than ever in news and commentary—they were simply searching it out in a different medium.

Friends of Journalists

It has been said that people are known by the company they keep, and sociologists have often measured the social circle as an indicator of professionalism: The more journalists spend leisure time with other journalists, the more they resemble members of other professions in their social habits. In this regard, the social life of journalists remained the same as it had been since 1971. About one-third of the typical journalist's social network comprised other journalists. As in previous surveys, the friendship patterns changed according to certain personal characteristics. Women journalists were more likely than men to have journalists in their social networks, as were younger and less experienced journalists and those with degrees in journalism.

Overall, the institutional structure of journalism in 2002 appeared stronger than it had in 1992, but not dramatically stronger. Readership of professional news and commentary seemed to be on the rise, thanks largely to the emergence of a popular Web site, and membership in professional organizations was up. Relative to other professions, however, journalism still lacked solidity. The next section probes more deeply into journalists' thoughts about the purpose of their work. Despite their lack of "professionalized" behavior, it is possible that journalists perceive their work to be of profound social importance.

JOURNALISTIC ROLE CONCEPTIONS

In his 2001 book title, Jay Rosen asked the question, "What Are Journalists For?"[17] which is the simplest way of summarizing this 30-year inquiry into journalists' perceptions of the functions or roles journalism plays in American society. The previous chapter showed that individual journalists embarked on their careers for a wide array of reasons, many of them altruistic, but how do they feel about the purpose of journalism in general?

Thirty Years of Attitudes About Journalistic Roles

Convulsive debate and civil unrest about the Vietnam war was the backdrop against which the Johnstone team carried out its large-scale national study of journalists in 1971. At that time, the lines between personal feelings about the war and the job of reporting the wrenching struggle to end it became harder to draw for many journalists. It is hardly surprising, then, that the 1971 study by Johnstone found evidence of two "pure" ideological types among working journalists. The dichotomy of values reflected old arguments about objectivity, detachment, involvement, and advocacy, which were made salient again by widespread public protest of the war. Johnstone and his colleagues characterized the competing belief systems as a neutral, "nothing-but-the-truth" orientation versus a participant, "whole-truth" mentality. However, the surprise was that fewer than one in five journalists could be classified as hard-line proponents of a single view. Most adhered to some parts of both "ideologies."[18]

By the time we were in the field in late 1982 for the first revisiting of the Johnstone study, the Watergate scandal had toppled the Nixon presidency, and investigative reporting, glamorized by the movie *All the President's Men*, seemed to have elevated journalism's respectability. By the end of 1970s, however, that glamour began to fade. Investigations into abuses of public power began evolving into investigations into the private lives of public figures. At the same time, satellite technology was enabling instantaneous coverage of global events, which had immediate effects on political life, diplomacy and terrorism. *Time* magazine summarized the emergent view of journalists during the period: "They are rude and accusatory, cynical and almost unpatriotic."[19] Michael O'Neill, then editor of *The New York Daily News*, deplored the rise in journalism of an "adversarial mindset" in his 1982 address to the American Society of Newspaper Editors.[20]

Another Study in an Adversarial Age

In our 1982–1983 survey, we added questions about adversarial stances toward government and business to the battery of role-related questions developed by the Johnstone team. The expanded list of items was subjected to factor analysis, a complex statistical procedure, to determine whether patterns, or clusters, of roles would emerge and whether they would resemble the neutral and participant stances found by Johnstone.

Given the tenor of the times, we expected a complex picture of journalist roles. Hugh Culbertson, then a journalism professor at Ohio University, studied

285 editors and writers on 17 newspapers in 1982, and he found three, as opposed to the earlier two, role conceptions. Our own analysis also suggested three: adversarial, interpretive, and disseminator clusters of attitudes about journalistic purpose. The surprise, however, was twofold. First, contrary to the critics, the adversarial conception was hardly dominant, with only 17% of the sample considering the role as central to their work. Second, the pluralism of the journalistic mindset was significantly greater than a decade earlier, with about a third of all journalists fully embracing both the interpretive and the disseminator roles. Only about 2% of the respondents were exclusively one-role oriented, compared with 18% in 1971.

In a Climate of Cynicism, A Third Look

The only thing 1992 seemed to have in common with the period of our 1982–1983 study was that another economic recession had upset the advertising revenue base of the field. The journalistic glory of Watergate was a distant memory, and Rush Limbaugh, a major figure in the emergence of "talk" radio in the 1980s, was drawing national attention to his conservative critique of the "liberal" press. It was also a time when some within the mainstream press worried that the widespread cynicism in American society was indeed partly the fault of journalists. Davis Merritt, a newspaper editor, and Jay Rosen, a journalism professor, argued for a change in the nature of reporting and a shift to "public journalism." They urged a style of journalism that would seek out the perspective of ordinary citizens, not solely the perspective of leaders and institutions, and then report in ways that would mobilize citizens to participate in "the public life."[21]

In the 1992 study, as in the two earlier studies, each of the questions about roles was considered individually. Then we aggregated them into larger clusters of functions to assess other, possibly broader, changes in the core philosophies of journalists. Despite enormous changes in the journalistic environment during the 1980s, the portrait of core functions in 1992 was fairly similar to that of 1982–1983. The two functions most strongly supported were the disseminator function and the interpretive function. The adversarial function again attracted only modest support, and a fourth function emerged from the analysis; we dubbed it "populist mobilizer"—a function that received the weakest support of the four, but substantive support nonetheless.

An Age of Information, and of Terrorism

Our most recent interviews of journalists were conducted in the summer and fall of 2002. Once again the economy had gone into decline, but this time partly as the result of an extraordinary event: the September 11, 2001, destruction of the World Trade Center and the attempted destruction of other targets in Washington, D.C., by the terrorist group Al Qaeda. The coverage of the tragedies associated with September 11 was generally considered respectful and at times even patriotic, and news-media credibility seemed to recover for the first time in a decade. Eighteen months later the Bush administration, unable to bring the Al Qaeda leadership to justice, turned the nation's attention to Iraq, an Islamic dictatorship portrayed by the White House to be supplying the terrorist world with "weapons of mass destruction." When the United States invaded Iraq in March 2003, hundreds of journalists were "embedded" with the U.S. troops, and the patriotic impulses of post–September 11 journalism flowered during this war.

Meanwhile, journalism was being challenged by emerging technologies as never before. Not only were Americans seeing more live coverage of war and terrorism than ever before, but they could now access it 24 hours a day. In 10 years, the Internet had grown from an obscure means of military communication to the country's dominant medium for written interpersonal communication and perhaps even for mass communication of news, information, and opinion. Its ubiquity by 2003 had several observers predicting the Internet would, at the very least, redefine the functions of the traditional news media. We were expecting changes in the journalists' conceptions of their roles and functions, but not changes as dramatic as these.

Journalistic Roles in the 21st Century

As in the past studies, journalists were asked how important several journalistic roles were to them. In the 2002 sample, each journalist responded to 15 questions such as this: "How important do you think it is for journalists to provide analysis and interpretation of international developments?" Responses included "extremely important," "quite important," "somewhat important," and "not really important." Most of the questions were identical to those asked in previous decades, which allowed us to compare journalists over the last 30 years. Then we aggregated them into larger clusters of functions to assess other, possibly broader, changes in the core philosophies of U.S. journalists.

Only 2 of the 15 journalistic roles were deemed "extremely important" by a clear majority in the 2002 study: getting information to the public quickly and investigating government claims (two others attracted slight majorities). These were the only two roles that garnered the same extremely important majorities in 1992, but the details reveal a significant change. In 1992, getting information to the public quickly had the highest "extremely important" percentage of all the roles; in 2002 that role had slipped to a distant second (see Table 4.3).

Getting information out quickly declined in importance for workers in all six media types, even television and radio (Table 4.5). The percentage for television journalists sank from 80% 10 years earlier (which was higher than journalists in any other medium except wire services) to 68%; for radio journalists, the response "extremely important" fell from 67% to 50%. Even for wire service journalists, who have prided themselves for more than a century on the immediacy

TABLE 4.3
Importance Journalists Assigned to Various Mass Media Roles

Media Roles	Percentage Saying Extremely Important			
	1971[a]	1982–1983[b]	1992[c]	2002
Investigate government claims	76	66	67	71
Get information to public quickly	56	60	69	59
Avoid stories with unverified content	51	50	49	52
Provide analysis of complex problems	61	49	48	51
Discuss national policy	55	38	39	40
Discuss international policy[d]	—	—	—	48
Concentrate on widest audience	39	36	20	15
Develop intellectual/cultural interests	30	24	18	17
Provide entertainment	17	20	14	11
Serve as adversary of government[e]	—	20	21	20
Serve as adversary of business[e]	—	15	14	18
Set the political agenda[f]	—	—	5	3
Let people express views[f]	—	—	48	39
Motivate people to get involved[d]	—	—	—	39
Point to possible solutions[d]	—	—	—	24
Total N	1,313	1,001	1,156	1,149

[a] Data are from John Johnstone, Edward Slawski, and William Bowman, *The News People*, p. 230.

[b] Data are from David Weaver and G. Cleveland Wilhoit, *The American Journalist*, p. 114.

[c] Data are from Weaver and Wilhoit, *The American Journalist in the 1990s*, p. 136.

[d] Not asked in the 1971, 1982–1983, or 1992 surveys.

[e] Not asked in the 1971 survey.

[f] Not asked in the 1971 or 1982–1983 surveys.

of their work, getting information out quickly dropped in importance from 81% to 71%. In 1992, satellite and mobile technologies were improving the immediacy of journalism, especially broadcast journalism, but in 2002, journalists found themselves in a new world. Perhaps the Internet had snatched journalists' franchise on being first with the latest, and the responses to the survey may reflect a concession that immediacy was no longer being considered the most important aspect of their work.

Only a few of the 15 roles increased in their "extremely important" tallies, and 2 of those were "investigate claims and statements made by the government" (from 67% in 1992 to 71% in 2002) and "be an adversary of businesses by being constantly skeptical of their actions" (from 14% in 1992 to 18% in 2002; Table 4.3). The latter role probably rose in the awareness of many journalists after a series of scandals involving high-ranking officers of U.S. corporations, but the continued popularity of the government watchdog role seems ironic in view of the relatively strong press support the Bush administration enjoyed between the September 11 tragedy and the war in Iraq.

Several other roles declined in importance between 1992 and 2002. It was less important to journalists to "provide entertainment and relaxation" and to "concentrate on news that's of interest to the widest possible audience" (Table 4.3). It was also less important to "give ordinary people a chance to express their views on public affairs." The biggest single decline over the 30 years of study, though, was in the "widest possible audience" role—from 39% in 1971 to 15% in 2002.

The journalists may have been saying over the years that the "mass" in mass media is disappearing. The emergence of cable television networks and channels by the hundreds, niche-market magazines by the thousands, and World Wide Web sites by the millions may have created a sense among journalists that media can succeed only when they target their offerings to specific audiences. Providing all things to all people brought success in the first three-quarters of the 20th century, but the media options are too many—and the interests of the American public too splintered—for that formula to appeal to many 21st-century journalists.

Journalistic Functions in the 21st Century

Using factor analysis, we aggregated the individual responses to the battery of 15 questions into broader attitudinal clusters: interpretive, disseminator, adversarial, and populist mobilizer. Two of these functions remained basically unchanged since the early 1990s in their positions in the journalistic "belief system"; one function increased its profile, and one suffered a dramatic decline. Each function and its implications are discussed next, beginning with the interpretive function.

The interpretive function remained the strongest perception among American journalists in 2002. As in 1982–1983 and 1992, most journalists perceived the interpretive role as essential to journalistic life. The interpretive function was a blend of responses to four items in the battery: providing analysis and interpretation of complex problems, providing analysis and interpretation of international developments, discussing national policy while it is still being developed, and investigating claims and statements made by the government. The item concerning international policy was new to the 2002 survey, but the other three items enjoyed slightly stronger support than they had in 1992. The strongest of the four, investigating government claims, rose from 67% saying it was "extremely important" in 1992 to 71% in 2002 (Table 4.4).

Thus, journalism's majority culture in 2002 continued to frame its basic purpose in terms resonant with the old recommendations of the Hutchins Commission on Freedom of the Press in 1947. While few journalists today would likely be familiar with the Hutchins report, most appeared to share the Commission's goal of investigating "the truth about the fact(s)" and providing "a context which gives them meaning."[22] The Commission would no doubt be encouraged to see that 55 years after its appeal for analysis, investigation, and interpretation, journalists adhere to this attitude far more than any other.

TABLE 4.4
The Interpretive Function: Percentages of Journalists of Various Media
Who Saw Its Dimensions as "Extremely Important"

Media Type	Investigating Official Claims (%)		Analyzing Complex Problems (%)		Discuss National Policy (%)		Discuss International Policy (%) [a]	
	1992	2002	1992	2002	1992	2002	1992	2002
News magazines	82	82	66	76	57	55	—	76
Wire services	76	93	55	69	50	62	—	70
Dailies	70	75	54	59	44	45	—	50
Weeklies	62	62	39	34	28	26	—	39
Television	62	63	37	36	26	29	—	37
Radio	46	54	25	33	22	33	—	35
Total [b]	67	71	48	51	39	40	—	48

[a] Not measured in the 1992 study.
[b] The overall N for 1992 was 1,156 and for 2002 it was 1,149.

Whereas 10 years earlier some media critics saw the strength of the interpretive function as a warning sign that journalists had become too cozy with political elites,[23] the sense among scholars in the 21st century is that the strength of the interpretive function is a response to technology's new capability to transport data instantaneously. Professor Jane Singer at the University of Iowa parsed the attitudes of 18 newspaper reporters and editors regarding online journalism and found a consistent sense among them that "as the explosion of information continues, there will be an increasing need for skilled journalists to sort through it, filter out what's important and help put it in perspective."[24]

The dramatic change in the alignment of these functions occurred with the steep decline in the importance of the disseminator function. This is a function whose elements changed since the factor analysis of the 1992 data. Ten years earlier, the disseminator function emerged because the journalists' responses clustered so closely on two items: getting information to the public quickly and avoiding unverifiable facts. With the 2002 data, however, this function seemed to represent a broader attitude. It consisted not only of the 1992 items but also included "concentrate on news that's of interest to the widest possible audience" and "provide entertainment and relaxation" (Table 4.5).

In other words, journalists who accorded high importance to the roles of getting news out quickly and accurately also gave high importance, in 2002, to reaching wide audiences, and with entertainment as well as information. The new attitude seemed to include not only the dissemination of news but dissemination of all kinds of editorial content to a mass audience. This had been a principal goal of daily journalism, whether newspaper or broadcast, for much of the 20th century. But here, for the first time since this series of studies began, the function appears not terribly important to most journalists. In both 1982–

TABLE 4.5
The Disseminator Function: Percentages of Journalists
Who Saw Its Dimensions as "Extremely Important"

Media Type	Getting Information to Public Quickly (%)		Avoid Unverified Facts (%)		Reach Widest Possible Audience (%)		Provide Entertainment and Relaxation (%)	
	1992	2002	1992	2002	1992	2002	1992	2002
Wire services	81	71	55	66	9	9	14	9
Television	80	68	49	58	31	27	7	3
Dailies	70	62	50	52	17	14	16	14
News magazines	67	50	32	33	5	5	10	13
Radio	67	50	50	53	33	15	10	5
Weeklies	53	45	48	48	24	16	17	10
Total[a]	69	59	49	52	20	15	14	11

[a] The overall N for 1992 was 1,156 and for 2002 it was 1,149.

1983 and 1992, the disseminator function was deemed very important by 51% of the respondents. As Figure 4.2 shows, that percentage eroded to less than 16% in 2002. It is possible that recent changes in market forces and rapid advances in technology have served to discount the notion of the ubiquitous news organ.

The adversarial function remained a minority attitude among the journalists, just as it had been ever since it was first measured in 1982–1983. This function consisted of two items: "Be an adversary of public officials by being constantly skeptical of their actions" and "Be an adversary of businesses by being constantly skeptical of their actions." We had anticipated that in the wake of dozens of scandals involving leaders of large corporations, the adversarial function would experience a surge. But the percentage of those according this cluster high importance rose only marginally over the 1992 level. As in past years, this result seemed puzzling in the context of the harsh criticism journalists receive for their negativity toward cherished American institutions and leaders. These findings represent either a popular misunderstanding of the nature of the American journalist or a widespread denial among journalists that they are skeptical adversaries of those in power (Table 4.6).

The other significant change in the appeal of the four functions is the increased affinity with the populist mobilizer function. This function first emerged in the 1992 factor analysis, and at that time, we considered it "tantalizing evidence" that public journalism may have established a foothold among the core values of a tiny minority of journalists. In 2002, this concept seems to have established a foothold with a larger minority, and because of the items that clustered together to create this function, we can identify it more clearly as an attitude of public journalism (Table 4.7).

TABLE 4.6
The Adversarial Function: Percentages of Journalists
Who Saw Its Dimensions as "Extremely Important"

Media Type	Adversary of Officials (%)		Adversary of Business (%)	
	1992	2002	1992	2002
News magazines	32	29	33	32
Dailies	26	23	17	20
Wire services	23	30	11	24
Television	17	14	9	12
Weeklies	11	15	8	13
Radio	8	10	7	9
Total[a]	21	20	14	18

[a] The overall N for 1992 was 1,156 and for 2002 it was 1,149.

TABLE 4.7
The Populist Mobilizer Function: Percentages of Journalists
Who Saw Its Dimensions As "Extremely Important"

Media Type	Let People Express Views (%)		Develop Cultural Interests (%)		Motivate People to Get Involved (%)[a]		Point to Possible Solutions (%)[a]		Set the Political Agenda (%)	
	1992	2002	1992	2002	1992	2002	1992	2002	1992	2002
Weeklies	58	48	17	20	—	44	—	24	3	4
Dailies	52	45	18	19	—	34	—	26	5	4
Radio	46	33	19	14	—	34	—	14	4	0
Television	39	29	18	12	—	25	—	25	4	2
News magazines	27	15	32	15	—	21	—	27	5	5
Wire services	26	23	14	13	—	25	—	17	2	3
Total[b]	48	39	18	17	—	33	—	24	5	3

[a] Not measured in the 1992 study.
[b] The overall N for 1992 was 1,156 and for 2002 it was 1,149.

Public (or "civic") journalism was the source of one of the most vigorous debates in the 1990s concerning journalism's function in American society. Media ethicist Edmund Lambeth offered a neutral definition. He wrote that public journalism is journalism that seeks to

1. listen systematically to the stories and ideas of citizens even while protecting its freedom to choose what to cover;
2. examine alternative ways to frame stories on community issues;
3. choose frames that stand the best chance to stimulate citizen deliberation and build public understanding of issues;

4. take the initiative to report on major public problems in a way that advances public knowledge of possible solutions and the values served by alternative courses of action;

5. pay continuing and systematic attention to how well and how credibly it is communicating with the public.[25]

But it did generate controversy. Whether the topic was public journalism's goals, its performance in implementing its goals, its relation to democratic theory, the nature of its practice or its impact on communities, the journalism reviews and scholarly journals were full of dispute.

Considering the historical context of this movement, however, it is hardly surprisingly that we would see so many different opinions. Public journalism crept upon the scene in the early 1990s without proclamation. The development of its theory, and the methods of its practice, has been under negotiation and revision ever since the movement began. Because there is no unifying theory or definition, let alone set of practical guidelines, the movement has been assigned a wide variety of ideas and manifestations, by both supporters and opponents. Some versions are straw figures whose creators have enjoyed knocking over with ease. Some versions conjure democratic paradises that no single profession or institution could be responsible for sustaining.

Until the late 1990s, many skeptical practitioners were dismissing public journalism as a fad—the pet project of a few out-of-the-loop editors and their friends in the academy. But most would now agree that public journalism, like it or not, survived its infancy. Between 1995 and 2002, news organizations sent summaries of more than 600 different public journalism projects to the Pew Center for Civic Journalism,[26] and it is likely that several hundred more efforts took place undetected by Pew. They encompassed a wide variety of projects seeking to learn the concerns of ordinary citizens, whether through town meetings, opinion polls, or other means; to motivate citizens to participate in local public life, such as by joining anticrime task forces, volunteering to tutor, or simply attending public meetings; and to focus on a process of community problem solving, rather than leaving readers and listeners with a list of seemingly overwhelming problems.

The Pluralistic Journalist

One of the most significant characteristics of these results is that most journalists still, as journalists did in the previous two studies, embrace more than one of these four role conceptions. The disseminator role may seem to stand in contradiction to the adversarial role, for example, but the two are far from mutually exclusive in the views of journalists. Figure 4.2 illustrates this point. We saw "overlap" in every possible combination of role conceptions. Two-thirds of those who rated the disseminator role as very important also rated the interpretive role as very important as well. Four-fifths of those who rated the adversarial role as very

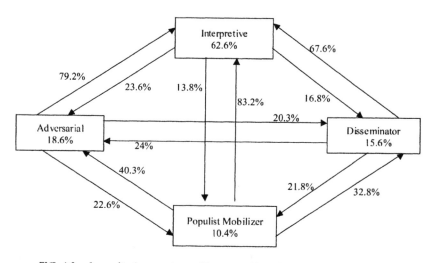

FIG. 4.2. Journalists' perceptions of functions. Note: Percentages in boxes indicate the proportions of journalists who rate each function as very important (the top quartile of each scale). Percentages along the arrows indicate the overlap in the proportions of journalists who strongly endorse both roles. For example, 79.2% of those journalists who consider the adversarial role very important also consider the interpretive role very important.

important also rated the interpretive role as very important. The greatest conceptual mismatch, between disseminator and adversarial, still showed substantial overlap: One-fourth of those embracing the adversarial role also embraced the disseminator role, while one-fifth of those embracing the disseminator role felt the same about the adversarial role.

Equally important is the observation that the overlap was never total between any two role conceptions. The highest degree of harmony was between populist mobilizers and interpreters: 83% of those who rated populist mobilizer as a very important role also rated interpretive as very important. Journalists have their priorities in terms of role conceptions, but these priorities are not exclusive. Not only do they recognize the existence or necessity of other journalistic roles; they accord those roles substantial importance. With that in mind, our investigation turned to the possibility that different factors could predict which role a journalist would endorse.

THEORETICAL "CAUSES" OF ROLE CONCEPTIONS

It is rarely possible to state with certainty what forces cause a journalist to adopt an interpretive, disseminator, adversarial, or mobilizer attitude in his or her view of journalism, but through the statistical procedures of multiple regression, it is possible at least to identify factors that are associated with those attitudes, even when other factors are held constant. These factors are often referred to as "predictors" of the survey results, because although we cannot say that one condition causes another to exist, we can still note that where one condition exists, the other condition also will regularly appear. Returning to the framework proposed by Shoemaker and Reese, we grouped the predictors of journalistic role conceptions into four categories, each representing a different level of analysis. Table 4.8 details these contexts.

Organizational Context

In a similar analysis 10 years earlier, organizational factors emerged as more important "predictors" of role conceptions than they had been in the past, and the influence of the organization stayed strong in this analysis as well. More organization-related factors emerged as statistically significant predictors of role conceptions than did individual, professional, or external factors. However, different aspects of organizations came to the fore this time. For example, in 1992, the journalist's salary and the state of the organization's ownership mattered: journalists with larger paychecks who worked at publicly traded corporations tended to endorse the interpretive role. This time ownership and income patterns had no effect on these attitudes. Instead, editorial staff size and the type of medium were strong predictors.

Journalists working on large staffs tended to embrace the interpretive and adversarial roles, whereas those at small news organizations embraced the populist mobilizer role. Also, journalists working in the print media tended to endorse the adversarial and populist mobilizer roles. Another, more subtle organizational factor we measured was whether the journalist felt his or her ethics were influenced heavily by editors and senior staff members. Those who said they took their ethical cues from more senior colleagues tended to endorse both interpretive and adversarial roles.

Other organizational factors—such as whether the organization was locally owned, the degree of autonomy the journalist felt, the perceived importance of profit, and whether the journalist had a say in who is hired or fired—predicted the adoption of a role conceptions. Most of these organizational factors predicted only one role conception, but taken together, they indicate that the journalist's work environment has a powerful impact on how he or she perceives the roles that the news media perform in today's society.

Individual Background

Other factors independent of organizational context were measured, such as gender, ethnicity, education, and religion. As a group, the individual-level factors did

TABLE 4.8

Predictors of Professional Values Among Journalists

Variables	Interpretive Values ($R^2 = .29$)		Disseminator Values ($R^2 = .19$)		Adversarial Values ($R^2 = .14$)		Populist Mobilizer Values ($R^2 = .33$)	
	Standardized Regression Coefficients	Correlation Coefficients	Standardized Regression Coefficients	Correlation Coefficients	Standardized Regression Coefficients	Correlation Coefficients	Standardized Regression Coefficients	Correlation Coefficients
Organizational Context								
Income								
Print Medium					.07	.17	.15	.17
Ownership—publicly traded								
Local ownership							-.07	-.09
Reporter								
Supervisor								
Staff size	.15	.22			.08	.13	-.12	-.12
Influence on hiring/firing	-.10	-.13						
Amount of comment from people above me	.09	.15						
Ethics influenced by editors/senior staffers	.20	.22			.08	.12		
Ethics influenced by staff peers							.07	.14
Ethics influenced by publisher/owner	-.20	-.16						
Organization does well informing public			.09	.13				
High profits important to organization			.12	.14				
My story ideas get covered			.08	.09				
My stories get a lot of editing								
Freedom in what to emphasize					.09	.16	.08	.09

Individual Background								
Private college	-.16				-.12	-.22	-.14	-.20
Being conservative	.12	-.25						
Education level		.21						
Majored in journalism			.07	.11			.06	.14
Importance of job security			.12	.22			.14	.21
Important to develop a specialty								
Journalistic Attitudes								
Importance of chance to influence public affairs	.12	.21			.09	.15	.18	.34
Importance of chance to help people		.25					.14	.29
Media should influence public affairs	.17				.06	.15	.18	.29
Media should influence public opinion					.07	.18		
OK to use official documents (unauthorized)	.12	.25	-.07	-.19				
OK to use hidden mics/cameras			-.10	-.17				
OK to use rape victims' names			-.08	-.17				
Influence of journalism training							.10	.18
Influence of wire budgets			.10	.19				
External Factors								
Get comments from audience	-.11						.09	.16
Audience mostly interested in breaking news		-.20	.09	.19				
Influence of audience research							.11	.18
Influence of friends								
Watch local TV news			.13	.19				
Watch PBS NewsHour			-.06	-.08				

Note. Only statistically significant (.05) betas and correlations are included.

not predict role conceptions to any great degree. Earlier studies had highlighted the importance of educational level, but the 1992 data showed a decrease in that influence, and these 2002 findings extended that decrease. Education predicted only one role endorsement: Those with higher levels of education tended to endorse the interpretive role. The stronger individual-level predictor of role attitudes was personal politics. The more liberal the journalist, the more likely he or she was to embrace the interpretive, adversarial, and populist mobilizer functions. This pattern is consistent with findings in the earlier studies.

Attitudes About Professionalism

Table 4.8 also includes a group of predictors concerned with the journalist's other attitudes about specific aspects of journalism which, taken together, create his or her belief system about what it means to be a professional journalist. These are opinions that are not necessarily a function directly of the journalist's work environment or individual traits but more likely the result of socialization that occurs through journalism education, learning from professional organizations (attending their meetings or reading their journals or Web sites), and any informal mentoring the journalist has enjoyed during a career.

Most influential among these were opinions on how important it is to them that their work has a chance to influence public affairs. Those who gave this factor high importance tended to embrace not only the interpretive and adversarial roles but especially the populist mobilizer role. Those who agreed that media should influence public opinion also embraced the adversarial and populist mobilizer roles. Sometimes stances on ethical issues predicted which journalistic role a journalist would identify with. The more likely the journalist was to approve of using unauthorized official documents, the more enthusiastically he or she embraced the interpretive or adversarial role, and the less likely that person was to embrace the disseminator role.

External Factors

Given the emergence of a more market-driven management of journalism in the 1990s,[27] we expected such factors as advertisers, audience, sources, and stockholders to emerge as influential on the journalists' role conceptions. A few did, but not with the force or frequency exhibited by the organizational or professional factors. Respondents were asked to what extent today's audiences are mostly interested in breaking news. Those who believed that audiences mostly are interested in breaking news endorsed the disseminator role and turned away from the interpretive role, unsurprisingly. Journalists who said they received lots of comments from their audience and who accorded influence to audience research tended to embrace the populist mobilizer role.

PROFILES OF JOURNALISTS EMBRACING DIFFERENT ROLES

Given that most journalists perceived more than one journalistic role to be extremely important, what characteristics describe the adherents to each of these four roles? Viewed from another angle, the data in Table 4.8 provide a profile of each category of journalist.

Interpreters: Who Were They?

Journalists embracing the interpretive role tend to be well-educated liberals at larger news organizations who learn from their immediate bosses and not from their owners. In fact, the most salient influences on the interpreters were the influences of editors and senior staff members, and of publishers or owners, on the journalists' sense of ethics. Interpreters said they look to their immediate superiors for ethical guidance with as much enthusiasm as they reject owners' and publishers' ethics. Interpreters are also journalists who say they receive a great deal of comment on their work by those same superiors and who feel they have little say as to who is hired or fired. They believe journalists' work should influence public affairs, and they relish the opportunity to do so. They are especially supportive of the use of unauthorized official documents to report an important story, and they reject the notion that audiences are mostly interested in breaking news. In short, interpreters seem to place great faith not only in the journalists they work with but in the important public service their sizeable news organizations are doing.

Adversarialists: Who Were They?

Those embracing the adversarial function were far fewer in number than the interpreters, but a profile of them emerged nonetheless. In many ways, the adversarialist resembles the interpreter. Both journalists tend to be politically liberal, work at a large news organization, support the use of unauthorized documents to report a story, take their ethical cues from senior staff members, and accord high importance to influencing public affairs. Unlike the interpreters, however, adversarial journalists tend to work in the print media, and they embrace the opportunity not just to influence public affairs but also to influence public opinion. They seem to embrace their "watchdog" attitude from the security of a large newspaper or magazine, surrounded by colleagues whose judgment they trust, insistent that their work influence the public.

Disseminators: Who Were They?

The disseminator presented a strikingly different profile. This is a more ethically cautious and traditional journalist. Disseminators tend to believe not only that high profits are important to their organizations but also that their organizations do a good job of informing the public. They tend to be people who majored in journalism in college, and people who place high importance on the notion of job security in general. They frown on the use of unauthorized official documents and hidden microphones or cameras to report a story, and they disapprove of using rape victims' names in stories. They say their news judgment is colored by wire-service budgets; they tend to watch local television news more than those embracing the other roles, and they watch the NewsHour on PBS less than the others.

Populist Mobilizers: Who Were They?

This role was associated with more predictors than any of the others. This is a journalist who is eager to connect with and influence the local community. The populist mobilizer tends to be a print journalist at a paper or magazine that is smaller than average but a publication that is not locally owned. This journalist also feels a higher degree of freedom in what to emphasize in his or her journalistic work. Populist mobilizers are personally liberal, and, more than the other types of journalists, they feel it is important professionally to develop a specialty. However, like the disseminators, populist mobilizers also place high importance on job security.

Populist mobilizers emerge as most distinctive in their attitudes about audience and community. They were the only group to display exceptional affinity with the media's opportunities to help people, as well as to influence public affairs and public opinion. The greatest influence on their news values tends to be their journalistic training—most likely, given the recent emergence of civic journalism, training in workshops and seminars since they left college. As for external influences, populist mobilizers were most likely to state they received comments from their readers or audience and most likely to accord importance to audience research.

These are summaries, however, of only the variables in this particular study that were associated with the role conceptions. Certainly dozens of other factors help shape these complex, underlying attitudes. And because they are underlying attitudes, we must be careful not to assume that the journalist who embraces one role over the other three will exhibit that role predominantly in his or her work. In our 1992 study, we asked respondents to send us samples of what they considered their best work, and a content analysis of those articles revealed that although the interpretive role was most popular at a conceptual level, the disseminator role was seen most often in the samples. Media researcher Tim P. Vos also found in his own survey that the same journalists who, in the survey, most often espoused the interpretive role most often did "disseminating" work.[28]

Clearly more investigation is needed here, but these results at least suggest that the role conceptions may represent an ideal type of journalism for the practitioner, but that the pressures of daily production necessitate the basic dissemination of the news before the more intricate and demanding work of interpretation, mobilization, or adversarial reporting can be undertaken.

NEWS VALUES

In the analysis of news production, nothing is more important than decisions about what is worthy of publication or broadcast. Dissatisfaction with the press, both within and outside the mass media, often is about news values and selection. The general public's impressions of the news media's choices took a roller-coaster ride at the century's turn, due in large part to the media coverage of the terrorist attacks of September 11, 2001.

For example, the Pew Research Center, which was polling the American public regularly with questions of press performance, found in 1999 that only 21% of Americans thought that journalists cared about the people they reported about.[29] In November 2001, shortly after the terrorist attacks, that percentage jumped to 47%—and slid back to 31% by the summer of 2003. Other perceptions of the news media showed a similar spike. In 1999, about 66% of Pew's respondents said the news media often try to cover up, rather than admit, their mistakes, and in 2003, the percentage was 62%. In November 2001, however, it had dropped to 52%. Asked whether the press is politically biased, 56% said yes in 1999 and 53% in 2003, but only 47% agreed with that assessment in November 2001.

Some aspects of the public's cynicism about the press have grown steadily over time. Asked whether the news media tend to favor one side, 53% said yes in 1985, and the percentage rose to 67% in 1997 and held about the same (66%) in 2003. Similarly, in 1985, 53% said the media are influenced by powerful people and organizations; that had risen to 63% by 1994, and 70% in 2003.

Yet people's perceptions of the media are not entirely negative. Their ratings of media professionalism stayed strong into the 21st century. In 1999 a slim majority, 52%, told Pew they thought news organizations were highly professional. That jumped to 73% just after September 11 and dropped down to 62% in 2003. But when Pew asked a question directly related to the Jayson Blair scandal in 2003—whether Americans felt that reporters at all news organizations either frequently or occasionally make up news stories, as occurred at the *Times*, 58% said yes (36% said reporters occasionally do, 22% said reporters frequently do). Small wonder there was little outrage outside journalistic circles over the *Times* scandal in the spring of 2003.

Are the media's attitudes and decisions important? The public seems to think so. The Pew Center found that 55% in 2003 believe the news media's influence to be increasing—a percentage that was consistent with Pew's findings going back to the mid-1980s.

Among journalists and scholars, notions about what makes something newsworthy are many: conflict, celebrity, impact, oddity, proximity, visual appeal, market appeal, and many more factors. Scarcely anyone believes, as some once claimed, that journalists simply "hold up a mirror on the world." However, still at the core of decisions on newsworthiness are the journalists themselves. What factors do they think influence their concept of newsworthiness?

As in the previous studies, we asked journalists in 2002 how influential a number of factors were in determining what was newsworthy in their day-to-day work. Overall, the influences on newsworthiness were fairly similar to those of a decade previous (see Table 4.9). Journalistic training, the top factor in the previous studies, emerged stronger than ever in 2002, with 79% of the respondents saying their training was very influential. Likewise, the influence of supervisors (56% saying very influential), sources (43%), peers (41%), and wire budgets (21%) remained about the same as in previous years.

There were some changes over time, however. The percentage citing audience research as influential had dropped from 42% in 1982–1983 to 35% in 1992, and it dropped again in 2002, to 30%. Local competing media as an influence on news judgment had been 36% in 1982–1983 but dropped to 25% in 1992 and 23% in 2002. The influence of large newspapers and network news had been at 28% in 1982–1983 and 27% in 1992 but dropped to 13% in 2002. We applied techniques of correlation and multiple regression to determine which characteristics of journalists "predict" their attributions of importance to the various influences on their concept of newsworthiness.

TABLE 4.9
Factors Influencing Concept of Newsworthiness, by Medium

Factor	Daily	Radio	Weekly	News Magazines	Wire	TV	Total 2002	Total 1992	Total 1982–1983
Journalistic training	79	83	77	68	87	80	79	73	77
Supervisors	60	41	50	67	62	49	56	51	58
Sources	39	50	50	47	32	50	43	40	43
Peers	40	38	47	52	41	41	41	41	43
Audience/readership research	29	32	38	12	15	34	30	35	42
Local competing news media	21	21	22	10	35	30	23	25	36
Network news/ Large papers	12	9	5	14	27	18	13	27	28
Wire budgets	27	11	4	6	42	17	21	20	22
Friends	20	12	17	13	10	5	5	—	—
Online sites	5	3	3	3	10	5	5	—	—
Cable networks	5	4	1	5	16	9	6	—	—
Polls	15	8	12	0	3	22	13	—	—

Note. Daily, N = 571; Radio, N = 105; Weekly, N = 179; News magazine, N = 62; Wire, N = 69; TV, N = 163; Total 2002, N = 1,136; Total 1992, N = 1,149; Total 1982–1983, N = 991.

Journalistic Training

At 79%, journalistic training was accorded more importance than any other single factor in influencing news judgment, and it was highest among the journalists at wire services (87% saying their training was very influential) and radio journalists (83%). The only relatively low mark given to training was given by newsmagazine journalists, who deemed their training (68%) about as influential as their supervisors (67%).

As in years past, more experienced journalists tended to see a strong connection between their journalistic training and their notions of newsworthiness. Journalists who had college experience on campus media or had taken journalism courses in college also valued their journalistic training highly. Unlike past years, however, gender and the size of the news organization seemed not to predict how important the journalists felt their training was.

News philosophy again was related to the salience of journalistic training. Journalists who embraced the populist mobilizer role of journalism, and who endorsed news organizations' techniques related to civic journalism, accorded strong influence to their journalistic training.

Supervisors and Peers

As they have been since 1982–1983, editors and other supervisors ranked second in the degree of influence on the journalists' conceptions of newsworthiness, with 56% saying they were very influential; 43% of the journalists surveyed said their peers had a strong influence on their news judgment. Magazine journalists considered their supervisors and peers more influential than those in other media: 67% said supervisors were very influential, and 52% said their peers were very influential. Broadcast journalists have a different take on their newsroom influences: In television news, only 49% cited high influence from their supervisors, and only 41% of radio journalists did. Radio journalists also accorded the least influence to newsroom peers—understandable, considering that relatively few radio journalists today have journalistic supervisors or colleagues.

Philosophy played a part again in predicting who would see a strong influence in their supervisors. Those who embraced the disseminator role said their supervisors and peers were very influential. Journalists who said they were very satisfied overall with their present jobs tended to say their newsroom culture influenced their news judgment. The younger the journalist, the more likely he or she was to cite the newsroom as influential. And the more often the journalist socialized with other journalists, the more influential his or her peers and supervisors seemed to be.

Sources

The journalists were asked how influential their news sources were on their concept of newsworthiness, and their responses reflected those of the previous surveys. About 43% said sources influence news judgment. Predictably, journalists at wire services felt the least influence of sources, at 32%. Sources seemed to have the greatest influence among radio and television journalists and those at weekly newspapers: In all three categories, 50% reported "very influential."

Only a few other characteristics were associated with rating sources as highly influential. Reporters tended to accord sources greater influence than did other kinds of journalists. And journalists who approve of various techniques of civic journalism also reported that sources influenced them a great deal.

Major Media

Critics of the news media often claim that American journalism's news judgment is dictated by decisions at a small number of elite news organizations: the television networks (including cable news networks), prestigious newspapers, the wire services, or popular Web sites. We asked the journalists to rate the influence of each of these, and their responses seem to defy the critics' claim. Only 5% of the respondents accorded strong influence to online sites, and only 6% said cable networks are influential. The networks and large newspapers garnered "very influential" ratings from 13%, but that percentage decreased from 28% in 1982–1983 and 27% in 1992. The influence of wire budgets basically held steady at 21%—still surprisingly low considering the pervasive presence of wire services in daily journalism.

For a regression analysis, we combined the influence of cable, online, broadcast network, and major newspapers, and a profile of sorts developed for the journalist who accords strong influence to the major media. Journalists who say they get a lot of reaction from readers or listeners tend not to feel influenced by the major media. Those who identify with the adversary role of the media do accord influence to the major media, as do those who work at large news organizations. Minority journalists also tend to credit the major media, as do journalists who say they socialize frequently with other journalists.

Audience Research

One of the most striking changes in the assigning of influence over news judgment is the 20-year decline of audience and reader research. At 42%, it was one of the most significant influences cited in the 1982–1983 study. Audience research has not entirely lost its luster, but it dropped to 30% in 2002. It was still strong among radio and television journalists, as we might expect, but the highest percentage was found among the weekly newspaper journalists at 38%. Weekly journalists also led in this category of influence in the 1992 study, which seems surprising in light of small newspapers' general lack of resources to conduct audience research. The phrase "findings of readership or audience research," however, may have simply connected with small papers' general orientation to their readers' concerns.

Regression showed that journalists who embrace the interpreter role of the media are very unlikely to accord influence to audience research, whereas those who approve of techniques of civic journalism tend to accord great influence to this kind of research. Also, journalists who say they get a lot of reaction from readers or listeners are more likely to rate audience research as very influential in determining newsworthiness.

Clearly the more personal contacts of journalists continue to influence their concepts of what is newsworthy. Newsroom supervisors and peers, as well as news sources, received much more credit than did the more distant factors of audience research and other media. Particularly noteworthy was the decline of influence of the television networks and major newspapers, but that decline may be more a shift to acknowledge the newer influences of cable networks and online sites (at the expense of the more traditional media leaders) rather than an overall decline in the influence of other media. The greatest influence by far, in the realm of concepts of newsworthiness, was accorded to the journalist's own training. The survey did not specify whether this was ongoing newsroom training or journalistic training undertaken several years earlier; respondents formed their own definitions of "journalistic training." The findings overall suggest that journalists' development of news judgment is a dynamic process with several competing influences, but the greatest influence is one over which news managers can exercise a good deal of control: training.

ETHICS IN JOURNALISM

Ethical and moral development for journalists has been in some journalism school curricula for at least half a century, long before the topic of applied ethics for professionals became fashionable in universities in the early 1980s. In 1924, Nelson A. Crawford, head of the Department of Industrial Journalism at Kansas State Agricultural College, published *The Ethics of Journalism* with the distinguished house of Alfred A. Knopf. His aim was to contribute to a "professional consciousness" and an ethical philosophy that was "realistic, discerning, intellectually honest, and applicable to the press as a social institution."[30] Crawford wisely realized that the goal was ambitious, but he could never have imagined that a recent textbook on media ethics, written by Conrad Fink, would state that "everywhere are signs of ethical deterioration."[31]

In our book on the 1982–1983 national study, we wrote that concern about journalism ethics was at a historic peak. The high-water mark, we thought, was the ill-fated Pulitzer Prize awarded to Janet Cooke, then of *The Washington Post*, for what turned out to be a fabricated story about the drug-infested world of an imaginary 8-year-old child. But the 1990s also saw no shortage of work for media ethicists. The rigged crash test of a GM truck for *Dateline NBC* became an ethical catastrophe for broadcast journalism. The O. J. Simpson trials, criminal and civil, brought charges that even the elite press was falling victim to the tawdry ethical standards of the supermarket tabloids. The press's relentless pursuit of photographs of Britain's Princess Diana was blamed by many critics for the automobile crash that took her life in 1997.

And there was no letup at the turn of the century. Janet Cooke's transgression has returned to haunt the journalism community. In two separate episodes, two columnists at *The Boston Globe* were found to have fabricated interviews and material. A writer for *The New Republic* was discovered to have committed similar breaches in several of his articles.[32] Other controversies occurred along the way. A reporter for the *Cincinnati Enquirer* was found to have used illegally obtained telephone messages to document parts of his exposé on Chiquita Brands International Inc. *The San Jose Mercury News* apologized to readers for jumping to the conclusion, in an investigative series, that the CIA was indirectly supplying drugs to the African American community in Los Angeles. Two reporters at *The Salt Lake Tribune* were found to have sold rumors regarding a story they were covering (about a high-profile kidnapping) to *The National Enquirer*.

In 2003, the United States invaded Iraq, and a debate ensued about the Department of Defense's practice of embedding reporters and photographers with the troops as they advanced on Baghdad. Critics like Alexander Cockburn felt the system led to unprecedented gullibility and bias on the part of the news media. Even *The New York Times* unquestioningly reported the Pentagon's assertion that Iraq had developed "weapons of mass destruction," despite lack of evidence before, during, and in the first years after the war. "That's the problem with 'embedfellows,'" Cockburn wrote. "Just one kiss is all it takes."[33]

Several more specific incidents were likewise scrutinized, most notably the rescue of Private Jessica Lynch from an Iraqi hospital. The initial stories about her capture and rescue spun a tale of heroism; facts discovered later revealed a fairly mundane procedure. Daphne Eviatar blamed the media's gullibility on the Fox network's ratings success in giving war coverage a patriotic twist; other news outlets soon followed suit.[34] But the most public debate over journalism ethics in the new century has been over Jayson Blair, the young reporter on *The New York Times* who was found to have copied major parts of a story of his from a previously published article. Further internal investigation revealed that Blair had committed plagiarism, fabrication, and misrepresentation in a number of stories.

Journalists and educators disagree over how ethics should be taught, or even whether ethics can be taught. Howard Good, a teacher of journalism ethics at the State University of New York, worried that the professional world of journalism had become so uninterested in upholding professional standards that ethics instruction may be futile. Mike Barnicle, for example, one of the columnists fired from *The Boston Globe* for fabrication, was soon back at work for *The New York Daily News*. "In the end," Good wrote, "it may not matter what happens in the classroom if newsrooms continue to practice no-fault ethics."[35] Lorraine Branham, director of the School of Journalism at the University of Texas, wrote that editors and news directors wrongly assume that young journalists have been adequately trained in ethical reasoning as part of their journalism education. Thus, Branham wrote, ethics discussions occur only rarely in most newsrooms. "We need to spend just as much time (teaching) ethics and values as we do reporting and writing," Branham concluded.[36]

What, then, are the foundations of journalists' notions of ethics? Our three national studies have asked journalists to consider the influences of their past or present circumstances on their ethical bearing. Specifically, the respondents were asked about the influence of a set of factors — ranging from family upbringing to Web resources — in shaping their ideas in matters of journalism ethics. The results suggest similar patterns of perceived influence over the two decades (see Table 4.10).

INFLUENCES ON ETHICS

As in previous years, newsroom learning topped the list, even though it slipped from 88% saying it was influential in the previous studies to 82% in 2002 (see Table 4.10). Family upbringing as an influence on ethics continued its upswing, rising from 72% in 1982–1983 to 78% in 2002. Ranking third in influence on ethics was the combination of senior editors, reporters, and directors, which,

TABLE 4.10
Sources of Influence on Ethics

	Percentage Saying Influential		
Source	1982–1983 (N = 1,000)	1992 (N = 1,155)	2002 (N = 1,136)
Newsroom learning	88	88	82
Family upbringing	72	74	78
Senior editors, reporters, directors	—[a]	—[a]	67
Senior editor	61	58	—[a]
Senior reporter	52	45	—[a]
Coworkers	57	—[a]	—[a]
Teachers, professors	—[a]	—[a]	45
College professors	50	21	—[a]
High school teachers	24	17	—[a]
Journalism seminar	—[a]	—[a]	21
Web resources	—[a]	—[a]	5
Religious training	35	36	30
Publishers, owners	25	17	14
Trade publications	—[a]	—[a]	12
College experience	—[a]	—[a]	29
Other respected organizations	—[a]	—[a]	38

[a] Not asked this year.

though phrased differently in the past studies, reflects previous years' rankings. The influence of owners and publishers on ethics continued its decline from 25% in 1982–1983 to 14% in 2002—likely a reflection of the decline in the number of independent owners who exert moral as well as business leadership at their news organizations.

In 2002, we added several new choices as sources of influence on ethics, and a few resonated. A factor we labeled "decisions of other news organizations you respect" received an "influential" nod from 38% of the respondents, and "experience in college news media" was deemed influential by 29%. Professional or trade publications, however, were accorded influence by only 12%, and Web resources seemed to influence the ethics of only 5%.

An intensive analysis of this list of influences suggested that the items could be clustered into four groups: newsroom context, family and religion, continuing education, and college experiences. These clusters were used to search for different patterns of influence on ethical orientations among journalists and to see which factors were associated with the tendency of some journalists to cite one of these clusters as their principal influence on ethics.

Newsroom Context

Overall, the newsroom context emerged again as the most powerful set of factors influencing journalists' ethics. Previous studies had found no significant differences among the different media, but in 2002, the wire-service journalists tended to give the newsroom factors especially high marks as influences on ethics, and those at weekly newspapers gave the newsroom context relatively low marks.

In a multiple regression analysis,[37] a number of factors related to the journalist's position in the newsroom were associated with the strength of newsroom in influencing ethics. Journalists who said they had a say in newsroom hiring and firing and who said they communicate frequently with reporters also gave high importance to the newsroom context for ethics. Respondents who said their work receives editing from others in the newsroom, unsurprisingly, said the newsroom context factors were influential. The larger the news organization, the more likely the journalist at the organization was to rate the newsroom as an influence on ethics. And of the four media functions, only those identifying with the interpreter role tended to rate the newsroom context as a strong influence—a turnabout from 10 years earlier.

Family and Religion

The influence of religious training continued its long-term decline, but its association with family upbringing created a powerful combination nonetheless—and a contradiction to the popular image of the journalist as hard-boiled and sacrilegious. The influence of family and religion on ethical orientation varied a great deal according to the type of news medium. Journalists at television stations and weekly newspapers were far more likely to rate family and religion highly than those at the other media. In the rest of the regression analysis, we found that the more conservative the journalist claimed to be, the stronger the influence of family and religion was on his or her ethics. Journalists who said they socialize frequently with other journalists were unlikely to credit family and religion. And journalists who approved of techniques of civic journalism were more likely to identify family and religion as influences on their ethics.[38]

Continuing Education

This cluster of factors emerged as a result of the addition of several new questions in the 2002 survey. It combined the influence ratings for journalism seminars, Web resources, trade publications, and "other respected organizations," to represent factors outside the immediate newsroom context that comprise the ongoing discussions of ethics in the journalist's developing career. Journalists at daily newspapers were the most likely to give high marks to these external influences, and those at news magazines were least likely. In the regression analysis, the strongest predictor, by far, was the journalist's positive appraisal of civic journalism practices. This is likely a function of civic journalism's spread through seminars, frequent articles in trade publications, Web discussions, and the leadership of certain news organizations. Journalists who belong to professional associations and minority journalists also accorded strong influence to these ongoing, external sources.[39]

College Experiences

The survey asked respondents to rate the ethical influence of their college professors and of experiences they had in college media, and each factor had substantive representation. Among the various media, only journalists at daily newspapers gave unusually high ratings to the college experience in shaping their ethics. In the multiple regression, the two leading factors associated with this were age and college major. The younger the journalist, the more likely he or she was to identify college as a key influence. And journalists who majored in journalism or communication were more likely—and therefore more likely to have some training in journalism ethics—to cite the college experience. In addition, journalists who said they socialize frequently with other journalists and those who said the media ought to influence public opinion gave high marks to the college experience as an influence on their ethics.[40]

The implication of the data on ethical influences is that, with the influence of the newsroom context as powerful as it is, newsroom managers have both an opportunity and an obligation to provide leadership in raising journalists' ethics consciousness. The last years of the 20th century saw a concerted effort among professional associations to revise codes of ethics, but it seems likely that journal-ists receive more effective guidance through personal conversations than through documents. The opportunity for journalism education is also apparent in these results. College classrooms and college newsrooms offer venues for relatively risk-free discussions about the issues of the day. Such discussions, on campus and in the business, would be lively. As the results in the next section demonstrate, jour-nalists display wide differences of opinion on ethical issues.

ETHICAL PERCEPTIONS
OF REPORTING PRACTICES

Media ethics, of course, covers a broad landscape, but nothing is more central than specific reporting practices. The tactics of journalists in obtaining informa-tion sometimes reflect their basic role orientations, as well as a zeal for a "good story." In our three surveys over 20 years, journalists were asked to think about 10 reporting situations, ranging from the possibility of paying for confidential information to going undercover to get a good story. The respondents indicated whether, given "an important story," the reporting practices "may be justified on occasion," or should not be approved "under any circumstances."

We understand that each question captures only a sliver of information, but it is important information. In journalistic life, the situations to which the various questions pertain are usually immensely complicated. An entire survey could be devoted to each one. The question used was not designed to measure preference among gradations of ethical options. Instead, it sets up "worst case scenarios" on which a journalist may say, in effect, "Here is a practice that I could never see myself or any other journalist doing regardless of the circumstances."

Table 4.11 shows how the approvals of these practices have changed over the 20 years.

Disclosing Confidential Sources

If there is a bedrock principle among journalists, it is that a commitment to a source's anonymity must be honored at all costs. In each of the three surveys, less than 10% of the journalists said that divulging the name of an anonymous source could be justified. This broadly held sentiment is in keeping with a 1991 decision by the U.S. Supreme Court, which declared that the First Amendment does not protect journalists who reveal the identities of sources who had been promised anonymity.[41] Over the years, reporters have made headlines far more often for going to jail to protect the identity of a source than for breaking a promise of con-fidentiality. However, the 1991 case and several other instances involving sourc-ing, including the Jayson Blair saga at *The New York Times*, have caused editors to use more caution in approving the use of confidential sources. Several newsrooms

TABLE 4.11
Journalists' Acceptance of Various Reporting Practices

Reporting Practice	Percentage Saying May Be Justified		
	1982–1983[a]	1992	2002
Getting employed in a firm or organization to gain inside information	67	63	54
Using confidential business or government documents without authorization	55	82	78
Badgering unwilling informants to get a story	47	49	52
Making use of personal documents such as letters and photographs without permission	28	48	41
Paying people for confidential information	27	20	17
Claiming to be somebody else	20	22	14
Agreeing to protect confidentiality and not doing so	5	5	8
Using hidden microphones or cameras[b]	—	60	60
Using re-creations or dramatizations of news by actors[b]	—	28	29
Disclosing names of rape victims[b]	—	43	36

[a] Data from Weaver and Wilhoit, *The American Journalist*, p. 128.
[b] Not asked in the 1982–1983 survey.

adopted policies in the late 1990s that narrowly specify the circumstances under which reporters would even be able to grant confidentiality to a source.[42]

Using False Identification

Claiming to be someone else in order to get a story has been a technique of investigative reporting for at least a century, and it was never more public than in Bob Woodward's and Carl Bernstein's Pulitzer-Prize-winning investigation of the Watergate scandal in 1973 and 1974. Since those glory days, the practice has come under a far more critical eye. The percentage of respondents justifying this practice has dipped since 1992, from 22% to 14% (Table 4.12).

The range among different media was surprisingly large, however, with 28% of magazine journalists saying that claiming to be someone else at times is justifiable, and only 9% of wire-service journalists allowing the practice. One of the most notable changes was in television journalists, whose 31% approval rate in 1982–1983 and 1992 dropped to 17% in 2002. Similarly, daily newspaper journalists' justification of the practice fell from 20% in 1992 to 11% in 2002.

Paying for Confidential Information

The early 1990s saw a spate of "checkbook journalism," and a corresponding spate of criticism of the practice. Lou Prato, writing in the *American Journalism*

TABLE 4.12
Opinion on Claiming to Be Somebody Else,
by Medium

| | Percentage Saying May Be Justified | | | | | |
| | 1982–1983 | | 1992 | | 2002 | |
	%	N	%	N	%	N
Television	31	121	31	137	17	163
News magazines	30	62	34	61	28	62
Radio	25	119	13	101	13	105
Daily	19	463	20	635	11	571
Wire	15	47	21	58	9	69
Weekly	12	183	22	162	19	179
Total	20	995	22	1,154	14	1,136

TABLE 4.13
Opinion on Paying for Confidential Information,
by Medium

| | Percentage Saying May Be Justified | | | | | |
| | 1982–1983 | | 1992 | | 2002 | |
	%	N	%	N	%	N
News magazines	35	62	25	61	23	62
Television	32	121	25	137	22	163
Wire	30	47	22	58	13	69
Daily	26	463	17	635	13	571
Radio	26	119	23	101	22	105
Weekly	23	183	24	162	24	179
Total	27	995	20	1,154	17	1,136

Review in 1994, said, "The practice of paying sources has become so rampant in television that it now threatens the fundamental credibility of TV news."[43] In the firmament of ethical controversies in journalism, this controversy had virtually disappeared by the turn of the century. It either has become so pervasive that media critics and journalists no longer consider it controversial, or it has become taboo among mainstream journalists (Table 4.13).

Recent survey results indicate that its support has declined over the years. Journalism researchers David Arant and Philip Meyer, in a lengthy study of changes in journalists' values, presented their respondents with a scenario involving payment to a source and found that only 6% would pay the source for the story.[44] Our own survey saw a similar decline in response to the more general concept of "paying people for confidential information." In 1982–1983, 27% could justify the practice; that dipped to 20% in 1992 and 17% in 2002. As in 1992, daily newspaper and wire-service journalists were especially intolerant of the practice, with only 13% saying they might justify it.

Badgering Sources

One of the reporting practices that seem to irritate media observers is that of badgering, the seemingly relentless pursuit of an unwilling source—or a line of questioning a source is unwilling to address. To many nonjournalists it seems rude at the very least and, at its extreme, an unconscionable invasion of privacy or dignity. To many journalists, badgering is a mark of integrity, a refusal to give up a dogged pursuit or line of independent questioning when it matters most—when the source is being elusive. Several media critics blamed the paparazzi in pursuit of photos of Princess Diana for her death in a car crash in 1997. Closer to home, television sports journalist Jim Gray took a spotlight for his live interview with retired baseball star Pete Rose during a game in the 1999 World Series. Rose had just been honored on the field for his inclusion in baseball's "All-Century Team," but in the interview, Gray tried repeatedly to get Rose to confess to gambling on baseball games—an accusation for which he had been banned from the Hall of Fame earlier. For his interviewing posture, Gray received as much public criticism as any single journalist did in the 1990s (Table 4.14).

As in the previous studies, we found sharply divided opinion on this practice. The percentage saying that badgering may be justified rose slightly from 47% in 1982–1983 and 49% in 1992 to 52% in 2002. The differences among media,

TABLE 4.14
Opinion on Badgering Sources, by Medium

	Percentage Saying May Be Justified					
	1982–1983		1992		2002	
	%	N	%	N	%	N
Wire	68	47	53	58	65	69
News magazines	67	62	59	61	75	62
Television	52	121	46	137	41	163
Daily	47	463	55	635	53	571
Radio	43	119	28	101	42	105
Weekly	38	183	36	162	53	179
Total	47	995	49	1,154	52	1,136

however, are striking. Television journalists were somewhat less supportive of this practice in 2002 as compared with 1992, perhaps reflecting the lingering effects of the Pete Rose fallout or the possibility that badgering's implicit rudeness is most obvious in a television interview. Only 41% of television and 42% of radio journalists said this practice might be justified in 2002, compared with 75% of news-magazine and 65% of wire- or news-service journalists.

Using Personal Documents Without Consent

The meaning of the term "personal documents" has certainly changed since this question was asked in the 1982–1983 survey. In the days before digital personal communication, this referred to personal letters or photographs, or perhaps mementos or keepsakes. By 2002, however, the prevalent personal document was the e-mail message, which can be forwarded to thousands of recipients with a few clicks of the mouse. Add to that the availability of databases containing private information, either for a fee or through a bit of ingenious "hacking," and the common understanding of personal documents is not nearly as quaint as in previous decades (Table 4.15).

In the 1990s, the profile of invasion of privacy as an ethical issue was raised considerably, thanks in large part to the power of the technology available to the news media. This may explain the reversal of the trend we spotted in the 1992 survey, when the percentage of those justifying the unauthorized use of personal documents nearly doubled since 1982–1983, to 48%. In 2002, that percentage declined to 41%.

The differences by medium did not change, however. As in 1992, the journalists most likely to justify this practice worked for news magazines and wire services (those news media most removed from local contact), and those least likely to

TABLE 4.15
Opinion on Unauthorized Use of Personal Documents,
by Medium

	Percentage Saying May Be Justified					
	1982–1983		1992		2002	
	%	N	%	N	%	N
Wire	49	47	53	58	58	69
Daily	33	463	54	635	44	571
News magazines	32	62	54	61	58	62
Television	26	121	45	137	41	163
Weekly	21	183	31	162	31	179
Radio	12	119	28	101	24	105
Total	28	995	48	1,154	41	1,136

endorse using personal documents worked for weekly newspapers and radio (those news media most likely to be in contact with local community members).

Using Unauthorized Business or Government Documents

Less controversial, certainly for journalists, is the practice of using unauthorized confidential documents from government agencies and businesses. In most discussions of the use of confidential documents, the question is usually raised as to whether the interest of privacy outweighs the public's interest in learning the information contained in the document. With personal documents such as e-mail messages, the public's "need to know" or "right to know" is often not apparent. But when the document is being used by public officials to conduct the business of government, or when the document provides evidence of wrongdoing by corporate executives or of a corporate policy that has direct impact on the public, the utilitarian justification moves more often to the fore.

Ever since the U.S. Supreme Court supported the publication of the Pentagon Papers—confidential Defense Department documents about the Vietnam war that were leaked to *The New York Times* and *The Washington Post* in 1971—the use of government and business documents has become a staple of investigative reporting. The source of the documents is often an organization insider, so usually the journalist's receipt of the documents is not illegal (Table 4.16).

Once in a while, however, the practice backfires and is seen as unethical and legally risky. Such was the case in 1998, when Mike Gallagher, the author of the *Cincinnati Enquirer's* exposé on Chiquita Brands International Inc., was found to have illegally obtained tapes of voice-mail messages to and from Chiquita executives. In the wake of the corporate community's outcry over the stolen tapes (and Chiquita's impending lawsuit), the paper disavowed the exposé, apologized to

TABLE 4.16
Opinion on Unauthorized Use of Business
or Government Documents, by Medium

	Percentage Saying May Be Justified					
	1982–1983		1992		2002	
	%	N	%	N	%	N
Wire	68	47	93	58	94	69
News magazines	67	62	90	61	94	62
Daily	62	463	89	635	82	571
Television	55	121	77	137	75	163
Weekly	46	183	67	162	65	179
Radio	33	119	57	101	61	105
Total	55	995	82	1,154	78	1,136

Chiquita on its front page, offered a multimillion-dollar settlement, and removed the stories from its Web site.[45] Supporters of Gallagher pointed out that the facts of his stories were never in dispute and that their conclusions were still valid, but the case has been remembered most as a cautionary tale about how reporters obtain confidential business documents.

Where the use of government documents is the issue, journalists are sometimes viewed as unpatriotic, especially since the attacks of September 11, 2001. Leaks of documents, for example, led to stories of significant civilian casualties in the United States' post–9/11 invasion of Afghanistan. After further stories that similarly embarrassed the Bush administration, the Pentagon restricted employees' contact with news reporters—with hardly any public outcry. Alex Jones, host of PBS's "Media Matters," wrote in *Editor & Publisher*, "We need for the public to understand that it is not unpatriotic to want government officials to leak information. That's how we—and our readers—find out about what Washington is really up to."[46]

Of the 10 ethical practices included in the survey, this one received the most support, but its support was hardly unanimous. In 2002, 78% of all journalists could justify using unauthorized business or government documents, but that included only 61% support from radio journalists and 65% support from weekly newspaper journalists. Those working for wire services and news magazines, however, almost unanimously supported the practice: 94% from each of the two.

Getting Employed to Get a Story

This practice is a variation on the previous theme, claiming to be someone else in order to get a story. But the level of acceptance of this practice, when the claim involves going undercover to work inside an organization, was remarkably higher than simply claiming to be someone else. The most notable example in recent years was the case involving an ABC report that a Food Lion supermarket in North Carolina was using unsanitary practices in its preparation of meat and other food for sale. In order to report the story "from the inside," ABC employees applied for and received jobs at the market without identifying themselves as journalists. Although a federal appellate court eventually reduced the original jury's award of $5.5 million to Food Lion to $301,000, the court agreed with Food Lion that ABC had committed fraud and trespass.[47]

In the wake of that ruling several news organizations tightened their rules on undercover reporting. Many now forbid such reporting unless the practice will prevent serious harm to individuals or illuminate a serious social problem, and unless all other means of reporting the story have been exhausted. Some newspapers, including *The Wall Street Journal* and *The Washington Post*, forbid reporters from misrepresenting themselves to get a story under any circumstances.[48]

The Food Lion case may explain the decline in support for going undercover, but overall support is still among the highest in this group of 10 questionable

TABLE 4.17
Opinion on Getting Employed to Gain
Inside Information, by Medium

| | Percentage Saying May Be Justified | | | | | |
| | 1982–1983 | | 1992 | | 2002 | |
	%	N	%	N	%	N
Television	78	121	65	137	59	163
Wire	77	47	55	58	55	69
News magazines	71	62	67	61	63	62
Daily	68	463	63	635	49	571
Radio	64	119	60	101	55	105
Weekly	58	183	62	162	69	179
Total	67	995	63	1,154	54	1,136

practices, as Table 4.17 indicates. In 2002, 54% of the journalists said they could justify getting employed to gain inside information, a drop from 63% in 1992 and from 67% in 1982–1983. Surprisingly, support for this practice in 2002 was lowest among newspaper journalists. Only 49% of them said going undercover could be justified, while 59% of the television journalists agreed that the practice might be justified.

Using Hidden Cameras and Microphones

Another variant of deceptive reporting practices is the use of hidden recording devices, which has become a staple of undercover reporting in television journalism, especially as technology has advanced to make the devices easier to hide. The practice first became common in the networks' prime-time "news magazines," but by the mid-1990s most local television news teams as well were using them to ferret out evidence for stories. As one reporter said, "With the hidden camera, viewers can see the corruption with their own eyes."[49] Trade publications in the new century were publishing, and professional seminars offering, tips on the craft of hidden-camera reporting.[50]

We therefore expected that television journalists would be the most supportive of the practice of using hidden devices to get important stories. After all, in 1992, 90% of television journalists said the practice could be justified. This was even more true in 2002, when 94% of the television journalists said hidden devices might be justified, far more than any other kind of journalist (see Table 4.18). The journalists least supportive of using hidden devices were from daily and weekly newspapers, and from radio stations.

TABLE 4.18
Opinion on Hidden Microphones
or Cameras, by Medium

	Percentage Saying May Be Justified			
	1992		2002	
	%	N	%	N
Television	90	137	94	163
Wire	59	58	68	69
News magazines	63	61	59	62
Daily	58	635	51	571
Radio	59	101	57	105
Weekly	45	162	55	179
Total	60	1,154	60	1,136

Using Re-Creations of News Events by Actors

In 1989, ABC caused an ethical stir with its dramatization of the spying behavior of American diplomat Felix S. Bloch. The network aired photographs of a man resembling Bloch handing over a briefcase to someone identified as a Soviet agent, without telling viewers that these were pictures of actors playing their roles in a re-enactment. The network apologized for the ethical lapse in not labeling the photographs, and after that episode, the use of re-enactments fell largely out of favor.

The practice is still common in "reality" shows, such as those that describe crimes in an effort to locate perpetrators, but re-creations are rarely seen in mainstream journalism. As expected, the practice was deemed most acceptable among television journalists. While 29% of all journalists said re-creations could sometimes be justified, 43% of the television journalists defended the practice "on occasion." The lowest levels of support came from wire-service and news-magazine journalists (see Table 4.19). Ten years earlier, 28% of all respondents said the practice might be justified.

Disclosing the Names of Rape Victims

The 1992 survey occurred at the height of a national discussion on the ethics of identifying victims of rape. The previous year, William Kennedy Smith had been accused of raping a woman whose identity was revealed first by a supermarket tabloid, then by The New York Times, and then by every news medium covering the trial. The debate that ensued had been fueled the year before when Geneva Overholser, then editor of the Des Moines Register, published a column arguing

TABLE 4.19
Opinion on Using Re-Creations
of News by Actors, by Medium

| | Percentage Saying May Be Justified[a] | | | |
| | 1992 | | 2002 | |
	%	N	%	N
Television	42	137	43	163
Wire	21	58	20	69
News magazines	23	61	21	62
Daily	22	635	24	571
Radio	42	101	29	105
Weekly	36	162	35	179
Total	28	1,154	29	1,136

[a] This question was not posed in the 1982–1983 survey.

that withholding rape victims' names mutes the public outrage against the crime and perpetuates the stigma that rape victims feel. Shortly thereafter, the paper published a Pulitzer-Prize-winning series in which a rape victim, named with her consent, described her ordeal.[51]

The previous year, the U.S. Supreme Court had ruled that a newspaper in Florida could not be punished after it published the name of a rape victim.[52] A smattering of law professors and media critics began predicting that a new era of insensitivity to rape victims was beginning, but evidence to that effect has not emerged. The incidence of rape in the United States has not abated: In 2002, researchers estimated that about 750,000 Americans are raped each year, 400,000 of whom are children.[53] Few of those crimes are reported to police; however, far fewer are reported in the news media, and only a small fraction of those stories name the victims. Media ethicist Kelly McBride reported in 2003 that the vast majority of rape victims still do not want to be named in news stories and that reporters and editors should name only those victims who unambiguously want to share their stories and their names.[54]

Opinions varied widely according to type of medium on this issue (see Table 4.20). Only about one-fourth of the television and radio journalists said naming a rape victim might be justified, but more than half of the wire-service journalists could justify the practice on occasion. The overall acceptance rate was 36%, down from the 43% recorded in the 1992 survey. In 1992, there seemed to be no difference in how men and woman responded to this item. In 2002, however, male journalists were significantly more likely to see a justification for naming rape victims than were female journalists.

TABLE 4.20
Opinion on Disclosing Names
of Rape Victims, by Medium

	Percentage Saying May Be Justified[a]			
	1992		2002	
	%	N	%	N
Television	34	137	27	163
Wire	59	58	55	69
News magazines	45	61	34	62
Daily	47	635	40	571
Radio	28	101	25	105
Weekly	38	162	29	179
Total	43	1,154	36	1,136

[a] This question was not posed in the 1982–1983 survey.

To sum up the changes in journalists' attitudes toward these controversial practices, significant decreases appeared in the journalists' acceptance of some deceptive practices, namely claiming to be someone else, going undercover to get a story, making use of personal documents without permission, and naming rape victims. Support for using hidden devices stayed strong, however. Lest anyone conclude that journalists are becoming altogether more respectful, or passive, or lethargic, we also note increases in tolerance, over the last 20 years, for the use of unauthorized documents of all kinds and for badgering unwilling sources. It seems the journalistic ethic is becoming more aggressive in the pursuit of important information but less deceptive (except in the case of hidden microphones or cameras) in how it conducts the pursuit.

CORRELATES OF ETHICAL PERCEPTIONS

What characteristics were typical of journalists in 2002 that were cautious, or aggressive, about the use of the various reporting practices? As our final piece of analysis of the ethically questionable practices, we combined the responses to all 10 to create an overall index of ethical "aggressiveness" and explored whether certain characteristics predict such aggressiveness. (See Table 4.21 for the regression results.)

The profile of the ethically aggressive journalist changed somewhat from the 1992 analysis. The earlier analysis showed strong correlations between the ownership of the news organization and the degree of tolerance for these reporting practices. Those connections disappeared in the 2002 analysis. Instead, we saw that television journalists were more likely to tolerate these practices than journalists in the other media. Those who believe their news organization is conservative, and those who believe their news organization informs the public well, tended *not* to tolerate these controversial practices. Journalists at the rank of editor also tended not to endorse them.

Broader attitudes, much like those in 1992, also predicted tolerance of these practices. As in the earlier analysis, those who identifed with journalism's disseminator function tended not to justify these controversial reporting practices. Those who identifed with the adversary function or the intepreter function tended to be more willing to say that the practices might be justified. Also, those journalists who felt that job security is important in evaluating a position tended to be less willing to say that these reporting methods might be justified.

TABLE 4.21
Predictors of Justification of Various Reporting Practices[a]

	1992 ($R^2 = .13$)		2002 ($R^2 = .17$)	
	Standardized Regression Coefficients (betas)	Correlation Coefficients	Standardized Regression Coefficients (betas)	Correlation Coefficients
Organizational Context				
Owned by publicly traded corporation	.06	.07		
Owned by private group	-.26	.03		
Independently owned	-.31	-.10		
Radio	-.14	-.10		
Weekly	-.09	-.13		
Television			.13	.09
Organization is conservative			-.07	-.06
Editor			-.07	-.09
Organization informs public well			-.09	-.10
Individual Background				
Age	-.12	-.11		
Education level	.10	.17		
Being conservative	-.09	-.16		
Professionalism				
Importance of job security	-.18	-.09	-.07	-.14
Important to help others			-.15	-.13
Disseminator function	-.10	-.12	-.21	-.25
Adversarial function	.12	.21	.09	.16
Interpretive function	.15	.23	.20	.20
Would like more training			.06	.07
External factors				
Influence of family, religion on ethics	-.07	-.09		
Amount of comment from sources	.08	.10		
Influence of cable news			.07	.07

[a] Only statistically significant (.05) betas and correlations are included.

CIVIC JOURNALISM IN PRACTICE

Earlier in the chapter, the journalistic function of populist mobilizer was seen to have established a foothold with a more substantial minority of journalists than it had 10 years earlier. As a concept, public (or "civic") journalism was the source of one of the most vigorous debates in the 1990s. Anticipating that public journalism may have become a more accepted notion, its controversy notwithstanding, we added a few questions in 2002 to gauge journalists' acceptance of public journalism in practice.

In an examination of 10 years' coverage of public journalism by the two leading journalism reviews (*American Journalism Review* and *Columbia Journalism Review*), researchers Tanni Haas and Linda Steiner concluded that the journals portrayed the movement as a threat to such traditional journalistic values as objectivity and editorial news judgment. Several commentators, they reported, framed public journalism as a manifestation of the incursion of business values into the newsroom. The common response was to isolate advocates and misrepresent the practice of public journalism.[55]

Despite the criticism, by the early 2000s, several commentators were arguing that many practical aspects of public journalism had become common practice in many newsrooms across the country.[56] Walker Lundy, a former editor of the *St. Paul Pioneer Press*, wrote in 2003 that his paper had begun its civic journalism with a grant from the Pew Center but that eventually public journalism "started being part of the culture of the newsroom."[57] The culture was manifest, Lundy wrote, in such practices as reporters' "seeking out real people" as sources for public-affairs stories, going into greater depth on public issues, showing readers how they could get involved in these issues, and talking more often with readers responding to published stories.

In our survey, we asked the journalists about public journalism at two different levels. Each of three broad, societal goals associated with civic journalism, the goals that contributed to the makeup of the populist mobilizer function, received solid majorities of approval. Giving ordinary people a chance to express their views on public affairs was considered either extremely or quite important by 72%; motivating ordinary people to get involved in public discussions of important issues by 65%, and pointing people toward possible solutions to society's problems garnered 57%, when journalists were asked how important it was for the news media in general to do or try to do these things.

But how would these lofty ideas play out in daily practice in the journalists' own newsrooms? We asked journalists how important they thought it was *for their own news organization* to engage in each of four practices commonly associated with civic journalism: conducting polls to learn citizens' priorities on issues, convening meetings of citizens and community leaders to discuss public issues,

TABLE 4.22
Journalists' Acceptance of Civic Journalism Practices
in 2002

Civic Journalism Technique	Percentage Saying Very Important[a]
Include ordinary citizens as sources	69
Motivate citizens to participate	46
Conduct polls to learn citizens' priorities	37
Convene meeting to discuss issues	32

[a] Very important is a combination of "extremely" and "quite" important answers.

making special efforts to motivate citizens to participate in decision-making on public issues, and making special efforts to include ordinary citizens as sources in public affairs stories.

As Table 4.22 shows, the results were mixed, suggesting that journalists in general didn't agree on how best to implement the broader goals associated with the populist mobilizer function. Only 32% said it was very important (defined as "extremely" or "quite" important) that their newsroom convene meetings to discuss issues; 37% said it was very important to conduct polls, and 46% said it was very important for their news organization to motivate citizens. Only one activity—making special efforts to include ordinary citizens as sources—was considered very important by a majority (69%). It is worth noting, however, that the results did not imply a wholesale rejection of these controversial practices. If the response "somewhat important" were added to the percentages who thought that each practice was very important for their news organizations, the approval for including ordinary citizens as sources would be 94%; for conducting polls, 82%; for motivating citizens to participate, 81%; and for convening meetings, 68%.

Correlates of Approval of Civic Journalism Practices

As with several of the other aggregate measures in this chapter, we used multiple regression to build a profile of sorts to describe the typical journalist who felt these four civic journalism practices were important for his or her news organization. Because those who responded favorably to one of these practices tended to respond favorably to the others,[58] we created an index of civic journalism approval for use in the regression analysis.

Several characteristics emerged with strong associations to this pro–civic journalism attitude, as Table 4.23 indicates. Journalists who worked at news magazines or wire service were the least likely to approve, and the larger the journalist's news organization was, the less importance he or she ascribed to these practices. Journalists who said their news organizations conducted a lot of audience research,

TABLE 4.23
Predictors of Approving Civic Journalism Practices
$(R^2 = .41)$ in 2002

	Standardized Regression Coefficients (betas)	Correlation Coefficients
Organizational Context		
Wire services	-.13	-.22
News magazines	-.14	-.26
Newspaper	.11	.19
Staff size	-.09	-.24
Lots of audience research here	.10	.18
Quality of journalism rising here	.08	.10
Newsroom resources shrinking here	.07	.09
Individual Background		
Income	-.09	-.20
Minority	.09	.14
Professionalism		
Influenced by ethics seminars	.11	.29
Important to develop a specialty	.10	.17
Important to help people	.08	.25
Media should influence public opinion	.08	.10
Disseminator function	.15	.31
Interpreter function	.11	.07
Would like more journalistic training	.06	.12
External factors		
Influenced by findings of audience research	.10	.39
Influenced by public opinion polls	.16	.30
Watch network newscasts	.07	.19
Watch Newshour with Jim Lehrer	.07	.08

and who said the quality of their newsroom's journalism was rising despite shrinking resources, tended to support these practices. At a more personal level, journalists of color were more likely than White journalists to approve of civic journalism practices, as were journalists with lower personal incomes.

Journalists who felt it was important to help other people and to develop a specialty in one's work also tended to endorse these practices, as did those who felt that ethics seminars are a strong influence on their sense of what's right and wrong in the newsroom. This type of journalist also identified strongly with both disseminator and interpreter functions of the media. Unsurprisingly, journalists who said their news judgment was influenced by polls and by findings of audience research also accorded importance to these civic journalism practices. Overall, we see a journalist who works at a smaller newspaper or radio or television station and doesn't make a great income, who is optimistic about his or her organization's work, and whose sense of professionalism is altruistic and strongly connected with his or her audience.

CONCLUSIONS

The institutional culture of journalism, never particularly strong, was weaker in 1992 than in the decade previous. Our latest survey in 2002, however, finds the professional culture of journalism to be somewhat stronger. In the 1990s journalists reversed a 20-year trend of declining membership in professional organizations, with 41% now saying they belong to at least one professional organization.

Readership of professional and trade publications, which had also declined in the 1980s, seems to have become stable. And, thanks to the Web, increasing numbers of journalists appear to be exposed to news and commentary about the field. Still, the unmistakable point is that no single professional organization or publication reaches more than a small minority in journalism, unlike other professions such as law, medicine, or accounting, where common literature and professional associations reach far greater numbers. This leaves the institutional culture of the field relatively weak in a time when the professionalism of journalists is challenged almost daily.

Of the 15 journalistic roles we explored in our survey, two—investigating government claims and getting information to the public quickly—have remained dominant in the perceptions of journalists over the years, but significant shifts are apparent. Getting information to the public declined significantly as an "extremely important" role for journalists in traditional media, apparently because of the Internet's strength with immediacy. This shift in journalists' "belief system" was even more evident when the battery of 15 role questions was aggregated into broader, functional clusters. Whereas most journalists continue to perceive the interpretive function as essential to journalistic life, the disseminator function showed significant decline, with only about one in six journalists perceiving it as very important in 2002. The adversarial function remained a minority attitude among journalists, just as it had since it was first measured in 1982–1983. Only about one-fifth of all U.S. journalists perceived the adversary role as very important.

The populist mobilizer function, although still a minority construct in the journalistic belief system, grew in perceived importance in 2002. About 1 in 10 of journalists saw this role as very important. This is clear evidence that the concept of public journalism has established a foothold with a larger minority of journalists. Whereas the more abstract ideas of public journalism seem to have garnered broad support, the organizational methods to implement these ideas received more cautious support. Even at the newsroom level, however, small minorities rejected public journalism strategies outright.

In general, the overall conclusion is that the typical journalist's mindset about journalistic roles is considerably less pluralistic now than it was in the 1980s and 1990s. The majority mindset is now more strongly interpretive than in the last quarter of the 20th century, largely, we think, because of the immense change in

the media landscape caused by the Internet and the number of competing channels of television news. Nevertheless, the dominant interpretive belief system
puts journalism more in line with the recommendations made a half century ago
by the Hutchins Commission on Freedom of the Press.

As in our 1992 study, more organization-related factors emerged as statistically significant "predictors" of journalistic role conceptions than did individual,
professional, or external factors. However, in 2002, media ownership and journalistic income patterns had no effect on the journalistic belief system. Instead,
editorial staff size and type of medium were strong predictors. Journalists on large
staffs were more likely to embrace the interpretive and adversarial roles, whereas
those at smaller news organizations tended to embrace the populist mobilizer
role. Also, journalists working in the print media were more likely to endorse the
adversarial and populist mobilizer roles than were their colleagues in the broadcast sectors.

On the important matter of journalists' development of news judgment—
how the concept of newsworthiness is defined—the findings overall suggest a
dynamic process with several competing influences. The greatest influence,
though, is newsroom training, something over which news managers can exercise
a good deal of control. And the perceived importance of that training on newsworthiness appears to be stronger now than in previous surveys. Other factors—
supervisors, news sources, and peers—are perceived to be of less importance than
newsroom training. The proportions of journalists citing audience research, local
competing media, large newspapers, and broadcast networks as important influences on news judgments continued to decline. Clearly, the more personal contacts of journalists continue to influence their ideas about what is newsworthy.
Newsroom supervisors and peers, as well as news sources, received much more
credit than did the more distant factors of audience research and other media.

Journalistic conceptions about media ethics are affected by four major factors:
newsroom context, family and religion, continuing education, and college experiences. By far the most important, however, is the newsroom context, learning
that takes place in the newsroom, and the interaction with supervisors and peers.
With the influence of the newsroom context as powerful as it is, newsroom managers have both an opportunity and an obligation to provide leadership in raising
journalists' ethical consciousness.

On perceptions of proper ethical practice, the 2002 study suggests significant
decreases in the acceptance of some of the 10 controversial reporting practices
asked about over the years. Specifically, claiming to be someone else and going
"undercover" to get a story are now tolerated by only small minorities of journalists. The proportion of those justifying the naming of rape victims has declined
as well. On the other hand, increases in tolerance appear, over the last 20 years,
for the use of unauthorized documents of all kinds and for badgering unwilling
sources. In general, television journalists are more likely to be tolerant of the
questionable practices, especially the use of hidden cameras and microphones,

than are their colleagues in other media. Editors tend to be less supportive of controversial reporting practices than are reporters.

Overall, our 2002 survey of U.S. journalists suggests somewhat more professionalism among journalists than 10 years ago, including more college graduates, better compensation, increased job satisfaction, and somewhat increased endorsement of the roles of investigating government claims, analyzing complex problems, and being skeptical of business actions. There is also less emphasis on the entertainment role and less willingness to justify a number of controversial reporting methods such as undercover employment and posing as someone else. As in 1992, there is a professional "mood" among U.S. journalists, but its influence resides mainly in individual newsrooms and news organizations, not in the larger institutions of journalism. There is too much variance among individual journalists and news organizations to claim a more professional journalism in the United States in general in 2002.

NOTES

1. Fred Brown, "Ethics Week Brought Plenty of Ethics Discussion," *Quill*, 91, 6 (July 2003), pp. 60–61.
2. Theodore L. Glasser, "Professionalism and the Derision of Diversity: The Case of the Education of Journalists." *Journal of Communication*, 42, 2 (Spring 1992), pp. 131–140.
3. James Bowman, "A Pretense of Professionalism." *New Criterion*, 15, 4 (December 1996), pp. 55–61.
4. Pamela J. Shoemaker and Stephen D. Reese, *Mediating the Message: Theories of Influences on Mass Media Content*, 2nd ed. (White Plains, NY: Longman, 1996).
5. Fred Brown, "A Classic Case of Good Reporter, Bad Reporter," *Quill*, 91, 2 (March 2003), pp. 28–29.
6. Brown, "A Classic Case of Good Reporter, Bad Reporter," pp. 28–29.
7. Stephen D. Reese, "Understanding the Global Journalist A Hierarchy-of-Influences Approach," *Journalism Studies*, 2, 2 (2001), pp. 173–187.
8. Randal A. Beam, "Journalistic Professionalism as an Organizational-Level Concept," *Journalism Monographs*, 121 (June 1990).
9. Richard C. Wald, "How To Worry About the Blair Affair," *Columbia Journalism Review*, 42, 2 (2003), p. 23.
10. Jonathan Alter, "An Erosion of Trust," *Newsweek*, 141, 21 (2003), p. 47.
11. James W. Carey, "Mirror of the *Times*," *Nation*, 276, 23 (2003), p. 13.
12. Linda Rashid, communications coordinator, American Medical Association Unified Service center, e-mail communication October 24, 2003.
13. Tracie Maxley, Market Research Dept., American Bar Association, e-mail communication October 28, 2003.
14. Kim Ellis, communications manager, American Institute of Certified Public Accountants, e-mail communication October 22, 2003.
15. American Association of University Professors, accessed on October 22, 2003, at www.aaup .org/aboutaaup/description.htm
16. Susan E. Tifft, "The Romenesko Factor," *Columbia Journalism Review*, 42, 2 (2003), p. 21.
17. Jay Rosen, *What Are Journalists For?* (New Haven, CT: Yale University Press, 1999).
18. Johnstone, Slawski, and Bowman, *The News People*, p. 102.

19. "Journalism Under Fire," *Time*, December 12, 1983, pp. 76–93.

20. Michael J. O'Neill, "A Problem for the Republic—A Challenge for Editors," address to the American Society of Newspaper Editors, May 5, 1982. Reprinted in *The Adversary Press* (St. Petersburg, FL: Modern Media Institute, 1983), pp. 2–15.

21. Davis (Buzz) Merritt and Jay Rosen, "Imagining Public Journalism: An Editor and Scholar Reflect on the Birth of an Idea," *Roy W. Howard Public Lecture #5* (Bloomington, IN: School of Journalism, April 13, 1995).

22. The Commission on Freedom of the Press, *A Free and Responsible Press* (Chicago: The University of Chicago Press, 1947), pp. 21–22.

23. See, for example, Stephen Bates, *Realigning Journalism with Democracy: The Hutchins Commission, Its Time, and Ours* (Washington, DC: The Annenberg Washington Program in Communications Policy Studies of Northwestern University, 1995).

24. Jane B. Singer, "Changes and Consistencies," *Newspaper Research Journal* 18, 1, (1997), p. 16.

25. Edmund B. Lambeth, "Public Journalism as a Democratic Practice," in E. B. Lambeth, P. E. Meyer, and E. Thorson (Eds.), *Assessing Public Journalism* (Columbia: University of Missouri Press, 1998), p. 17.

26. Lewis Friedland and Sandy Nichols, "High Impact Logged in 600 Civic Projects," *Civic Catalyst*, 4, 6 (Summer 2002), p. 4.

27. See, for example, Doug Underwood, *MBAs in the Newsroom* (New York: Columbia University Press, 1993); and John H. McManus, *Market Driven Journalism* (Thousand Oaks, CA: Sage Publications, 1994).

28. Tim P. Vos, "The Enactment of Journalists' Role Conceptions," paper presented to the Association for Education in Journalism and Mass Communication, August 2002, Miami, FL.

29. The Pew Center's poll results could be found at its Web site: The Pew Research Center: The People and the Press, http://people-press.org/reports/index.php3?TopicID=1

30. Nelson Antrim Crawford, *The Ethics of Journalism* (New York: Alfred A. Knopf, 1924), pp. viii, 114.

31. Conrad C. Fink, *Media Ethics* (Boston: Allyn & Bacon, 1995), p. xiii.

32. Tom Winship, "Whistle Blowers Try to Save Journalism From Itself," *Editor & Publisher*, 131, 30 (July 25, 1998), pp. 3–4.

33. Alexander Cockburn, "The Decline and Fall of American Journalism," *Nation*, 276, 18 (May 5, 2003), p. 9.

34. Daphne Eviatar, "The Press and Private Lynch," *Nation*, 277, 1 (July 7, 2003), pp. 18–20.

35. Howard Good, "We Need Ethics Examples," *Quill*, 89, 3 (April 2001), p. 40.

36. Lorraine E. Branham, "Learning Takes Time," *Quill*, 91, 6 (July 2003), p. 9.

37. Each of the four clusters of influence (newsroom context, family and religion, continuing education, and school experience) was used as the dependent variable in an analysis of 22 possible "predictors" of the strength of each cluster as an influence on ethics. For Newsroom Context, the cumulative $R^2 = .15$. The analysis found these predictors: frequency of communication with reporters (beta = .12); Influence over hiring and firing decisions (beta = .14); Amount of editing done on respondent's own work (beta = .12); Belief that media should influence public opinion (beta = .11); Interpreter role of media (beta = .18), and size of news organization (beta = .11).

38. In the regression on Family and Religion, the cumulative $R^2 = .38$. The analysis found these predictors: Ideology to the right (beta = .18); Socialize with other journalists (beta = -.10), and approve of civic journalism techniques (beta = .18).

39. In the regression on Continuing Education, the cumulative R^2 was .48. The analysis found these predictors: Belong to journalism associations (beta = .16); ethnic minority (beta = .13), approve of civic journalism techniques (beta = .26), and ability to get newsroom follow-up of what the journalist thought was a good story idea (beta = -.12).

40. In the regression on College Experience, the cumulative R^2 was .45. The analysis found these predictors: Large role in deciding play of stories (beta = -.10); Media should influence public

opinion (beta = .07); Socialize with other journalists (beta = .07); age (beta = -.25); journalism/communication major in college (beta = .24), and approve of civic journalism techniques (beta = .11).

41. *Cohen v. Cowles Media Co.*, 501 U.S. 663 (1991).

42. See, for example, the excerpts from various news organizations' codes of conduct regarding unnamed sources, in Jay Black, Bob Steele, and Ralph Barney, *Doing Ethics in Journalism: A Handbook with Case Studies*, 3rd ed. (Boston: Allyn & Bacon, 1999), pp. 283–289.

43. Lou Prato, "Tabloids Force All to Pay for News," *American Journalism Review*, 16(7) (September 1994), p. 56.

44. M. David Arant and Philip Meyer, "A Survey of Daily Newspaper Staff Members," *Nieman Reports*, 51, 3 (Fall 1997), pp. 55–62.

45. Associated Press, "*Cincinnati Enquirer* to pay $10 million to Chiquita," *Wall Street Journal*, June 29, 1998, p. B7, and in other newspapers as well.

46. Alex S. Jones, "Why Do Many Readers Hate Us Again?" *Editor & Publisher*, 135, 31 (Sept. 2, 2002), p. 12.

47. *Food Lion v. Capital Cities/ABC Inc.*, 984 F. Supp. 923 (1997).

48. Susan Paterno, "The Lying Game," *American Journalism Review*, May 1997, pp. 40–45.

49. Shellee Smith, "Shoptalk," *Scripps Howard News*, May/June 1995, p. 15.

50. See, for example, Gerry Lanosga and Kathleen Johnston, "Hidden Camera: Undercover Work Shows Sheriff Drinking, Driving," *IRE Journal*, 25, 3 (May/June 2002), pp. 33, 43.

51. Conrad C. Fink, *Media Ethics* (Boston: Allyn & Bacon, 1995), pp. 252–254.

52. *Florida Star v. B.J.F*, 491 U.S. 524 (1989).

53. Kelly McBride, "Before You Publish a Rape Victim's Name," *American Editor*, April 2003, pp. 24–25.

54. McBride, p. 25.

55. Tanni Haas and Linda Steiner, "Fears of Corporate Colonization in Journalism Reviews' Critiques of Public Journalism," *Journalism Studies*, 3, 3 (2002), pp. 325–341.

56. See, for example, Al Cross, "A Powerful Experiment," *Quill*, 90, 5 (June 2002), pp. 4–5, or Jeffrey D. Mohl, "Changing Times, Changing Needs," *Quill*, 91, 2 (March 2003), p. 3.

57. Walker Lundy, "Civic Journalism 101," *Editor & Publisher*, 136, 17 (April 28, 2003), p. 46.

58. The reliability of this pattern was measured as a Cronbach's alpha of .70.

Chapter 5

Women Journalists

In our 1992 study, we concluded that journalists then were no more likely to be female than a decade earlier, despite dramatic increases in women journalism students in U.S. universities and an emphasis on hiring more women. As we will see in this chapter, women have made some gains since 1992, but in many ways, the picture looks much the same in 2002 as it did a decade earlier.

During the decade of the 1990s, women made some gains in the U.S. workforce at large. According to the 2000 Census,[1] women inched up 1.4 percentage points, to 47% of the civilian workforce of 137.67 million. This means about 64.7 million women were working, up from about 57 million in 1991. (Minorities were up 5 percentage points, from 22% in 1990 to 27% in 2000.) By 2000, as noted in Chapter 1, women accounted for about 30% of lawyers and judges in the country (though only 16% of law partners),[2] about 28% of medical doctors, 23% of architects, and 19% of dentists.[3] As we saw in Chapter 1, women made up a third of the overall news media workforce, the same as a decade earlier.

Even as women advanced as participants in the workforce at large and in the professions, there were signs that no revolution was under way and that, in some cases, women were opting out of advancement as defined by supervisory and management positions and the higher salaries that go along with these positions.[4]

BACKGROUNDS

Education

The gap in formal education between men and women journalists—significant 30 years ago—had closed by 2002. At the same time, the level of education for

TABLE 5.1
Amount of Formal Education of U.S. Journalists (Percentage in Each Category)

Highest Educational Attainment	1971[a]		1982–1983[b]		1992[c]		2002	
	Men	Women	Men	Women	Men	Women	Men	Women
Some high school	2.0	1.3	0.6	—	—	0.3	0.0	0.0
High school graduate	10.6	18.4	6.2	10.1	3.6	5.4	1.8	1.8
Some college	27.4	29.5	19.1	16.3	15.0	11.0	9.2	8.2
College graduate	41.4	32.6	53.6	57.3	63.5	66.5	68.0	68.1
Some graduate training	10.2	11.6	8.3	9.2	6.3	5.9	4.4	5.3
Graduate degree	8.4	6.6	12.1	7.1	11.7	11.0	16.6	16.6

[a] From Bowman, *Distaff Journalists*, p. 132.
[b] From Weaver and Wilhoit, *The American Journalist*, 2nd ed., p. 166.
[c] From Weaver and Wilhoit, *The American Journalist in the 1990s*, p. 178.

both men and women had increased. As noted in Chapter 1, a college degree is virtually a requirement for journalism work in the 21st century. In 2002, 89% of male journalists and 90% of female journalists held a college degree, had some graduate training, or held a graduate degree. The comparable figures from earlier decades are shown in Table 5.1.

By 2002, 56% of students enrolled in U.S. colleges and universities and 64% of students in America's journalism programs were women.[5] While women have been a majority in undergraduate programs since at least 1977–1978, they now approach two-thirds of journalism programs' graduation figures. According to the University of Georgia's 2002 national survey of journalism and mass communication enrollments, 64.6% of the bachelor's degrees, 64.2% of the master's degrees, and 50.3% of the doctoral degrees were awarded to women.[6] Journalism and mass communication programs have broadened their scope over the years, and an increasing percentage of students plan careers in public relations or advertising—not in news.

Becker's 2002 study found that of the graduates, women were more likely than men to say they wanted careers in public relations (29% of women and 20% of men), and about a quarter of all journalism and mass communication graduates said they wanted careers in advertising. That means that less than half of the women who attend these programs plan careers in news, and slightly more than half of the men do.

Race and Ethnicity

As was true in 1992, among racial and ethnic minorities women made up a larger percentage of each of the groups measured than the 33% figure for all journalists and the 31.5% figure for non-Hispanic White journalists. Compared to a decade ago, however, only African American and Asian American journalists showed a slight increase: In 2002, 54.1% of African American journalists were women, compared with 53.2% in 1992, and 55.5% of Asian American journalists were women, compared with 52.5% in 1992.

There were some slight declines among the other groups: In 2002, 46.2% of Hispanic journalists were women, compared with 48.1% in 1992, and 38.9% of Native American journalists were women, compared with 42.9% in 1992. Among non-Hispanic White journalists, 31.5% were women in 2002, as compared with 33.3% in 1992. As was true in 1992, increasing the number of racial and ethnic minorities in mainstream news media seems likely to also result in an increase in women, especially among African American and Asian American journalists.

Family Life

We noted that by 1992, women had made some gains in balancing family life with a journalistic career but that differences persisted between men and women in family life measures. Those differences continued in 2002. Men were more likely to be married than were women (67% of men were married, compared with 48% of women). These figures are nearly identical to those of 1992: 65% of men were married then, and 48% of women were. In 2002, nearly 10% of women, but only 4% of men, reported being "unmarried but living with a partner." Nearly a third of women (32.5%) said they had children living at home, up from 28% in 1992. Almost half (46%) of men had children at home, up slightly from 44% in 1992. Change toward a sort of equality in family life seems to be occurring, but the pace seems more glacial than revolutionary.

Age

As in 1992, the largest increase in women journalists in 2002 was in the youngest age group (see Table 1.7). Women made up 60% of the under-25 journalism workforce, and, for the first time, they reached more than 40% of the 25–34 age group (at 45%), suggesting an increase in retention of women over time. Beyond age 34, however, the percentage of women remained low (and much below the labor force in general), and, unlike 1992, the 2002 survey found drops in both the 35–44 and 45–54 age groups. Indeed, in this latter group, the percentage of women in the journalistic workforce, 23.8%, is comparable to that in 1971, when it was 22.5%.

The one group where increases continued was the 55–64 age group, where, in 2002, a third of the journalists were women. This increase suggests that some women may return to journalism, perhaps after a career change or interruption for family or other reasons, or that a dedicated core group of women finish their careers in journalism whereas a growing number of younger women leave to pursue work in other fields. Without having panel data on the same women over time, it's not possible to directly test these speculations.

JOBS

Work Experience

We measured the proportion of women journalists in the workforce by age group and also by years of experience. As Figure 1.1 in Chapter 1 shows, with the exception of the lowest level of experience (0–4 years), women continued to lag behind men in each group. The 2002 figures, in fact, are much the same as those in 1992, with women making up 41.2% of the 5–9 year group, 34.4% of the 10–14 year group, and a quarter of the 15–19 year group. It's at the 0–4 year group where women, for the first time, surpass men, at 54.2%.

Paired with the figures for age (previous section), these years-of-experience figures suggest that more women are hired early and are perhaps staying with journalism a bit longer but are, as in past decades, leaving journalism at about the same rate.

News Medium

The proportion of women journalists in each news medium has varied over the years. The biggest jump, in all news media, occurred between 1971 and 1982–1983. The 2002 data generally showed a drop in the proportion of women in the various media, as Table 1.6 indicates. The one exception was television news, where women made up 37% of TV journalists in 2002, compared with 25% in 1992. (Women were at about a third in the 1982–1983 survey, so the 2002 figures show a bit of a gain over the 1980s.) As Table 1.6 shows, the percentage of women dropped in radio, wire services and weekly newspapers from 1992 to 2002 but remained about the same in news magazines and daily newspapers.

Income

As median salaries increased over the decade, the salary gap between men and women remained the same in 2001 as it was in 1991: The median salary for women was 81% of men's median salary. The gap, which narrowed 17 percentage points from 1970 to 1991, is largely explained by years of experience. Men and women with 15 or fewer years of experience have comparable salaries as Figure 3.7 shows. For those with 15 to 19 years of experience, the gap is $4,444. Among those with 20 or more years of experience, the gap widens to $7,265.

As we saw in Chapter 3 (Table 3.18), the difference between men's and women's salaries is partially explained by a number of factors. Women tend to have fewer years of experience, work for smaller news organizations, and be less likely than men to be managers. These factors all were associated with lower salaries, but even after controlling for all of these and others statistically, being female was still a statistically significant predictor of lower income.

Managerial Influence

Are women shying from positions in management? Some studies from the late 1990s and early years of the 21st century suggest many are.[7] Our study found a decrease in the percentage of women in supervisory roles, if not in all areas of managerial influence.

The gains women made during the 1980s appear to largely have been lost by 2002. In 1992, 41% of women journalists said they supervised news or editorial employees (43% of men identified themselves as having supervisory roles); in 2002, only one-third (34%) of women said they supervised, as compared to 45% of men.

At the same time, there may be some differences among the media. For example, data collected by the Media Management Center at Northwestern University in 2002 shows a marked increase in the number of women publishers at daily newspapers with a circulation of more than 85,000—18% in 2002, compared with 14% in 2001 and just 8% in 2000.[8] The same study found women editors at 22% in 2002, compared with 25% of senior managers and 28% of junior managers in our 2002 study (see Table 3.4).

Our own data from 2002 show some definite differences among news media, with 30% of the women at daily newspapers supervising other newsroom employees, 39% at weekly newspapers, 33% at television stations, 26% at news magazines, 43% at news-service bureaus, and 50% at radio stations.

In terms of perceived influence on hiring and firing, Table 5.2 shows that women, as in previous years, were less likely than men to think they had "a great

TABLE 5.2
Male and Female Newsroom Managers' Perceived Influence on Hiring
(Percentage in Each Category)

	1992				2002			
	Print		Broadcast		Print		Broadcast	
Influence	Men (n = 253)	Women (n = 128)	Men (n = 74)	Women (n = 33)	Men (n = 260)	Women (n = 96)	Men (n = 82)	Women (n = 31)
A great deal	39.9	35.2	40.5	21.2	45.4	37.5	46.3	38.7
Some	20.9	22.7	20.3	27.3	23.1	30.2	28.0	19.4
A little	18.2	16.4	25.7	27.3	17.3	17.7	14.6	12.9
None at all	20.9	25.8	13.5	24.2	14.2	14.6	11.0	29.0

deal" of influence on hiring and firing decisions. In contrast to 1982–1983 and 1992, however, women in broadcast management positions were as likely as women in print managerial positions (38.7% and 37.5%) to perceive such influence. Women still trailed men overall, however, despite a notable gain in broadcast newsrooms from 1992 to 2002. More than one-quarter (29%) of women broadcast managers said they had no influence at all in hiring and firing decisions, compared with only 11% of men.

In print media, however, the percentages of men and women who thought they had no, or only a little, influence were identical, and women were more likely than men to perceive some influence on hiring and firing, suggesting an increase in women holding positions of more managerial responsibility in print media during the decade of the 1990s.

Editorial Influence

For men and women, in both print and broadcast newsrooms, the decade between 1992 and 2002 brought a decline in perceived freedom to determine selection of stories, as Table 5.3 shows. Whereas in 1992, women in broadcast journalism were more likely than men to say they "almost always" could select the stories they worked on, by 2002, men were more likely than women to say this (40% of men, compared with only 31% of women).

Likewise, both men and women in print media experienced a drop in perceived freedom to select the stories they work on. In 1992, 46% of women in print journalism said they "almost always" could choose the stories they worked on, but that figure had dropped to about 40% in 2002; for men, the comparable figures were 47.5% in 1992 and 35% in 2002.

In 2002, combining the top two categories ("a great deal" and "almost complete" freedom), the figures come to about 80% for both men and women in print

TABLE 5.3
Amount of Freedom Men and Women Had in Being Able to Select Stories
(Percentage in Each Category)

	1992[a]				2002			
	Print		Broadcast		Print		Broadcast	
Amount of Freedom	Men (n = 583)	Women (n = 328)	Men (n = 172)	Women (n = 63)	Men (n = 580)	Women (n = 291)	Men (n = 184)	Women (n = 84)
Almost complete	47.5	46.0	44.8	54.0	35.0	39.9	39.7	31.0
A great deal	37.7	36.6	43.0	39.7	45.2	38.8	41.3	35.7
Some	14.1	16.8	11.6	6.3	17.9	16.2	17.4	31.0
None at all	0.7	0.6	0.6	0.0	1.9	5.2	1.6	2.4

[a] Question wording in 1992 was "How often are you able to select the stories you work on?" with categories "almost always," "more often than not," "only occasionally," and "don't make such proposals."

journalism. In broadcast journalism, however, men seemed to have more autonomy than did women—81% of men said they had either "a great deal" or "almost complete" freedom to select stories compared with only two-thirds of women.

Table 5.4 suggests that women broadcast managers lost a little ground in the last decade in terms of the amount of editing they did, whereas men held steady. Women had made a significant jump between 1982–1983 and 1992, from about 20% to 35% saying they did "a great deal" of editing, but the figure for 2002 was 30%. Male newsroom managers in broadcast, meantime, still trailed women, with 23% saying they did "a great deal" of editing. The 2002 figures for print media male and female managers were comparable to those of a decade earlier—40% of women and 36% of men said they did a great deal of editing—but notably higher than those for broadcast managers, as was generally true in 1992. In addition, women print managers were notably more likely to say they did "some" editing in 2002 than in 1992 and less likely to say they did "none at all," suggesting that women made some gains in print media editing positions during the 1990s.

The 2002 data suggest a continuing decline in perceived editorial autonomy among those with editing duties, as well as with those just described. Women editors in the print media were a bit less likely than men to think they had almost complete freedom in deciding how to use stories written by others, but in the broadcast media, women were much less likely to think this, as Table 5.5 shows. In both print and broadcast news media, the percentage of women saying they had almost complete freedom in determining how stories would be used dropped considerably from 1992 to 2002, but men fared better, increasing slightly in print and notably (from 25% to 36%) in broadcast news. Male editors perceived considerably more freedom than women in broadcast, with about three-quarters of men in broadcast media saying they had almost complete or a great deal of freedom in deciding how stories would be used, as compared with only half of the women with editing duties. The figures for print were more comparable—half of men versus 43% of women.

TABLE 5.4
Amount of Editing Performed by Male and Female Newsroom Managers
(Percentage in Each Category)

	1992				2002			
	Print		Broadcast		Print		Broadcast	
Amount of Editing	Men (n = 585)	Women (n = 329)	Men (n = 173)	Women (n = 63)	Men (n = 584)	Women (n = 295)	Men (n = 184)	Women (n = 84)
A great deal	39.1	42.6	20.8	34.9	36.3	39.3	22.8	29.8
Some	37.1	29.5	60.1	41.3	40.8	39.3	51.1	50.0
None at all	23.8	28.0	19.1	23.8	22.9	21.4	26.1	20.2

Job Dimensions

While the overall ranking of job dimensions didn't change much in the decade between 1992 and 2002, some shifting occurred, as Table 5.6 shows. Pay and fringe benefits remained at the bottom of the rankings for both men and women, with fringe benefits being seen as "very important" to a larger percentage of both men and women than pay. Less than a fifth of men and women said pay was "very important," and a little more than a quarter of each group saw fringe benefits as very important. But for both men and women, these dimensions of work declined in importance over the decade.

TABLE 5.5
Amount of Freedom Men and Women With Editing Duties Had in Deciding
How Stories Would Be Used (Percentage in Each Category)

| | 1992 | | | | 2002 | | | |
| | Print | | Broadcast | | Print | | Broadcast | |
Amount of Freedom	Men (n = 428)	Women (n = 230)	Men (n = 138)	Women (n = 48)	Men (n = 443)	Women (n = 227)	Men (n = 135)	Women (n = 65)
Almost complete	15.9	21.3	24.6	41.7	18.1	12.8	35.6	18.5
A great deal of	33.9	33.0	30.4	37.5	32.2	30.4	39.3	32.3
Some	35.3	28.3	37.0	16.1	31.8	33.5	18.5	33.8
None at all	15.0	17.4	8.0	4.2	17.8	23.3	6.7	15.4

TABLE 5.6
Importance of Job Dimensions for Journalists
(Percentage Who Rated Each Dimension Very Important)

| | 1971 | | 1982–1983 | | 1992 | | 2002 | |
Dimension	Men	Women	Men	Women	Men	Women	Men	Women
Pay	28.7	15.3	24.5	18.9	22.2	19.7	18.3	15.6
Fringe benefits	25.6	23.3	25.8	25.1	33.2	37.7	28.4	29.8
Chance to get ahead in the organization	52.4	38.7	43.9	52.8	38.3	40.5	32.9	40.1
Job security	50.9	52.5	56.6	57.7	62.3	58.1	58.3	56.3
Chance to develop a specialty	43.5	48.8	41.9	50.4	38.9	41.9	37.5	46.7
Chance to help people	65.0	73.1	56.6	68.9	57.2	67.9	57.8	73.9
Editorial policies of the organization	48.9	62.3	54.1	62.3	66.8	71.8	66.3	75.1
Freedom from supervision	52.4	54.8	38.1	39.3	—[a]	—[a]	—[a]	—[a]
Amount of autonomy	55.4	54.9	50.1	51.1	49.1	54.5	54.9	59.5
Chance to influence public affairs	—[a]	—[a]	—[a]	—[a]	—[a]	—[a]	35.9	44.1

[a] Not asked in this year.

The editorial policies of their news organizations were "very important" for the largest percentages of both men and women (for 75% of women and 66% of men). A chance to help people has remained highly important over the decades for both genders, though more so for women. In 2002, nearly three-quarters of women said this dimension was very important, compared with 58% of men.

Although job security has remained important for men and women over time, a decreasing percentage of men see having a chance to get ahead in the organization as very important (just a third in 2002 as compared with half in 1971, 44% in 1982, and 38% in 1992), perhaps because male journalists tend to be older on average (median age of 42, compared to 35 for women) and to have achieved higher positions. By contrast, 40% of women in 2002 said advancement was very important to them, about the same percentage as in 1992.

Job Satisfaction

Chapter 3 analyzes various factors that contribute to job satisfaction for journalists. Although journalists, in general, expressed a higher level of satisfaction with their work in 2002 than they did a decade earlier, the intensity of satisfaction varied somewhat based on a number of conditions. (We measured satisfaction directly, by asking how satisfied the respondent was, and indirectly, by asking whether he or she planned to remain in journalism "in 5 years." We also asked an open-ended question to allow respondents to elaborate.)

As Figure 3.8 in Chapter 3 shows, women were slightly less satisfied with their jobs than were men — 79% of women said they were either "very" or "fairly" satisfied, as compared with 87% of men, but both men and women were, on balance, much more satisfied than dissatisfied with their work as journalists. Women were also a bit more likely to say they planned to leave journalism within 5 years. One-fifth of women (21%) said they planned to leave, compared with 16% of men, slightly less than in 1992 when 25% of the women and 21% of the men said they would like to be working outside the news media in 5 years. But, again, both men and women were much more likely to plan to stay in journalism than to leave in the next 5 years.

Why did one-fifth of women journalists say they planned to leave journalism? We asked an open-ended question about this, and the reasons varied, some having to do with changing practices of the field, some with more personal issues. One woman journalist put it this way: "Because it's not the profession that it was when I went into it. . . . It has lost . . . what I regard as a sense of honor. I feel it's become more concerned now with the bottom line, not the truth." Said another: "It is very stressful; it's demanding. [It] takes a lot of energy, and at times it's pretty discouraging. I think a lot of newspapers are being homogenized into a corporate identity."

A Hispanic female journalist said this: "I think as a published author, I could be more independent and not be controlled by whoever is the one that is controlling the media. As an author, it's just you and whatever you can say. It's not easy to publish, but if you can do it, it would be a lot freer." An African American female journalist said: "It gets old: the schedules, the news business becomes your life. As fulfilling as it may seem, you miss out on things in your life."

Satisfaction with one's work in journalism, as we saw in Chapter 3 (Table 3.23), was linked to a number of factors having to do with both the workplace and medium and with personal characteristics. Gender, apart from other characteristics, was not a significant predictor of job satisfaction once other possible predictors were controlled statistically. That means that rather than being attributed to gender, the apparent differences we see were more attributable to such things as size and ownership of the media organization, feelings about the performance of the news organization in informing the public, beliefs about the quality of journalism at one's organization, perceived autonomy and clout, years of experience, and income.

PROFESSIONAL VALUES

Role Perceptions

Over the decades, there has been a consistency of ratings of various roles of the media, both for men and women, and between men and women (Table 5.7). The largest differences between men and women were in their views about the role of the media in providing analysis of complex problems (women, at 57%, were more likely than men, at 48%, to see this as extremely important) and getting information to the public quickly. Women were, again, more likely to view this as extremely important than were men: 63% to 57%.

TABLE 5.7
The Importance Journalists Assigned to Various Mass Media Roles
(Percentage Who Rated Each Role Extremely Important)

Role	1982–1983		1992		2002	
	Men	Women	Men	Women	Men	Women
Investigate government claims	64.0	68.6	68.1	64.8	69.0	73.4
Get information to public quickly	57.8	63.3	67.5	70.7	56.7	63.1
Avoid stories with unverified content	45.8	58.0	47.3	52.1	50.4	55.3
Provide analysis of complex problems	49.2	49.1	48.9	47.1	47.9	57.0
Discuss national policy	39.5	39.6	39.5	37.2	40.2	39.9
Develop intellectual/cultural interests	23.5	25.7	17.7	19.7	15.8	19.3
Provide entertainment and relaxation	18.2	23.1	15.3	11.5	10.8	9.8
Serve as an adversary of government	21.0	18.7	22.2	19.6	20.4	19.4
Serve as an adversary of business	15.1	16.0	14.7	14.0	17.7	17.2

As in earlier studies, sizable majorities of both men and women journalists have rated investigating government claims as being "extremely important," although in 2002, women were more likely than men—and much more likely than they were a decade ago—to say so. The role least likely to be rated as important, again for both men and women, was providing entertainment and relaxation. This role seems to lose importance by the decade as the entertainment content of various media seems to increase. Men and women rated the adversarial role of journalism, whether toward government or toward business, about the same, as Table 5.7 indicates.

Ethical Standards

Ethical lapses make the news, and the past decade has seen its share of lapses, with cases of fabrication and plagiarism perhaps chief among them, as noted in Chapter 4's discussion of the Jayson Blair case at *The New York Times* and the Stephen Glass fabrications at *The New Republic*.

The American Journalist studies have tracked journalists' views of various reporting practices over time since 1982–1983. As noted in Chapter 4 (Table 4.11), among all journalists in our study, there was a drop in perceived acceptability of a number of practices between 1992 and 2002, including using personal documents without permission, claiming to be someone else, getting employed in a firm or organization to gain inside information, and disclosing the names of rape victims.

Similar to 1992, the 2002 findings in Table 5.8 show minimal differences by gender in journalists' opinions about numerous reporting methods, even for the reporting of the names of rape victims. The rankings for men and for women were

TABLE 5.8
Journalists' Opinions on Reporting Practices (Percentage
Saying Each Practice May Be Justified on Occasion)

Reporting Practices	Men (n = 768)	Women (n = 379)[a]
Using confidential business or government documents without authorization	79.2	74.9
Getting employed to gain inside information	54.2	52.1
Using hidden microphones or cameras	60.1	58.8
Badgering unwilling informants to get a story	52.3	51.5
Using personal letters and photographs without permission	42.7	37.7
Disclosing names of rape victims	36.8	33.6
Using re-creations of news by actors	27.6	30.7
Claiming to be somebody else	13.8	15.1
Paying for confidential information	18.7	14.3
Agreeing to protect confidentiality and not doing so	8.7	4.8

[a] Ns vary slightly by item. The largest Ns are reported here.

identical for the four practices ranked as most likely to be "justified on occasion" if the situation involved was an "important story," though women were slightly less likely than men to say each of these was justifiable.

The rankings of men and women were also identical for the next three practices — using personal letters and photographs without permission, disclosing the names of rape victims, and using re-creations of news by actors — although less than a majority of both men and women saw these as possibly justifiable. As in past studies, the least justifiable practice, to both men and women, was going back on a promise to a source of confidentiality, and women were slightly less willing than men to say that this might be justified. This was one of the few practices where there was a slight increase from the 1992 figures for both men and women, however.

The largest changes from 1992 for women journalists were in the decline of those willing to justify getting employed to gain inside information, using personal letters and photographs without permission, disclosing the names of rape victims, and claiming to be someone else. For men, the largest declines were for getting employed to gain inside information, disclosing the names of rape victims, and claiming to be someone else. These declines suggest some agreement among both men and women journalists about stricter ethical standards of reporting based on undercover employment, the naming of rape victims, and impersonation.

CONCLUSIONS

It's clear that women have made significant gains in journalism over the 30 years of the American Journalist studies. The last decade has seen some change, though perhaps not as much progress as many might have predicted.

Backgrounds

Women now make up the majority of U.S. college graduates and a significant majority of journalism and mass communication majors and graduates. By 2002, women and men were entering news media positions at about the same rate. Women were not, however, staying in at levels at all comparable to men. Overall, women made up one-third of the media workforce, the same as in 1992. But the representation of women, as in the past, diminished with years of experience. That is, when one looks at people with the most years of experience, there are many fewer women than there are men. (See Figure 1.1 in Chapter 1.)

Women were better represented among each of the minority journalist groups than in the majority White group. More than half of the Asian and Black journalists were women in 2002, and nearly half of the Hispanic journalists were women. Increasing the number of minority journalists is likely to increase the number of women journalists at the same time.

By 2002, women journalists were still less likely than men to be married and to have children. Journalism is certainly not alone among the professions in not being particularly conducive to traditional family life. Our longitudinal data suggest that time has not served to greatly improve family-life dimensions of news journalists.

Occupational Experience

The income gap between men and women remained the same in 2002 as it was in 1992: Women made 81% of what men made. It's notable that entry salaries for men and women are comparable, however, and when other predictors (size of organization, years of experience, managerial responsibilities) are held constant, the pay gap is virtually gone. What is significant, though, is that these other predictors are indicators that women are leaving—opting out—before they achieve the years of experience and managerial responsibilities that lead to higher salaries.

During the years of the American Journalist studies, women have had a larger presence in news magazines and weekly newspapers than in the other media. In 2002, news magazines remained the medium with the largest percentage of women, and women regained some of the ground they'd lost in television news.

Women continued to have less influence in newsrooms than men. They held fewer supervisory roles and reported somewhat less autonomy than men in making various editorial decisions. At the same time, satisfaction levels for both men and women increased over the decade from a low in the early 1990s. Differences between men and women—women were slightly less satisfied with their jobs and a bit more likely than men to say they planned to leave the profession—were explained less by gender than by other workplace factors.

Professional Roles and Ethics

As in earlier studies, the 2002 survey data show only slight differences between men and women in terms of their views of journalistic roles and ethical practices. Women were a bit more likely than men to think that a number of media roles were extremely important (investigating government claims, getting information to the public quickly, avoiding stories with unverified content, and providing analysis of complex problems), but women's ranking of these roles in relation to one another was nearly identical to that of men.

In terms of the ethics of various questionable reporting practices, men and women were very close in the percentages saying that each practice might be justified in the case of an important story, and the rankings from most to least acceptable were identical for the first seven and nearly identical for the remaining three practices. There were notable drops in the percentages from 1992 to 2002 who considered a number of the practices justifiable, and these declines suggest some agreement among both men and women journalists about stricter ethical standards of reporting.

It's clear from Chapter 4 that the stronger predictors of which roles journalists consider most important and which reporting practices they consider most justifiable do not include gender. In fact, most are measures of organizational context, such as type of medium, type of ownership, size of newsroom, type of position (editor, reporter, etc.), feedback from others in the newsroom, and perceptions of how well the organization performs, the political leanings of the organization, and the amount of freedom a journalist has. The next most numerous predictors of roles and reporting ethics are journalistic attitudes about the different dimensions of their jobs, followed by external factors, such as frequency of audience and news source feedback, the influence of friends and family and religion, and the influence of other news media. Among individual-level predictors, only educational level, political views, type of college, major in college, and age were significant.

As in our 1982–1983 and 1992 studies, these findings raise the question of whether news coverage is likely to change much as more women enter journalism and assume positions of increasing responsibility. Our studies, and those of others such as Beam, Hirsch, and Shoemaker and Reese, have found that most journalists work within the constraints of specific news organizations.[9] As such, most realize that they must meet organizational, occupational, and audience expectations. In addition, the news organizations within which journalists work are influenced by external societal and cultural environments. Given these layers of influences, it was not too surprising that, once again, we found that gender did not correlate strongly with beliefs about the roles and ethics of journalistic work. But gender may matter more in the long run in changing the nature of news organizations and specific news coverage than in changing the more abstract attitudes and beliefs that were measured in this survey, as Kay Mills has suggested.[10]

NOTES

1. D'Vera Cohn and Sarah Cohen, "The Doors to Professions Widen," *The Washington Post National Weekly Edition*, January 5–11, 2004, p. 31.
2. Lisa Belkin, "The Opt-Out Revolution," *The New York Times Sunday Magazine*, October 26, 2003, accessed October 30, 2003, at http://www.nytimes.com/2003/10/26/magazine/26WOMEN.html?pagewanted-print&position=
3. U.S. Bureau of the Census, *Statistical Abstract of the United States 2001* (Washington, DC: U.S. Government Printing Office, 2001), p. 380.
4. Lisa Belkin, "The Opt-Out Revolution."
5. Lee B. Becker, "Gender Equity Elusive, Surveys Show," accessed January 2, 2004, at http://www.freedomforum.org/templates/document.asp?documentID=17784
6. Tudor Vlad, Lee B. Becker, Jisu Huh, and Nancy R. Mace, "2002 Annual Survey of Journalism & Mass Communication Enrollments," presented at the 2003 convention of the Association for Education in Journalism & Mass Communication, August 1, 2003, Tables 17, 18, and 19. See also the following Web site: www.grady.uga.edu/annualsurveys/

7. Lisa Belkin, "The Opt-Out Revolution," and Laura D'Andrea Tyson, "New Clues to the Pay and Leadership Gap," *Business Week*, October 27, 2003, p. 36.

8. Joe Strupp, "Women Take the Reins," *Editor & Publisher*, November 3, 2003, accessed November 21, 2003, at http://www.editorandpublisher.com/editorandpublisher/features_columns/article_display.jsp?vnu_content_id=2030399

9. Randal A. Beam, "Journalistic Professionalism as an Organizational Level Concept," *Journalism Monographs*, 121 (June 1990); Paul M. Hirsch, "Occupational, Organizational, and Institutional Models in Mass Media Research," in Paul M. Hirsch, Peter V. Miller, and F. Gerald Kline (Eds.), *Strategies for Communication Research* (Beverly Hills, CA: Sage, 1977); Pamela J. Shoemaker and Stephen D. Reese, *Mediating the Message: Theories of Influences on Mass Media Content*, 2nd ed. (White Plains, NY: Longman, 1996).

10. Kay Mills, "What Difference Do Women Journalists Make?" In Pippa Norris (Ed.), *Women, Media, and Politics* (New York: Oxford University Press, 1997), pp. 41–55.

Chapter 6

Minority Journalists

Diversifying newsrooms by race and ethnic background has remained a major challenge for U.S. news organizations, and numerous studies during the decade have attempted to identify both doors and barriers to the hiring and retention of journalists of color.

In Chapter 1, we reported a slight increase in minority representation in the U.S. mainstream news media, from 8.2% in 1992 to 9.5% in 2002. The percentage was still well below the overall percentage of minorities in the United States (30.9%, according to the 2000 U.S. Census). Even considering only those with a four-year college degree—effectively a minimum requirement for U.S. journalists—the percentage of minorities still lagged. Twenty-four percent of minorities nationwide held college degrees in 2000. Further, given the general downsizing of news organizations in recent years and the thin pipeline of minority journalists provided by journalism programs around the nation, the challenge for improving these percentages remains formidable.

The representation of journalists of color looks far better if years of experience are considered. As we saw in Chapter 1, 16.9% of journalists with 0 to 4 years of experience were racial or ethnic minorities, far higher than the 9.5% overall, but the percentages for those with more years of experience show that retention remains a problem (see Figure 1.2).

Chapter 1 also looked at minority representation by type of news medium and reported that in all media, except radio, the percentage of minorities increased between 1992 and 2002. Daily newspaper representation rose by 2 percentage points, to 9.6%. Figure 1.3 in Chapter 1 shows that the lowest representation, as in 1992, was in weekly newspapers, where minorities made up 5.6% of the workforce, still a notable increase from 1.9% in 1992. The largest representation, in television, at 14.7%, is consistent with representation of minorities in college journalism programs.[1] In addition, the 2002 annual national survey of journalism and mass communication graduates by Lee Becker and colleagues found that minority students were considerably more likely to seek jobs in television (28%) than in any other news medium (daily newspapers were second at 22%) and also more likely than nonminority students (21%) to look for jobs in television.[2]

BACKGROUNDS

Generalizing between White journalists and minority journalists as a single group can be misleading because, in a number of areas, the variation among minority groups themselves is significant.[3] Taken as a whole, however, minority journalists were more likely to be female than the majority, less likely to be Republican or Republican-leaning, more likely to be younger and more likely to work for larger news organizations (except for Native Americans) and to be members of a journalism organization.[4]

To get a sense of some characteristics of minority journalists, we present a brief description of a "typical" news worker from each of the groups we surveyed.

The "typical" African American journalist was female, Protestant, a college-degree holder, either married or single and living with a partner, a Democrat earning a median salary of $53,333 a year, a member of at least one journalistic organization, and an employee of a large (an average of 153 news people), group-owned organization.

The "typical" Asian American journalist was also female, the holder of at least a bachelor's degree and more likely than any other group to hold a graduate degree, not affiliated with any religion, married or living with a partner, a Democrat, someone with fewer than 10 years of journalistic experience, a median salary of $52,300, a member of at least one journalistic organization, and an employee of a very large (an average of 308 news people), group-owned organization.

The "typical" Hispanic journalist was male, the holder of a bachelor's degree, married or living with a partner, someone with more than 10 years of experience, a median salary of $49,167, Catholic, a member of a journalistic organization, and an employee of a large (an average of 185 news people), group-owned organization.

Finally, the "typical" Native American journalist was a male, married or living with a partner, a bit older and with more years in the profession than the other minority groups but also with a lower median salary ($37,300), not a member of a mainline religion but a member of a journalistic organization, and a worker in a small (an average of 65 news people) news organization that was not owned by a larger corporation.

Let's look at some further details.

TABLE 6.1
Amount of Formal Education of U.S. Journalists
(Percentage in Each Category)

Highest Educational Attainment	Minorities (n = 310)	Non-Hispanic White (n = 1,072)
Some high school	0.0	0.0
High school graduate	0.3	1.9
Some college	11.3	8.3
College graduate	64.8	67.8
Some graduate training	5.2	4.9
Graduate degree	18.4	17.1

Education

Table 6.1 shows that slightly fewer journalists of color held college degrees in 2002 than did white majority journalists, but minority journalists were slightly more likely to hold a graduate degree. Overall, the formal education level, for both majority and minority journalists, has increased over time, so that by 2002, nearly 90% of all journalists held at least a college degree and about 17% held a graduate degree.

There were some differences among the individual minority groups, however. Native Americans and Asian Americans were less likely to have taken courses in journalism as undergraduates (60% and 64%, respectively) than others (from 72% for Whites to 77% for Hispanics and African Americans). Native American and Hispanic journalists were less likely than the others to have gone to private undergraduate schools (11% and 22% to private schools vs. 39% and 44% for Asian Americans and African Americans, respectively), and Native Americans were less likely than the others to have earned a master's degree (none of the Native American journalists held master's degrees, as compared with 15% of Hispanics and 21%–24% of Asian Americans and African Americans).

Overall, the percentage of minority and majority journalists who held graduate degrees (MAs or PhDs) in 2002 was considerably higher than a decade earlier. Although the figure for minorities as a group was 18.4%, that number masks the differences between groups from 2.8% for Native American journalists to 24.5% for Asian American journalists. Among majority Whites, 17.1% held a graduate degree of some kind. As in 1992, journalists of color, with the exception of Native Americans, were somewhat more likely than majority journalists to have attended an Ivy League college at both undergraduate and graduate levels.

Continuing Education

Minority journalists as a group (85%–90%, up from 70%–80% a decade ago) were more likely than majority journalists (75%, up from 60% in 1992) to say they would like additional training in journalism. African American journalists were more likely than others (80% vs. 64%–69%) to have taken courses or workshops since becoming a journalist. Overall, interest in improving one's professional skills has increased, with minority journalists expressing the most interest and, correspondingly, taking the most advantage of formal programs.

Family Life

As a group, journalists of color were less likely than majority journalists to be married, as in 1992. Minority journalists were also more likely to be women and more likely to be younger than the majority journalists. Among the groups, 46% to 53% were married (54%–58% were either married or living with a partner), as compared with 63% of Whites (69% of Whites were either married or living with a partner). The most likely of the minority groups to be married were Native Americans (53%).

Native Americans were also the most likely of the minority groups to have children living at home (44%, similar to 42% for Whites), and Asian Americans were least likely, at 29%. Asian Americans and African Americans were more likely than the other groups to be female (about 55%).

Age

Overall, the U.S. news worker population is aging. Whereas in 1992 the median age of majority journalists was 37, the comparable figure in 2002 was 42. That figure was higher than for any of the minority journalists, except Native Americans, whose median age was 43. Median ages for the other groups ranged from 36 for Asian Americans to 39 for Hispanics to 41 for African Americans. The relatively low median age, 36, for Asian Americans suggests that journalism has been attracting more young members of that group in recent years.

JOBS

Work Experience

In 1992, journalists of color were more likely than Whites to have 10 or fewer years of experience, about as likely to have 11 to 15 years of experience, and much less likely to have more than 15 years of experience. By 2002, it appeared as if minorities who had begun their careers earlier were staying in journalism longer. That is, whereas the minorities were still more likely to have 10 or fewer years of experience and were about as likely to have 11 to 15 years of experience, they were *more* likely to have 16 to 20 years of experience (Table 6.2).

It is not yet clear whether this persistence will continue. In 2002, minority journalists were still less likely than Whites to have more than 21 years of expe-

TABLE 6.2
Years of Experience in Journalism
(Percentage in Each Category)

Experience	Minorities (n = 310)	Non-Hispanic White (n = 1,064)
1–5 years	19.4	15.9
6–10 years	25.8	18.8
11–15 years	13.9	14.0
16–20 years	18.1	14.2
21–25 years	12.9	14.9
26–30 years	5.8	11.5
31–35 years	2.6	6.5
36–40 years	1.3	2.3
More than 40 years	0.3	2.0

rience. Further, depending on how one cuts the age categories, there was wide variation among minorities. For example, whereas nearly half of Asian American journalists had fewer than 10 years of experience, a little less than one-fourth of African Americans had less than 10 years experience. These figures alone can't tell us much about long-term persistence rates for any particular group, but other studies have found that African American journalists, in particular, are less inclined to say they plan to stay in journalism than are White journalists. Our own data support this: One-third of African American journalists in our sample said they planned to be out of the news media within five years, but only 13% to 17% of the other minority groups said they planned to leave the news business in the next five years.

Income

The overall analysis of U.S. journalists' 2001 personal income in Chapter 3 shows that there was little impact of race or ethnicity (see Table 3.18). Instead, the major predictors of income were size of news organization, years of experience, and type of news medium (news magazines paid most and radio and weekly newspapers least). Supervising other employees, working for a publicly owned organization, having more education, and belonging to a journalism organization were also significant predictors of higher income.

Table 6.3 compares 2001 income levels of minorities as a group with majority journalists. The picture looks somewhat different depending on how these income categories are grouped. About half of the minorities made less than $50,000 a year, compared with nearly 60% of Whites. And a larger percentage of minorities (26%) made $70,000 or more than did Whites (21%). Compared with 1991 salary estimates, it's clear that minority journalists made significant progress

TABLE 6.3
Income of Journalists
(Percentage in Each Category)

Income	Minorities (n = 302)	Non-Hispanic White (n =1,011)
Less than $15,000	1.3	1.5
$15,000–$20,000	3.3	2.6
$20,000–$25,000	3.3	8.2
$25,000–$30,000	6.3	9.2
$30,000–$35,000	6.3	10.5
$35,000–$40,000	10.9	9.9
$40,000–$45,000	11.6	8.2
$45,000–$50,000	6.3	8.5
$50,000–$55,000	6.6	7.1
$55,000–$60,000	8.3	6.8
$60,000–$65,000	4.3	3.6
$65,000–$70,000	5.3	3.1
$70,000–$75,000	3.3	2.7
$75,000–$85,000	7.6	3.6
$85,000–$100,000	7.7	4.5
More than $100,000	7.6	10.0

on salaries, increasing from 6% in 1991 to 26% in 2001 making $70,000 or more, compared with an increase among Whites from 4% to 21%.

These figures, however, mask differences among minority groups. African American journalists had the highest median income, $53,333, and Native American journalists the lowest, $37,300. Asian Americans' median income was just below that of African Americans, at $52,300, and Hispanic journalists earned a median income of $49,167 in 2001. The comparable figure for non-Hispanic Whites was $45,795. Again, our analysis found the differences among the minority groups had more to do with organizational factors, education level, and years of experience than they did with race or ethnicity. As noted in Chapter 5, gender was also a predictor of salary, with women journalists earning, on average, 81% of what men earned.

Managerial Influence

As in 1992, of all the minority groups, Native Americans were most likely to say they supervised others in the newsroom (50%) and were most likely to work for a small news organization, which likely enhanced their odds of being a supervisor. African American journalists were least likely to report they supervised others (only 29.5% said they did); Hispanics were next at 33%, and Asian Americans and Whites, at 41% and 44%, respectively.

Perceived influence in hiring decisions is another indicator of managerial influence. Table 6.4 shows that minorities in both print and broadcast were less likely than majority journalists to say they had "a great deal" of influence in hiring. The findings for print media represent a decline for minorities because in 1992 minorities and Whites were nearly as likely to say they had a great deal of influence (37% of minorities and 39% of Whites). Even more than in 1992, broadcast hiring seemed to be influenced by White males (see Chapter 5, Table 5.2), although a larger percentage of minorities were working in broadcast media than in print (see Chapter 1, Figure 1.3).

Editorial Influence

During the decade of the 1990s, all journalists, regardless of race or ethnicity, perceived a reduction in freedom to select the stories they worked on. This was true in both print and broadcast news media. Table 6.5 shows that minorities in both print and broadcast were less likely than Whites to say they had "almost complete freedom" to select stories and more likely to perceive "some freedom" to do so.

The amount of editing done by minority and White journalists did not differ greatly (Table 6.6). Majority journalists in print media were slightly more likely than minorities to say they did "a great deal" of editing, and minorities in broadcast news were slightly more likely than Whites to say they did a great deal

TABLE 6.4
Minority and White Newsroom Managers' Perceived Influence
on Hiring (Percentage in Each Category)

	Print		Broadcast	
Influence	Minorities (n = 68)	Non-Hispanic White (n = 344)	Minorities (n = 32)	Non-Hispanic White (n = 101)
A great deal	32.4	45.1	37.5	45.5
Some	27.9	24.4	15.6	25.7
A little	23.5	16.3	21.9	14.9
None at all	16.2	14.2	25.0	13.9

TABLE 6.5
Amount of Freedom to Select Stories Worked on (Percentage in Each Category)

	Print		Broadcast	
Amount of Freedom	Minorities (n = 215)	Non-Hispanic White (n = 804)	Minorities (n = 76)	Non-Hispanic White (n = 236)
Almost complete freedom	29.8	37.3	27.6	37.7
A great deal of freedom	42.3	42.8	34.2	40.3
Some freedom	23.7	16.8	30.3	20.3
None at all	4.2	3.1	7.9	1.7

TABLE 6.6
Amount of Editing Performed by Minority and White Journalists
(Percentage in Each Category)

Amount of Editing	Print		Broadcast	
	Minorities (n = 219)	Non-Hispanic White (n = 816)	Minorities (n = 64)	Non-Hispanic White (n = 248)
A great deal	31.1	37.6	28.1	24.6
Some	34.2	40.4	46.9	52.8
None at all	34.7	21.9	25.0	22.6

TABLE 6.7
Amount of Freedom Those With Editing Duties Had in Deciding
How Stories Would Be Used (Percentage in Each Category)

Amount of Freedom	Print		Broadcast	
	Minorities (n = 139)	Non-Hispanic White (n = 625)	Minorities (n = 59)	Non-Hispanic White (n = 178)
Almost complete freedom	10.8	17.6	20.3	31.5
A great deal	29.5	32.2	37.3	37.1
Some	33.1	32.5	30.5	22.5
None at all	26.6	17.8	11.9	9.0

of editing. Perhaps more notable is what appears to be an increase (from 28% to 35%) of minorities in print who said they did no editing at all, and an increase in minorities in broadcast media (from 40% to 47%) who did some editing.

Table 6.7 reports on the perceived amount of freedom editors had in making decisions about the use of stories. In both print and broadcast news media, journalists of color were less likely to perceive almost complete freedom than were Whites but equally likely to think they had a great deal of freedom. In the print media, the percentage of minority journalists claiming almost complete freedom dropped from 16% in 1992 to 11% in 2002, whereas it increased (from 12% to 20%) for minorities in broadcast. Those saying they had "almost complete freedom" or "a great deal" of freedom (the top two categories) reached 40% for minorities in print and 58% for minorities in broadcast. These data, along with those for women (Chapter 5), suggest some significant gains during the decade for minorities in broadcast news, but they also indicate that White males are still in the majority in the management and editorial control of broadcast news organizations.

Job Dimensions

We asked a number of questions to gauge how journalists viewed various aspects of their jobs. Table 6.8 compares perceptions of minorities and Whites on these

TABLE 6.8
The Importance of Job Dimensions for Journalists
(Percentage Who Rated Each Dimension "Very Important")

Dimension	Minorities (n = 311)[a]	Non-Hispanic White (n = 1,069)[a]
Pay	26.4	16.6
Fringe benefits	33.3	28.4
A chance to get ahead in the organization	51.8	34.0
Job security	64.3	56.5
Chance to develop a specialty	51.0	39.5
Chance to help people	80.4	61.1
Editorial policies of organization	73.5	69.6
Chance to influence public affairs	51.6	38.0
Amount of autonomy	58.4	56.0

[a] Ns vary slightly by item. The largest Ns are reported here.

dimensions. As in 1992, minority journalists were more likely than Whites to rate "a chance to get ahead in the organization" and a "chance to influence public affairs" as very important. In 2002, minorities were also more likely than Whites to see pay, a chance to develop a specialty, and a chance to help people as very important.

Overall, Whites and minorities agreed on their top three job dimensions — the editorial policies of their organizations, the chance to help people, and job security. The percentages saying each dimension was "very important" varied, however, as seen in Table 6.8.

Job Satisfaction

In 1992, we reported a significant decline in the percentage of journalists saying they were "very satisfied" with their jobs (from 49% in 1971 to 40% in 1982–1983, to 27% in 1992). Although satisfaction levels haven't returned to the levels of the 1970s, the overall numbers were up in 2002, as Table 3.19 in Chapter 3 shows. Overall, about one-third of journalists said they were very satisfied in 2002, and the percentages of minorities who said they were "very" or "fairly" satisfied with their jobs were slightly lower than for White journalists (see Chapter 3, Tables 3.19 and 3.21).

For minorities, the "very satisfied" figure was highest for Native American journalists. More than half (53%) reported being very satisfied, which was a major increase from 33% in 1992 and well above the 34.5% for the White majority. Of the other minority groups, African Americans showed the biggest increase in the percentage saying they were very satisfied (from about 20% to about 30%). For all groups except Hispanics and African Americans, the percentage of those expressing some or much dissatisfaction decreased over the decade. Nearly one-fourth

TABLE 6.9
Job Satisfaction of Journalists (Percentage in Each Group)

Level of Satisfaction	Asian American (n = 110)	African American (n = 61)	Hispanic (n = 132)	Native American (n = 36)	Non-Hispanic White (n =1,120)
Very satisfied	28.2	29.5	26.5	52.8	34.5
Fairly satisfied	52.7	47.5	51.5	38.9	50.0
Somewhat dissatisfied	19.1	21.3	20.5	5.6	13.8
Very dissatisfied	0.0	1.7	1.5	2.8	1.7

of Hispanics and African Americans said they were somewhat or very dissatisfied with their jobs, as Table 6.9 shows.

Their reasons? Some took issue with management style and practice. Some complained about the lack of autonomy "to do what you have to do when you need to do it without having to deal with red tape," as one Hispanic journalist said. Another Hispanic television journalist spoke about the intersection of management and autonomy: " I don't have as much autonomy as I would like to have. I think the craft is in somewhat of a decline and not enough attention is being paid to it. I think that there are not enough resources put into helping people become better journalists."

An African American daily newspaper journalist expressed the sentiment of others: "I would like more money. I would like the opportunity for more autonomy and also would like to have more opportunities for advancement." And a Native American daily newspaper journalist said: "We're cutting back staff, we're being forced to do more with less, we're not given the resources we need to do the job we do, and more is always expected of us."

Commitment to Journalism

We also measured journalists' satisfaction with their work by asking where they would most like to be working in five years. For all groups except African American journalists, between 80% and 85% said they hoped to be working in the news media in five years. For African American journalists, however, nearly a third (32%) said they would like to be working somewhere else in five years. This figure is much larger than any of the other minority groups (and the majority White group), and it presents a dichotomy in need of exploring: One-third of African American journalists say they want to leave the profession, but 30% say they are "very satisfied" with their jobs.

Open-ended responses to our question of "why" journalists wish to leave mirror the findings of other studies during the decade that point to a number of life-style and workplace issues. "After doing this for 10 years, you start thinking about other fields that may be more conducive to a family," said one Asian American television journalist. Others mentioned the lack of flexible hours and the sheer stress of doing journalism. An African American daily newspaper journalist summed up points made by others: "I think that really the craft of journalism has been lost in our rush to attract new readers, younger readers. We've really lost sight of the craft and it's really a disturbing trend to me; it's a trend I don't see ending soon."

Rating of Organization

In past studies, as in the current one, one of the strongest predictors of job satisfaction was how good a job journalists thought their organizations were doing in informing the public (see Chapter 3, Table 3.23). Although there was no significant difference between men and women on this measure (12.5% of men and 13.2% of women said their organization was doing an "outstanding" job, and nearly two-thirds of each group thought their organizations were doing either a very good or an outstanding job), there were some differences among minority groups.

Native Americans stood out among all groups in saying their organizations were doing an outstanding job. Nearly one-fourth—22%, compared with 12% to 15% for other groups—of Native Americans thought their organizations were doing an outstanding job. Said one, a television journalist: "We keep in touch with our viewers through public opinion research as well as through our staff of reporters to make sure we do stories that are of interest to them and that affect them." Likewise, Native Americans were more likely than others to express satisfaction with their work. Interestingly, of all groups, Native Americans had the lowest median pay (see the section on income, earlier in this chapter).

African American journalists were most likely of all groups to say they wanted to leave journalism and were most likely to rate the work of their organization as low. Their median salaries, however, ranked highest among all the minority groups and Whites. Some of those who responded to the open-ended question evaluating their news organizations praised their news teams for trying to cover the people and issues of their region, but others were less positive. Said one television journalist: "I don't think (my news organization) gives enough ordinary citizens opportunity to participate in the process, I don't think that it gives as wide a range of views as it should on major issues, and I don't think it is as open to diverse ideas as it should be."

Organizational Memberships

On the whole, minority journalists were more likely than White journalists to be members of a union, though the figures for each group varied. About 15% of the majority White journalists said they were union members compared with 28% of Asian American, 26% of African American, and 22% of Native American journalists. Only Hispanics, at 13%, were less likely than the majority to be union members. Comparing with 1992, however, union membership appears to be down for some groups, most notably Asian Americans, who were at 46% in 1992.

As in our past studies, minority journalists were more likely than majority White journalists to be members of a professional journalism organization. Additional samples of minority journalists in this study were drawn from the membership lists of professional organizations, so it's therefore not surprising that these minority journalists belonged to an organization. However, even in the main probability sample, which was drawn from a random sample of news organizations and not from membership lists, some minority journalists were more likely than Whites to belong to a professional organization. Whereas 40% of White journalists said they belonged to a journalism professional organization, 69% of African American, 64% of Asian American, 80% of Native American, and 39.5% of Hispanic journalists in the main sample said they did.

If belonging to a professional association is a sign of professional identity or commitment, then African American, Asian American, and Native American journalists were more likely to demonstrate such commitment in 2002 than were other U.S. journalists.

PROFESSIONAL VALUES

Role Perceptions

One indicator of journalistic values is the priority journalists assign to various roles of the news media. As discussed in Chapter 5, differences between men and women on these measures were not great. Though the rankings were similar, women were slightly more likely than men to rate as extremely important the top four roles (investigating government claims, getting information to the public quickly, avoiding stories with unverified content, and providing analysis of complex problems).

Minority journalists varied somewhat from Whites on several measures, and we found some differences among minority groups (Table 6.10). Like majority journalists, minorities placed high importance on the roles of investigating government claims and getting information to the public quickly, although all groups rated this latter role of less importance than they had a decade earlier. Minorities were more likely than majority journalists to see as important analyzing complex problems (59% vs. 51% saying it was "extremely important"); developing intellectual and cultural interests of the community (31% vs. 16%); seeing journalists as adversaries of public officials (27% vs. 20%) and business (24% vs. 18%); and including news of the widest possible interest (25% vs. 14.5%).

As in 1992, the largest difference between these groups of journalists was in developing the intellectual and cultural interests of their publics. Minority jour-

TABLE 6.10
The Importance Journalists Assigned to Various
Mass Media Roles (Percentage Who Rated
Each Role Extremely Important)

Journalistic Role	Minorities ($n = 311$)[a]	Non-Hispanic White ($n = 1072$)[a]
Investigate government claims	75.2	71.0
Get information to public quickly	58.7	59.1
Avoid stories with unverified content	59.5	50.5
Provide analysis of complex problems	59.2	51.3
Discuss national policy	42.4	41.5
Develop intellectual/cultural interests	30.9	16.2
Provide entertainment and relaxation	10.9	10.6
Serve as an adversary of public officials	27.2	19.7
Serve as an adversary of business	24.0	17.6
Use news of widest interest	25.1	14.5
Set the political agenda	4.8	3.0
Let ordinary people express their views	49.2	38.4

[a] Ns vary slightly by item. The largest Ns are reported here.

nalists were much more likely than Whites to rate this role as extremely important, as Table 6.10 shows. This role was part of a larger approach to journalism
that we called the populist mobilizer function in Chapter 4. Minorities were also
more likely than majority Whites to consider as extremely important another
populist mobilizer or "civic" role of letting ordinary people express their views
(49% vs. 38%). Although the samples were too small to make confident gener-
alizations about differences among minorities, it appears as if Native American
journalists were more likely than others to rate as extremely important this role
of giving ordinary people a chance to express their views.

In our 1992 study, we speculated that minority journalists might be particularly interested in the cultural interests of their publics because of a perception of
dominance by the mainstream Anglo American culture. The data from our 2002
study also support this speculation, although we have no way of testing it directly
because no open-ended question was included to ask journalists why they rated
the various roles as more or less important.

Ethical Standards

As we noted in Chapter 5, there was virtually no difference between the way men
and women journalists considered controversial or questionable reporting practices. This was true in 1992 as well. And it was true in cases in which one might
expect to see differences between men and women, such as the appropriateness of
disclosing the names of rape victims. We did find differences, some striking, however, among the different minority groups in 2002. In some cases, some practices

are considered *less* acceptable than in 1992, in other cases, *more* acceptable, and in some cases, the picture is mixed.

For example, Table 6.11 shows that on the technique of using confidential business or government documents without authorization, Asian Americans were more likely than other groups, and Native American journalists less likely, to say that this might be justified. Likewise, Asian Americans were more likely, and Native American and Hispanic journalists less likely, to say that badgering sources might be acceptable. African American journalists were less likely than others to say it was acceptable to claim to be someone else in order to get a story, and they were much less likely than they were in 1992 to think this practice might be justifiable (nearly 25% of the African American sample said so in 1992; only about 10% said so in 2002). Native American journalists were less likely than the other minority groups to approve of naming rape victims, using recreations of news by actors, and agreeing to protect the confidentiality of sources and then not doing so. Native American journalists were, however, more likely than the others to say it might be justified to get employed by an organization to gain inside information.

What explains these differences? As we suggest in Chapter 4, some of the apparent differences might be explained by organizational factors and the workplace norms they engender, as well as differing cultural backgrounds. Asian American journalists tended to work for the largest news media (usually daily newspapers or news magazines), which helps explain their willingness to use con-

TABLE 6.11
Journalists' Opinions on Controversial Reporting Methods
(Percentage of Each Category Saying May Be Justified on Occasion)

Reporting Method	Asian American (n = 110)	African American (n = 61)	Hispanic (n = 132)	Native American (n = 36)	Non-Hispanic White (n = 1,120)
Using confidential business or government documents without authorization	82.4	71.7	77.9	69.4	78.5
Getting employed to gain inside information	50.5	50.0	45.5	66.7	53.8
Using hidden microphones or cameras	60.9	67.2	58.3	44.4	59.8
Badgering unwilling informants to get a story	60.6	52.5	40.5	33.3	52.3
Using personal letters and photographs without permission	41.3	32.8	32.1	41.7	42.5
Disclosing names of rape victims	41.3	39.3	32.1	19.4	36.6
Using re-creations of news by actors	33.0	36.1	37.8	25.0	27.9
Claiming to be somebody else	14.5	9.8	15.2	13.9	14.3
Paying for confidential information	13.6	16.4	15.9	11.1	17.7
Agreeing to protect confidentiality and not doing so	10.1	11.5	9.1	0.0	7.3

fidential business or government documents without authorization (see Chapter 4, Table 4.16). Native American journalists, on the other hand, tended to work for the smallest news media (often weekly newspapers or radio stations), which helps to explain their relative reluctance to justify badgering informants or disclosing the names of rape victims (see Chapter 4, Tables 4.14 and 4.20). Whatever the reasons for these differences, it's clear that that there were more differences of opinion about the acceptability of various questionable reporting practices by race and ethnic background than by gender.

CONCLUSIONS

Minority representation in American media has inched up over the years but, at 9.5% by 2002, remained much below the minority percentage of the U.S. population and also below the college-educated minority population. The American Society of Newspaper Editors has long since revised its goal of achieving parity in newspaper newsrooms by 2000. The new goal is to reach parity (estimated at 38%) by 2025, but even that goal, judged by progress so far, seems remote.[5]

A hopeful sign (shown partly in Chapter 1, Figure 1.2) is that minorities were being hired at a faster rate than in earlier decades. We found that about 17% of *all* journalists with 0 to 4 years of experience were minorities (see Chapter 1, Figure 1.2), and we found some evidence of persistence among those hired before 1990. We also found that the minority presence in television is increasing. Still, other factors, some from our study, continue to suggest that hiring and retaining minority journalists will be difficult.

One challenge has been a retrenchment in newspaper newsrooms. The growth of earlier days simply no longer is occurring. Another is the lack of a significant pipeline of young minority journalists coming out of journalism schools. A third is the finding that minority journalists, especially African American journalists, voice unhappiness with opportunities for advancement and are notably more likely than others to say they intend to leave the news media in the next five years.

Generalizations

Our study found that minority journalists were more likely than majority Whites to be women and to be younger. They also were more likely to be Democrats. But we also found that generalizing about all the minority groups served to mask distinct differences. For example, whereas on the whole minority journalists were more likely to be women than men, that's not so of Native American journalists, who tended to be a little older and were more likely to be men. On the whole, minority journalists made a bit more than White journalists, except for Native American journalists, whose median salary of $37,300 was well below that of

Whites' $45,795. But African American journalists had the highest median salary of all the groups—about $53,000.

In terms of roles of journalists, we found that minority journalists expressed some different sentiments, on the whole, than majority journalists in terms of the roles journalism should play in society. Minorities, more than Whites, saw as important the adversarial roles of journalism, the role of analyzing complex problems, and developing the intellectual interests of the community. Further, they, more than Whites, saw as important the role of allowing ordinary citizens to express their views.

Of course it's impossible to predict the future. To the extent that the past is a good guide, we presume news organizations will continue to work at hiring and retaining minority and women journalists. Our findings over time suggest that the task will continue to be a difficult one if those who manage news organizations—most often men and most often White men—do not make strong efforts to create the sort of working environments that convince minority and women journalists that this is an occupation they wish to dedicate themselves to throughout their careers.

NOTES

1. Lee B. Becker and Thomas E. Engleman, "Class of 1987 Describes Salaries, Satisfaction Found in First Jobs," *Journalism Educator*, 43 (Autumn 1988), p. 6.
2. Lee B. Becker, Tudor Vlad, Jisu Huh, and Nancy R. Mace, "2002 Annual Survey of Journalism & Mass Communication Graduates," presented at the 2003 annual convention of the Association for Education in Journalism & Mass Communication, August 1, 2004, Table S20. See also the following Web site: www.grady.uga.edu/annualsurveys/
3. Whenever references are made to White or majority journalists in this chapter, we are referring to non-Hispanic Whites. We are aware that some Hispanics consider themselves to be White in terms of race, and we have treated Hispanic ethnic background separately from race in our data analysis.
4. It should be remembered that the findings about minority journalists we report in this chapter are mostly based on combinations of the main probability sample and the additional samples from the membership lists of minority journalism associations, so these are not strictly probability samples and they may not provide a representative picture of the population of U.S. minority journalists. The figures about minorities cited from Chapter 1 are based only on those minority journalists in the main probability sample, so they should be more representative of the larger population of U.S. journalists.
5. Jeffery D. Mohl, "Lessons in Diversity," *Quill*, 91, 6 (August 2003), p. 3.

Chapter 7

Online Journalists

Online journalism has been discussed and analyzed extensively in the past five years or so, as more and more news media organizations have developed their own Web sites. As online media scholar Jane Singer has written, "The World Wide Web has had a tremendous impact on traditional media outlets and the people who work for them."[1]

At the same time, the potential online news audience is growing very rapidly. As of March 2004, Nielsen/NetRatings estimated that there were more than 114 million active Internet users in the United States and more than 209 million with Internet access.[2] Traffic to leading Internet news sites has increased dramatically, and it has been predicted that the proportion of Americans who go online for news will increase to nearly 75% by 2007.[3]

In spite of all the growth in online news sources on the Internet and in the online news audiences, there has not been much research on the U.S. journalists who produce online news, except for studies by Singer and a few others. Given the increasing importance of the Web as a news medium since our last study in 1992, we decided to include a separate sample of online journalists in this survey, in addition to those who fell into the main random sample, much as we did for minority journalists in 1992 and again in 2002. We begin by analyzing the demographics of all these online journalists, as compared with those working for more traditional print and broadcast media; then we examine educational backgrounds, political views, income, attitudes about work, work environments, views about professional roles, and opinions about the use of various questionable reporting methods.

BACKGROUNDS

Who are online journalists? Do they differ significantly from those working for more traditional print and broadcast news media in terms of gender, age, race, and education?

Gender

Table 7.1 suggests that women comprise about one-third of all online journalists, just as they do for the traditional print news media. Women are a bit less numerous among broadcast journalists, as was illustrated in Chapter 1 in Table 1.6, where it is clear that women are least represented among radio and wire- or news-service journalists and most represented among those working for news magazines. The percentage of women working as online journalists is almost equal to the percentage working for daily newspapers (33.0%), which is not surprising considering that daily newspapers are quite likely to have their own Web sites and to employ journalists who work online.

Age

Online journalists are a bit younger on average (39) than are those working for traditional print and broadcast news organizations (41 and 40), and considerably more likely to fall into the 35- to 44-year-old range, as Table 7.2 illustrates. But overall there are not many notable differences in age between online and other journalists, despite the sometimes common assumption that those working online are likely to be considerably younger than those working for more traditional news media in the United States. In fact, there were no online journalists younger than 25 in our sample.

Race

Because of the relatively small sample size of online journalists, it was not possible to reliably categorize the online journalists into specific racial/ethnic groups, but

TABLE 7.1
Gender of Online Journalists
(Percentage in Each Category)

Gender	Online (n = 100)	Print (n = 879)	Broadcast (n = 268)
Men	66.0	66.4	68.7
Women	34.0	33.6	31.3

TABLE 7.2
Age of Online Journalists
(Percentage in Each Category)

Age	Online (n = 100)	Print (n = 880)	Broadcast (n = 267)
Under 25	0.0	4.3	4.9
25–34	30.0	28.5	31.8
35–44	36.0	27.6	28.8
45–54	24.0	29.1	25.5
55–64	9.0	8.1	7.1
65 and older	1.0	2.4	1.9
Total	100.0	100.0	100.0
Median age	39.0	41.0	40.0

TABLE 7.3
Race of Online Journalists
(Percentage in Each Category)

Race	Online (n = 100)	Print (n = 872)	Broadcast (n = 268)
Non-Hispanic White	93.5	91.4	87.7
Minority	6.5	8.6	12.3

Table 7.3 does indicate that online journalists were slightly less likely to be racial or ethnic minorities than print journalists, in general, and about half as likely to be minorities as journalists working for broadcast news media. Overall, however, the differences in racial or ethnic backgrounds between online journalists and other journalists were not large, and these differences are within the margin of sampling error. Minority online journalists were about evenly split between Hispanics, African Americans, and Asian Americans. There were no Pacific Islanders and almost no Native Americans or Alaskan Americans.

Education

Online journalists were considerably more likely than mainstream media journalists to have had some graduate education and to have earned a graduate degree, as Table 7.4 indicates. Altogether, 36% of online journalists had had some graduate education, compared to about 23% of print and 16% of broadcast journalists. And 27% of online journalists had earned a graduate degree, compared to 18% of print and 10.5% of broadcast journalists. Thus, there is little doubt that U.S. online journalists as a group tend to be more highly educated than U.S. journalists working for more traditional news media.

TABLE 7.4
Education of Online Journalists
(Percentage in Each Category)

Level of Education	Online (n = 100)	Print (n = 881)	Broadcast (n = 268)
Completed high school	0.0	1.6	2.6
Some undergraduate	8.0	8.1	11.2
Undergraduate degree	56.0	67.4	70.1
Some graduate	9.0	4.4	5.6
Master's degree	22.0	17.1	9.0
Doctorate, law, or medical degree	5.0	1.2	1.5

TABLE 7.5
Major of Online Journalists
(Percentage in Each Category)

Major in College	Online (n = 100)	Print (n = 865)	Broadcast (n = 268)
Journalism major	37.0	38.7	27.5
Not journalism major	63.0	61.3	72.5

Online journalists were about as likely as print journalists in general to have majored in journalism in college (37%) and considerably more likely to have done so than broadcast journalists, as Table 7.5 shows. And online journalists were slightly less likely to want additional training or education (73%) than were print (77%) or broadcast (76%) journalists, although this difference is not significant statistically. Sixty percent of online journalists had had additional training beyond college courses compared to two-thirds of the print journalists and 57% of the broadcast journalists, so there were no significant differences on this measure.

Political Party Preference

Online journalists in our sample were considerably more likely to identify with the Democratic party, and less likely to prefer the Republican party, than other print or broadcast journalists, as Table 7.6 illustrates. Online journalists were also somewhat less likely to consider themselves political Independents and somewhat more likely to prefer another political party besides the two major parties in the United States. Taken together, these findings suggest that online journalists were more liberal politically than journalists working for more traditional print and broadcast media.

Overall, then, the online journalists in our sample were likely to be White men between 25 and 54 years old, who had completed at least an undergraduate

TABLE 7.6
Political Party Identification of Online
Journalists (Percentage in Each Category)

Political Party	Online (n = 98)	Print (n = 857)	Broadcast (n = 257)
Democrat	50.0	39.6	28.8
Republican	6.1	16.5	25.7
Independent	26.5	33.5	33.5
Other	17.3	10.5	12.1

college degree and had not majored in journalism, and who tended to identify with the Democratic party. The online journalists were about as likely to be men or women as journalists working for more traditional news media, to be about the same age, to be a bit less likely to be a racial or ethnic minority, to be more highly educated, and to somewhat more liberal politically.

JOBS

Work Experience and Income

Online journalists in our sample had worked an average of 16 years in journalism, virtually the same as all journalists in our main sample. The online journalists were somewhat more likely to have worked 5 to 14 years and somewhat less likely to have worked 20 or more years, or less than 5 years, in the field. In other words, they were more likely to be midcareer journalists. In spite of this, the online journalists were the highest paid on average of any category of journalist in our study except for those working at news magazines and wire or news services, with a median annual income of $64,000 in 2001, compared to a median income of $43,500 for all journalists. Online journalists tended to work at larger news organizations (median staff size of 60) than broadcast journalists (media staff size of 20), but at about the same size organizations as print journalists (median staff size of 60).

Job Satisfaction and Commitment

Online journalists were a bit more satisfied with their jobs than print journalists, as their higher average pay might predict, but not more than broadcast journalists, as Table 7.7 shows. The similarity in job satisfaction levels among all three groups is striking. And online journalists were about as likely to plan to keep working in the news media (84%) as print (81%) and broadcast (84%) journalists.

TABLE 7.7
Job Satisfaction of Online Journalists
(Percentage in Each Category)

Level of Satisfaction	Online (n = 97)	Print (n = 881)	Broadcast (n = 268)
Very satisfied	38.0	30.8	41.8
Fairly satisfied	49.0	52.4	44.4
Somewhat dissatisfied	10.0	14.9	13.1
Very dissatisfied	3.0	1.9	0.7

TABLE 7.8
Autonomy of Online Journalists (Percentage in Each Category)

Measure of Perceived Autonomy	Online (n = 100)	Print (n = 879)	Broadcast (n = 265)
Can almost always get a subject idea covered	35.7	49.8	42.3
Almost complete freedom to select stories they work on	30.9	36.5	36.9
Almost complete freedom to decide story emphasis	35.1	35.8	47.0

Note. Ns vary slightly by item.

Perceived Autonomy

In spite of similar levels of job satisfaction and higher average levels of income, online journalists were less likely than more traditional print and broadcast journalists to think that they could almost always get a subject covered or that they had almost complete freedom to select stories to work on (see Table 7.8). The difference between online and print journalists on perceived ability to get a subject covered was particularly noteworthy (14 percentage points), as was the difference between both online and print journalists and broadcast journalists on deciding story emphasis.

Part of the reason for these differences in perceived freedom is undoubtedly due to the nature of online journalism work as compared with more traditional news media work. Online journalists were much less likely to do reporting regularly (27% said so) than journalists in general (65% said so) and much more likely to supervise other employees (63%) than journalists in general (41%). Online journalists were also less likely to communicate with reporters daily or more often (40%) than journalists in general (58%) and less likely to be able to get a subject covered (36%) than journalists in general (48%). Because of these differences in work patterns, online journalists would be less likely to be able to initiate news articles than other journalists who do more reporting.

Interactions With Others

Online journalists were about as likely as other journalists to get comments regularly on their work from people above them in their news organizations (50% said so, compared to 45% of all journalists), but they were less likely to hear from news sources regularly (20% said so, compared to 32% of all journalists), and online journalists were much more likely to regularly hear from audience members (64% said so, compared to 48% of all journalists). Thus, online journalists seem to be more isolated from news sources than other journalists but more in touch with readers, viewers, and listeners.

PROFESSIONAL VALUES

Role Perceptions

As noted in Chapter 4, an important indicator of professional values is the priority that journalists assign to various roles of the news media. Tables 7.9 through 7.12 compare the percentages of online, print, and broadcast journalists who saw these various roles as extremely important, and these tables also group the roles into the more general functions of journalism suggested in Figure 4.2 in Chapter 4.

Beginning with the roles that comprise the disseminator function of journalism in Table 7.9, it seems that online journalists were as likely as other journalists to perceive getting information to the public as extremely important, but they were less likely to consider factual verification and reaching the widest possible audience as extremely important. Online journalists were also slightly less likely than print journalists to think that providing entertainment and relaxation is an extremely important role for the news media. Taken together, these findings suggest that online journalists were somewhat less likely than print and broadcast journalists to think that the disseminator function was extremely important.

When asked about the four roles of the interpretive function, however, online journalists were more likely than either traditional print or broadcast journalists

TABLE 7.9
The Disseminator Function: Percentages of Journalists
Who Saw Its Dimensions as "Extremely Important"

Type of Journalist	Getting Information to Public Quickly	Avoid Unverifiable Facts	Reach Widest Possible Audience	Provide Entertainment and Relaxation
Online	60.0	41.4	6.0	6.0
Print	58.3	50.8	13.3	12.5
Broadcast	60.7	56.2	22.4	3.7

to consider these extremely important, as Table 7.10 indicates. This was especially true for the roles of investigating government or official claims and discussing national policy. In all cases, online journalists were much more likely than their colleagues in the broadcast media to consider these roles extremely important but only slightly more likely than print journalists to consider analyzing complex problems and discussing international policy extremely important. Overall, this interpretive approach to journalism was the one most favored by online journalists, as was true for all journalists in general (see Figure 4.2).

Online journalists were less likely than those working for traditional print media to consider the roles of the populist mobilizer function extremely important, as Table 7.11 shows. For these roles, the online journalists were closer to the broadcast journalists in their evaluations, and both groups were less likely to consider these roles extremely important as compared with those of the disseminator and interpretive functions—especially the role of setting the political agenda, which received by far the least support of any of the roles we asked about. Online journalists were also notably less likely than broadcast or print journalists to consider pointing out possible solutions to problems as extremely important. In general, online journalists were less likely to endorse several of the roles related to civic journalism.

Online journalists were slightly more likely to consider the adversarial role of journalism extremely important, as Table 7.12 indicates, and they were much more similar to print journalists in this regard. About one-fifth of both groups strongly endorsed this role, compared with only about one-tenth of the broad-

TABLE 7.10
The Interpretive Function: Percentages of Journalists
Who Saw Its Dimensions as "Extremely Important"

Type of Journalist	Investigating Official Claims	Analyzing Complex Problems	Discuss National Policy	Discuss International Policy
Online	78.0	58.0	51.0	52.0
Print	73.9	55.9	42.9	50.8
Broadcast	59.3	34.7	31.0	36.6

TABLE 7.11
The Populist Mobilizer Function: Percentages of Journalists
Who Saw Its Dimensions as "Extremely Important"

Type of Journalist	Let People Express Views	Develop Cultural Interests	Motivate People to Get Involved	Point to Possible Solutions	Set the Political Agenda
Online	26.0	14.0	23.0	13.0	1.0
Print	41.3	18.1	34.5	24.7	4.0
Broadcast	31.0	13.1	28.5	21.0	1.1

TABLE 7.12
The Adversarial Function: Percentages of Journalists
Who Saw Its Dimensions as "Extremely Important"

Type of Journalist	Adversary of Officials	Adversary of Business
Online	20.0	18.0
Print	22.3	19.5
Broadcast	12.4	10.9

cast journalists. Thus, online and print journalists were most likely to consider the watchdog function of journalism extremely important, although this support was less than that for the interpretive and some aspects of the disseminator functions.

In sum, online journalists were more similar to print journalists in their support of the interpretive and adversarial functions of journalism and more similar to broadcast journalists in their evaluations of the populist mobilizer function. Online journalists were less likely than both other groups of journalists to consider the neutral disseminator function extremely important. Online journalists generally favored getting information to the public quickly, investigating government claims, analyzing complex problems, and discussing national and international policy. They tended to downplay reaching the widest audience, providing entertainment, setting the political agenda, pointing to possible solutions, and developing cultural interests. It was somewhat surprising that online journalists were less likely than others to emphasize motivating people to get involved and letting people express their views, given the increased interactive possibilities of online media as compared with more traditional news media.

The increased emphasis on the interpretive function of journalism by online journalists is not very surprising, given their increased likelihood of holding a graduate degree (see Table 7.4) and their more liberal political leaning, both of which are predictors of interpretive values for all journalists combined (see Chapter 4, Table 4.8). Online journalists were also more likely to work for larger news organizations (median staff size of 60) than were broadcast journalists (media staff size of 20), and larger staff size is another significant predictor of interpretive values.

Ethical Standards

Most of our questions regarding journalistic ethics centered on questionable or controversial reporting practices. As noted earlier, online journalists were much less likely than other journalists to do reporting regularly, so we might expect some differences in their answers to these questions. In fact, there are some substantial differences, especially between online and print journalists.

TABLE 7.13
Ethical Dilemmas Presented to Online Journalists
(Percentage in Each Category Who Say "May Be Justified on Occasion")

Reporting Method	Online (n = 100)	Print (n = 879)	Broadcast (n = 265)
Pay for confidential information	23.5	15.7	22.1
Use confidential documents without authorization	90.0	80.4	69.3
Claim to be somebody else	20.0	13.8	15.7
Not protect confidentiality after agreeing to do so	11.0	6.5	10.4
Badger informants	55.0	55.4	41.0
Use personal documents without permission	49.0	43.1	34.1
Get employed at a firm to gain inside information	52.0	52.7	57.3
Use hidden microphones or cameras	62.0	53.5	79.4
Use recreations or dramatizations of news	32.7	25.8	37.6
Disclose names of rape victims	39.6	38.7	26.2

Note. Ns vary slightly by item.

Table 7.13 compares the percentages of online, print, and broadcast journalists who said that various reporting practices "may be justified on occasion," given an important story. For nearly every practice, online journalists were more likely to say it might be justified than were print journalists (except for badgering informants or undercover employment). In a number of cases, the differences in percentages were insignificant, but there appeared to be more substantial differences on paying for information, using confidential business or government documents without authorization, claiming to be somebody else, using personal documents without permission, using hidden microphones or cameras, and using re-creations or dramatizations of news.

When compared with broadcast journalists, however, there were fewer instances of online journalists who were more willing to use questionable reporting methods and a few cases where the broadcast journalists were more accepting of such methods (undercover employment, use of hidden microphones or cameras, and use of dramatizations of news). Online journalists were notably more likely than were broadcast journalists to justify using confidential business or government documents without authorization, to badger informants, to use personal documents without permission, and to disclose the names of rape victims.

Overall, then, online journalists came across as more willing to use a variety of questionable or controversial reporting methods than did journalists working for more traditional print and broadcast news media, possibly because of less reporting and less contact with news sources than other journalists. Personal contact with news sources may tend to reduce a journalist's willingness to use questionable reporting methods, although the data in Chapter 4, Table 4.21 suggest that amount of comment from news sources is a positive (although quite weak) predictor of willingness to justify the various questionable reporting practices for all journalists combined. Stronger predictors included endorsement of the interpretive function (positive) and endorsement of the disseminator function (negative) of the news media, and the previous section has shown that online journalists were more likely to consider the interpretive function as extremely important than were other journalists and less likely to emphasize the disseminator function.

CONCLUSIONS

This brief report on online journalists suggests that they are similar to other U.S. journalists in gender, age, and race, but they are slightly younger on average and slightly less likely to be people of color. Online journalists were considerably more likely than traditional mainstream media journalists to have had some graduate education and to have earned a graduate degree, more likely to identify with the Democratic party, and less likely to prefer the Republican party.

Overall, then, U.S. online journalists in our sample were likely to be White men between 25 and 54 years old who had completed at least an undergraduate college degree and had not majored in journalism, and who tended to identify with the Democratic party. They were more likely to be midcareer journalists and to be the highest paid on average of any type of journalist in our study except for those working at news magazines and wire services. They were a bit more satisfied with their jobs than traditional print journalists and about as likely to plan to keep working in the news media as other journalists.

Online journalists were less likely than those working at more traditional news media to perceive complete freedom to select stories to work on and to think that they could almost always get a subject idea covered, probably because they were much less likely to do reporting regularly and much more likely to supervise other employees than journalists in general. Online journalists were also less likely to communicate with reporters daily or more often and less likely to be able to get a subject covered. They were less likely to hear from news sources regularly and much more likely to hear regularly from audience members. Thus, online journalists seemed to be more isolated from news sources than other kinds of journalists but more in touch with readers, viewers, and listeners.

In terms of journalistic roles, online journalists were somewhat less likely than other U.S. journalists to think that being a neutral disseminator was extremely important and more likely to emphasize an interpretive function. Overall, the interpretive approach to journalism was the one most favored by online journalists, as was true for all journalists in general. But online journalists were less likely than others to consider the roles of the populist mobilizer function as extremely important, especially setting the political agenda and pointing out possible solutions to public problems. They were slightly more likely than more traditional journalists to consider the adversarial or watchdog function of journalism as extremely important.

Online journalists emphasized getting information out quickly, investigating government claims, analyzing complex problems, and discussing policy. It was surprising that online journalists were less likely than more traditional journalists to emphasize motivating people to get involved and letting people express their views, given the increased interactive capability of online media as compared with more traditional news media.

As for the possible use of questionable or controversial reporting methods, online journalists were generally more willing to use these than were other print and broadcast journalists, possibly because online journalists considered the interpretive function more important and the disseminator function less so.

In short, online journalists were more similar to, than different from, journalists working in more traditional print and broadcast news media, but there were some notable differences, mainly in work-related attitudes and behaviors, confirming the importance of the organizational environment. Our study suggests that U.S. online journalists in 2002 were not dramatically different from more traditional mainstream media journalists in demographics, education, political attitudes, or views about journalistic roles and the ethics of reporting practices.

NOTES

1. Jane B. Singer, "Who Are These Guys? The Online Challenge to the Notion of Journalistic Professionalism," *Journalism: Theory, Practice and Criticism* 4, 2 (May 2003), p. 139.
2. Nielsen/NetRatings, "United States: Average Web Usage Week Ending March 14, 2004," accessed on March 15, 2004, at http://www.nielsen-netratings.com/reports.jsp?section=pub_reports
3. Vin Crosbie, "Weak Online Economics Threaten Quality of All Journalism, Pew Study Finds," *Online Journalism Review*, March 17, 2004, at http://www.ojr.org/ojr/business

Journalists' Best Work

Traditional notions about news came under assault during the decade leading up to the latest American Journalist survey. The rapid growth of media organizations built around cable television and the World Wide Web altered the concept of the news cycle and, in the view of some observers, changed what passed for "news."

In 1992, the year that the last American Journalist survey was conducted, CNN had the cable-TV news business largely to itself. Within 4 years, however, there would be two other 24-hour cable news networks—MSNBC and the Fox News Channel—to compete against CNN.[1] At about the same time, the World Wide Web began to emerge as a force in the news business. *The Chicago Tribune* established what is believed to be the first Internet newspaper service (through America OnLine) in 1992. By the end of 1996, CNN had launched what it claimed to be the first major news and information site on the Web;[2] Time Warner had established the Pathfinder.com site to distribute information from *Time* and other magazines;[3] and *The New York Times, The Washington Post, USA Today* and other daily newspapers had invaded cyberspace with Web sites that showcased their content.[4]

Smaller dailies and weeklies quickly followed, and today thousands of newspapers have Web sites.[5] With the growth of cable TV channels and Web sites devoted to news, those wanting the latest developments no longer had to wait for a regularly scheduled newscast or the arrival of the morning or afternoon paper. News junkies could get their fix "24/7"—24 hours a day, 7 days a week.

As Internet publishing tools became simpler to use and Web domain names cheaper and easier to come by, the business of collecting, editing, and distributing news to consumers became less exclusive, and the definition of a "journalist" more flexible. Someone with a story to tell no longer needed to work for a company that owned expensive presses or broadcast transmitters. A talented "Matt

Drudge" could set up a simple Web site and, with good fortune and perseverance, publish material that vied for attention with the dispatches from the experienced reporters of the big news magazines or the highly trained correspondents of the national TV networks. The neighbor down the block with an understanding of HTML, a personal computer, and a Web address could report the news from Any-town, USA, just like the hard-working professionals at the local newspaper or TV station.

Former journalists Bill Kovach and Tom Rosenstiel have suggested that during the 1990s, a new "mixed media culture" emerged, leaving journalism in "a state of disorientation brought on by rapid technological change, declining market share, and growing pressure to operate with economic efficiency."[6] The perpetual news cycles of cable TV and the Internet created an enormous appetite for the latest news and information.

In the movie "Live From Baghdad," which chronicles a television news crew's efforts to cover the 1991 Gulf War, actor Michael Keaton's character, CNN producer Robert Wiener, calls this phenomenon "feeding the beast." To draw a sizable audience, journalists constantly need to be feeding something compelling to the Web site or cable channel. The ferocious competition among media organizations for the audience's ears and eyes, coupled with unrelenting profit demands of their corporate owners, has brought under assault the standards for news, according to Kovach and Rosenstiel.

"In a sometimes desperate search to reclaim audience, the press has moved more toward sensationalism, entertainment, and opinion," they write in their book *Warp Speed: America in the Age of Mixed Media*.[7] What is at risk, they argue, is journalism based on the traditional news values of verification, proportion, relevance, depth, and quality of interpretation. In its place, they fear a "journalism of assertion" will take over—a journalism that de-emphasizes determining whether a claim is valid and encourages putting an assertion into the arena of public discussion as quickly as possible.[8]

THE IMPORTANCE OF "BEST WORK"

It is within this nascent "mixed media culture" that we asked journalists to talk briefly about an example of their best work. It's useful to examine their choices and the reasons for those choices, because they presumably embody the professional standards that journalists most cherish. "Best work" provides insights into the journalistic values that were driving the production of news at the start of the new millennium. If those values were changing, one result might be that the work that journalists believe represents their best effort would be changing, too.

In the 1982–1983 and 1992 American Journalist surveys, we asked respondents to submit examples of what they considered their best work. In the 1992 survey, about 14% complied with that request, mailing in a copy of a story or script.[9] Because of that relatively low compliance rate, another approach was taken in the latest survey. Each journalist was asked to think about one of the best stories on which he or she had worked during the previous year and to give a brief description of it to the interviewer.[10] More than 90% of the journalists in the main sample of 1,149 responded to that question. From among those responses, 336 were selected randomly for analysis, and they constitute the basis for the findings described in this chapter.

Journalists' responses to the best-work question were categorized by topic. Originally, 20 specific content categories were used, and they are listed in Table 8.1. Six broader categories, combining topics from among the original 20, were used in some analyses. Each journalist also was asked to say why the story he or she had chosen was particularly good. Those rationales were put into 12 categories, and they are shown in Table 8.2. Because this method for assessing best work differs substantially from that used in 1982–1983 and 1992, direct comparisons with the two earlier studies were impossible. Still, information from the earlier surveys is reported to provide a sense of what journalists saw as their best work in previous decades and how their opinions then compare, at least informally, with the work of which they were proudest in 2002.

THE IMPACT OF 9/11 ON STORY TOPICS

The horror that has become known as 9/11 was the nation's dominant news story in the months leading up to this latest American Journalist survey. Perhaps it should be no surprise, then, that accounts of the September 11, 2001, terrorist attacks and their aftermath were the most frequently cited examples of the best work that journalists said they had done in the year prior to the survey. Though 9/11 stories constituted the largest single category of exemplary work, journalists' best efforts covered a broad array of topics, and the reasons that they gave for singling out that work were equally wide ranging. In those two respects, the best-work findings in this survey parallel those of the earlier studies.

The stories on 9/11 and the war on terrorism accounted for almost 16% of the mentions among the responses analyzed. Many journalists spoke with evident pride about the ways that their news organizations responded to both that event and its consequences. "It was a great example of my station providing a true public service," said a 36-year-old television anchor from Ohio. "We brought our (local) viewers to New York and showed how their efforts helped ease a national tragedy." Or this from a 42-year-old news-service journalist from New York: "I think our coverage of September 11 and the aftermath was exemplary. It drew upon our global network. It was fast and analytical." A 27-year-old reporter for a Northeastern daily newspaper was proud of work that examined the effects of 9/11. "Probably the best stuff I've worked on in the past year were things dealing with the September attacks with racism and bigotry," she said. "We urged

TABLE 8.1
Topics of "Best Work" by Type of Medium

Topic	All Media[a] (%)	Print[b] (%)	Broadcast/Cable[c] (%)
9/11, terrorism	15.8	15.7	16.0
General human interest	13.1	12.3	16.0
State and local government or politics	9.8	9.2	12.0
Crime, courts, or law enforcement	8.9	8.4	10.7
Social problems or protests	8.0	8.0	8.0
Business or finance	6.8	8.0	2.7
Education or schools	6.0	5.7	6.7
Environment, energy, utilities, or transportation	6.0	6.1	5.3
Sports	4.8	5.4	2.7
Accidents or disasters	4.5	2.7	10.7
Consumer advice or information	3.0	3.1	2.7
Medicine or health care	2.7	3.1	1.3
Arts, leisure, or travel	2.4	2.7	1.3
Religion	2.1	2.7	0.0
National government or politics	1.8	2.3	0.0
International affairs	0.6	0.4	1.3
Science or space	0.6	0.8	0.0
Celebrities or personalities	0.3	0.4	0.0
Humor	0.3	0.4	0.0
Miscellaneous	2.7	2.7	2.7

[a] N = 336.

[b] N = 261; category includes respondents from daily and weekly newspapers, news magazines, and news services.

[c] N = 75; category includes respondents from radio and television organizations (broadcast and cable).

our readers not to get involved in bigoted, prejudiced acts in the wake of the attacks."

The kinds of 9/11 stories ranged widely. Journalists from New York and Washington, D.C., often cited news coverage of the event itself. A Virginia writer said his story examined the impact on travel. A radio reporter from California did a first-person commentary about her husband's service in the National Guard. Other stories examined the implications of the 9/11 attacks for civil liberties, for the lives of individuals caught up in the tragedy, for the social fabric of the country, for the Bush administration's war on terrorism, and for local communities.

Though 9/11 was the most prevalent topic among the responses analyzed, those stories constituted only a small fraction of the work that journalists said exemplified their best efforts. Human-interest stories—profiles of unusual people, features about community activities, accounts of individuals facing adversity—constituted the second-largest category of best work, followed by stories on state and local government or politics; crime, courts, and law enforcement; and social problems or protests.

Though the methods of analysis here are different from 1982–1983 and 1992, the rankings across the three surveys are remarkably similar. Social problems, general human interest, and state and local government news were all in the top five categories in all the surveys. Ranking much farther down the list in 2002 were stories about celebrities or personalities, which had been a top-five category in both 1982–1983 and 1992. Generally, journalists at the two broad types of news organizations—print and broadcast/cable—tended to value about the same kinds of stories (Table 8.1). The top four categories were the same for both kinds of organizations. Only one difference is worth mentioning: Broadcast journalists were more likely than print journalists to identify stories about accidents or disasters (excluding 9/11) as examples of their best work. About 11% of the "best" broadcast stories were about accidents or disasters—roughly four times the percentage for print journalists. Those stories, of course, play to the strengths of broadcast journalism. They are visually compelling, well suited to the immediacy of broadcast news cycles and high in perceived audience interest or impact.

REASONS FOR CONSIDERING WORK "BEST"

As with the topics of the best work, print and broadcast/cable journalists offered similar reasons for describing their best work as exemplary. Table 8.2 shows the categories of reasons. Two rationales ranked ahead of the rest for both print and broadcast journalists: the belief that a story had strong audience interest or impact, and the belief that a story addressed a key issue or served the public

TABLE 8.2
Reason Work Is Exemplary by Type of Medium

Reason Work Is Best	All Media[a] (%)	Print[b] (%)	Broadcast/Cable[c] (%)
Strong audience interest or impact	22.2	20.2	29.3
Performed public service, addressed key issue	21.3	19.8	26.7
Revealed something surprising, unknown	13.8	14.0	13.3
Emotionally appealing, touching, humorous	13.2	15.1	6.7
Required extraordinary information gathering	6.9	8.5	1.3
Well-executed professional work	6.6	6.6	6.7
Offered perspective or context	5.1	5.8	2.7
Timely	3.0	3.1	2.7
Strong visual, auditory content	1.2	0.8	2.7
Rare or unusual occurrence	1.2	0.8	2.7
Actionable information for audience	0.3	0.4	0.0
Miscellaneous	5.1	5.0	5.3

[a] N = 333

[b] N = 258; category includes daily and weekly newspapers, news magazines, and news services.

[c] N = 75; category includes radio and television organizations (broadcast and cable).

interest. Those two categories accounted for more than 40% of the responses analyzed. Audience impact ranked first or second in both of the 1982–1983 and 1992 studies as well. Through the years, it has been a consistent rationale for choosing a story as an example of best work.[11]

The worldwide impact of 9/11 was so pervasive that it was hard *not* to cite that as a rationale for a story being an example of best work. "Because it affected every single person in the United States," said a 30-year-old wire service reporter from Washington, D.C., who was proud of her 9/11 coverage, ". . . people really wanted to know what was going on and wanted to know what the U.S. was doing in the aftermath of the attacks." Or this rationale from a 56-year-old television reporter-anchor from Illinois: "It was a story that affected everyone, and to be able to do stories that help people understand their own reactions to September 11, or get more information about what they could do to help themselves, is exactly the kind of responsibility I see for myself as a journalist."

Many other topics also were selected because of their audience appeal. An analysis of Social Security retirement benefits was chosen because the writer, a 36-year-old magazine journalist based in New York, believed that it was on the minds of many readers. "It tapped into an issue that a lot of people were worried about at the time and it raised awareness of issues people hadn't considered," he explained.

What story topics were associated with the most common rationales for selecting something as best work? Table 8.3 organizes the 20 content categories into six broader groups, and it shows the distribution across those six groups for journalists who said their best work was good because it

- Had strong audience interest or impact;
- Had performed a public service or addressed a key issue; or
- Was emotionally appealing.

Almost a fifth of the stories judged to have strong audience interest or impact were examples of traditional public-affairs journalism—stories about government, politics, social problems, or education. Apparently journalists believed that it was possible for public-affairs stories to be compelling, despite their reputation for being dull. By comparison, the soft-news category—celebrities, arts, leisure, travel, humor, advice, and general human-interest stories—accounted for only 11% of the best work that was judged to have strong audience interest or impact. Within the strong-appeal category, the largest group of stories was on crimes, accidents, and disasters—mainly the 9/11 stories.

As might be expected, journalism that was chosen as exemplary because it provided a public service or addressed a key social concern was most often a public-affairs story. About 45% of the best works chosen because they were significant were about government, politics, social problems, or education. Virtually tied for the second-place ranking were the categories of general news and soft

TABLE 8.3
"Best Work" in Content Categories by Reason Work Was Exemplary

Type of Content	Strong Audience Interest, Impact (%)[a]	Public Service, Key Issue (%)[b]	Emotionally Appealing (%)[c]	All Reasons (%)[d]
Soft news[e]	10.8	19.7	43.2	19.0
Traditional public affairs[f]	18.9	45.1	6.8	25.6
General news[g]	17.6	21.1	9.1	18.8
Crimes, accidents, disasters[h]	43.2	11.3	34.1	29.2
9/11 articles as percentage of total[i]	28.4	4.2	25.0	15.8
Sports news and features[j]	8.1	0.0	6.8	4.8
Miscellaneous	1.4	2.8	0.0	2.7

[a] N = 74.
[b] N = 71.
[c] N = 44.
[d] N = 333.
[e] This category includes best work on celebrities, human interest, arts, humor, and advice.
[f] This category includes best work on education, government, politics, and social problems.
[g] This category includes best work on business, medicine, energy and the environment, international affairs, science, and religion.
[h] This category includes best work on crimes, accidents, disasters, and 9/11.
[i] 9/11 coverage is a subset of the crimes, accidents, and disaster category.
[j] This category includes best work for all sports coverage.

news. (General news included the topics of business, medicine, energy and environment, international affairs, science, and religion.) The high ranking for soft news was somewhat surprising. Many journalists appear to believe that stories on what traditionally have been considered soft topics often can be as substantive as what's published or broadcast on public affairs, foreign affairs, science, business, and the like.

Two other rationales accounted for a substantial percentage of the reasons that a story was designated "best work." The "scoop" still has cachet. Almost 14% of the responses said a story represented exemplary work because it revealed something that was surprising or not previously known. Emotional appeal was another key reason for choosing an example of best work, though that mattered more to print journalists than broadcast journalists. Among the journalists who characterized their best work as emotionally appealing, more than 40% singled out a soft-news story and another 25% chose a 9/11 story.

BEST WORK AND JOURNALISTIC ROLES

The conceptions that journalists have about their professional roles seem likely to have some association with their ideas about their best work. We presumed

TABLE 8.4

"Best Work" in Content Categories by Journalists' Roles

Type of Content	Disseminator Role[a]		Adversarial Role[b]		Interpretive Role[c]		Mobilizer Role[d]	
	Weaker (N = 139) %	Stronger (N = 197) %	Weaker (N = 185) %	Stronger (N = 148) %	Weaker (N = 149) %	Stronger (N = 187) %	Weaker (N = 152) %	Stronger (N = 184) %
Soft news	18.7	19.3	25.4	11.5	20.8	17.6	19.1	19.0
Traditional public affairs	30.2	22.3	24.9	27.0	22.8	27.8	21.7	28.8
General news	15.1	21.3	15.7	20.9	16.1	20.9	18.4	19.0
Crimes, accidents, disasters	28.1	29.9	26.5	33.1	32.2	26.7	33.6	25.5
9/11 articles as percentage of total[e]	16.5	15.2	10.3	23.0	15.4	16.0	19.1	13.0
Sports news and features	3.6	5.6	5.9	3.4	4.7	4.8	5.3	4.3
Miscellaneous	4.3	1.5	1.6	4.1	3.4	2.1	2.0	3.3

[a] Weaker and stronger categories based on responses to item asking how important it is to get information to the public quickly.

[b] Weaker and stronger categories based on responses to items asking how important it is to be an adversary of public officials and to be an adversary of businesses by being skeptical of their actions.

[c] Weaker and stronger categories based on responses to items asking how important it is to provide analysis and interpretation of complex problems and to provide analysis and interpretation of international developments.

[d] Weaker and stronger categories based on responses to item asking how important it is to motivate ordinary people to get involved in public discussions of important issues and to point people toward possible solutions to society's problems.

[e] 9/11 coverage is a subset of the crimes, accidents, and disaster category.

that journalists would value stories that seem consistent with the journalistic roles that they embrace most strongly. Table 8.4 shows how journalistic roles and the choices of best work relate to one another. The table is based, in part, on answers that journalists gave to seven questions that probed their thinking about four professional roles identified in previous chapters: the disseminator, adversarial, interpretive, and populist mobilizer roles.[12]

The seven questions, described in the notes section of Table 8.4, were used to determine the degree to which a journalist embraced a particular professional role. Those roles are not mutually exclusive; that is, a journalist could strongly embrace none, some, or even all of the roles. Here are the noteworthy findings from those analyses:

- Journalists who more strongly endorsed the disseminator role—who believed that it was crucial to get information out to the public as quickly as possible—were somewhat less likely to select a traditional public-affairs story as an example of best work than those with a weaker belief in the disseminator role. This may reflect the fact that many public-affairs stories are long, detailed reporting projects, not breaking news that needs to be shared quickly with the public.

- Those who more strongly embraced an adversarial role were drawn less to soft news and more to some type of hard news—crimes, accidents, disasters, business, medicine, science, environment, international affairs, and religion. The more strongly adversarial journalists also were more likely to cite 9/11 stories as an example of their best work. There was no appreciable difference, however, when it came to public-affairs journalism.

- Journalists who more strongly supported the interpretive role as an analyst of problems differed little in their choice of best work from those who were less enthusiastic about an interpretive role.

- Journalists who more strongly believed that they had an obligation to mobilize public discussions of significant issues or to point people toward solutions to society's problems were slightly more likely to list public-affairs journalism as exemplary work and slightly less likely to cite a story about a crime, accident, or disaster.

All in all, a journalist's support of a particular professional role occasionally seemed to have a modest association with the kind of story he or she chose as exemplary work. That also is an apt summary about the relationship between support for a professional role and the rationale used to explain the choice of best work. For the most part, there was no clear association between these two factors, with a couple of exceptions:

- Journalists who embraced the interpretive role were more likely to give examples of exemplary work that they said revealed something unknown.

At the same time, they were somewhat less likely to cite best work that they believed had strong audience interest or impact.

• Journalists who supported the disseminator role tended to say that their best-work example had strong audience appeal and were somewhat less likely to say that it addressed a key issue or provided a public service.

COMMITMENT TO JOURNALISM

The impact of news companies' business practices on the quality of U.S. journalism has been a recurring source of concern within the profession. The *Newspaper Research Journal* devoted an entire issue to the topic in 2004, with many of the articles expressing concern that journalistic quality was falling victim to corporate profit goals.[13] A 1999 article in *Fortune* described the staff cutbacks imposed on network news divisions in an effort to improve profitability.[14] Almost half of the journalists responding in a 1999 national survey[15] said that bottom-line pressures were damaging the quality of journalism at their news organizations. Others have voiced similar complaints, but perhaps none more dramatically than Jay Harris. Harris quit in March 2001 as publisher of the *Mercury News* in San Jose, California, announcing publicly that he would not accede to demands by the paper's owner at the time, the Knight Ridder Corp., to cut costs to improve profits. In resigning, Harris said he feared that Knight Ridder's insistence on higher profits would hurt the newspaper's quality.[16]

Some have suggested that bottom-line pressures could tempt news organizations to emphasize journalism that's cheaper and easier to do, that's targeted at the audiences that advertisers desire most, and that's intended more to entertain than to inform. Others have suggested that the bottom-line pressures put at risk investigative journalism or comprehensive analyses of social problems, which are more expensive because they require more time to produce.[17]

In the most recent American Journalist survey, we included three items that asked journalists to assess the commitment that their news organizations had to producing high-quality journalism. Those items asked respondents to say how strongly they agreed or disagreed with assertions that, at their news organization, profits were a higher priority than good journalism; that the quality of journalism at their organization had been rising steadily during the previous few years; and that newsroom resources had been shrinking at their organization during the previous few years.[18] Those questions were used to create a scale to assess the trend in organizational commitment to quality journalism, at least as perceived by the journalists we asked. Using that scale, we divided the sample of journalists whose best-work responses we've been examining into two groups.[19] One group included the journalists who reported that their news organization had a stronger commitment to journalistic quality and the other included journalists who reported a weaker commitment to journalistic quality. Then we looked for differ-

TABLE 8.5
"Best Work" in Content Categories by Commitment to Quality Journalism

Content Categories	Stronger Journalistic Commitment (%) [a]	Weaker Journalistic Commitment (%)
Type of content		
Soft news[b]	17.0	21.3
Traditional public affairs[c]	27.8	23.9
General news[d]	16.5	20.6
Crimes, accidents, disasters[e]	32.4	25.8
9/11 articles as percentage of total[f]	18.8	12.3
Sports news and features[g]	4.0	5.8
Miscellaneous	2.3	2.6
Reasons for choice of best work[h]		
Strong audience interest or impact	23.0	20.1
Performed public service, addressed key issue	23.0	20.1
Revealed something surprising, unknown	14.9	12.3
Emotionally appealing, touching, humorous	12.1	14.9
Required extraordinary information gathering	6.9	7.1
Well-executed professional work	5.2	8.4
Offered perspective or context	5.2	5.2
Timely	2.9	3.2
Strong visual, auditory content	0.6	1.3
Rare or unusual occurrence	0.6	1.9
Actionable information for audience	0.6	0.0
Miscellaneous	5.2	5.2

[a] N = 176 for "stronger" category and 155 for "weaker" category.

[b] This category includes best work on celebrities, human interest, arts, humor, and advice.

[c] This category includes best work on education, government, politics, and social problems.

[d] This category includes best work on business, medicine, the environment, international affairs, science, and religion.

[e] This category includes best work on crimes, accidents, disasters, and 9/11.

[f] 9/11 coverage is a subset of the crimes, accidents, and disaster category.

[g] This category includes best work for sports coverage.

[h] N = 174 for "stronger" category and 154 for "weaker" category.

ences in the examples of best work and in the rationales for choosing best work from journalists in those two groups.

Table 8.5 shows the differences in the topics and rationales. The comparisons show more similarities than differences between the groups. For both, the top reasons for choosing a story as an example of best work were its strong audience appeal or its capacity to perform a public service. Stories that revealed something previously unknown or that touched an emotional chord also were highly regarded by both groups. The striking similarity in these rationales seems to imply that the criteria for judging high-quality journalism are widely shared within the profession and are not influenced significantly by the organizational environment in which a journalist works. In other words, it didn't matter whether journalists worked for "good" news organizations or "bad" news organizations. The reasons for selecting something as an example of best work were about the same in each organizational environment.

A few minor differences surfaced in the topics of the best-work stories, however. At organizations perceived to have a stronger commitment to good journalism, the best work was slightly more likely to be traditional public-affairs journalism and slightly less likely to be a soft-news story or a general-news article on such things as business, medicine, science or the environment. In addition, journalists from the more "committed" organizations were somewhat more likely to cite a 9/11 article as an example of their best work. These results make sense if one assumes that public-affairs journalism tends to be expensive and if a stronger journalistic commitment translates into more reporting resources. Still, if the public-affairs and general-news categories were combined, the percentages between the "stronger" and "weaker" groups would be about the same. That leaves only two small differences between the groups: Organizations with a stronger journalistic commitment were associated with more examples of 9/11 coverage, and organizations with a weaker commitment were associated with more examples of human-interest or soft-news articles.

CONCLUSIONS

In an age of mixed media, serious articles reflecting longtime news values still dominate the work that journalists say represents their best efforts. Certainly the findings here do not necessarily contradict the argument that the "journalism of assertion" has gained a toehold within the news media and represents a threat to traditional professional standards. Nor do they necessarily disprove claims that news organizations are becoming addicted to celebrity gossip, enamored with lightweight features or dependent on cheaply produced, event-driven news coverage. Those kinds of stories may be common—perhaps even abundant—in newspapers and news magazines and on newscasts and news Web sites. We didn't assess quantity here, just one example of quality in the form of descriptions of best work.

These findings do suggest, however, that many journalists still value news over softer human-interest articles or features when thinking about the best work that they do. Roughly 70% of the 336 best-work descriptions that were examined in this study fell into the broad category of news. Of the 10 content categories with the highest number of mentions, 8 were news categories. And even though general human-interest stories constituted the single largest category of mentions, outside of 9/11 stories, they often focused on people who were emblematic of broader social problems—individuals grappling with the health-care system, parents facing problems with adoption, teens struggling with anorexia. In sum, most journalists seemed to prize substantive work over trivial work.

The most common reasons that journalists gave for judging stories to be best work were substantive, too. Their best-work examples were rarely chosen because they were titillating or entertaining. In fact, it was far more likely that a journalist chose an example of exemplary work because it performed a public service, revealed something previously unknown, offered perspective or context, or involved extraordinary information gathering rather than because it was touching or emotionally appealing (though many examples of excellent journalism have those qualities, too). Those first three categories together accounted for roughly half of the rationales offered for choosing an example of best work— triple the number of times that a story was chosen because it was emotionally appealing or humorous. Even the work chosen because of its high audience interest or impact tended to be serious journalism—often 9/11 stories but also articles on child abuse, homelessness, housing, education, and so forth.

Though the methods for analysis were different from those used in 1982–1983 and 1992, what was discovered tracked with the findings from those earlier surveys. In general, the journalists whose responses were examined here selected examples of serious journalism as their best work, and they chose those examples for reasons other than their entertainment value.

NOTES

1. Dan M. Flournoy and Robert K. Stewart, *CNN: Making News in the Global Market* (Luton, UK: University of Luton Press, 1997), pp. 135, 141.
2. David Carlson, *Online Timeline*. Accessed on June 29, 2004, at http://iml.jou.ufl.edu/carlson/1990s.shtml.
3. Kate Maddox, "Net Access Luring Cable Firms." *Interactive Age*, May 22, 1995, p. 4.
4. Carlson, *Online Timeline*.
5. No exact count of newspaper Web sites is available, according to Eric Meyer, managing partner of Newslink.org. In 2000, Meyer estimated 10,792 newspaper Web sites existed. By 2004, that figure approached about 25,000. Personal correspondence, June 28, 2004.
6. Bill Kovach and Tom Rosenstiel. *Warp Speed: America in the Age of Mixed Media*. (New York: Century Foundation Press, 1999), p. 2.
7. Kovach and Rosenstiel, *Warp Speed*, pp. 2, 9.
8. Kovach and Rosenstiel, *Warp Speed*, p. 8.
9. David H. Weaver and G. Cleveland Wilhoit, *The American Journalist in the 1990s: U.S. News People at the End of an Era* (Mahwah, NJ: Lawrence Erlbaum Associates, 1996), pp. 217–218.
10. See Appendix II for exact wording. Question 47 asks about an example of the journalist's best story and Question 48 asks why the journalists thinks that story is particularly good.
11. Whether a story served the public interest or dealt with a significant issue was not directly examined in the 1982–1983 and 1992 studies.
12. For a more complete examination of journalists' professional roles, see Chapter 4 of this book.
13. Geneva Overholser, "Good Journalism, Good Business: An Industry Perspective," *Newspaper Research Journal*, 25, 1 (Winter 2004), pp. 8–17.

14. Marc Gunther, "The New Face of Network News," *Fortune*, Feb. 1, 1999, p. 76.
15. Pew Research Center for the People & the Press, "Introduction and Summary," *Striking the Balance, Audience Interests, Business Pressures and Journalists' Values*, May 30, 1999. Accessed on June 29, 2004, at http://people-press.org/reports/display.php3?ReportID=67
16. Howard Kurtz, "Bottom-Line News: San Jose Publisher Quits to Protest Emphasis on Profits Before Journalism." *The Washington Post*, March 20, 2001, p. C1.
17. James D. Squires, *Read All About It! The Corporate Takeover of America's Newspapers* (New York: Times Books, 1993), pp. 207–234; Gilbert Cranberg, Randall Bezanson, and John Soloski, *Taking Stock: Journalism and the Publicly Traded Newspaper Company* (Ames: Iowa State University Press, 2001), pp. 12–15; Lucia Moses, "Profiting From Experience: New Studies Seek to Show that 'Quality' Can Pay Off. There's Just One Problem: No One Agrees on What 'Quality' Means." *Editor & Publisher*, Feb. 3, 2003, p. 10; Gunther, "The New Face of Network News."
18. See Appendix II for exact wording of these questions (40A, 40B, and 40C).
19. A simple additive scale was created. Values on the scale ranged from 3 to 15. The sample was divided into two groups at approximately the median, with 48% of the valid responses falling into the weaker-commitment group and 52% into the stronger-commitment group.

Chapter 9

Conclusions

In the book reporting the findings of our 1992 national survey of U.S. journalists, we wrote that the three studies of 1971, 1982–1983, and 1992 suggested that the world around journalists "had changed much more than they have."[1] We noted that one reason for this was that we had defined journalists in these studies to focus squarely on traditional news media. Another reason was that our portrait of journalists was based largely on what individual journalists told us rather than on a systematic study of their news organizations, although we did include questions about the backgrounds of journalists and the type, size, ownership, goals, and practices of the organizations for which they worked.

The picture of U.S. journalists in 2002 that we have provided in this book is also one marked more by stability than change, even though we have included separate samples of online and minority journalists to compensate for their relatively small numbers among journalists working for traditional mainstream news media in the United States. This chapter briefly reviews our main findings and comments on their implications for journalism in the United States.

DEMOGRAPHICS

Among the similarities with previous studies, we found, in 2002, that the bulk of U.S. journalists were still concentrated in the print news media, especially in daily newspapers, and their geographic distribution matched the overall U.S. population fairly closely, especially in the South and West. Journalists in 2002 were no more likely to be women than in 1992 or 1982–1983, even though there was an increase in women with less than 5 years of experience. Women journalists were still less likely to be married than men and less likely to have children living with them.

There were some notable differences from 1992, however, including a decrease in the size of the journalistic workforce in traditional U.S. news media, an increase in average age of U.S. journalists, and slight growth in the proportions of racial and ethnic minorities (especially among journalists hired between 1998 and 2002, and especially in television news). U.S. journalists also changed in terms of religious backgrounds and reflected the overall U.S. population less closely than in earlier decades. There was a notable drop in the proportion coming from a Protestant background and an increase in those claiming to be brought up in no religion or something other than Protestant, Catholic, or Jewish. Journalists in 2002 were also much less likely than the U.S. population to practice any religion or to rate religion or religious beliefs as very important.

These demographic findings suggest some progress in recent years in the recruitment of women and minorities, but they also suggest some problems for young people who want to advance in mainstream U.S. news organizations. Because the size of this journalistic labor force shrunk during the 1990s, many of the most desirable jobs in U.S. journalism are held by those in their late 40s or early 50s who are still years away from retirement. Without new growth in these news media, there will be relatively few opportunities for advancement for the next decade or so, and this will make it difficult to retain the brightest and most ambitious young journalists, especially women and people of color.

These findings also suggest that U.S. journalists in 2002 differed from the U.S. population and workforce at large in terms of age, gender, marital status, parental responsibilities, race, ethnic origins, and religion. For many occupations, these differences would be considered of little interest or relevance, but not so for journalism, where these characteristics are assumed to be correlated with interests and perspectives that are reflected in news coverage.

MEDIA USE

The New York Times and *The Wall Street Journal* were still the most regularly read newspapers among U.S. journalists, and *Newsweek* and *Time* remained their favorite magazines. As in past decades, only a handful of newspapers and magazines were read regularly by more than 10% of all journalists, and all but one were based on the East Coast, reinforcing the dominance of the East Coast media in U.S. journalism.

Compared with the early 1990s, there was a slight decline in the average number of local and network television news shows watched each week by U.S. journalists and an increase in the viewing of cable TV network news. Again, these patterns of media use are assumed to influence the news coverage of journalists, or to reduce the diversity of interests and views reflected in the news, so they are of interest to those outside journalism.

POLITICS

Journalists have been portrayed as social reformers who are likely to be more liberal than conservative politically.[2] In our 1982–1983 national survey of U.S. journalists, we found a slight left-leaning tendency, but it was much less pronounced than that found in Lichter and Rothman's early 1980s study of Northeastern elite journalists.[3] In our 1992 study, we found a more pronounced tilt to the left. In 2002, we found U.S. journalists somewhat less likely to place themselves on the left and somewhat more likely to claim to be a little to the right than in 1992. But compared with the general population, journalists in 2002 were less likely to think of themselves as on the right side of the political spectrum and much more likely to consider themselves on the left.

Neither journalists nor the general public changed dramatically in political leanings from 1992 to 2002, although journalists in 2002 were less likely to identify with the Democratic party than a decade earlier and slightly more likely to identify with the Republican party. It should be noted that journalists' political views and political party identification varied considerably by gender, race and ethnicity, and type of news medium, so there is not a monolithic political mindset among U.S. journalists. This is important to remember, given the perennial charges of political bias in news coverage and the widespread assumption that the political views of individual journalists influence their news coverage.

EDUCATION

In 1971, John Johnstone and his colleagues found substantial diversity in the educational backgrounds of U.S. journalists but predicted that differences in these backgrounds would become less pronounced as those in the oldest age groups were replaced by younger journalists.[4] This prediction was supported by our 1982–1983 study and even more strongly by our 1992 and 2002 surveys. By 2002, there were very few U.S. journalists without a college degree (only 11%) as compared with 1971 (42%), and the percentage of all journalists who majored in journalism–mass communication (53%) was about twice what it was in 1971. This was one of the greatest changes in individual characteristics of U.S. journalists in the 30-year period, in addition to an increasing median age.

Differences in proportions of college graduates by media type and size were markedly less in 2002 than in 1971 or 1982–1983, but differences in college major by region of the country still persisted, with journalists who studied in the Northeast much less likely to have majored in journalism–mass communication than those who attended college in another region of the country. As in 1992, news magazines were by far the least likely of all the news media to employ graduates of journalism–mass communication programs, although they were the most likely to hire college graduates and those with graduate degrees.

Even though more journalists in 2002 had graduated from college and more had majored in journalism or communications as undergraduates, it should be remembered that in most undergraduate journalism programs the major totaled only about one-fourth of all classes taken, and, in a number of these programs, a second major or concentration was required. In 2002, we found a few differences between those who majored in journalism and other subjects but many more similarities.

Nevertheless, the educational backgrounds of U.S. journalists have become less diverse since Johnstone et al.'s 1971 study, and there is a concern that college graduates, who are a minority of the total population, may not be able to be sufficiently sensitive in their news coverage to the concerns of the majority of the population who are not college graduates. This difference in educational backgrounds is one of the largest we found between U.S. journalists and the overall U.S. population, and it raises again the question of whether journalists are "elites."[5]

WORK

The news media's embrace of the Internet, the graying of its labor force, the struggles to maintain profit levels during a recession, the ongoing consolidation in ownership, and the battle to hang on to audiences during the decade of the early 1990s to the early years of the 21st century all seemed to suggest big changes in American journalists' views about their work and their newsrooms. But the overall findings from our 2002 study regarding these views are more suggestive of stability or perhaps small shifts in attitudes and working conditions.

Journalists in 2002 were a bit more satisfied with their work than they were a decade earlier, and the percentage planning to leave the news media during the next five years dropped. Journalists rated their news organizations' efforts to inform the public somewhat higher than in 1992 and tended to agree that the quality of work was rising at their news organizations. In addition, median salaries outpaced inflation during the 1990s, and supervisors were perceived as meeting more often with their staffs in 2002 than in 1992.

Not all of our findings regarding journalistic work and workplaces were positive, however. We also found that women journalists rated their job satisfaction lower than did men, and the youngest journalists tended to be considerably more pleased with their jobs than journalists in the next age group (25–34), raising concerns about the ability of the news media to retain their younger recruits. We found that even though salaries did rise faster than inflation in the 1990s, the actual average purchasing power of U.S. journalists in 2002 still remained below that of the early 1970s, and the pay gap between all men and women journalists did not shrink during the 1990s. These gender disparities in pay and job satisfaction will not help to recruit and retain women journalists, but it is encouraging that the median salaries of men and women U.S. journalists hired during the 1990s were essentially equal.

Reporters' perceived autonomy and influence in the newsroom declined during the 1990s, continuing a downward trend from the early 1980s. Both perceived autonomy and influence are predictors of higher levels of job satisfaction, and, more important, both could have serious implications for the freedom and diversity of news coverage. If reporters are not able to cover stories they think are important, this can negatively impact the ability of journalists to provide a full and fair account of the day's events—something that is necessary for an informed citizenry in a democracy.

A number of findings concerning the work and newsrooms of U.S. journalists in 2002 suggest a pattern of more stability than of change, however. These include the proportions of journalists involved in news gathering, news processing, and news supervision; the amount of feedback from news sources and the public; the median size of news organizations; and the reasons that journalists cited for choosing this occupation and for planning to leave it. Thus, for the most part, U.S. journalists in 2002 saw their work environment in much the same way as they saw it in 1992.

PROFESSIONALISM

Our 2002 study found the professional culture of U.S. journalists to be somewhat stronger than in 1992. A 20-year trend of declining membership in professional organizations was reversed, and readership of professional and trade publications stabilized. Thanks to the World Wide Web, increasing numbers of journalists appeared to be exposed to news and commentary about the field of journalism. Still, no single professional organization or publication reached more than a small minority of U.S. journalists in 2002, unlike other professions such as law, medicine, or accounting, where common literature and professional associations reach far greater proportions.

Thus, the institutions of U.S. journalism are relatively weak at a time when the professionalism of journalists is questioned almost daily. As in 1992, there is a professional mindset among U.S. journalists, but its influence is found mainly in individual news organizations rather than in the larger institutions of journalism. There is too much variation among individual journalists and news organizations to claim a more professional journalism in the United States in general in 2002 as compared with earlier decades.

ROLES

The perceived importance of various roles could be considered another measure of the professionalism of journalists. Two of the 15 journalistic roles we asked about in our 2002 survey have remained dominant in the minds of U.S. journalists over the years: investigating government claims and getting information to the public quickly. But the timely information role declined significantly in perceived importance during the 1990s, perhaps because of cable TV news and the speed of the Internet. This shift was even more evident when the 15 role questions were grouped into broader functions of journalism. Whereas most journalists continued to think of the interpretive function as most important, the neutral disseminator function showed a significant decline from the early 1990s and the adversarial function remained very important to only a minority of journalists, just as it has since it was first measured in our 1982–1983 study.

A relatively new function, which we have called populist mobilizer, grew in perceived importance during the 1990s, although only a minority of journalists in 2002 regarded it as very important. Still, this is evidence that the related concept of public (or civic) journalism had established a foothold with a larger minority of journalists in 2002 than a decade earlier. Although the more abstract ideas of public journalism received wide support, the methods to implement these ideas (such as convening meetings of officials and citizens and conducting public opinion polls) received notably less support.

In general, the typical journalist's thinking about roles was considerably less pluralistic in 2002 than in the 1980s and 1990s. The majority in our latest study are now more strongly in favor of an interpretive role than in the last quarter of the 20th century, probably in large part because of the immense change in the media landscape caused by the Internet and the proliferation of television news channels. This interpretive bent puts journalism more in line with the recommendations made a half century ago by the Hutchins Commission on Freedom of the Press for a more socially responsible news media that would provide "a truthful, comprehensive, and intelligent account of the day's events in a context which gives them meaning," among other things.[6] But it should be remembered that journalists working at larger news organizations were more likely to embrace the interpretive and adversarial roles, whereas those at smaller news media were more likely to endorse the populist mobilizer role, and those working in the print media were more likely to consider important the adversarial and populist mobilizer roles than were those at broadcast news media.

NEWS VALUES AND ETHICS

Our findings suggested that the largest influence on news judgment was newsroom training, and this influence seems to be stronger than in previous surveys. Clearly the more personal contacts of journalists continued to influence their ideas about what is newsworthy. Newsroom context was also the most important influence on journalists' views of which reporting practices might be justified given an important story, emphasizing the importance of learning in the newsroom and the responsibility of editors, news directors, and other managers to provide leadership in raising journalists' ethical consciousness and getting them to think more carefully about what should be and should not be considered newsworthy. This responsibility appears in 2002 to fall more heavily on individual news organizations than on journalistic institutions, as we noted earlier, for better or worse.

Perhaps this responsibility is being taken more seriously in 2002 than in 1992, because our most recent findings show significant decreases in the justification of some of the 10 questionable reporting practices we have asked about since 1982. Claiming to be someone else and paying people for confidential information were justified by only small minorities of journalists, and the proportions justifying undercover employment, making use of personal documents without permission, and disclosing the names of rape victims all declined from 1992 to 2002.

Overall, our 2002 survey of U.S. journalists suggests somewhat more professionalism than 10 years earlier, including more college graduates, better compensation, increased job satisfaction, and somewhat increased endorsement of the roles of investigating government claims, analyzing complex problems, and being skeptical of business actions. There was also less emphasis on the entertainment role. But, as noted earlier, these indicators vary substantially by individual news organizations, so one must be cautious in claiming a more professional (or perhaps more conservative?) journalism in the United States in 2002 than a decade earlier.

It's clear from our findings that the stronger predictors of which roles journalists consider most important, and which reporting practices they are most likely to consider justifiable, are measures of organizational context, such as type of medium, type of ownership, size of newsroom, type of position (editor, reporter, etc.), amount of feedback from others in the newsroom, and also journalists' perceptions of how well their organizations perform, the political leanings of their newsrooms, and the amount of freedom they have to select stories and emphasize certain aspects. These findings raise questions about how much U.S. journalism and news coverage will (or should) change if more women and racial/ethnic minorities are hired or if more journalists work for online news media, unless these journalists change the news organizations for which they work in fundamental ways.

In spite of considerable diversity of organizational settings, our findings regarding journalists' descriptions of their best work suggest that serious articles reflecting longtime news values still dominate the work that U.S. journalists say represents their best efforts.[7] These findings suggest that many journalists still value news over softer human-interest articles or features when thinking about the best work that they do. Even though general human-interest stories constituted the single largest category of mentions outside of stories about the September 11, 2001, terrorist airplane attacks on New York City and Washington, D.C., they often focused on people who were emblematic of broader social problems such as the health-care system, problems with adoption, or teens struggling with anorexia.

The most common reasons that journalists cited for considering certain stories to be examples of their best work were also substantive. Such examples were rarely chosen because they were titillating or entertaining, but rather because they performed a public service, revealed something previously unknown, offered perspective or context, or involved unusual information gathering. Even the work chosen because of its high audience interest or impact tended to be serious journalism dealing with the 9/11 terrorist attacks and subjects such as child abuse, homelessness, housing, education, and so forth.

As did John Johnstone and his colleagues in 1976, we conclude this 2002 study of U.S. journalists with both concern and optimism. There are more positive findings in 2002 than in 1992, as noted earlier, and the questions on journalists' best work suggest that the public service values of U.S. journalism are still alive and well in the minds and hearts of many U.S. journalists. But there is also reason for concern about retaining young women and people of color in journalism and in protecting the editorial freedom and autonomy of journalists from corporate pressures and interests that often come into conflict with the public interest.

In our 1992 study, we concluded that the pluralism we found in the mindset of American journalists suggested that they had accepted the challenge of trying to create a world "in which a classical notion of democracy would make sense" and of shining a "searchlight of publicity" on powerful official and private interests.[8] We questioned, however, whether the culture of the modern, corporate newsroom would be able to sustain this democratic altruism and provide the resources needed to shine this searchlight on these powerful private and governmental interests that might conflict with the public good. Many of the findings from this 2002 study give us hope that even in this age of very large multinational corporations, the public service and investigative values of U.S. journalism are still alive and well. But other findings give us pause for concern, especially the declines in perceived autonomy of many journalists in this country and the cuts in newsroom resources at some organizations.

We hope that the journalism of this 21st century and this new millennium will be "a journalism of sense making based on synthesis, verification, and fierce independence," in the words of Bill Kovach and Tom Rosenstiel, and that it will not "be subsumed inside the world of commercialized speech."[9] We also hope that the journalist of this new century will live up to the description of the journalist written in the early 20th century by Frank Crane:

> I am the journalist. . . .
> I do not judge. I record. I do not praise or blame. I tell. . . .
> The ethics of my profession may be told in one word—truth. . . .
> No man can buy my light. No man can buy my silence. . . .[10]

NOTES

1. David H. Weaver and G. Cleveland Wilhoit, *The American Journalist in the 1990s: U.S. News People at the End of an Era* (Mahwah, NJ: Lawrence Erlbaum Associates, 1996), p. 231.
2. Leo Rosten, *The Washington Correspondents* (New York: Harcourt, Brace and Company, 1937; reprint ed. Arno Press, 1974), p. 191; William L. Rivers, "The Correspondents After Twenty-five Years," *Columbia Journalism Review*, 1 (Spring 1962), p. 5; Stephen Hess, *The Washington Reporters* (Washington, DC: The Brookings Institution, 1981), pp. 87–90; Robert Lichter and Stanley Rothman, "Media and Business Elites," *Public Opinion* (October/November 1981), pp. 42–46, 59–60; Bernard Goldberg, *Bias: A CBS Insider Exposes How the Media Distort the News* (New York: HarperCollins, 2003).
3. David H. Weaver and G. Cleveland Wilhoit, *The American Journalist: A Portrait of U.S. News People and Their Work* (Bloomington: Indiana University Press, 1986), pp. 25–32; Lichter and Rothman, "Media and Business Elites," p. 43.
4. John W. C. Johnstone, Edward J. Slawski, and William W. Bowman, *The News People: A Sociological Portrait of American Journalists and Their Work* (Urbana: University of Illinois Press, 1976), pp. 31–32.
5. David H. Weaver and G. Cleveland Wilhoit, "Journalists—Who Are They, Really?" *Media Studies Journal*, 6, 4 (Fall 1992), pp. 63–79; Ted Gup, "Who's a Journalist?–I," *Media Studies Journal*, 13, 2 (Spring/Summer 1999), pp. 34–37; and Weaver and Wilhoit, *The American Journalist in the 1990s*, pp. 232–242.
6. The Commission on Freedom of the Press, *A Free and Responsible Press* (Chicago & London: University of Chicago Press, 1947) p. 20.
7. These findings are based on a random sample of 336 of the journalists in our main probability sample who responded to the open-ended questions asking them to describe a story that represented some of their best work and to tell us why they thought that this story was particularly good. More than 90% of the journalists in the main sample of 1,149 responded, so this random subsample should be representative of the population of U.S. journalists within the limits of sampling error (about 5.5 percentage points at the 95% level of confidence).
8. Michael Schudson, *The Power of News* (Cambridge, MA: Harvard University Press, 1995), p. 223.
9. Bill Kovach and Tom Rosenstiel, *The Elements of Journalism* (New York: Crown Publishers, 2001), p. 193.
10. Frank Crane, *Four Minute Essays* (Vol. 6) (New York and Chicago: Wm. H. Wise & Co., 1919), pp. 42–43.

Bibliography

Abbott, Julie. (2003). Does employee satisfaction matter? A study to determine whether low employee morale affects customer satisfaction and profits in the business-to-business sector. *Journal of Communication Management.* 7(4), 333–339.

Alter, Jonathan. (2003). An erosion of trust. *Newsweek.* 141(21), 47.

American Association of University Professors. (2003, October 22). [Official Web Site of the American Association of University Professors]. Accessed on October 22, 2003, at http://www.aaup.org/aboutaaup/description.htm

American Press Institute and Pew Center for Civic Journalism. (2002, September). *The great divide: Female leadership in U.S. newsrooms.* Accessed on September 1, 2005, at http://www.asne.org/index.cfm?id=4051

Arant, David M., & Meyer, Philip. (1997, Fall). A survey of daily newspaper staff members. *Nieman Reports.* 51(3), 55–62.

Associated Press. (1998, June 29). *Cincinnati Enquirer* to pay $10 million to Chiquita. *Wall Street Journal,* p. B7.

Bagdikian, Ben H. (1997). *The Media Monopoly* (5th ed.). Boston: Beacon Press.

Bandler, James. (2004, April 23). Report cites "virus of fear" at *USA Today. Wall Street Journal,* p. B1.

Barron, Jackie. (2000, Winter). Multimedia reporting in a never-ending news cycle: A Tampa reporter covers a murder trial for TV, newspaper and the web. *Nieman Reports.* 54(4), 52–53.

Bates, Stephen. (1995). *Realigning Journalism With Democracy: The Hutchins Commission, Its Time, and Ours.* Washington, D.C.: The Annenberg Washington Program in Communications Policy Studies of Northwestern University.

Beam, Randal A. (1990, June). Journalism professionalism as an organizational-level concept. *Journalism Monographs* (No. 121).

Beam, Randal A. (1998, Summer). What it means to be a market-oriented newspaper. *Newspaper Research Journal.* 19(3), 2–20.

Beam, Randal A. (2003, Summer). Content differences between daily newspapers with strong and weak market orientations. *Journalism & Mass Communication Quarterly.* 80(2), 368–390.

Becker, Lee B., & Engleman, Thomas E. (1988, Autumn). Class of 1987 describes salaries, satisfaction found in first jobs. *Journalism Educator.* 43(3), 4–10.

Becker, Lee B., & Kosicki, Gerald M. (1993). *Summary results from the 1992 annual enrollment & graduate surveys.* Paper presented at the 1993 convention of the Association for Education in Journalism, Kansas City, MO. Table 2.

Becker, Lee B., & Kosicki, Gerald M. (1993, Autumn). Annual census of enrollment records fewer undergrads. *Journalism Educator*. 48(3), 56–57.

Becker, Lee B., Vlad, Tudor, Huh, Jisu, & Mace, Nancy R. (2003, August 1). *2002 annual survey of journalism & mass communication graduates*. Paper presented at the 2003 convention of the Association for Education in Journalism & Mass Communication, Kansas City, Missouri. Tables S1, S20. See also the following Web site: http://www.grady.uga.edu/annualsurveys/

Becker, Lee B., Vlad, Tudor, Huh, Jisu, & Mace, Nancy R. (2003, Autumn). Annual enrollment report: Graduate and undergraduate enrollments increase sharply. *Journalism & Mass Communication Educator*. 58(3), 273–300. See also the following Web site: http://www.grady.uga.edu/annualsyrveys/

Becker, Lee B., Vlad, Tudor, Huh, Jisu, & Mace, Nancy R. (2003, December 15). Gender equity elusive, surveys show. *Freedomforum.org*, pp. 1–6. Accessed September 5, 2005, at http://www.freedomforum.org/templates/document.asp?documentID=17784

Belkin, Lisa. (2003, October 26). The opt-out revolution. *The New York Times Sunday Magazine*. Accessed October 30, 2003, at http://www.nytimes.com/2003/10/26/magazine/26WOMEN.html?pagewatned-print&position=

Black, Jay, Steele, Bob, & Barney, Ralph. (1999). *Doing Ethics in Journalism: A Handbook with Case Studies* (3rd ed.). Boston: Allyn & Bacon.

Blalock Hubert M., Jr., (1972). *Social Statistics* (2nd ed.). New York: McGraw-Hill Book Co.

Bolner, Crystal. (2003, April 9). Women want out of newsrooms more than men. *The American Society of Newspaper Editors Reporter*, Reston, VA, p. 18. Also available online at http://www.asne.org/index2.cfm?id=4499

Bowman, James. (1996, December). A pretense of professionalism. *New Criterion*. 15(4), 55–61.

Bowman, William (1974). *Distaff Journalists: Women as a Minority Group in the News Media*. Dissertation, University of Illinois at Chicago Circle.

Branham, Lorraine E. (2003, July). Learning takes time. *Quill*. 91(6), 9.

Brown, Fred. (2003, March). A classic case of good reporter, bad reporter. *Quill*. 91(2), 28–29.

Brown, Fred. (2003, July). Ethics week brought plenty of ethics discuss. *Quill*. 91(6), 60–61.

Buchanan, Brian J., Newton, Eric, & Thien, Richard. (1993). *No train, no gain: Continuing training for newspaper journalists in the 1990s*. Arlington, VA: The Freedom Forum.

Buchholz, Michael. (1998). Yellow journalism. In M. A. Blanchard (Ed.), *History of the Mass Media in the United States*. Chicago: Fitzroy Dearborn Publishers.

Carey, James W. (2003). Mirror of the *Times*. *Nation*. 276(23), 13.

Carlson, David. *Online Timeline*. Accessed on June 29, 2004, at http://iml.jou.ufl.edu/carlson/1990s.shtml.

Case, Tony. (2000, October 30). Nowhere but up. *Editor & Publisher*, pp. 20–25.

Case study: At the vanguard of successful recruitment. (1998, May). *HR Focus*. 75(5), 9.

Chunovic, Louis. (2004, July 12). Close up: ABC stations group. *Broadcasting & Cable*, p. 28.

Cockburn, Alexander. (2005, May 5). The decline and fall of American journalism. *Nation*. 276(18), 9.

Cohn, D'Vera, & Cohen, Sarah. (2004, January 5–11). The doors to professions widen. *The Washington Post National Weekly Edition*, p. 31.

Colamosca, Anne. (1999, July/August). Pay for journalists is going up. *Columbia Journalism Review*, pp. 24–28.

Coldford, Paul D., & Jenkins, Evan. (2003, July/August). The *Times* after the storm: Jayson Blair, Howell Raines, and the rest of us. *Columbia Journalism Review*, pp. 14–17.

Commission on Freedom of the Press. (1947). *A Free and Responsible Press*. Chicago: University of Chicago Press.

Committee of Concerned Journalists. (2003, December 19). About CCJ. Accessed on December 19, 2003, at http://www.journalism.org/who/ccj/about.asp

Cranberg, Gilbert, Bezanson, Randall, & Soloski, John. (2001). *Taking Stock: Journalism and the Publicly Traded Newspaper Company*. Ames: Iowa State University Press.

Crane, Frank. (1919). *Four Minute Essays* (Vol. 6). New York & Chicago: Wm. H. Wise & Co.

Crawford, Nelson Antrim. (1924). *The Ethics of Journalism.* New York: Alfred A. Knopf.

Crosbie, Vin. (2004, March 17). Weak online economics threaten quality of all journalism, Pew study finds. *Online Journalism Review.* Accessed on March 17, 2004, at http://www.ojr.org/business

Cross, Al. (2002, June). A powerful experiment. *Quill.* 90(5), 4–5.

Croteau, David, & Hoynes, William. (2001). *The Business of Media: Corporate Media and the Public Interest.* Thousand Oaks, CA: Pine Forge Press.

Cunningham, Brent. (2000, May/June). In the lab. *Columbia Journalism Review,* pp. 29–31.

Dow Jones Newspaper Fund. (1984). *1984 Journalism Career and Scholarship Guide.* Princeton, NJ: Dow Jones Newspaper Fund.

Duin, Juli. (2001, September 28). Newsrooms' distaff divide. *The Washington Times.* Accessed on September 28, 2001, at www.washtimes.com

Eviatar, Daphne. (2003, July 7). The press and private Lynch. *Nation.* 277(1), 18–20.

Fink, Conrad C. (1995). *Media Ethics.* Boston: Allyn & Bacon.

Flournoy, Dan M., & Stewart, Robert K. (1997). *CNN: Making News in the Global Market.* Luton, UK: University of Luton Press.

Friedland, Lewis, & Nichols, Sandy. (2002, Summer). High impact logged in 600 civic projects. *Civic Catalyst.* 4(6), 4.

Gade, Peter J., & Perry, Earnest L. (2003, Summer). Changing the newsroom culture: A four-year case study of organizational development at the St. Louis Post-Dispatch. *Journalism & Mass Communication Quarterly.* 80(2), 327–347.

Gallup, George H. (1973). *The Gallup Poll: Public Opinion, 1972–1977.* Wilmington, DE: Scholarly Resources.

Gallup Organization. (1982). *Public Opinion, 1982.* Wilmington, DE: Scholarly Resources.

Gallup Organization. (2002). National telephone survey of U.S. adults, May 6–9. *The Gallup Poll: Public Opinion Two Thousand Two,* p. 204.

Gallup Organization. (2002). National telephone survey of U.S. adults, October 14–17. *The Gallup Poll: Public Opinion Two Thousand Two,* p. 327.

Gallup Organization. (2002). National telephone survey of U.S. adults, December 9–10. *The Gallup Poll: Public Opinion Two Thousand Two,* p. 397.

Glasser, Theodore L. (1992, Spring). Professionalism and the derision of diversity: The case of the education of journalists. *Journal of Communication.* 42(2), 131–140.

Goldberg, Bernard. (2003). *Bias: A CBS Insider Exposes How the Media Distort the News.* New York: HarperCollins.

Good, Howard. (2001, April). We need ethics examples. *Quill.* 89(3), 40.

Gunther, Marc. (1999, February 1). The new face of network news. *Fortune,* p. 76.

Gup, Ted. (1999, Spring/Summer). Who's a journalist?—I. *Media Studies Journal.* 13(2), 34–37.

Haas, Tanni, & Steiner, Linda. (2002). Fears of corporate colonization in journalism reviews' critiques of public journalism. *Journalism Studies.* 3(3), 325–341.

Hansen, Kathleen A., Neuzil, Mark, & Ward, Jean. (1998, Winter). Newsroom topic teams: Journalists' assessments of effects on news routines and newspaper quality. *Journalism & Mass Communication Quarterly.* 75(4), 803–821.

Hess, Stephen. (1981). *The Washington Reporters.* Washington, DC: The Brookings Institution.

Hickey, Neil. (2001, September/October). Morale matters: Low and getting lower. *Columbia Journalism Review,* pp. 37–39.

Hirsch, Paul M. (1977). Occupational, organizational, and institutional models in mass media research. In Paul M. Hirsch, Peter V. Miller, and F. Gerald Kline (Eds.). *Strategies for Communication Research* (pp. 13–42). Beverly Hills, CA: Sage.

Johnstone, John W. C., Slawski, Edward J., & Bowman, William W. (1976). *The News People: A Sociological Portrait of American Journalists and Their Work.* Urbana: University of Illinois Press.

Jones, Alex S. (2002, September 2). Why do many readers hate us again? *Editor & Publisher*. 135(31), 12.

Journalism under fire. (1983, December 12). *Time*, pp. 76–93.

Jurkowitz, Mark. (2003, August 27). More women in J-school doesn't translate to jobs. *The Boston Globe*, p. C1.

Kim, Meesook, & Cho, Kyung-Ho. (2003, April). Quality of life among government employees. *Social Indicators Research*. 61(1), 387.

Kovach, Bill, & Rosenstiel, Tom. (1999). *Warp Speed: America in the Age of Mixed Media*. New York: The Century Foundation Press.

Kovach, Bill, & Rosenstiel, Tom. (2001). *The Elements of Journalism*. New York: Crown Publishers.

Kurtz, Howard. (2001, March 20). Bottom-line news: San Jose publisher quits to protest emphasis on profits before journalism. *The Washington Post*, p. C1.

Lambeth, Edmund B. (1998). Public journalism as a democratic practice. In E. B. Lambeth, P. E. Meyer, & E. Thorson (Eds.). *Assessing Public Journalism* (pp. 15–35). Columbia: University of Missouri Press.

Lanosga, Gerry, & Johnston, Kathleen. (2002, May/June). Hidden camera: Undercover work shows sheriff drinking, driving. *IRE Journal*. 25(3), 33, 43.

Laventhol, David. (2001, May/June). Profit pressures: A question of margins. *Columbia Journalism Review*, pp. 18–19.

Lichter, Robert, & Rothman, Stanley. (1981, October/November) Media and business elites. *Public Opinion*. 4(5), 42–46, 59–60.

Liebling, A. J. (1961). *The Press*. New York: Ballantine Books.

Lindley, William R. (1975). *Journalism and Higher Education: The Search for Academic Purpose*. Stillwater, OK: Journalistic Services.

Lundy, Walker. (2003, April 28). Civic journalism 101. *Editor & Publisher*. 136(17), 46.

Maddox, Kate. (1995, May 22). Net access luring cable firms. *Interactive Age*, p. 4.

McBride, Kelly. (2003, April). Before you publish a rape victim's name. *American Editor*, pp. 24–25.

McManus, John. (1994). *Market-Driven Journalism: Let the Citizen Beware?* Thousand Oaks, CA: Sage Publications.

Merritt, Davis, & Rosen, Jay. (1995, April 13). *Imagining Public Journalism: An Editor and Scholar Reflect on the Birth of an Idea*. Roy W. Howard Public Lecture Number 5. Bloomington: School of Journalism, Indiana University.

Mills, Kay. (1997). What difference do women journalists make? In Pippa Norris (Ed.), *Women, Media, and Politics* (pp. 41–55). New York: Oxford University Press.

Mitchell, Greg. (2002, January 7). Outlook: The worst may be over. *Editor & Publisher*, pp. 10–13.

Mohl, Jeffrey D. (2003, March). Changing times, changing needs. *Quill*. 91(2), 3.

Mohl, Jeffrey D. (2003, August). Lessons in diversity. *Quill*. 91(6), 3.

Moses, Lucia. (2000, March 20). Nervous in the newsrooms. *Editor & Publisher*, pp. 4–6.

Moses, Lucia. (2003, February 3). Profiting from experience: New studies seek to shown that "quality" can pay off. There's just one problem: No one agrees on what "quality" means. *Editor & Publisher*, p. 10.

Newspapers face ongoing challenges. (2002, July/August). *Quill*, 90(6), 8.

Newsroom Training: Where's the Investment? "News Staffers Interview: Topline Results." (2002). Miami, FL: John S. and James L. Knight Foundation.

Newsroom Training: Where's the Investment? "Twelve Key Findings." (2002). Miami, FL: John S. and James L. Knight Foundation.

Nielsen/NetRatings. *United States: Average Web Usage Week Ending March 14, 2004*. Accessed on March 15, 2004, at http://www.nielsennetratings.com/reports.jsp?section=pub_reports

O'Neill, Michael J. (1982, May 5). *A Problem for the Public—A Challenge for Editors*. Address to the American Society of Newspaper Editors. Reprinted in *The Adversary Press* (1983, pp. 2–15). St. Petersburg, FL: Modern Media Institute.

Outing, Steve. (1999, April 3). News site audiences closing in. *Editor & Publisher*, p. 29.

Outing, Steve. (2001, January 29). An inevitable mix: Old and new media. *Editor & Publisher*, pp. 115–116.

Overholser, Geneva. (2002, October 22). *What Is Good Journalism? Fighting to Keep It Working for Us*. Comments delivered to the Anvil Freedom Award, Estlow Lecture, University of Denver, Denver, CO.

Overholser, Geneva. (2004, Winter). Good journalism, good business: An industry perspective. *Newspaper Research Journal*. 25(1), 8–17.

Paterno, Susan. (1997, May). The lying game. *American Journalism Review*, pp. 40–45.

Pavlik, John V. (1997, July/August). The future of online journalism: Bonanza or black hole? *Columbia Journalism Review*, pp. 30–36.

Peterson, Paul V. (1972, January). Journalism growth continues at hefty 10.8 per cent rate. *Journalism Educator*, 26(4), pp. 4, 5, 60.

Peterson, Paul V. (1981). *Today's Journalism Students: Who They Are and What They Want to Do*. Columbus: School of Journalism, Ohio State University.

Peterson, Paul V. (1983, Winter). J-school enrollments hit record 91,016. *Journalism Educator*. 37(4), 3–8.

Pew Research Center. [Official Web Site of The Pew Research Center: The People and the Press]. Accessed on July 15, 2004, at http://peoplepress.org/reports/index.php3?TopicID=1.

Pew Research Center for the People & the Press. (2004). *Striking the Balance, Audience Interests, Business Pressures and Journalists' Values*. Accessed on June 29, 2004, at http://people-press.org/reports/display.php3?ReportID=67

Podmolik, Mary Ellen. (2002, May 8). Numbers crunch. *Advertising Age*, pp. S12–S13.

Potter, Deborah. (2004). Local TV news project—2002: Pessimism rules in TV newsrooms. Accessed on Feb. 26, 2004, at http://www.journalism.org/resources/research/reports/localtv/2002/pessimism.asp

Prato, Lou. (1994, September). Tabloids forcea ll to pay for news. *American Journalism Review*, 16(7), p. 56.

Reese, Stephen D. (2001). Understanding the global journalist: A hiearchy-of-influences approach. *Journalism Studies*. 2(2), 173–187.

Reinhold, Robert. (1981, April 16). *Washington Post* gives up Pulitzer, calling article on addict, age 8, fiction. *The New York Times*, p. A1.

Risser, James. (2000, January/February). Lessons from L.A.: The wall is heading back. *Columbia Journalism Review*, pp. 26–27.

Rivers, William L. (1962, Spring). The correspondents after twenty-five years. *Columbia Journalism Review*. 1, pp. 4–10.

Rosen, Jay. (1999). *What Are Journalists For?* New Haven: Yale University Press.

Rosenstiel, Tom. (1997, September 14). U.S. press: Paying for its sins. *The Washington Post*, p. C-3.

Rosenstiel, Tom, Gottlieb, Carl, Brady, Lee Ann, & Rosenheim, Dan. (2000, November/December). Time of peril for TV news. *Columbia Journalism Review*, pp. 84–93.

Rosten, Leo. (1937). *The Washington Correspondents*. New York: Harcourt, Brace and Company. Reprint of the 1937 ed. published by Arno Press. (1974).

Rothman, Stanley, & Lichter, Robert. (1983, Spring). Are journalists a new class? *Business Forum*, p. 15.

Schudson, Michael. (1995). *The Power of News*. Cambridge, MA: Harvard University Press.

Shoemaker, Pamela J., & Reese, Stephen D. (1996). *Mediating the Message: Theories of Influences on Mass Media Content* (2nd ed.). White Plains, NY: Longman.

Singer, Jane B. (1997). Changes and consistencies. *Newspaper Research Journal*. 18(1), 16.

Singer, Jane B. (2003, May). Who are these guys? The online challenge to the notion of journalistic professionalism. *Journalism: Theory, Practice and Criticism*. 4(2), 139.

Smith, Shellee. (1995, May/June). Shoptalk. *Scripps Howard News*, p. 15.

Squires, James D. (1993). *Read All About It: The Corporate Takeover of America's Newspapers*. New York: Times Books.

Strupp, Joe. (2000, August 21). Three point play. *Editor & Publisher*, p. 18.

Strupp, Joe. (2003, November 3). Women take the reins. *Editor & Publisher*. Accessed on November 21, 2003, at http://www.editorandpublisher.com/editoandpublisher/features_columns/article_display.jsp?vnu_content_id=2030399

Taylor, Humphrey. (2001, November 21). The impact of recent events and fears about the economy on employee attitudes. *The Harris Poll* #57. Accessed on October 27, 2003, at http://www.harris interactive.com/harris_poll/index.asp?PID=268

Tifft, Susan E. (2003). The Romenesko Factor. *Columbia Journalism Review*. 42(2), 21.

Toossi, Mitra. (2004, February). Labor force projections to 2012: The graying of the U.S. workforce. *Monthly Labor Review*, p. 54.

Tyson, Laura D'Andrea. (2003, October 27). New clues to the pay and leadership gap. *Business Week*, p. 36.

Underwood, Doug. (1993). *When MBAs Rule the Newsroom*. New York: Columbia University Press.

U.S. Bureau of the Census. (1971). *Statistical Abstract of the United States, 1971*. Washington DC: U.S. Government Printing Office.

U.S. Bureau of the Census. (1982–1983). *Statistical Abstract of the United States, 1982–1983*. Washington DC: U.S. Government Printing Office.

U.S. Bureau of the Census. (1991). *Statistical Abstract of the United States, 1991*. Washington DC: U.S. Government Printing Office.

U.S. Bureau of the Census. (2001). *Statistical Abstract of the United States, 2001*. Washington DC: U.S. Government Printing Office.

U.S. Bureau of the Census. (2003). *Statistical Abstract of the United States, 2003*. Washington DC: U.S. Government Printing Office.

U.S. Bureau of Labor Statistics. (2002). *Employee Tenure in 2002*. Accessed on July 2, 2002, at http://www.bls.gov/news.release/tenure.t06.htm.

U.S. Bureau of Labor Statistics. (2002). *National Compensation Survey: Occupational Wages in the United States*. Accessed July 20, 2004, at http://www.bls.gov/ncs/home.htm

Vlad, Tudor, Becker, Lee B., Huh, Jisu, & Mace, Nancy R. (2003, August 1). *2002 annual survey of journalism & mass communication enrollments*. Paper presented at the 2003 convention of the Association for Education in Journalism and Mass Communication, Kansas City, Missouri: Tables 17, 18, and 19. See also the following Web site: www.grady.uga.edu/annualsurveys/

Vos, Tim P. (2002, August). *The enactment of journalists' role conceptions*. Paper presented to the Association for Education in Journalism and Mass Communication, Miami, FL.

Wald, Richard C. (2003). How to worry about the Blair affair. *Columbia Journalism Review*. 42(2), 23.

Weaver, David H., & Wilhoit, G. Cleveland. (1986). *The American Journalist: A Portrait of U.S. News People and Their Work*. Bloomington: Indiana University Press.

Weaver, David H., & Wilhoit, G. Cleveland. (1991). *The American Journalist: A Portrait of U.S. News People and Their Work* (2nd ed.). Bloomington: Indiana University Press.

Weaver, David H., & Wilhoit, G. Cleveland. (1992). Journalists—Who are they, really? *Media Studies Journal*. 6(4), 63–79.

Weaver, David H., & Wilhoit, G. Cleveland. (1996). *The American Journalist in the 1990s: U.S. News People at the End of an Era*. Mahwah, NJ: Lawrence Erlbaum Associates.

Whitman, Janet. (2003, November 5). Gannett takes aim at younger readers. *The Wall Street Journal*, p. 1.

Winship, Tom. (1998, July 25). Whistle blowers try to save journalism from itself. *Editor & Publisher*. 131(30), pp. 3–4.

Wu, Denis H., & Bechtel, Arati. (2002, Spring). Web site use and news topic type. *Journalism & Mass Communication Quarterly*. 79(1), 73–86.

Methods

This 2002 national telephone survey of 1,149 U.S. journalists (plus additional separate samples of 315 minority and online journalists) was designed to be a partial replication of three earlier ones—the 1971 national telephone survey of 1,328 U.S. journalists by John Johnstone and his colleagues,[1] the 1982–1983 national telephone survey of 1,001 U.S. journalists by Weaver and Wilhoit,[2] and the 1992 national telephone survey of 1,156 U.S. journalists by Weaver and Wilhoit.[3] Hence, we closely followed the definitions of a journalist, the sampling methods, and the question wording of these previous surveys. This was necessary to be able to make direct comparisons with the findings from 1971, 1982–1983, and 1992. We used many of the same questions asked in these earlier surveys but added some to reflect the changes in U.S. journalism during the past decade.

As in the 1992 study, we deliberately added separate samples of journalists from the four main minority journalism associations—the Asian American Journalists Association (AAJA), the National Association of Black Journalists (NABJ), the National Association of Hispanic Journalists (NAHJ), and the Native American Journalists Association (NAJA)—to ensure adequate numbers for comparison with each other and with majority White journalists. We also added a separate sample of online or Internet journalists from the Online News Association (ONA) to make sure we had enough of this kind of journalist to analyze separately. These separate samples were not included with the main random sample of 1,149 when making comparisons with the earlier studies.

POPULATION

As in the earlier studies, the population of our 2002 main sample comprised full-time news people responsible for the information content of English-language traditional general-interest news media in the United States. This study included only journalists who worked for English-language news media targeted at general audiences rather than special interest or racial/ethnic groups. These mainstream traditional news media included daily and weekly newspapers, news magazines, radio and television stations (as well as one television network operation), and general news services (such as the Associated Press and Reuters) based in the United States.

We included those persons who produced news, information, and opinion, rather than those who created fiction, drama, art, or other media content. We also limited our study to those news media that disseminated information more frequently than once a month, as was true in the earlier studies. Thus, no monthly or less frequently published periodicals were included in our main sample. Only news magazines published more than once a month were included.

DEFINITION OF A JOURNALIST

Following the earlier studies, we defined *journalists* as those who had responsibility for the preparation or transmission of news stories or other timely information—all full-time reporters, writers, correspondents, editors, news announcers, columnists, photojournalists and other news people. In broadcast organizations, only those working in the news and public-affairs departments were included. Our 2002 definition of journalists included editorial cartoonists, as in 1992, but not comic-strip cartoonists. We did not include librarians, camera operators, or video and audio technicians because of the reasoning from the earlier studies that they do not usually have direct responsibility for news content in the various media. We did include photojournalists, as in 1992, because they often work independently to create news content.

SAMPLING—MAIN PROBABILITY SAMPLE

We used a three-stage sampling plan similar to that used in the three previous studies.

1. The first step was to compile lists of daily and weekly newspapers, news magazines, news or wire services, and radio and television stations in the United States. We used the Audit Bureau of Circulation's *Circulation 2001* report for the list of daily newspapers, the 2001 *Editor & Publisher International Yearbook* for lists of weekly newspapers and news-service bureaus, the 2001 *Gale Directory of Publications and Broadcast Media* for the lists of television and radio stations (and also a list of radio stations with news programs from the Center for Radio Information), and *Bacon's Directory 2002* for the list of news magazines. We also relied on the

Summer 2001 *News Media Yellow Book* for our lists of news-magazine and television-network journalists (www.leadershipdirectories.com).

The lists of daily and weekly newspapers, and radio and television stations, involved no judgment on our part: We simply used what was provided in the directories. But the lists of news services and news magazines did require decisions as to what constituted legitimate news services (as opposed to purely feature, picture, and comics services, which are also listed with news and press services in the *Editor & Publisher International Yearbook*), and which magazines were genuine *news* magazines. We chose the news magazines from five categories in *Bacon's Directory*: General Interest Consumer/General Editorial, General Interest Consumer/General Editorial Metro, News Magazines, Political and Social Opinion, and Business and Commercial/General Business. Our final list of news magazines included the following 16: *Barron's, Business Week, Forbes, Fortune, People, The New Yorker, Insight, Newsweek, Time, U.S. News & World Report, The American Prospect, In These Times, The Nation, National Review, The New Republic,* and *The Weekly Standard.* This list is quite similar to the one from the 1992 study.

Our final selection of news services included The Associated Press, Reuters America, and United Press International bureaus, as listed in the *Editor & Publisher Year Book.* We also received helpful information from the headquarters of these news services on numbers of full-time journalists and bureaus.

From these sources, we used systematic random sampling to compile lists of 156 daily newspapers (stratified by circulation so that we drew about 10% of the number of dailies in each circulation category),[4] 120 weekly newspapers (every 5th one), 16 news magazines (all that we classified as such), 36 news service bureaus (every fifth one), 88 radio stations (every 19th one of those with a news format), and 98 television stations (every 10th one) plus one TV network operation.

In all, our random sample of news organizations included 515 from an estimated 10,870 in the United States (not counting radio stations with no news format or non-news magazines), or about every 21st one.

2. The second task was to obtain lists (or at least total numbers) of all full-time journalists working for the 515 news organizations in our sample. This was done in three steps. First, letters were sent to all editors or news directors of the 515 news organizations in our sample from mid-February until early March of 2002. These letters explained the importance of this decennial survey and asked for the total number of all news or editorial people working in each organization. We defined what we meant by *news people* both in print and broadcast, and we also asked for the names and job titles of all full-time journalists as well as their telephone numbers and e-mail addresses, or at least a list of all news positions and the number of persons in each one. We audited the lists of journalists we received for job titles we considered not fitting our definition of journalist, such as receptionist, librarian, camera operator, and so on.

The response to this first letter was very disappointing—less than 10%—so we sent a follow-up letter to all who had not responded in March 2002. Again, the response was low, so we began to search the Web sites of the various news organizations, some of which contained lists of all journalists with contact information. We also began telephone calls to those who had not responded and who did not provide the information we needed on their Web sites. We found that these calls resulted in a much better response than did the letters. We also used the *News Media Yellow Book* to get names and phone numbers of journalists working for news magazines, news services, and the one television network in our sample.

In all, we obtained numbers and/or lists of full-time journalists from 242 (47%) of the 515 news organizations in our sample, but we were able to increase this number substantially by going to the Web sites of some organizations. Nevertheless, this was a substantial decrease from the 80% response in 1992—and a telling indication that news organizations have become substantially less willing to respond to surveys such as ours in this age of the Internet, information overload, and increased concern about identity theft. The best response was from radio stations (64%) as in the 1982–1983 and 1992 studies, and the worst response was from weekly newspapers (25%).

3. The third task was to draw a random sample of individual journalists from the lists of names and positions collected in Step 2. We first used the total number of journalists working for the news organizations that responded to estimate the total numbers working for all news media throughout the United States. We did that by calculating the percentage of each type of news organization responding (daily newspapers, television, radio, etc.), then multiplying the total number of full-time journalists working for each type of organization by 100 divided by the percentage of these organizations in our sample.

For example, we obtained the numbers of full-time journalists working for 42 randomly selected television stations (4.29%) of the 980 in the United States. We divided 100% by 4.29% and got a multiplier of 23.3. Multiplying the total number of journalists from the 42 stations in our sample by 23.3 yielded an estimate of about 18,820 full-time television station journalists in the United States. We added the number of TV network journalists (1,468) obtained from the Leadership Directory's *News Media Yellow Book* to this figure to obtain our final estimate of 20,288 U.S. television journalists. This basic procedure was followed for each of the other types of news media to arrive at our total estimate of 116,148 full-time U.S. journalists.

Once we had estimated the total number of journalists, we calculated the percentage working for each type of medium by dividing our estimated total number of journalists (116,148) by our estimates of the total number working for each type of news medium. We then used these percentages to estimate how many journalists from each type of news medium should be included in our national probability sample.

After going through this procedure, we found that using the percentages of total estimated U.S. journalistic workforce would result in only about 12 news-magazine and 6 news-service journalists in a probability sample of 1,250. Because we wanted to compare journalists working for different media, we increased the news-magazine sample from 12 to 96 (every 12th name) and the news-service sample from 6 to 91 (every 7th name). This oversampling of these journalists meant that we had to undersample journalists from some other types of news media. We chose to reduce the number of daily newspaper, weekly newspaper, and radio journalists somewhat, but we also added some journalists in other categories, making the main probability sample 1,466 rather than the 1,250 we had originally planned.

A total of 1,149 interviews were completed from these 1,466, for an overall response rate of 78.4%. When those who were incapacitated, ill, deceased, never available, or no longer journalists were subtracted from the total sample of 1,466, and replacement names were chosen randomly from our original lists, the adjusted response rate was 79%.

We ended up with percentages in each medium that were close to those estimated in the total workforce. The largest differences were for the major news services of AP, UPI, and Reuters (5.5 percentage points above the estimated percentage in the total workforce) and for news magazines (4.4 percentage points above), which we oversampled because of their relatively small numbers. The largest undersampling was for weekly newspapers (-3.3 percentage points) and for television (-3.3 points). Thus, no group of journalists was either over- or undersampled by more than 6 percentage points, as was true in 1982 and 1992, leading us to conclude that weighting by medium type was not necessary.

The maximum sampling error at the 95% level of confidence for this main probability sample is plus or minus 3 percentage points. It is higher, of course, for the individual media groups because of their smaller sizes, especially the news-service and news-magazine samples. This main sample of 1,149 included 571 daily newspaper journalists, 179 from weekly or nondaily newspapers, 163 from television stations and networks, 105 from radio, 69 from the wire services, and 62 from news magazines.

SAMPLING—MINORITY
AND ONLINE JOURNALISTS

As in 1992, we included separate samples from the four most well-established minority journalists associations to ensure enough journalists of color to compare with each other and with White majority journalists. We knew from previous studies that we would not obtain enough minorities from the main probability sample for these comparisons. In fact, our main probability sample of 1,149 U.S. journalists contained only 42 African Americans, 38 Hispanics, 11 Asian

Americans, 6 Native Americans, 2 Pacific Islanders, and 10 who classified themselves as "Other Minority." In all, then, our main probability sample included 109 journalists (9.5%) who classified themselves as belonging to a racial or ethnic group other than non-Hispanic White. Likewise, there were only 24 journalists in our main sample (2.1%) who identified themselves as full-time online journalists.

To increase the number of minority journalists in our study, we drew random samples from the membership lists of the Asian American Journalists Association (AAJA), the National Association of Black Journalists (NABJ), the National Association of Hispanic Journalists (NAHJ), and the Native American Journalists Association (NAJA). We obtained mailing lists from all of these associations, but only the list from the Asian American group included telephone numbers, so we sent letters to the other journalists asking them to call the Survey Research Center's 800 (toll-free) number to volunteer to participate in our telephone survey. The Hispanic Journalists association list included the news organization for which they worked, so we were able to find telephone numbers for most of these organizations. All journalists in all the minority journalism associations received letters explaining the study before they were called, as was true for the main sample.

From these efforts, the Indiana University Survey Research Center completed interviews with an additional 99 Hispanic, 97 Asian American, 30 Native American, and 13 African American journalists, totaling 239 minority journalists in the separate samples, for an overall response rate of 26.5%.

To increase the number of online journalists in our study, we used the membership list of the Online News Association (ONA) to draw a random sample of 342. Because this list included only the e-mail addresses of members, we had to contact them via an e-mail letter asking them to call the Center for Survey Research at its toll-free number. In the end, the CSR was able to complete interviews with 76, for an overall response rate of 22.2%.

When those minority and online journalists who were incapacitated, ill, deceased, never available, no longer journalists, and whose telephone numbers could not be ascertained were subtracted from the total initial samples, however, the adjusted response rate for these separate samples of minority and online journalists combined was 82.2%. Taken together, the maximum sampling error for these additional samples of 315 minority and online journalists was plus or minus 5.8 percentage points at the 95% level of confidence. It is higher for the individual groups because of their smaller sizes, especially the Native American and African American journalists.

Combining the main sample and separate samples yielded 137 Hispanic, 108 Asian American, 55 African American, 36 Native American, and 100 online journalists from a total of 1,464 interviews in the main probability sample (1,149) and the separate oversamples (315).

INTERVIEWING

Telephone interviews averaging 51 minutes in length were completed with these 1,464 U.S. journalists working full time for some 515 daily and weekly newspapers, radio and television stations, wire services, and news magazines throughout the United States. All but 72 of these interviews were conducted from July 12 to November 30, 2002, by trained interviewers at the Center for Survey Research at Indiana University's Bloomington campus. The other 72 interviews were completed with additional oversamples of Native American and online journalists from January 17 to March 2, 2003, by the Center.

Two weeks before the interviews were conducted, letters were sent to all journalists in the sample explaining the study and urging them to cooperate. In addition, the questionnaire was pretested on a small sample of local journalists in early July 2002. The data collection staff included 23 supervisors and 41 interviewers. All interviewers received at least 15 hours of training in interviewing techniques before actually beginning the survey. Interviewers were monitored by the supervisors using the CSR facilities that do not allow the interviewers to know they are being monitored. Monitoring was conducted randomly, with each interviewer being monitored at least once during each 3-hour shift.

Interviewers were instructed to ask each respondent for a convenient time for the interview and to reschedule if necessary. All cases with confirmed valid telephone numbers were called up to 24 times, unless the respondent refused. Cases of unknown validity (persistent no answers or answering devices) were called a minimum of 14 times during the morning, afternoon, evening, late evening (after 9 P.M.), and weekend. Each "refusal" was attempted to be converted to a completed interview twice—at the first instance of refusal and again after a few days. Substitutions were allowed only if the original respondent had left journalism or could not be reached. If they had moved to another news organization, interviewers were instructed to track them. Substitutions were made with another person holding the same job title in the original media organization whenever possible.

NOTES

1. John W. C. Johnstone, Edward J. Slawski, and William W. Bowman, *The News People: A Sociological Portrait of American Journalists and Their Work* (Urbana: University of Illinois Press, 1976).
2. David H. Weaver and G. Cleveland Wilhoit, *The American Journalist: A Portrait of U.S. News People and Their Work* (Bloomington: Indiana University Press, 1986; 2nd ed., 1991).
3. David H. Weaver and G. Cleveland Wilhoit, *The American Journalist in the 1990s: U.S. News People at the End of an Era* (Mahwah, NJ: Lawrence Erlbaum Associates, 1996).
4. The daily newspaper circulation categories were (1) over 500,000; (2) 250,001–500,000; (3) 100,001–250,000; (4) 50,001–100,000; (5) 25,001–50,000; and (6) 25,000 or less.

2002 Journalists Survey Questionnaire

RECORD WHETHER THIS INTERVIEW IS FROM THE NATIONAL PROBABILITY SAMPLE OR FROM ONE OF THE FIVE GROUP MEMBERSHIP LISTS:

National probability sample — 1
Asian American Journalists Association (AAJA) — 2
National Association of Black Journalists (NABJ) — 3
National Association of Hispanic Journalists (NAHJ) — 4
Native American Journalists Association (NAJA) — 5
Online News Association (ONA) — 6

RECORD TYPE OF NEWS ORGANIZATION:
(Ask if not known from sample lists of journalists)

Daily newspaper 1	Newsletter 8
Weekly newspaper 2	Other (SPECIFY) . 9
News magazine 3	Don't Know 0
News agency/Wire service . 4	
TV station. 5	
Radio station. 6	
Online or Web news site . . 7	

Thank you for agreeing to participate.

1.   In this survey, I will ask a number of questions about your news organization (NAME). Is there another name that you use to refer to it?
Yes . . . 1 (GO TO ORGN.)
No . . . 5

ORGN. What name do you use? (ENTER NAME)

1.a.   First, what is your exact job title at (NAME OF ORGANIZATION)?
        JOB TITLE:

2.   In what year did you become a full-time employee of (NAME OF ORGANIZATION)?
        YEAR: _____   Not full-time (GO TO END)
        Don't Know (DK) . . . 9998   Refused (RF) . . . 9999

3.   How long have you worked in journalism?
        YEARS: _____   Can't estimate . . . 97   DK . . . 98   RF . . . 99

4.   In looking back, why did you become a journalist? (PROBE IF NECESSARY: "Any
        other reasons?")
        (RECORD VERBATIM)

5.   Where would you most like to be working in five years—in the news media or
        somewhere else?
        In news media (GO TO Q. 6) 3
        Somewhere else (GO TO Q. 7) . . . 1
        VOLUNTEERED:
        Retired/No longer working. 2
        Don't know 9
        Refused 0

6.   In which of the news media—newspapers, magazines, radio, television, the Web,
        or other news services?
        Newspapers 1
        Magazines 2
        Radio. 3
        Television 4
        Web (online) 5
        News/Wire Services 6
        (VOLUNTEERED)
        Other—where? (SPECIFY). . . 7
        Don't Know. 9
        Refused 0

(SKIP TO Q. 9 AFTER ASKING Q. 6)

7.   In what field or occupation would you like to be working?

8.   Why do you want to work outside the news media? (RECORD VERBATIM)

9.   I'd like to find out how important a number of things are to you in judging jobs
        in your field—not just your job. For instance, how much difference does the pay

make in how you rate a job in your field—is pay very important, fairly important, or not too important?

	VERY IMPORTANT	FAIRLY IMPORTANT	NOT TOO IMPORTANT	DK	RF
A. the pay?	5	3	1	9	0
B. fringe benefits?					
C. the editorial policies of the organization?					
D. job security?					
E. the chance to develop a specialty?					
F. the amount of autonomy you have?					
G. the chance to get ahead in the organization?					
H. the chance to help people?					
I. the chance to influence public affairs?					

10. All things considered, how satisfied are you with your present job—would you say very satisfied, fairly satisfied, somewhat dissatisfied, or very dissatisfied?

Very satisfied 7   Very dissatisfied. . . . 1
Somewhat dissatisfied . . .3   Don't know . . . . . . 9 (GO TO Q. 12)
Fairly satisfied 5   Refused . . . . 0 (GO TO Q. 12)

11. What are the most important reasons you say you are (very satisfied, fairly satisfied, etc.) with your present job?

12. Now I'd like to read you a list of ways some journalists use computers in their work. For each one, please tell me whether you do this daily, several times a week, weekly, less often than that, or don't do this at all.

Daily (8)   Several times/week (7)   Weekly (5)   Less often than that (3)
Don't do this at all (1)   DK (9)   Refused (0)

A. Find names or addresses of sources using the Web
B. Interview sources via e-mail
C. Get background information for stories from the Web or computer databases such as Lexis/Nexis
D. Search for story ideas from the Web or from list-serves
E. Check facts in a story using the Web or computer databases such as Lexis/Nexis
F. Keep up with the news by reading the Web sites of other news organizations
G. Search for or receive press releases via e-mail or the Web
H. Communicate via e-mail with readers, viewers or listeners
I. Download raw data from computer databases
J. Use spreadsheets or statistical programs to analyze data from government agencies or other sources

13.A. Now I'd like to ask about your work. How often do you get reactions or comments on your work from people who are *above* you in your organization—would you say regularly, occasionally, seldom or never?

Regularly (7)   Occasionally (5)   Seldom (3)   Never (1)   DK (9)   Refused (0)
Not Applicable (8)

B. How often do you get reactions or comments on your work from *news sources*—
    regularly, occasionally, seldom or never?

C. How often do you get reactions or comments on your work from *readers, listeners,
    or viewers*—regularly, occasionally, seldom or never?

14. Do you supervise any news or editorial employees?

    Yes (ASK Q. 15)......3
    No (SKIP TO Q. 18)...1
    DK...9   RF...0   (GO TO Q. 18)

15. About how many do you supervise, directly or indirectly? (ENTER ACTUAL
    NUMBER)

16. About how often do you communicate with individual reporters to discuss future
    stories—would you say several times a day, daily, several times a week, weekly, or
    less often than that?

    Several times a day.......7
    Daily 6
    Several times a week......5
    Weekly 4
    Less often than that 3
    (VOLUNTEERED)
    Don't meet with reporters. . 8
    DK...9   RF...0

17. How much influence do you have in decisions on hiring and firing news or edito-
    rial employees? Would you say:

    A great deal...7
    Some........5
    A little, or....3
    None at all ...1
    dk...9   RF...0

18. How much editing or processing of other people's work do you do? Would you say:

    A great deal..............5
    Some...................3
    None at all (SKIP TO Q. 20) ..1
    DK...9   RF...0   (GO TO Q.20)

19. How much freedom do you usually have in deciding how the stories written by
    others will be used in (FILL IN MEDIUM)? Would you say:

    Almost complete freedom ..7
    A great deal of freedom 5
    Some freedom, or 3
    None at all 1
    DK...9   RF...0

20. How often do you do reporting? Would you say:

Regularly (ASK Q. 21). 7
Occasionally (ASK Q. 21) . . 5
Seldom, or. . . . . 3 (GO TO Q. 24)
Never . . . . 1 (GO TO Q. 24)
DK . . . 9   RF . . . 0   (GO TO Q. 23)

21. Do you usually cover a specific "beat" or subject area, or do you usually cover different things?

Cover a specific "beat" . . 3 (GO TO Q. 22)
Cover different things. . . 1 (GO TO Q. 23)
DK . . . 9   RF . . . 0   (GO TO Q. 23)

22. (IF SPECIFIC BEAT) Which beats or areas do you usually cover?

23. How much editing do your stories get from others at (FILL IN ORGANIZATION)? Would you say:

A great deal. . . 5
Some, or 3
None at all . . . 1
DK . . . 9   RF . . . 0

24. Next, a question on journalistic freedom. On the whole, what do you consider to be the most significant limits on your freedom as a journalist? (RECORD VERBATIM)

25. If you have a good idea for a subject which you think is important and should be followed up, how often are you able to get the subject covered? Would you say:

Almost always. 5
More often than not, or 3
Only occasionally 1
Don't make such proposals . . . 8
DK . . . 9   RF . . . 0

26. How much freedom do you usually have in selecting the stories you work on? Would you say:

Almost complete freedom . . . 7
A great deal. 5
Some, or 3
None at all 1
DK . . . 9   RF . . . 0

27. How much freedom do you usually have in deciding which aspects of a story should be emphasized? Would you say:

Almost complete freedom . . . 7
A great deal. 5
Some, or 3
None at all 1
DK . . . 9   RF . . . 0

28. Do you belong to a journalists' union?

> Yes 3
> No 1
> Don't know . . . 9
> Refused 0

29. Does your news organization employ someone either full- or part-time as a writing coach?

> Yes 3   Don't know . . . 9
> No 1   Refused 0

30. Here are some statements about your (readers, viewers, listeners). Please indicate whether you strongly disagree, somewhat disagree, somewhat agree, or strongly agree with these statements or are you neutral?

> A. . . . .(Readers, viewers, listeners) are more interested in the day's breaking news than in analysis. Do you:
> Strongly disagree 1
> Somewhat disagree . . . 2
> Somewhat agree 4
> Strongly agree, or 5
> Are you neutral? 3
> DK 9
> RF 0

> B. The majority of (readers, viewers, listeners) have little interest in (reading about, viewing, listening to) social problems such as racial discrimination and poverty. Do you: (Strongly disagree, etc., as in Q. 30.A.)

> C. (Readers, viewers, listeners) are gullible and easily fooled. Do you: (Strongly disagree, etc., as in Q. 30.A.)

Next, some questions on influence of the media and public opinion. For each statement, I would like you to use a zero-to-ten rating scale to indicate the amount of influence.

31. First, how strong do you think the influence of the media is on the formation of public opinion? Please choose a number from zero to ten, where zero means no influence and ten means very great influence.

> No Influence   Very great influence
> 0   1   2   3   4   5   6   7   8   9   10
> Don't know . . 98
> Refused 99

32. And how strong do you think the influence of the media *should* be on public opinion? Again, please choose a number from zero to ten, where zero means no influence and ten means very great influence.

> No Influence   Very great influence
> 0   1   2   3   4   5   6   7   8   9   10
> Don't know . . 98
> Refused 99

33. Given an important story, which of the following, if any, do you think may be justified on occasion and which would you not approve under any circumstances?

	Justified on occasion	Would not approve	Not sure	DK	RF
A. First, paying people for confidential information. Is it justified on occasion, or would you not approve it under any circumstances?	3	1	9	8	0

B. Using confidential business or government documents without authorization. Is it (etc. as in 33.A.)

C. Claiming to be somebody else. Is it (etc.)

D. Agreeing to protect confidentiality and not doing so. Is it (etc.)

E. Badgering unwilling informants to get a story. Is it (etc.)

F. Making use of personal documents such as letters and photographs without permission. Is it (etc.)

G. Getting employed in a firm or organization to gain inside information. Is it (etc.)

H. Using hidden microphones or cameras. Is it (etc.)

I. Using re-creations or dramatizations of news by actors. Is it (etc.)

J. Disclosing the names of rape victims. Is it (etc.)

34. How influential have the following been in shaping your ideas in matters of journalism ethics?

First, how influential have high school or college teachers been in developing your ideas about what's right and wrong in journalism? Would you say extremely influential, quite influential, somewhat influential, or not very influential in developing your ideas about what's right and wrong in journalism?

	Extremely Influential	Quite Influential	Somewhat Influential	Not Very Influential	DK	RF
	7	5	3	1	9	0

A. Teachers?
B. Family upbringing?
C. Religious training?
D. Day-by-day newsroom learning?
E. Senior reporters, editors or news directors?
F. Publishers, owners or general managers?
G. Seminars on ethics for journalists?
H. Web resources?
I. Professional or trade publications?
J. Experience on college newspapers or other college news media?
K. Decisions of other news organizations that you respect

35. Next, I'd like to ask you how important you think a number of things are that the news media do or try to do today. First, get information to the public quickly.

Is that extremely important, quite important, somewhat important, or not really important at all?
(THEN ASK B–O: Is that extremely important, etc.?)

	Extremely Important	Quite Important	Somewhat Important	Not Really Important	DK	RF
A. Get information to the public quickly.	7	5	3	1	9	0

B. Provide analysis and interpretation of complex problems.
C. Provide entertainment and relaxation.
D. Investigate claims and statements made by the government.
E. Provide analysis and interpretation of international developments.
F. Stay away from stories where factual content cannot be verified.
G. Concentrate on news that's of interest to the widest possible audience.
H. Discuss national policy while it is still being developed.
I. Develop intellectual and cultural interests of the public.
J. Be an adversary of public officials by being constantly skeptical of their actions.
K. Be an adversary of businesses by being constantly skeptical of their actions.
L. To set the political agenda.
M. Give ordinary people a chance to express their views on public affairs.
N. Motivate ordinary people to get involved in public discussions of important issues.
O. Point people toward possible solutions to society's problems.

36. Using the same scale, how important is it to you that your news organization should do, or try to do, each of these things:

   A. Conduct polls to learn citizens' priorities on issues? Is that extremely, quite, somewhat, or not really important?

   B. Convene meetings of citizens and community leaders to discuss public issues. Is that extremely, quite, somewhat, or not really important?

   C. Make special efforts to motivate citizens to participate in decision making on public issues. Is that extremely, etc.?

   D. Make special efforts to include ordinary citizens as sources in public affairs stories. Is that extremely, etc.?

37. Next, I'd like to ask about your news organization. How good a job of informing the public do you think your own news organization is doing? Would you say outstanding, very good, good, fair or poor?

   Outstanding . . . 5   Good . . . 3   Poor . . . 1   Refused . . . 0   (GO TO Q. 39)
   Very good . . . 4   Fair . . . 2   DK . . . 9   (GO TO Q. 39)

38. Why do you think your news organization is doing a (outstanding, very good, good, etc.) job of informing the public? (RECORD VERBATIM)

39. How important would you say the following goals are to the owners or senior managers of your news organization? Would you say that they are extremely important, quite important, somewhat important, or not really important?

Extremely Important	Quite Important	Somewhat Important	Not really Important	DK	RF
7	5	3	1	9	0

A. Earning high, above-average profits?

B. Maintaining or securing high, above-average employee morale?

C. Keeping the size of your audience as large as possible?

D. Producing journalism of high, above-average quality?

40. Here are some statements that express some journalists' attitudes or beliefs about the organizations for which they work. Please indicate whether you strongly disagree, somewhat disagree, somewhat agree, strongly agree, or are you neutral?

Strongly Agree	Somewhat Agree	Neutral	Somewhat Disagree	Strongly Disagree	DK	RF
5	4	3	2	1	9	0

A. At my news organization, profits are a higher priority than good journalism. Do you strongly disagree, etc.?

B. The quality of journalism at my news organization has been rising steadily over the past few years. Do you strongly disagree, etc.?

C. At my news organization, newsroom resources have been shrinking over the past few years. Do you strongly disagree, etc.?

D. My news organization does a lot of audience research to learn what kinds of information our audience wants or needs. Do you strongly disagree, etc.?

41. Currently, in your day-to-day job, how influential is each of the following on your concept of what is newsworthy? Please use a scale from one to five, where one means not at all influential and five means very influential. (CHOOSE ONE NUMBER FOR EACH ITEM.)

	NOT AT ALL INFLUENTIAL			VERY INFLUENTIAL	VOLUNTEERED N/A	DK	RF
A. Your peers on the staff?	1	2	3	4	5	8	9	0

B. Your supervisors?

C. Your friends and acquaintances?

D. Your journalistic training?

E. Findings of readership or audience research?

F. News sources?

G. Priorities of TV network news?

H. Local competing news media?

I. Wire service budgets?

J. Public opinion polls?

K. Priorities of large newspapers?

L. Priorities of independent (NOT NEWS MEDIA OWNED) online news or information sites?

M. Priorities of cable network news?

42. The media are often classified politically in terms of left, right and center. On a scale from zero, which means extreme left, to one hundred, which means extreme right, where would you place the editorial policy of your organization?

RECORD POSITION: (0–100)   DK . . . 998   RF . . . 999

43. And where on this scale would you place yourself, keeping in mind that zero means extreme left and one hundred means extreme right?

RECORD POSITION: (0–100)   DK . . . 998   RF . . . 999

44. Overall, then, does this mean that you consider yourself:

Pretty far to the left 1
A little to the left 2
In the middle of the road . . . 3
A little to the right, or 4
Pretty far to the right 5
Don't know 9
Refused 0

45. Next I'd like to ask your views on two controversial issues. Do you think abortions should be legal under any circumstances, legal under only certain circumstances, or illegal in all circumstances?

Legal, any circumstances 5   No opinion . . . 9
Legal, certain circumstances. . . . 3   Refused 0
Illegal, all circumstances. 1

46. In general, do you feel that the laws covering the sale of firearms should be made more strict, less strict, or kept as they are now?

More strict . . . 5   Kept as they are now . . . 3   DK . . . 9   RF . . . 0
Less strict . . . 1

47. I'd like to talk with you about a story you think represents some of your best work. Please pick one of the best stories you've been involved in during the past year and tell me briefly what it was about.

Story described (SPECIFY AND RECORD VERBATIM) . . . 1
No story mentioned—(GO TO Q. 49) 0

48. Why do you think that this story is particularly good? (RECORD VERBATIM)

49. Which professional journalism publications, if any, do you read *regularly*—that is, almost every issue? (RECORD ALL MENTIONED. TRY TO GET FULL TITLES.)

50. Which professional journalism publications, if any, do you read or look at *occasionally?* (RECORD ALL MENTIONED. TRY TO GET FULL TITLES.)

51. Which Web sites for journalists, if any, do you read regularly—that is, almost every time they're updated?

52. Which newspapers do you read regularly—that is, at least once a week?
(LIST EACH PAPER—FULL NAME, CITY AND STATE OF PUBLICATION)

53.   Which ones, if any, do you read online? (LIST NAME, CITY, AND STATE OF
      NEWSPAPERS)

54.   How many days a week do you usually watch the early evening network newscasts
      on TV—that is CBS, NBC or ABC?

      0   1   2   3   4   5   6   7   DK—8   RF—9

55.   How many days a week do you usually watch cable news networks such as CNN,
      MSNBC, CNBC, or FOX?

      0   1   2   3   4   5   6   7   DK—8   RF—9

56.   How many days a week do you usually watch the Jim Lehrer Newshour on public
      television?

      0   1   2   3   4   5   6   7   DK—8   RF—9

57.   How many days a week do you usually watch local TV newscasts?

      0   1   2   3   4   5   6   7   DK—8   RF—9

58.   Please tell me the magazines you read regularly—that is, almost every issue.
      (LIST FULL NAMES OF ALL MAGAZINES.)

59.   Now a few questions about your background and we'll be through. What is the
      highest grade of school or level of education you have completed?

      No school or kindergarten (SKIP TO Q. 72) 0
      Grades 1–11 (SKIP TO Q. 72) .... (1–11)
      Completed high school (SKIP TO Q. 72)..........................12
      1–3 years of college (ASK Q. 60–65)....................... (13–15)
      Graduated from college (ASK Q. 60–65) 16
      Some graduate work, no degree (ASK Q. 60–69) 17
      Master's degree (ASK Q. 60–71) 18
      Doctorate, law, or medical degree (ASK Q. 60–71) 19
      Vocational or technical school beyond high school (SKIP TO Q.72) 97
      Don't Know..98
      Refused 99

(IF TAKEN ONE OR MORE YEARS OF COLLEGE)

60.   In which state or country did you do most of your undergraduate studies?
      (RECORD STATE OR COUNTRY, IF NOT THE U.S.A.)

61.   As an undergraduate, did you attend a public or private school?

      Public . . . 1   Private . . . 3   DK . . . 9   RF . . . 0

62.   Was it an Ivy League college?

      Yes . . . 3   No . . . 1   DK . . . 9   RF . . . 0

63.   As an undergraduate, did you take courses in journalism?

      Yes . . . 3   Don't know . . . 9
      No . . . 1   Refused 0

63A. Did you work on a college newspaper or other campus news medium?

Yes . . . 3   Don't know . . . 9
No . . . 1   Refused 0

64.   What was your undergraduate major?

Journalism or Broadcast Journalism 1
Journalism and other major (SPECIFY) 2
Telecommunications or Radio/TV 3
Communication or Mass Communication. . . 4
Other major(s)—what was it? (SPECIFY) 5
(VOLUNTEERED)
Did not have a major 7
Don't Know. 9
Refused 0

65.   What was your undergraduate minor?

Journalism or Broadcast Journalism 1
Journalism and other minor 2
Telecommunications or Radio/TV 3
Communication or Mass Communication. . . 4
Other minor(s) 5
(VOLUNTEERED)
Did not have a minor 7
Don't Know. 9
Refused 0

(IF SOME GRADUATE WORK OR GRADUATE DEGREE(S))

66.   In which state or country did you do most of your graduate studies?
      (RECORD STATE, OR COUNTRY IF NOT THE U.S.A.)

67.   Was it a public or private school?

Public . . . 1   Private . . . 3   Don't Know . . . 9   Refused . . . 0

68.   Was it an Ivy League college?

Yes . . . 3   No . . . 1   DK . . . 9   RF . . . 0

69.   What field did you study in graduate or professional school?

Journalism or Broadcast Journalism 1
Telecommunications or Radio/TV 2
Communication or Mass Communication. . . 3
Other (RECORD FIELD OF STUDY). 4
Don't Know . . . 9   Refused . . . 0

(IF GRADUATE DEGREE(S))

70.   Which graduate degrees do you hold? (FIRST MENTION)

MA 1   MD. 5
PhD. 2   Other—what? . . . . 7 (SPECIFY)
JD, law. . . . 3   Don't know 9
MBA 4   Refused 0

71. Which graduate degrees do you hold? (SECOND MENTION)

    MA 1   MD. 5

    PhD. 2   Other—what?. . . . 6 (SPECIFY)

    JD, law. . . . 3   Don't know 9

    MBA 4   Refused/No second mention   0

72. Would you like additional training in journalism or other subjects?

    Yes . . . . 3 (GO TO Q. 73)
    No . . . . 1 (SKIP TO Q. 74)
    Don't Know. . . . 9 (SKIP TO Q. 74)
    Refused . . . . 0 (SKIP TO Q. 74)

73. What kind of training would you like?
    (RECORD ANSWER VERBATIM.)

74. Have you had any short courses, sabbaticals, workshops or fellowships since becoming a journalist?

    Yes . . . . 3 (GO TO Q. 74A)
    No . . . . 1 (SKIP TO Q. 75)
    Don't Know. . . . 9
    Refused 0

74A. Were they mostly in-house, at a different location, or both?

    Mostly in-house . . . 1   Mostly at a different location . . . 2   Both . . . 3
    DK . . . 9   RF . . . 0

75. Altogether, about what percentage of the people you see socially are connected in some way with journalism or the communications field?

    PERCENTAGE: (0 to 100)
    Can't estimate. . . . 997
    Don't know 998
    Refused 999

76. In what year were you born? _____

    Don't know 9998
    Refused 9999

77. Are you Spanish, Hispanic or Latino?
    Yes . . . 3   No . . . 1   DK . . . 9   Refused . . . 0

78. In which one of the following racial groups would you place yourself?

    White (Caucasian) 1
    Black or African-American 2
    Asian or Asian-American 3
    American Indian or Alaska Native . . . 4
    Pacific Islander 5
    Other (SPECIFY). 6
    Don't know 9
    Refused 0

79. In what religion, if any, were you brought up?

Protestant 1
Evangelical Christian 2
Catholic 3
Jewish 4
Other. . . . . .5 (SPECIFY)
None at all 7
Don't know 9
Refused 0

80. What religion, if any, do you practice now?

Protestant 1
Evangelical Christian 2
Catholic 3
Jewish 4
Other. . . . . .5 (SPECIFY)
None at all 7
Don't know 9
Refused 0

81. How important is religion or religious beliefs to you?
     Would you say:

Very important 7
Somewhat important 5
Not very important, or . . .3
Not at all important 1
Don't know 9
Refused 0

82. What is your marital status? Are you:

Now Married. . . . 7	Unmarried but living with a partner. . . . 3
Widowed. 6	Single, that is, never married 1
Divorced 5	Refused. 9
Separated 4	Other (SPECIFY) 0

83. Do you have any children living with you?

Yes. . . . . 3 (GO TO Q. 84)
No . . . . 1 (SKIP TO Q. 85)
Sometimes. . . . 2 (GO TO Q. 84)
Refused . . . . . . 9 (SKIP TO Q. 85)

84. How many children are currently living with you? (SPECIFY)

Don't know . . . 98
Refused 99

85. As of today, are you a Democrat, a Republican, or what?

    Democrat . . . . .1 (SKIP TO Q. 87)
    Republican 3
    (VOLUNTEERED)
    Independent/no party . . . .5 (GO TO Q. 86)
    Other (SPECIFY). . . . . .7 (SKIP TO Q. 87)
    Don't know 9
    Refused 0

86. (IF INDEPENDENT OR NO PARTY) Which of the following best describes your political leanings?

    Lean toward the Republican party 3
    Lean toward the Democratic party, or . . . 1
    Lean toward neither major party 5
    (VOLUNTEERED)
    Other (SPECIFY). 7
    Don't know 9
    Refused 0

87. Do you belong to any organizations or associations that are primarily for people in journalism or the communications field?

    Yes . . . . .3 (GO TO Q. 88)
    No . . . . .1 (SKIP TO Q. 89)
    Don't know . . . .9 (SKIP TO Q. 89)
    Refused . . . . . . .0 (SKIP TO Q. 89)

88. (IF YES) Which ones? (RECORD COMPLETE NAMES OF EACH ONE) Any others?

89. Is your (FILL IN NEWS ORGANIZATION) owned by a public corporation whose shares are traded on a stock exchange?

    Yes 3
    No 1
    Don't know 8
    Refused 9

90. Is your news organization owned by a larger company?

    Yes . . . . .3 (GO TO Q. 91)
    No . . . . .1 (GO TO Q. 92)
    Don't know . . . .8 (GO TO Q. 92)
    Refused . . . . . . .9 (GO TO Q. 92)

91. Which company is that? (RECORD FULL NAME)

92. Is the person or company that owns your news organization located in your town or city?

    Yes 3
    No 1
    Don't know 9
    Refused 0

93. Now I'd like to ask you some financial information. I'd like to mention once again that all information you give us will be treated in strict confidence, and neither you nor your organization will ever be linked by name to this information.

    Would you please tell me what your total personal income was, before taxes, from your work in journalism during 2001? Was it:

Less than $15,000	01	Between 60 and 65,000	11
Between $15,000 and $20,000	02	Between 65 and 70,000	12
Between 20 and 25,000	03	Between 70 and 75,000	13
Between 25 and 30,000	04	Between 75 and 80,000	14
Between 30 and 35,000	05	Between 80 and 85,000	15
Between 35 and 40,000	06	Between 85 and 90,000	16
Between 40 and 45,000	07	Between 90 and 95,000	17
Between 45 and 50,000	08	Between 95 and 100,000	18
Between 50 and 55,000	09	Between 100 and 105,000	19
Between 55 and 60,000	10	Between 105 and 110,000	20
Between 110 and 115,000	21	Between 130 and 135,000	25
Between 115 and 120,000	22	Between 135 and 140,000	26
Between 120 and 125,000	23	Between 140 and 145,000	27
Between 125 and 130,000	24	Between 145 and 150,000	28
		150,000 and over	29
		Don't know	99
		Refused	98

94. (INTERVIEWER: RECORD RESPONDENT'S GENDER. ASK ONLY IF NECESSARY.)
I'm required to ask all questions. Are you:

Male, or...... 1
Female....... 3
DK/Refused ... 9

95. How many full-time news and editorial people are employed at your organization?
NUMBER OF NEWS-EDITORIAL PEOPLE: _____
(VOLUNTEERED)
Can't estimate....997
Don't know......998
Refused.........999

96. During the past few years, has the size of your news staff grown, shrunk, or remained about the same?

Grown....................5
Remained about the same....3
Shrunk 1
Don't Know..............9
Refused..................0

97. Do you have any final comments?
Yes....1 (SPECIFY—RECORD VERBATIM)
No....9

Thank you very much for your time and cooperation!

Coding Schedule for Questions Regarding Journalists' Best Work

I. General Story Topic Categories

a. 9/11, terrorism (01)
b. general human interest (02)
c. state or local government, or politics (03)
d. crime, courts, or law enforcement (04)
e. social problems or protests (05)
f. business or finance (06)
g. education or schools (07)
h. environment, energy, utilities, or transportation (08)
i. sports (09)
j. accidents or disasters (10)
k. consumer advice or information (11)
l. medicine or health care (12)
m. arts, leisure, or travel (13)
n. religion (14)
o. national government or politics (15)
p. international affairs (16)
q. science or space (17)
r. celebrities or personalities (18)
s. humor (19)
t. miscellaneous/other (20)

II. Reasons for Considering Best Work

(Journalists were asked to describe an example of their best work and to say why they considered it exemplary work. Their verbatim responses were classified using the following categories):

a. Extraordinary effort or commitment: comments alluding to intensive research, good sourcing, or overcoming difficult reporting challenges (01)
b. Public-affairs commitment a: comments that the work addressed a significant or controversial issue of public concern (02)
c. Public-affairs commitment b: comments that the work performed a public service, changed policy, or executed the media's watchdog role (03)
d. Audience appeal: characterizations of the work as addressing a matter of widespread interest, or as having a wide impact on audience, or as having great audience appeal (04)
e. Service: comments that the work provided advice to readers (05)
f. Immediacy: characterizations of the work as timely or immediate (06)
g. Human interest: characterizations of the work as humorous, emotional, touching, sad, or personal (07)
h. Rarity: comments suggesting that the work dealt with something unusual or rare (08)
i. Perspective: comments about the work providing context or perspective, or suggestions that the work discussed a matter in depth (09)
j. Visual/auditory appeal: characterizing the work as having strong visual or auditory appeal (10)
k. Professionalism: characterizations of the work as well executed, well written, professionally done, or balanced (11)
l. Not categorized (12)

About the Authors

Randal Beam is Associate Professor of Communication at the University of Washington in Seattle. A former newspaper copy editor and manager, his research focuses on the work environment of journalists and on the ways that business and economic factors influence the news. His research has been published in *Journalism & Mass Communication Quarterly*, *Journalism Monographs* ("Journalism Professionalism as an Organizational Level Concept") and the *Newspaper Research Journal*. He also was a contributor to the *Handbook of Media Management and Economics*. He previously held faculty positions at Indiana University and the University of Oregon. He received his master's degree from Syracuse University and his Ph.D. from the University of Wisconsin–Madison.

Bonnie Brownlee is Associate Professor and Associate Dean for Undergraduate Studies at Indiana University's School of Journalism. She holds bachelor's and master's degrees from Indiana University and a Ph.D. in mass communication from the University of Wisconsin–Madison. Her teaching, research, and service focus on global media and issues of journalism education in the United States and abroad. She has been a consultant for various communication and rural development projects in Central America and South America, and she has worked for Regional Educational Radio in Puerto Cabezas, Nicaragua. She has published articles in the *Journal of Ecology of Food and Nutrition*, *Gazette*, *Journalism Educator*, and *Latin America and Caribbean Contemporary Record*.

Paul S. Voakes has been Dean of the School of Journalism and Mass Communication at the University of Colorado–Boulder since 2003. His Ph.D. is from the University of Wisconsin–Madison, and before Colorado, he served on the faculty of the Indiana University School of Journalism for 9 years. His research and teaching specializations are in mass media law and ethics, news writing, reporting and editing, and math/statistics for journalism. Before entering academia, he was a journalist for 15 years at three newspapers in the San Francisco Bay Area, most recently as an editorial writer for the *San Jose Mercury News*. In the summer of 2000, he was a political reporter at the Portland *Oregonian*, as an American Society of Newspaper Editors fellow. He is the author of *The Newspaper Journalists of the '90s* (ASNE, 1997) and has published his research in *Journalism & Mass Communication Quarterly*, *Journal of Mass Media Ethics*, *Newspaper Research Journal*, *Communication Law & Policy*, and *The National Civic Review*. He is a coauthor of *Working With Numbers and Statistics: A Handbook for Journalists* (Lawrence Erlbaum Associates, 2005).

David H. Weaver is the Roy W. Howard Professor in Journalism and Mass Communication Research at Indiana University's School of Journalism, where he has taught since 1974. He holds bachelor's and master's degrees in journalism and sociology from Indiana University and a Ph.D. in mass communication research from the University of North Carolina. He has worked as a journalist for four daily newspapers in Indiana and North Carolina. He has been involved in writing or editing 10 books about journalists, news media's influence in elections, and mass communication research. He has written numerous book chapters and articles on these subjects as well as on newspaper readership, foreign news coverage, and journalism education. He is a past president of the Association for Education in Journalism & Mass Communication and the Midwest Association for Public Opinion Research.

G. Cleveland Wilhoit is Professor Emeritus of Journalism at Indiana University, where he taught from 1967 to 2004. He was director of the Bureau of Media Research (1967–1976 and 1993–1996) and associate director of the I.U. Institute for Advanced Study (1988–1993). He holds bachelor's and master's degrees and a Ph.D. in mass communication research from the University of North Carolina. He is coauthor (with David Weaver) of *The American Journalist: A Portrait of U.S. News People and Their Work* (Indiana University Press, 1986), *The American Journalist in the 1990s: U.S. News People at the End of an Era* (Lawrence Erlbaum Associates, 1996), and *Newsroom Guide to Polls and Surveys* (American Newspaper Publishers Association, 1980, and Indiana University Press, 1990). He was editor of the first two volumes of the *Mass Communication Review Yearbook* (Sage Publications, 1980 and 1981) and a winner (with David Weaver) of The Society of Professional Journalists' Sigma Delta Chi Award for Research About Journalism in 1987 and 1997 for the two American Journalist books.

Name Index

Subject Index

N

O

L, M

Printed in the USA
CPSIA information can be obtained
at www.ICGtesting.com
LVHW022157140224
771912LV00007B/197